This Book Was Purchased as a Gift

For _____

By _____

SECRETS
TO
FINANCIAL
SUCCESS
IN
MARRIAGE

John C. Shimer
and
Successful Financial Planners, Inc.

FIRST EDITION

Grateful acknowledgment is made for permissions granted by:

Cavett Robert, Inc. for use of various stories and inspirations which appear in Chapter Seven.
Doris Wood, President of MLMIA, for allowing a reprint of her article, "The Right MLM Company" which appears in Appendix F.
Pam Hait, for allowing the use of excerpts from her article "Time and Love" in Chapter Five. "Time and Love" originally appeared in *Ladies Home Journal* in November 1985.
Williamson Music, for use of the quote from the musical *South Pacific* found on page 43 from:
>   **"HAPPY TALK"**, by Richard Rodgers
>   and Oscar Hammerstein II.
>   Copyright (C) 1949 by Richard Rodgers
>   and Oscar Hammerstein II.
>   Copyright Renewed. International Copyright Secured.
>   ALL RIGHTS RESERVED.
>   WILLIAMSON MUSIC owner of publication and allied rights throughout the world.

Penguin USA, for various excerpts from and references to:
>   THE RICHEST MAN IN BABYLON by George S. Clason
>   Copyright (C) 1955 by George S. Clason
>   Copyright Renewed (c) 1983 by Clyde Clason.
>   Used by permission of the publisher, Dutton, an imprint of New American Library, a division of Penguin Books USA Inc.

Scott Daley, for the quote from POGO found on page 119:
>   From POGO by Walt Kelley.
>   Copyright (C) 1992 by O.G.P.I.

Irving Music, Inc. for the quote from "I AM WOMAN" found on page 297:
>   I AM WOMAN
>   Words by Helen Reddy / Music by Ray Burton
>   Copyright (C) 1971, 1972 Irving Music, Inc. / Buggerlugs Music Co.
>   All Rights Reserved, International Copyright Secured.

Library of Congress Cataloging-in-Publication Data

Shimer, John C.
    Secrets To Financial Success In Marriage

ISBN 0-9633044-3-7

Library of Congress CIP Number 1992   92-60786

To Cay Fortune
My Partner
My Friend
My Lover
My Wife

Table of Contents

This book does not have an index. The reason is because most couples try to manage the challenge of discussing money in a haphazard manner, jumping around from subject to subject with no agreed upon agenda. This is a self-defeating process, and an index tends to encourage this haphazard approach to money discussions. The contents of this book offer a carefully planned path for my readers to follow. Those who follow this path faithfully will reap the greatest reward.

• Financial Law No. 7: You Can't Take It With You • How Property Can Pass To Other People At Death • Financial Strategy No. 1 for Harmonizing with Financial Law No. 7: Preparing Your Wills • The Benefits of Wills • Misconceptions About Wills • The Role of An Executor • Taking Care of Minor Children Through Your Will • Drafting Your Wills • When To Change Your Wills • What Is Probate and How Can It Be Avoided? • Financial Strategy No. 2 for Harmonizing with Financial Law No. 7: The Effective Use of Trusts • The High Cost of Dying • A Final Word (or two) of Advice

Appendices

Acknowledgments

It has been said that those who want to go somewhere in life had better get on the train. I hesitated getting on the author train for seven years after I published *Secrets To Financial Success In Marriage* as a cassette tape album. When I finally started writing, I realized that while the trip I was taking would eventually result in a published book, I also understood that I wasn't on this train alone. Some of my fellow passengers on this trip made important contributions that will always be appreciated.

David Harner, my editor and dear friend.

Eldon Doty, who illustrated this book and kept me mindful of the fact that one of the most important secrets to getting along with other people (and one of the secrets to financial success in marriage) is a good sense of humor.

Carol Wright, and Word Graphics Inc., who set the type.

Jim Sutton, who designed the cover.

My co-authors, who spent the time required to read and make important suggestions to every chapter.

Pam Hait, whose article in Ladies Home Journal (November, 1985), "Time and Love," convinced me that my cassette tape course on *Secrets To Financial Success In Marriage* could be presented successfully as a book.

William Griffen, who counseled me on self publishing.

Valerie Ryan, who counseled me and proofread every page.

Sheryn Hara, who counseled me through pre-publication.

Cavett Robert, the man who taught me so many important lessons about life and people.

Jay H. Cowles, CFP, who offered several important ideas to improve the readability of this book.

Cindy Shimer, who offered many suggestions that improved the readability of this book and who offered many prayers on my behalf.

Christian Shimer, who kept me laughing and encouraged me through the many months of writing. His music will someday eclipse anything that I may accomplish as an author.

Mike and Mary Shimer, my mother and father, who through their marriage planted many of the seeds of truth which my readers will harvest.

The Philanthropists of this world, those dozens of unnamed, wonderful people who shared with me their secrets to successful partnership and exposed me to the laws that govern financial success.

Cay Fortune, to whom this book is dedicated. Her gift of trust and love through partnership inspired me to share the truths and wisdom of this book with a much larger audience.

Dear Reader:

Successful Financial Planners, Inc. encourages the use of this book as a teaching tool for those who provide pre-marital and marriage counseling. While members of our firm are available for public lectures, we do not offer seminars and workshops and we do not charge a licensing fee or royalties for those who wish to use this book for teaching and counseling. If you are interested in bringing a member of our team to your area, please contact our agent:

Sheryn Hara
P.O. Box 19732
Seattle, WA 98109
(206) 285-1512

I regret that I am unable to answer individual letters, phone calls, or provide financial counsel to my readers. I do read my mail, however, and if you have feedback or responses to this book, I'd be happy to hear from you. Simply drop a note to:

Successful Financial Planners, Inc.
Attention: John Shimer
2405 Carillon Point
Kirkland, WA 98033

In the spirit of Love,

John C. Shimer

Introducing:

Eldon C. Doty—Humorous Illustrator

The wonderful illustrations in this book have been provided by Eldon C. Doty—Humorous Illustrator. Mr. Doty was born and raised in Seattle, Washington. He graduated from the University of Washington in 1966 and worked as a policeman for over 12 years. In 1978 he left police work and began to pursue a career in art and humorous illustration. He attended the San Francisco Academy of Art and began free lance illustration for such diverse clients as Chevron, IBM, Trump Casino and Gallo Wines. In addition to advertising, his work has appeared in various magazines as well as numerous educational publications. Eldon has also illustrated the Children's book ZOO CLUES. He currently resides in Redmond, a small town outside of Seattle where he conducts business from his electronic cottage. His home sits on the top of a hill that provides him a spectacular view of the Cascade Mountains. However, the beauty of nature is not the source of his inspiration. Blessed with an eye for seeing the humor in people and life situations, Eldon, through his illustrations, has helped us share a secret to financial success in marriage that could be conveyed in no other way—the importance of a sense of humor.

Preface

*"Human freedom involves our capacity to pause
between stimulus and response and, in that pause,
to choose the one response toward which
we wish to throw our weight."*
.... Rollo May
"The Courage To Create"

The inspiration to write *Secrets to Financial Success in Marriage* first came to me in 1976 while I was mourning the end of my own marriage. It was a very sad time for me. I was only thirty-three years old and my marriage had lasted nine years. I was the first person in my immediate family ever to have been divorced. To this day, my brothers and my sister remain married to their original partners.

"Why me?" is what I wanted to know. My self-confidence was at an all time low. I was angry *and* frightened. And for a while, I was completely cynical.

My parents had taught me never to fear failure, but to learn from it. For awhile, their teachings were eclipsed by the dark feelings of grief that hung over my life. But then, as the clouds of sadness slowly lifted, it occurred to me that I *could* learn something from all that had happened. After all, I had an entire lifetime ahead of me. "Maybe," I thought, "I had *better* learn something or end up making the same mistakes all over again." It took fifteen more years to learn everything contained in these pages. Now, remarried, I am discovering with delight the power and productivity of the *"secrets to financial success in marriage."* However, these "secrets" are completely powerless without a common commitment to throw the weight of both husband and wife behind them and apply them every day in married life. Without the shared commitment of my partner to the principles and values that I teach in this book, I would have little to write about and even less to teach.

The hardest lessons for me to learn were the ones contained in the first five chapters. Learning the "rules of the financial road" (the subject of Chapters Six through Ten) was easy by comparison. I suspect you will find the lessons in Chapters One through Five more than a little difficult, too. They are not lessons that one might call obvious.

The field work for this book occurred every day in my career as a professional fundraiser. In this line of work, I was in daily contact with men and women who were financially *very* successful. They had to be. They were *giving away* money. Many of them were married, but not all of them happily. My relationship with them was not shallow. I specialized in developing huge gifts (from $50,000 up to a million dollars or more). This kind of generosity doesn't come to pass by picking up a telephone and dialing a number. I really got to *know* these people.

I learned the lessons in the first five chapters from those who were both financially successful *and* happily married. Often, I could talk openly with them about their secrets, but frequently I had to deduce them. No one ever sat me down and told me everything that is in this book. Ultimately, I had to distill these lessons from both the spoken and unspoken conversations I had with these people.

Those who were financially successful and unhappily married taught me a lot, too. One should never underestimate the value of a negative example. However, life can be a lot more enjoyable if you avoid becoming a negative example. As Mark Twain used to point out, a cat that sits on a hot stove learns to avoid hot stoves, but won't sit on a cold one either. That cat gets completely out of the business of sitting on stoves. I've used some negative examples in this book so you can learn from them and avoid the more harsh experiences of managing money as a married couple.

Your greatest opportunity to benefit from this book may come as you learn about and discuss the universal spiritual laws that stimulate the dynamics of cooperation—the dynamics that must dominate your life as a married couple in order to be successful with money. I personally believe that a loving, caring God is the author of the universal spiritual laws presented here, and that the life and teachings of Jesus Christ reveal the very essence of these laws. I also know that you don't have to be a Christian to grasp the moral truth and power contained in them. The unanswered question is, "Will you adopt and apply these spiritual laws in your personal life and in your marriage?"

Nothing I say in this book has the power to help you make moral and ethical decisions about how to live your life and how to relate to your marriage partner. I fully appreciate that morality is a choice that everyone (and every couple) can and will (and ultimately must) make for themselves. However, if reading this book only helps you to appreciate the *power of choice* that you have in selecting your values and deciding how to behave toward one another, then I believe you will end your reading of this book more fully "free." That, for me, would be reason enough for writing this book and sharing it with you.

The Agreement Checks *throughout* the book are my way of empowering you to make your *own* decisions about every topic of discussion presented *in* the book. As you complete each Agreement Check, remember that there are no right or wrong answers; there are only *your* answers. Don't answer any of the questions in the book as you think they should be answered; answer them honestly, according to what you know, feel and believe. While it may be easier to let others make decisions for you, I am thoroughly convinced that you will gain much more if you make your own decisions about what is "right" for *your* marriage.

While at first glance this book may seem long, it reads quickly. Don't let the amount of material to be covered delay your reading and sharing every topic in these pages. Make your decisions about the subjects in this book sooner, instead of later. Otherwise, you may make the unhappy discovery that so many other couples have made: **Later is often too late.**

John C. Shimer

Why Read This Book?

Chapter One

"Toto, I've a feeling we aren't in Kansas any more."
Dorothy to her dog Toto in *The Wizard of Oz*

Mark and Kathy *were seemingly the All-American couple when they took their marriage vows. They had a big church wedding, a reception for 200 people, and a five day honeymoon in Las Vegas—all compliments of their parents. Kathy's Aunt Rachel gave them $500 dollars for spending money on their trip. They gambled it all away before they went to bed on their first night in Vegas.*

That experience on their honeymoon seemed to set the financial tone for the first year of their marriage. They both worked and made good money—Kathy was a computer analyst for a mail order firm. She made an annual salary of $28,500, and her future with her company looked promising. Mark was an estimator for a contractor who built shopping malls. He made an average of $31,000. He also received a once-a-year bonus from $1,000 to $5,000, depending on how the company did that year.

They leased a townhouse in a fashionable development in the suburbs near the University campus. Before they moved in, they had a garage sale to sell the modest furniture that each had owned before their marriage, and bought coordinated pieces for each

room. Kathy's boss recommended an expensive interior decorator who happened to be her close friend. Mark didn't want to offend his wife's boss so they spent several hundred dollars for the decorator's advice.

Mark and Kathy's places of business were on opposite ends of town. That was excuse enough, they reasoned, to buy two cars. Kathy bought a sporty-looking Buick with all the bells and whistles. Kathy's father helped them make the down payment. Kathy was his only child. Mark bought a pickup—four-wheel drive, special wheel package, custom paint, tinted windows, electric everything! It added to his "successful contractor" image, he thought. Mark teased her about her "sissy" computerized instrument panel. She teased him about his "macho super truck."

Time passed quickly that first year. The couple celebrated their first anniversary in style (by throwing a "small party" for about 35 friends). The catering bill, including liquor, came to slightly more than $715. A week after the party, they got a notice from the utility company stating that unless they paid their bill in person within 4 days, their electricity would be disconnected. That night, Mark and Kathy had a serious argument. Actually, it was more like a shouting match, and it was only one (although the most irrational one) in a series of arguments that had been occurring more and more frequently. It was about money. Mark accused Kathy (who paid the bills from her account with major contributions from Mark) of not paying enough attention to their family finances and spending too much money on her wardrobe. Kathy angrily responded by calling Mark cheap and selfish, pointing out that on a weekend fishing trip with his buddies, he had spent nearly $500 for his share of a rented houseboat, food, liquor, and fishing equipment. The argument got more serious when Mark proposed putting both of their incomes in one bank account—his. He wanted to write all of the checks from now on, citing Kathy's failures to "keep track of things."

Kathy, stung by Mark's accusations and lack of confidence in her, let Mark have his way, but didn't speak to him for two full days—and nights. And, by the end of the month, Mark discovered a very important fact when he made out checks for their expenses. Their major bills—rent, the two car payments, and the payment on the bank loan for their furniture—devoured almost all of both paychecks. Utilities, gasoline, and food just weren't being covered. They had managed to cover these expenses by not paying one or more of their major debts on time. The maneuvers Kathy and Mark had used to get by had finally caught up with them. If they should face a major car repair or some other major, unexpected expense, they had no savings to pay it.

Mark went to see if his Dad would lend them money. He had financial problems of his own because of a slumping sales volume in his electron-

ics store. He could not help them.

Mark and Kathy went together to see Kathy's father. Mark wasn't proud of having to ask his father-in-law for help, but something had to be done. Kathy's father was smiling until they told him why they needed the money. He wrote a check to bring their major debts current, but warned them that it was the last money he would give them until they got their act together. They needed, he said, rather forcefully, to "grow up financially!"

"...Not In Kansas Anymore"

Mark and Kathy are finding out that when it comes to money, they aren't "...in Kansas any more." They are no longer under the protective wings of their parents; they are somewhere in a financial Land of Oz, the real world, where life is not always pleasant, not always secure, where financial realities have to be faced and planned for—together.

Consider this.

The two most fundamental goals of married life are to provide companionship and economic security.

That's right! Even having children and raising a family is optional in today's world.

What can be said for how well couples are prepared to manage the financial side of marriage?

Factually, we know this: In marriages that fail, 9 out of 10 report that money problems contributed heavily to the breakup. Yet, our education system offers few courses for married couples on how to manage money. As you might expect, most couples get off to a rocky start with money management.

The question is, "Will you be any different, or will you make a commitment from the beginning of your married life to be successful with money?" Before you try to answer that question, see if you believe the following couple has a better chance at succeeding than Mark and Kathy.

John and Melanie were born and raised in a small town. In fact, they had known each other since kindergarten. They married quite young. He was 19; she was 18. They had agreed to get married the moment Melanie finished high school. They did—two days after graduation.

They both knew things were going to be tough—financially, anyway. John worked in a small factory that made custom artificial marble products—shower stalls, bath fixtures, that sort of thing. He started working there a year ago, during the summer after he graduated. John considered himself fortunate. His boss liked him and appreciated his hard-working, no-nonsense attitude. Although he had started at minimum wage, he had received raises every quarter, and now made $6.85 an hour. His boss had even given them a wedding gift—a check for $200.

Melanie's job prospects were not as good. There just weren't that many jobs available—of any kind. She finally settled for two part-time jobs, working as a receptionist for the town's only doctor during his peak office hours in the morning and stocking groceries at Conway's Market in the afternoon. She received the minimum wage for her seven hour day. Their combined take-home pay averaged $260 a week, approximately $1040 a month. They discovered a small, one-bedroom apartment above a store for $375 a month, including utilities. They found a few pieces of furniture at yard sales and auctions. John bought a washing machine and dryer at an appliance repair shop in the large town 20 miles away. The appliances had a few dings and scratches, but they worked just fine and came with a three-month warranty. They slept on the bedroom floor on a mattress that Melanie's parents gave them. Bed frames and box springs, for some reason, were hard to come by—used ones, at least. They agreed that they wouldn't go into debt for a new set.

John had an older Jeep that he bought when he was a high school senior. He rebuilt the engine as a Shop Class project and had the vehicle paid for by the following Christmas. It wasn't pretty; it was a little drafty during the winter months; but it ran perfectly. He had received an "A" on the project.

Neither John nor Melanie's parents were well-to-do. John's father worked as a mechanic in the local Chevy garage; Melanie's parents were struggling to keep the family farm from going under. But in exchange for some weekend machinery repair from John, her parents gave the couple enough pork and beef packages from their freezer so that the young couple didn't have to buy much meat. The owner of their building let them plant a small

3

garden in the vacant lot behind the store.

Melanie and John were quite financially conservative for young people. For example, both firmly believed (as did their parents) that buying anything with credit was a bad idea. In a small town, a cash economy is easier to live by than in a larger city. Everybody in town knew if someone were a poor financial risk. Most people used barter when cash was in short supply—exchanging services for goods, and vice versa. As a result of all these factors, John and Melanie were able, by careful planning, to put nearly $200 a month into savings. Their biggest worry was medical expenses. Fortunately, both were healthy, and minor problems were taken care of, free, by Melanie's doctor employer.

After their first year of marriage, John and Melanie spent several hours talking about their financial situation and made plans for the future. They had agreed at the beginning of their marriage to make all major financial decisions together. As a result, they had decided together that in two years of careful planning and saving that they could open a small auto repair shop. They laughed about their "early poverty" apartment furnishings, but decided appearances weren't as important as financial independence.

Making Decisions Together

John and Melanie, contrary to what a lot of people might believe, are actually quite fortunate as far as their financial situation is concerned. A strong value system about money was instilled in them by both sets of parents, a system which they accepted

and adopted. While this system might not work for everyone, it has worked well for them in their particular environment. The important thing to realize about this young couple is that they adopted this financial value system *together*. They discussed and agreed *together* how they felt about money, how they would deal with it, and what it could mean to them later on. John and Melanie have grown up financially well in advance of their years and experience.

When you picked up this book, it was probably because you have or are ready to make a commitment to share the rest of your life with someone you love. Or, perhaps you have been married for a short time and have found out, like Mark and Kathy, that you really haven't grown up financially, and can see the clouds of financial trouble out there on your horizon. Maybe, like John and Melanie, you were fortunate enough to have financial examples set by your parents that helped you to establish, early on, sound attitudes and values where money is concerned. Or, maybe you have been married for a year or more and have found that financial problems are robbing beauty and fun from your marriage. It's possible you are starting married life for the second time and don't want to repeat some of the mistakes that may have helped to destroy your first marriage.

If any of these situations describes your life right now, this book is for you. It is not a magical book. It does not offer a quick fix or a Band-Aid approach to the challenge of managing the financial side of marriage. If you have scanned its pages, you already know that it won't be as easy to read as a romance novel or a spy thriller. It will take a considerable amount of your time, particularly if you both conscientiously complete all the exercises and use all the written tools that the book provides.

But, hold on a minute! Here's why you *should* read this book.

Reduce Financial Stress

Planning for and succeeding to develop a financially successful marriage will reduce many of the normal stresses that threaten marriages—often to the breaking point. With less stress from financial problems, you can give more time and attention to the "romance" of marriage. You owe it to yourselves to avoid some myths about married life. One of the most common myths is the one that says money should not be important in a marriage. "You can live on love," this fairy tale says, "and the money can come later." "As long as you have each other, money just isn't important." A variation on this theme is the fable that says, "Two can live as cheaply as one." I am a firm believer in romance. However, there is little romance in having to struggle constantly, living from paycheck to paycheck, always worrying about how to pay bills, put food on the table and provide clothing and shelter for yourselves and your children.

Develop Communication Skills

Unlike other books that teach money management, this one was written specifically to help engaged or married couples learn how to create a financial life *together*. A great deal of

this book is devoted to helping you learn about what you each want out of life and how to communicate about money. And, because communicating about money is not easy, you can gain enormously from working through the exercises and "Agreement Checks" found throughout this book. You can gain by coming to a better understanding of yourself. You can gain in your understanding of one another and how to talk with one another about every subject relating to financial management. And, you can gain financially.

For, in the end, the kind of life that you'd really like to live, the things that you'd really like to see happen, will require money—in some cases, lots of money.

By the time you finish reading Chapter Seven, you'll know several new ways to increase the flow of money into your marriage.

Make Your Dreams Come True

Early on, this book will help you discover that you have dreams—for your life and for your marriage. And those dreams *are* important. You will also learn that your success with money will, to a large extent, determine whether those dreams and ambitions ever become more than just dreams.

Making dreams come true in marriage is a great way to put romance into married life.

By learning how to talk about dreams and by working to make them come true, you'll discover that every day of your life can be filled with excitement and romance. When dreams are shared and a promise is made to help make one another's dreams come true, you can become each other's best cheerleader. There's nothing more romantic than having an encouraging partner to cheer you on toward the goal of making dreams come true.

Take Control of Your Life

Another reason you should read this book is that you and your partner deserve to be a cut above the ordinary. The world is full of couples who are just getting by, just providing for their basic needs, just living for the immediate pleasures of life. Financial planning is of no interest to them at all. These couples have no idea where they are going financially. They often pretend they are doing well, and even try to look successful. Yet, when it comes to mastering the business of making and managing money, these couples don't even come close.

The question is, do you want to be different from them?

If you and your marriage partner could look into an imaginary mirror and see your lifestyle, your standard of living, twenty years from now, what do you think you would see?

That look into the future might show that you had done very well, that through careful planning and hard work you had built a wall of financial security around your marriage and lots of your dreams had come true. Or, you could see a couple still struggling, living from paycheck to paycheck, feeling disappointed that their dreams seemed financially shipwrecked.

Of course, one day you will wake up and it *will* be the future. Whether or not you like what you see will depend on a decision you make at the beginning of your marriage. That decision can be faced by asking yourself a basic question: *Do you really want to make the financial side of your marriage a success?*

Think carefully about the answer. Many couples say "Yes," but are not ready to make the investment of time and energy in learning how to do it. To be successful with money in marriage, you must have a strong desire, some reason to learn all the lessons in this book, and then keep right on learning and developing your money management skills. I believe the first three chapters of this book will help you discover that desire. After that, it's up to you.

Make The Most Of Your Marriage

I really believe that every one of you has the ability to reach financial success in some way. Maybe not in the sense that all of us can become millionaires. That's just not realistic. But I do believe that all of my readers can gain a basic knowledge of financial principles that can help make their lives more happy, more enriched.

This book is designed to help you make the most of yourselves and your marriage. Adopting its principles will give you an incredible amount of freedom and independence. Consider it one of your first investments—an investment of time that will repay itself many, many times over in the years to come. After completing this book, continue to build on the knowledge you gain here. Read the books suggested at the end of each chapter, attend classes and seminars and work with professional advisors to strengthen your money management skills. Because of changing forces and conditions in your economic lives, the financial strategies you choose in order to make dreams come true today may be out of date tomorrow. Continue to learn, grow and change so you can keep up and be prepared to take advantage of financial opportunities.

Just one more thing. I said earlier that I was a romantic. I am, but I'm a realist, too. To get the most out of this book, you absolutely must read and work through the exercises *together* and have the conversations with each other that are suggested.

If one of you is reluctant to invest the time to read and to work in order to make your lives and your marriage more successful, then it is up to the other to bring the reluctant partner along in a spirit of love and caring. It may be one of the most important acts of your life.

I wish you a happy and successful learning experience. You will soon discover how to pace yourselves and how much you can accomplish in each learning session. The important thing is to get started and to set aside a special time each week so you can share the wisdom contained in these pages. If you find that writing down the exercises is too difficult, you may wish to use a tape recorder. Either approach will work successfully. So get going— start your journey toward financial success in marriage *today!*

Notes

In Search of "Happily Ever After"

Chapter Two

"So off to the palace went Cinderella in the King's own coach, with the happy Grand Duke by her side...Soon she was princess of the land. And she and her husband, the charming Prince, rode to the palace in a golden coach to live...'Happily Ever After.'"

From *Cinderella*

Remember the story of Cinderella? Of course you do. Everyone who has ever heard or read the story of Cinderella is fascinated by the idea of "Happily Ever After." When we're very young, we may not know exactly what "Happily Ever After" means, but we're sure we want it (Doesn't everybody?). And when we grow up, we all try to find it. Yet, somehow it always seems to be just out of reach.

My intent in this book is to give you a specific definition of "Happily Ever After" and to help you use that definition to set up the financial side of your married life.

Before you finish reading this book, you'll have a chance to explore many ideas related to money and marriage. Hopefully, each idea I discuss will challenge you to think deeply and, in the end, make your own decisions about how to build a financial life together. But accepting the definition I offer of "Happily Ever After" is the key

to launching you successfully on this journey of learning. If, at any time, the journey seems long or hard, stop and think back to the lessons in the first three chapters. If just beginning the journey seems hard, keep in mind that "the journey of a thousand miles begins with a single step." So, let's begin.

First, since this book is one in which your participation is needed to get the most out of it, take a few minutes to complete the questions on the next few pages. Don't worry about form, grammar, or spelling; they are not important anywhere you may be asked to write in this book.

9

Your Definition of "Happily Ever After"

Without looking ahead in the book, examine your own ideas about "Happily Ever After." Dig deep and see if you can bring to the surface any assumptions about marital happiness that you have been carrying around with you—probably since childhood.

Since marriage is made up of two people, your spouse or intended spouse should complete this statement as well. Without letting your partner look at your response, let him or her complete the same statement.

Her definition of "Happily Ever After" is:

_____

_____

_____

_____

_____

His definition of "Happily Ever After" is:

_____

_____

_____

_____

_____

After completing your answers, ask each other *these* questions:

1. Are there any major differences in our answers?

2. How do we feel about the differences in our answers? Do any of these "differences" really matter?

3. Are we both willing to make a fresh start here, accept our differences, and begin to learn and grow together?

It is important to share with each other your responses to all of these questions. Why? Because as this book continues, there will be many dialogues and conversations that you will be asked to share.

Why? Because...

In the course of this book, we will do this together, step-by-step. Frequently, we will stop to allow you and your partner to have what I call "Agreement Checks." The purpose of these checks is not to force you to be of one mind about each subject or idea that is presented, but to allow you to appreciate each other's unique points of view, thoughts and observations. In the end, I hope your discussions of each topic will lead you to develop enough *agreements* to establish a *solid* foundation of common understanding. If that happens, you can go on from there to build your entire financial house—one that will keep you safe and comfortable through the financial storms life may send your way.

...deciding what role money will play in your marriage can be handled successfully only by building a foundation of common understanding.

11

For Love and Money

If you are already married, or are about to marry, you have discovered, or are about to discover, that marriage is always for love *and* money. Let's find out what this means.

Love, above all else, is what brought you together. Yet, by forming a marital union, you also formed a "financial community."

A financial community is one in which financial resources, financial decisions, and financial consequences are *shared*.

How you develop the structure of your marital financial community will greatly determine your success or failure in marriage. It can be a positive experience, or it can be negative.

If you build your financial community on correct principles and right values, then you have a much better chance of avoiding the kinds of financial problems that plague many marriages.

Most experts agree that the number one source of domestic squabbles is money management. But the experts don't agree on why this is true or what to do about it. The primary assumption of this book is that the challenge of mixing love and money has to be addressed *at the beginning* of married life to avoid the problems that most couples face. Furthermore, if a marriage is to flourish and prosper, a married couple must be aware of and bring their life into harmony with the principles, values and financial laws presented in this book.

Now, it's time for one of those Agreement Checks I mentioned earlier. How much in agreement are you with this first presentation of ideas?

Agreement Check:

1. We understand and accept that through marriage we have formed (or are about to form) a financial community.

☐ Agree ☐ Disagree

2. We acknowledge that the majority of marital problems involve conflict over money.

☐ Agree ☐ Disagree

3. We would like to limit our conflicts about money as much as possible. In fact, we would like to see the financial side of our marriage flourish and prosper.

☐ Agree ☐ Disagree

4. We are both willing to spend the time and make the effort required to read, complete the exercises and have the discussions in this book so our marriage can have the best possible chance to experience financial success.

☐ Agree ☐ Disagree

5. Before you go on to the next section, take some time to discuss any thoughts, ideas or feelings you have about this first set of understandings. Remember, it is not important to settle all of your differences as you have these discussions. Right now, it is more important to become aware of each other so you can appreciate the uniqueness of your individual differences as well as the common points of view that you share.

Notes

_____

_____

_____

_____

_____

_____

_____

How Prepared Are You?

If you agree that marriage, in fact, establishes a financial community, it is important to make an assessment of your readiness to live in that community. The best way to do this is to look at how you developed your financial personality.

Financially speaking, the person you are today is the product of many influences. Three important influences are (1) the example set by your parents, (2) your formal training and personal experiences with money, and (3) the culture in which you live. These influences are not equally weighted, however.

The most signifcant influence on your financial personality and, therefore, on your readiness to form a marital financial community, is the example set by your parents.

Parents are nearly god-like role models to children. What your parents told you about money and how they behaved in relation to money made a powerful impression on you—more powerful than any other influence in your life. When you were a child, the money messages you received from your parents were accepted unconsciously—without critical thought. Now, however, you are fully grown adults who can think for yourself. So, in the following pages I'm going to give you the opportunity to look back at the messages about money given to you by your parents, and ask you to re-evaluate them. You may decide that many of those messages no longer have mean-

ing for your life. Or, you may still accept some of them as valid and quite helpful. The important point to remember is that today, you are fully able to make these decisions freely, consciously, and rationally.

As you grew from childhood to young adulthood, you developed your thinking abilities and were exposed to many educational opportunities to learn about money. These experiences also had a powerful effect on shaping your financial personality. Your classes in school provided most of this training. A relative or some other adult role model may also have helped you learn about money. If you had good teachers or good role models, you picked up basic knowledge (maybe even advanced knowledge) about money in this way.

Those of you fortunate enough to participate in a free-enterprise experience while growing up learned about money in a special way. For example, if you had your own lemonade stand, a paper route, a summer job, a baby-sitting experience, or even if you only helped your parents run a garage sale, you learned fundamental principles about money. Your employment experiences as an adult have also contributed to your financial education. I hope these have all been positive experiences. Yet, whether positive or negative, these experiences gave powerful lessons that shaped your present financial personality.

Your culture has also influenced your financial personality. Cultural influences include religion, the government, the economy, the education system, and the media (the messages you get about money from newspapers, radio, television, etc.). While these influences are important, they don't usually have anywhere near the impact on shaping your financial personality as the other two, more primary influences. Cultural messages about money affect each person in different ways, and there is a perfectly good reason for this.

Usually, each of us "selects" from a wide range of cultural messages those that will _reinforce_ ideas and attitudes about money that are already established by the two more powerful influences. Normally, this "selection" process is also an unconscious tendency— something we do without critical thought.

In Chapter Five, you'll discover that there is one additional influence on financial personality—a more primitive and even a more primary influence than any of the three just discussed. How-

ever, let's hold off reviewing that influence until later. While the first five chapters of this book teach the philosophical and psychological secrets to financial success in marriage, it helps to learn these secrets in sequence—logically building the foundation of common understanding that I said you'll need in order to achieve financial success in _your_ marriage.

Before launching you down a new path of learning, I want you to look back and consider how the three influences identified above helped shape the person you are today, financially speaking. This look back is meant to help you appreciate your individual financial histories and to prepare you for an important discussion. Begin by completing the exercise on the following page—reviewing the financial example set by your parents. After completing that exercise, go right on to the next ones. Both of you should complete these exercises, but do them separately. Don't compare notes or discuss your answers yet.

Parental Examples of Money Management

As you were growing up, the primary influence on the development of your financial personality came from your parents. They are also your primary example of how to handle the financial side of marriage. Describe below the way you recall that your parents managed their financial life as a married couple. Did they sit down and talk about money? Did they have positive talks or did they argue? How did they handle the checkbook? Were they good at saving? Did either one overspend? What money messages did they give to *you?* Which of those messages did you accept? Which ones would you like to challenge or change? Write down every detail you can remember. (Remember, don't compare notes or discuss your answers yet.)

Her answer:

_____

_____

_____

_____

_____

_____

_____

_____

_____

_____

_____

_____

_____

_____

_____

_____

His answer:

_____

_____

_____

_____

_____

_____

_____

_____

_____

_____

_____

_____

_____

_____

_____

_____

_____

Remember, Son, a penny saved is a penny earned!

Your Training and Experience In Money Management

The second most powerful influence on your financial personality is your formal training and personal experiences with money. In the space below and on the next page, list the formal training in money management that you had in high school or college *and* any training you received from a close relative or some other significant adult role model. Also identify and list here the most important personal experiences you have had with money—both your growing up experiences and your experiences from employment opportunities prior to marriage. Explain how these experiences shaped your ideas and attitudes about money. Also tell how these experiences helped prepare you for managing the financial side of married life. Provide as much detail as possible. (Remember, you both need to complete these exercises. Use additional paper if necessary.)

Her answer:

_____

_____

_____

_____

_____

_____

_____

_____

_____

_____

_____

_____

His answer:

_____

_____

_____

_____

_____

_____

_____

_____

_____

_____

_____

_____

_____

_____

_____

A Look at Cultural Influences On Your Financial Personality

As stated earlier, cultural influences *usually* act to reinforce the money messages that you received from your parents or the money messages that you received from your formal training and personal experiences with money. But this is not always true.

Those who grew up in the Great Depression of 1929 were dramatically affected by the current economy. In that case, the economy played a more powerful influence than usual on shaping of financial personalities. Another example of how cultural influences can become unusually powerful is seen when a person is deeply involved with a religious organization. In those cases, parents often get replaced as primary role models by the teachings of the church. Such a shift in role models frequently results in major changes in a person's financial personality.

No matter what money messages are sent by the culture, your selection of these messages is what shapes your particular financial personality.

In the space on the following page, I want each of you to review how you have allowed cultural messages to affect your financial personality. To stimulate your thinking on this subject, review the list of typical cultural messages about money presented below. Identify those, or others that come to mind, that make sense to you—that express your ideas and attitudes about money. (Remember, hold off sharing your answers just yet.)

Typical Cultural Messages About Money:

"The one who has the gold makes the rules."

"A penny saved is a penny earned."

"The love of money is the root of all evil"

"A fool and his money are soon parted."

"All that you earn is a gift from God."

"You'll never have as much as your parents."

"The rich get richer, the poor get poorer."

"What you give, you will receive."

"It's a man's place to 'bring home the bacon.'"

"No family can survive in today's economy without two incomes."

"A woman's place is in the home."

"A woman's place is in the House...and in the Senate."

"I'm expensive, but worth it."

"If you're rich, I'm single."

"The one who dies with the most toys wins."

"The American Dream is dead."

Cultural Influences On My Financial Personality—His

_____

_____

_____

_____

_____

_____

_____

Cultural Influences On My Financial Personality—Hers

_____

_____

_____

_____

_____

_____

_____

Assessing Your Financial Strengths and Weaknesses

Each of you has lived with your financial personality for a long time, so you should know a lot about yourself financially. Based on this self-knowledge, use the space on the following two pages to take inventory of your financial strengths and weaknesses— as *you* see them. This inventory will allow you to appreciate more fully who you are today, financially speaking. (Remember, you both must complete one of these inventories. Once again, wait to share your answers.)

My Financial Strengths—Hers:

1. _____

Why I feel this is a strength _____

_____

2. _____

Why I feel this is a strength _____

_____

3. _____

Why I feel this is a strength _____

_____

My Financial Weaknesses—Hers:

1. _____

Why I feel this is a weakness _____

_____

2. _____

Why I feel this is a weakness _____

_____

3. _____

Why I feel this is a weakness _____

_____

My Financial Strengths—His:

1. _____

Why I feel this is a strength _____

_____

2. _____

Why I feel this is a strength _____

_____

3. _____

Why I feel this is a strength _____

_____

My Financial Weaknesses—His:

1. _____

Why I feel this is a weakness _____

_____

2. _____

Why I feel this is a weakness _____

_____

3. _____

Why I feel this is a weakness _____

_____

If you need more space for completing your answers, simply use a sheet of lined notebook paper and fasten your additional notes to this page. Remember, take your time. Don't discuss your answers yet. Once you complete this exercise, go right on.

Converting Weaknesses Into Strengths

One of the benefits you should gain from this book is learning how to develop a plan of action to turn your weaknesses into strengths. Before going on in this chapter, develop a list of possible strategies you could use to reach this goal.

You can return to this section at any time and add new ideas, but for now, use your own mental resources to set a positive course to get rid of any financial weaknesses you believe you have. Use the space below to help you make notes:

Plans & Strategies for Getting Rid of Financial Weaknesses:

Her Plan:

_____

_____

_____

_____

_____

_____

_____

His Plan:

_____

_____

_____

_____

_____

_____

_____

_____

Sharing Your Answers—
Beginning To Share A Financial Life

The exercises you just went through won't really help your marriage unless you both complete them and then talk about them. Talking about your answers may present some complications, because if you are like most couples, you won't know how to talk about money. It helps if you set up some ground rules for these talks. The rules on the opposite page are designed to help you have this first talk and any future discussions about money. So, right now, I want you to read through those rules before discussing your answers from the last few pages.

Rules for Discussing Money

Rules in the context used here are simply guidelines. Guidelines or rules help establish a framework for fair play. If you stick to these guidelines, they will make your discussions about money much easier. However, they won't get rid of your individual differences, and they won't get rid of misunderstandings or disagreements about money. If you are determined to keep misunderstandings and disagreements *to a minimum*, these guidelines will be very helpful.

Rule No. 1   Agree on a time and place to have discussions about money. Avoid unplanned discussions.

Rule No. 2   *Never* have your discussions about money in the bedroom. We all assign meaning to places where events occur. Financial discussions should be business discussions—cool, calm, and collected.

Rule No. 3   Have agendas for your money discussions and stick to them.

Rule No. 4   Share all financial information with one another—there can't be any secrets.

Rule No. 5   Take turns talking. Listen very carefully to what your partner has to say and *don't interrupt until he or she has finished.*

Rule No. 6   Don't dictate to one another—negotiate. Negotiating means presenting your wants to each other, and then working out solutions that allow each of you to realize as many wants as possible.

Rule No. 7   If discussions even *start* to become emotional, stop talking about money and talk about your feelings. Don't have discussions about feelings in the same room where you discuss money (for the same reasons identified in Rule Number Two).

Rule No. 8   If a discussion about money has to be stopped for any reason, agree on a time when you will resume the discussion.

Rule No. 9   Always remember that the purpose of your relationship is to love each other, and through your love to grow and prosper.

Rule No. 10   End every discusssion about money by telling your partner that you love him or her, and by giving each other some physical sign of affection.

Why Rules Help

Because you each have different financial histories, those *differences* are bound to be expressed in your financial personalities. Your financial personalities show up most clearly in your *styles* and *strategies* for managing money. Your financial styles and strategies are your way of expressing your personal expectations about life—what you value in life and what you want from life. Your financial styles and strategies also reflect what you *know* about money—how to earn it, save it, spend it or invest it. Until now, you may not have fully disclosed your financial styles and strategies to your partner—or even to yourself.

What typically happens is that each partner attempts to introduce into marriage the same (or the opposite) strategies and styles for managing money that their parents had. Just as your selection of parental messages about money is unconscious, so too is this tendency.

Attempting to blend different financial styles and strategies usually creates a big problem for young married couples. However, I don't want you to worry about this because there *is* something you can do about it.

By reading this book together, you will learn the secrets that make possible financial success in marriage. In learning these secrets, and by applying them in *your* marriage, you can *consciously* shape your financial styles and strate-

gies and take full charge of your financial ship of life. As a result, you can avoid some of the common mistakes that most couples make with money management—including the mistakes your parents may have made. You'll have to stretch your thinking and do a lot of communicating to profit from these lessons, but I know you can do that.

The rules I've given you on the previous page will allow you to explore subjects relating to money (including every subject in this book) in a safe and caring way. You may wish to think of these rules in the same way you think about the rules for driving your car. Such rules are designed to help you get where you're going with the least amount of fear and anxiety. Since there are a lot of miles to travel in this book (and many more miles to travel in your financial life as a married couple), adopting these rules for your money talks will start you off on the right foot and help you stay on course as you learn and grow financially.

Now, applying the "Rules For Discussing Money," I want you to share your answers to the last few exercises. Carefully answer (and discuss with one another) each of the questions in the following Agreement Check. Then go right on to the next section in this chapter and learn about the Four Dimensions of Love. Only then will you be fully prepared to learn about a new definition for "Happily Ever After."

Agreement Check

1. How did the example set by your parents influence your ideas and attitudes regarding money? What problems did they have that you would like to avoid? What aspects of your parents' financial life did you like? How did parental influences help you prepare to be a financial team member in your own marriage?

_____

_____

_____

_____

_____

2. How has your training in financial management and your personal experience with money influenced your ideas and attitudes regarding money? How did these experiences help develop your skills with money? How did these experiences help you prepare for working as a financial team member in marriage?

_____

_____

_____

_____

_____

3. How has your selection of cultural money messages served to reinforce your ideas and attitudes regarding money? How has your selection of these messages affected your ability to work as a financial team member in marriage?

_____

_____

_____

_____

_____

4. What does money mean to you now (before reading this book)? What are your personal ideas about money; how to earn it, save it, manage it and spend it? How do you see yourself applying these ideas to married life? Are these ideas negotiable (are you willing to look at them objectively and modify them if that will help your marriage)?

_____

_____

_____

_____

_____

5. After reviewing each other's personal assessment of financial strengths and weaknesses, are you optimistic about combining your financial strengths to form a strong financial community? Explain why and how?

_____

_____

_____

_____

_____

The Four Dimensions of Love

If you are going to be able to learn and profit from a new definition for "Happily Ever After," you will first need to learn about and accept a way of looking at love that may be new to you. I call this new way of looking at love, "the four dimensions of love." As each dimension is presented, you will be encouraged to go through some Agreement Checks with your partner. Go slowly through this section and take as much time as you need to discuss fully the ideas presented.

Each of the four dimensions of love is presented as a simple expression or statement. It is then followed by a short essay explaining its meaning. The four dimensions of love are expressed as:

"I Love Me."

"I Love The Me I See In You."

"I Love The You I Don't See In Me."

"In Your Happiness, I Find My Happiness."

31

The First Dimension of Love: "I Love Me."

When we are born into this world, Mother Nature equips us for survival by giving us the capacity to love ourselves. "I Love Me" is part of the natural order of things, and in a healthy home this form of loving is encouraged. We need to love ourselves in order to protect ourselves, and to demand food, clothing and shelter. We also need to love ourselves in order to respect our own personal goodness, value and originality.

With a healthy love of yourself, you have a basic sense of caring, interest in and affection for yourself.

The emotionally healthy person always has a sense of self love. When you love yourself in a healthy way, you know you have a right to be alive, that you matter, and you take time each day to meet your personal needs. You know your own plan for life, you talk about that plan with your partner and you work on it every day. Healthy self love allows you to take pride in your appearance, in the way you allow others to treat you and in your own accomplishments, even while fully aware that you are not perfect.

When self love is severely reduced, your ability to survive is reduced as well. Weak or distorted self love can also destroy a marriage. If you do not love yourself in a healthy way, you cannot love another person in a healthy way either.

When self love becomes the only focus of a person, we say that he or she is selfish, self-centered, egocentric, narcissistic, or thoughtless.

Those who think too much about getting love for themselves may very well be obsessed with themselves and with getting what they want without considering the needs of others.

In marriage, if one partner is stuck in this dimension of love (or if self love is weak or distorted), the marriage cannot possibly experience "Happily Ever After." Why not? Because the self-loving one will be unable to work as a team member or to share truly in any important way. Even if large amounts of money come into the marriage, the marriage itself will be at constant risk.

Agreement Check:

Take time to discuss your answers to the questions that follow. Remember, these discussions are intended to help you learn about one another. *There are no right or wrong answers.*

1. In what ways does this description of the first dimension of love make sense to us as a couple?

2. What conflicts do either of us see in this description of loving with ideas or beliefs we now hold?

3. What examples can we think of to prove the truths we see in this presentation about love?

4. What examples can we identify from our lives that in some way disprove the presentation made above?

Notes

_____

_____

_____

_____

_____

_____

_____

_____

_____

_____

_____

_____

_____

The Second Dimension of Love:
"I Love The Me I See In You."

As we grow and mature, we begin to notice that our brothers and sisters or our friends have qualities that are similar to our own. We may first notice physical similarities. Then we may notice patterns of behavior that are similar.

Often our first close friends are those who are "like us" in some way. This recognition of similarities, and the bonding that occurs between individuals who acknowledge these similarities, is a behavior pattern that remains with us all our lives.

Couples may first be attracted to one another because of similarities.

You may have noticed couples who work very hard at stressing their similarities—even going so far as to dress alike. You may have seen couples who had striking similarities in hair color, skin color or other physical traits. Others may find their similarities in interests, such as careers, or the way they spend their leisure time, or in their political or religious views. All of these "similarities" are expressions of the kind of bonding that occurs in the dimension of love expressed as "I Love the Me I See In You."

This form of loving is also perfectly natural. It is a deeper expression of love than "I Love Me," but it will not keep a marriage relationship going and growing over a lifetime. The reason for this is simple. The truth is that, in spite of similarities, none of us are *exactly* the same. In marriage, because of the great amount of time that couples spend together, the differences between marriage partners, which may have been overlooked or ignored during courtship, become more and more obvious. These differences, which might appear as little irritations to others, tend to cause great discomfort for the person who hasn't progressed beyond this dimension of loving. For example, leaving the cap off the toothpaste, or leaving the toilet seat cover up, register an eight on the Richter scale of incompatible differences. A different point of view or an independent thought is seen as an outright attack.

For those who have not advanced beyond this dimension of loving, the discovery of differences (both minor and major) in a partner often leads to a complete breakdown of the original bond that brought a couple together.

Without developing a deeper understanding of love than "I Love the Me I See in You," the discovery of differences in your partner will threaten the marriage itself.

As soon as I saw you I knew we were made for each other!

34

Agreement Check:

Take time to discuss your answers to the questions that follow. Remember, these discussions are intended to help you learn about one another. *There are no right or wrong answers.*

1. In what ways does this description of the second dimension of love make sense to us as a couple?

2. What conflicts do either of us see in this description of loving with ideas or beliefs we now hold?

3. What examples can we think of to prove the truths we see in this presentation about love?

4. What examples can we identify from our lives that in some way disprove this presentation about love?

Notes

_____

_____

_____

_____

_____

_____

_____

_____

_____

_____

_____

_____

The Third Dimension of Love:
"I Love The You I Don't See In Me."

Life has a wonderful way of presenting people to us who are different from ourselves. Those we respect and admire for their differences often become the people we love.

In these situations, we find ourselves in love with some quality that our partner brings to our life that we may not possess, but which enriches us through our appreciation of that quality.

These partners often possess some talent, characteristic or quality that we would like to have ourselves. By bringing this wonderful person into a closer relationship, we acquire that quality we admire.

This dimension of loving is deeper than either of the first two because it requires us to appreciate someone for being different from us. Once again, this dimension of love is perfectly natural and can truly make our lives richer. The more we can appreciate and enjoy another's differences without being threatened, the more enriched life is for us.

Yet, even this dimension of loving is not enough to hold a marriage together and make it grow over a lifetime.

In truth, we each want a dimension of love that goes beyond being appreciated for our special qualities.

We all know that in addition to the qualities our partner may admire, we also have qualities that he or she may not admire. More important to those that are stuck in this dimension of loving, is the fact that our admirable qualities may change. We may lose interest in a talent and want to try something new. We will all grow old and our looks will change. There will be ups and downs that affect our personalities over time. There will be stresses or crises that change us overnight from "pollyannas" who always see the bright side of life, to "Oscar The Grouches" who see life from the inside of a garbage can. As our wants, our needs, our hopes, our dreams and ambitions change (and they *will* change) the relationship may change, too. If loving in marriage is based too heavily on appreciation and enjoyment of a unique, admirable quality in another person, then we may someday discover that love has gone when that quality changes for some reason.

You're the most unique lady I've ever met!

36

Agreement Check:

Take time to discuss your responses to the questions that follow. Remember, these discussions are intended to help you learn about one another. *There are no right or wrong answers.*

1. In what ways does this description of the third dimension of love make sense to us as a couple?

2. What conflicts do either of us see in this description of loving with ideas or beliefs we now hold?

3. What examples can we think of to prove the truths we see in this presentation about love?

4. What examples can we identify from our lives that in some way disprove this presentation about love?

Notes

_____

_____

_____

_____

_____

_____

_____

_____

_____

_____

_____

_____

_____

The Fourth Dimension of Love:
"In Your Happiness, I Find My Happiness."

Have you ever felt the joy of helping to make another person happy? This experience is not known to everyone. Some people never learn this dimension of loving. But it *is* a real experience—one that has a most uplifting effect on the one who is loved *and* on the lover.

To love someone in this way begins with a sincere desire to find out what is important to someone else, what will make them happy.

It also requires learning and accepting that it is impossible to experience true happiness unless you live in harmony with universal laws that govern successful human relations. These laws, presented in Chapter Four of this book, are the foundation on which financially successful married couples build their values and on which they form the guidelines for all of their behavior toward one another.

As you will learn, these laws also serve as a standard against which you and your marriage partner can measure the goodness and the rightness of your wants, desires, and your behavior towards others. This means that "In your happiness, I find my happiness" requires moral and ethical decisions as part of the loving process. While it is not always easy to live by a moral or ethical code, it *is* possible and it is the only way to gain certain inner qualities of life that produce true happiness.

When the wants and desires of a marriage partner are heard, understood, *and fully accepted* as "good" and "right" (compatible with universal laws), then this fourth dimension of love says, "I'll be your cheerleader and your helpmate, so you can truly find what you seek from life. When you meet disappointment and get discouraged, I'll be there for you and help you get back on track." This deep, committed kind of love celebrates the fun, the excitement, and the joy of success that comes from seeing another person work for and actually achieve his/her life goals.

In marriage, the desire to help each other find happiness is the dimension of loving that can keep a marital relationship going over an entire lifetime. Furthermore, this dimension of love is the key that unlocks the door to "Happily Ever After" as it is defined in this book.

Learning to experience this fourth dimension of love does not mean you must give up the other three dimensions of loving. In fact, a healthy expression of this fourth dimension of loving uses the other three in a balanced way. You *must* keep on loving yourself enough to make sure you are meeting *your* needs. You *should* go right on enjoying your similarities with your partner while, at the same time, learning to appreciate your unique differences. However, by sharing the fourth dimension of love, you tune into and really listen to, encourage, and share with your partner, the fun and joy involved in helping one another to achieve happiness—in good times and in hard times.

To know real fulfillment in marriage, you must develop your capacity for loving to this deeply mature and caring state—a state where you both truly enjoy helping make one another happy in ways that are compatible with the universal laws presented in this book.

Agreement Check:

Take time to discuss your responses to the questions that follow. Remember, these discussions are intended to help you learn about one another. *There are no right or wrong answers.*

1. In what ways does this description of the fourth dimension of love make sense to us as a couple?

2. What conflicts do either of us see in this description of loving with ideas or beliefs that we now hold?

3. What examples can we think of from our own lives to prove the truths we see in the above presentation?

4. What examples can we identify from our lives that in some way disprove this presentation about love?

Notes

_____

_____

_____

_____

_____

_____

_____

_____

_____

_____

_____

"Happily Ever After" Defined

O.K., I've kept you in the dark long enough. It's time to share with you the meaning of "Happily Ever After." The definition of "Happily Ever After" presented in this book is offered with a humble spirit. It is not the product of a carefully organized scientific investigation. It is simply the distilled wisdom of more than twenty years of my own experience in working with some of the most financially successful and happily married couples in our nation. Your first reaction to it may be skeptical. Or, you may have an "Aha!" reaction and find that you are anxious to learn more. In any case, I invite you to try it on for size, and to test it against your own life experience. The moment you find it doesn't work, or if you find a better one, throw this one away.

"Happily Ever After" is the process of working together to make one another's dreams come true, both the shared dreams of married life and the unique, individual dreams that are special to each partner.

Observation has shown me and experience has convinced me that every man and every woman entering marriage has his or her own personal list of dreams that they hope will come true in the course of life with their partners. Usually, however, these dreams are not expressed out loud. Too often, they are hidden away in a secret chamber of the heart. This fact alone almost guarantees that many of those dreams will *not* come true.

In this life, dreams really *can* and frequently *do* come true. In marriage, this can happen only when couples talk about and share their dreams, convert them into goals, and work and sacrifice together to make those dreams (goals) come true.

However, working to make dreams come true as a couple will produce a better marriage *only when* the dreams you seek to make come true are "right" dreams or *love-filled dreams.* As you will discover in the next Chapter, dreams that are based on wrong principles and misguided values can actually destroy a marriage. Couples who have discovered this secret find that on the way to making "right" dreams come true, they actually grow closer together as a married couple. Even after years of living and observing the lives of others, I can not say how this occurs. I only know that it *does* occur. When the love in you and in your dreams is shared, and when you work together to make love-filled dreams come true, you *will* enrich your lives (both individually and as a married couple).

Couples who have learned how to make dreams come true in their marriage also know that every dream has a price tag. This means that dreams cost money—sometimes lots of money.

To be able to afford to make dreams come true requires that a married couple learn how to be successful with money. To be successful with money, you must both understand and live by *all* the secrets to financial success in marriage presented in this book. The first step you can take in that direction is to fully grasp (and ultimately accept) the definition I have given you for "Happily Ever After." So, to further make this definition clear, let me state emphatically what it *does not* mean.

"Happily Ever After" *does not* mean "keeping up with the Joneses."

Keeping up with the Joneses is one of the most common detours along the road to "Happily Ever After." This detour leads to a financial Dead End. During this detour, all effort goes into appearing to be financially successful, an often frantic exercise that has nothing whatsoever to do with making love-filled dreams come true. Besides making the Joneses miserable, getting lost on this detour will make you miserable, too. The only time it is correct to keep up with the Joneses is when you *are* the Joneses. As a married couple, *you* must decide what your goals are, how much love is in your dreams, and how you will reach them through taking charge of your own financial life. No one else has the right or the power to make these decisions for you.

"Happily Ever After" *is not* the pursuit of money for its own sake.

Chasing money for its own sake is also a detour that leads to a Dead End. The error of this path is that it confuses the goal itself with the way you reach the goal. When the goal is money, instead of possessing money, you become possessed *by* money. This sounds like an easy truth, but it is a truth that is easy to forget. If you're from a religious background, you'll remember the Bible says that "the love of money is the root of all evil." I suspect that the root of evil runs much deeper than the love of money, but evil is a real force that can destroy a marriage. Evil means becoming dishonest and living out of harmony with the life enriching principles and values that you'll learn about in Chapter Four. When you do that, your life becomes filled with pain and suffering. Although I'm not a biblical scholar, I don't believe the Bible teaches that striving to make love-filled dreams come true is evil.

But, as I have said, making dreams come true requires *money*. Traditional marriage vows declare that the union of two people is "for richer, for poorer." This does not mean, however, that couples should avoid the goal of achieving financial success. *Poorer is not better!* Poverty and its cousin, financial disaster, do nothing to make a marital relationship better. And unless you learn (and live by) the "rules of the financial road" presented in the second half of this book, you will never achieve financial success.

Ultimately financial success in marriage can have any definition you want to give it. And, ultimately, you alone will decide what definition of financial success will guide your marriage. Yet, my experience has been that, when a couple sets out to achieve financial success in order to make love-filled dreams come true, and if they do so in a way that is compatible with the principles and values presented in this book, they experience a type of love that builds a stronger and stronger bond each and every day. This bond is the glue that keeps couples together *and* keeps them excited about every today and every tomorrow.

Think about it. Do you really know your partner's dreams? Are you interested in learning about them? Or, are you so caught up in your own dreams that you haven't taken time to tune in to those of your partner? How about your own dreams? Have you tested them against the universal laws that govern true happiness? Do you have the courage to do that before blindly pursuing them? Don't let another day pass without reading the next two chapters of this book. I assure you, you'll be glad you did.

Agreement Check:

Discuss with one another your reactions to the definition for "Happily Ever After" offered in this chapter. Ask and answer the following questions:

1. Does this definition make sense to us?

2. Is this definition in conflict with our own beliefs?

3. Do we have a better definition to use at this time?

4. Are we willing to explore further to see if these ideas can have practical meaning in our marriage?

Notes

_____

_____

_____

_____

_____

_____

_____

_____

_____

"You Gotta Have A Dream"

Chapter Three

*"You gotta have a dream
'Cause if you don't have a dream,
How you gonna have a dream come true?"*
Rogers and Hammerstein
South Pacific

Throughout history, humans have needed their dreams in order to experience the fullest measure of being alive. Without dreams, life is reduced to mere survival, and no person or society can last long with survival as the only goal. Dreams fill our hearts with inspiration and hope. Hope, above all else, is the magic that makes life worth living. When dreams are combined with the hope that they can actually come true, they act as powerful motivators.

Dreams are the magic that bring excitement and romance into the daily routine of married life.

When you and your partner work hard to make a dream come true, your dream becomes a powerful way to fan the flames of married love. First, however, a couple must be willing to share their deepest dreams with each other. Only then can they begin the exciting process of creating a financial plan that will allow them to make their dreams come true—and strengthen their marriage.

The following exercise is designed to help you and your partner begin the process of sharing your dreams. Have fun!

"The Lottery"

Imagine that your door bell rings one day and you receive a registered letter telling you and your partner that you have won the lottery. Your prize? $1.5 million dollars!! The taxes have already been paid on the money. It's yours, tax free! Excited? You better believe it! Now, calm down long enough to answer these questions. However, don't let your partner see your answers. Not yet. Have your partner answer the same questions—on a separate sheet of paper.

A. What three things would you buy—things that you have always wanted but felt you could never afford—until now? Be sure to list what you think is the approximate cost of each selection.

1. _____ Cost $ _____

2. _____ Cost $ _____

3. _____ Cost $ _____

Now, what follows is tricky. Try to guess what three things your partner will list. Don't try to look over his or her shoulder—just give your best guess!

1. _____ Cost $ _____

2. _____ Cost $ _____

3. _____ Cost $ _____

B. What things would you like to do—things you always wanted to do but couldn't afford—until now? Consider activities such as travel, sports, hobbies, education, etc. Be sure to list what you think is the approximate cost of each one.

1. _____ Cost $ _____

2. _____ Cost $ _____

3. _____ Cost $ _____

Now, once more, try to guess what your partner would list.

1. _____ Cost $ _____

2. _____ Cost $ _____

3. _____ Cost $ _____

C. What acts of caring for others or sharing with others would you do? List those things you have always wanted to do for someone else—either people, organizations or institutions. For example, would you send your parents to Hawaii? Fund a scholarship for a needy student? Give a generous gift to your place of worship? Use your own ideas. Be sure to give an approximate amount for each of these acts of caring or sharing.

1. _____ Cost $ _____

2. _____ Cost $ _____

3. _____ Cost $ _____

One more time, try again to guess what your partner will list.

1. _____ Cost $ _____

2. _____ Cost $ _____

3. _____ Cost $ _____

Wasn't it fun spending all that money? Hopefully, you each made out these lists without sneaking a peek at your partner's answers.

These lists are called "wish lists." Sharing your lists and talking about them will give you important insights about yourself, your partner, and how you see each other. As a bonus, since there are no right or wrong answers, sharing your wish lists should be fun.

So go ahead, exchange your lists and see how close you came to guessing one another's answers. If you were way off, don't worry about it or make it a big deal. I suggest you ask your partner to share more details about the items listed on his or her wish list. Remember not to make any judgmental comments while listening to your partner.

If you're like most young couples, you'll be absolutely amazed to learn your partner's answers. (You may be just as amazed to learn how each of you is perceived by the other.)

Just remember, you're two separate people, and like towels, your answers to this exercise will be monogrammed "His" and "Hers."

After sharing your lists, go on to the next exercise—filling out a simple financial profile.

45

Your First Financial Profile

Completing your first financial profile will be simple; but it is very important. You should use the outline provided. It isn't necessary to be extremely accurate about every bit of information you are asked to provide. Just give the best information that you can. Do this exercise together.

Our Present Yearly Income Is:

Husband's annual income: $_____
Wife's annual income: $_____
Other income–yearly total: $_____

Total Annual Income: $_____

What We Own:

Total amount we have in savings: $_____
Present balance in our
checking account: $_____
Total value of our investments:
(Include cash value of any
life insurance, the value of your
home, cars, jewelry, stocks,
bonds, etc.) $_____

Total Assets: $_____

What We Owe:

Total of all outstanding loans: $_____
Balance on our mortgage: $_____
Owed to family members: $_____
Total of all credit card balances: $_____

Total Liabilities: $_____

Our Estimated Net Worth: $_____ *

Figure your net worth by subtracting your total liabilities from your total assets. The amount remaining should be your approximate net worth. Use the example on the next page as a guideline.

Ann and Ken's First Financial Profile

*When **Ann and Ken** decided to estimate their net worth, they had both thought that the process might be difficult. However, once they got started, they found, instead, that the process was easy. Each made $13,500 a year. They had no other kind of income, so their Total Annual Income was $27,000.*

They had $800 in savings and $650 in their checking account. They had owned their own home for two years. Its market value (which they determined from looking at sales prices of similar houses in their neighborhood) was $85,000. Their car would bring about $5,500 if they had to sell it. Ann had a life insurance policy that her folks had taken out for her when she was a teenager. Its cash value was now $2,000. Adding these items made their Total Assets $93,950. Both Ken and Ann were impressed.

They owed the bank $1,700, the balances remaining on their car and furniture loans. $62,500 remained on their house mortgage. They owed Ken's brother $400, and they had a $360 balance on their VISA card. Their Total Liabilities were $76,960. They subtracted their Total Liabilities from their Total Assets to compute their Estimated Net Worth—$16,990. Ann and Ken thought their Net Worth was pretty low compared to their Total Assets.

After you complete your first financial profile, take a look at the big picture. Compare your fantasies with your finances. Can any of the items on your wish lists be provided based on the financial snapshot taken by completing your first financial profile? Maybe so, and maybe not. If you feel discouraged, you are missing the point. If you feel too happy about the results of your profile, you are probably also missing the point.

What is the point? The point is that we all have to start here and now, the way we are, and put together our own plan to make some of our dreams come true. By following the principles and processes in this book, you can learn how to make your dreams come true by providing the money needed to pay for them.

So, if you're ready, let's take the next step!

47

Fantasies and Dreams

Everything we want in life can be divided into three categories: necessities, fantasies, and dreams. Most married couples focus the majority of their time and energy on providing necessities such as food, shelter and clothing. Fantasies and dreams are seldom discussed because they are more difficult subjects. However, this tendency must be overcome to be successful in managing the financial side of married life. Why?

Because just focusing on providing the necessities in life will not give meaning to your marriage—not the kind of meaning needed to get you out of bed in the morning and fill your life with excitement and enthusiasm.

Only focusing on making dreams come true can do that.

To help you start discussing your dreams, it's worthwhile to distinguish between dreams and fantasies. A fantasy is definitely not a dream. A fantasy is something that sounds and looks attractive, but it always has one missing quality—the ability to focus the full power of your mind and heart. A fantasy is something that you might include on your wish list (the list you created in the lottery exercise), and there may be some fantasies on the lists you completed.

A dream, while similar to a fantasy, not only has the ability to focus the power of your heart and mind, it will also enrich your life and the lives of others. Furthermore, dreams have the power to cause you to act—to work and to sacrifice in order to change them to realities.

Believe it or not, it is easy to confuse fantasies with dreams. As you refine your own thinking on this subject, consider asking the following questions of yourself. What in this world are you truly willing to go after with all your might? If you came up against discouragement, is this dream something you would still fight for? Would you be willing to give this dream enough time to put it all together? How patient would you be in the pursuit of this dream? What would you be willing to give up in order to make this dream come true? How would making this dream come true enrich your life? How might it enrich the lives of others?

You don't have to answer all of these questions right now, but keep them ever present in the back of your mind. They will come up again and again as you refine your thinking.

The next exercise helps you to separate real dreams from mere wishes or fantasies and will also start the process of making your dreams come true.

Separating Dreams From Fantasies

I've already said that a dream is different from a fantasy in several respects. Dreams are those things that mean so much to us that we are willing to truly dedicate all our energy to them. Deep down, we know that our dreams will truly enrich our lives—even if we have never identified exactly how. Often we see in our dreams a way to enrich the lives of others.

Our dreams are a reflection of our values, and making them come true is one way we have of sensing that we are on course in our life and that our values are working for us.

Putting dreams in writing begins the process of making them come true. It's fun, too! So, if you have never had the fun of focusing on your dreams, here is your chance.

List your personal dreams on the following page. Feel free to list more than the space allows. In fact, your list can be as long as you like. Just remember that what you list should be honest and sincere.

What you write on these lists should also reflect what you are willing to work very hard and sacrifice for.

Don't be surprised if some items you listed from the lottery exercise don't appear on this next list. Remember, the objective this time is to separate your dreams from your fantasies.

Of course, both of you need to complete this exercise. Don't compare lists until you have both had a chance to make them independently. By the way, when it comes to identifying the cost of your dreams on the next two pages, just make your best guess.

My Big Dreams—Hers:

_____ Cost $_____

_____ Cost $_____

_____ Cost $_____

_____ Cost $_____

My Medium-Size Dreams:

_____ Cost $_____

_____ Cost $_____

_____ Cost $_____

_____ Cost $_____

My Small Dreams:

_____ Cost $_____

_____ Cost $_____

_____ Cost $_____

_____ Cost $_____

My Really Small (But Still Important) Dreams:

_____ Cost $_____

_____ Cost $_____

_____ Cost $_____

_____ Cost $_____

My Big Dreams—His:

_____ Cost $ _____

_____ Cost $ _____

_____ Cost $ _____

_____ Cost $ _____

My Medium-Size Dreams:

_____ Cost $ _____

_____ Cost $ _____

_____ Cost $ _____

_____ Cost $ _____

My Small Dreams:

_____ Cost $ _____

_____ Cost $ _____

_____ Cost $ _____

_____ Cost $ _____

My Really Small (But Still Important) Dreams:

_____ Cost $ _____

_____ Cost $ _____

_____ Cost $ _____

_____ Cost $ _____

Sharing Your Dreams With One Another

Finished? O.K. Now it's time to have a real heart-to-heart talk. Set aside some special time when you are relaxed, when you won't be interrupted, and choose some place where you can enjoy plenty of privacy. **But remember the rule—discussions about money should never take place in the bedroom!**

Take turns talking about your dreams. For each dream, explain to your partner what that dream means to you and why it is important in your life. Be sure to explain how making this dream come true will enrich your life. The stakes are much higher now. This time you're telling your partner about something that is deeply meaningful and important, not just a fantasy.

When it is your turn to listen, ask as many good questions as you can about your partner's dreams. I also urge that if possible, you take notes about what each other says regarding each dream. Listen carefully to what is said and don't make judgments. By being a good listener, you are telling your partner that you respect him or her and that you respect this special, intimate kind of sharing.

Do not return to this book until you have finished talking about every dream on both of your lists.

Can Dreams Be "Wrong?"

Dreams can be "right" and they can also be "wrong." However, the ultimate decision about whether a dream is "right" or "wrong" can only be made by the one who has the dream.

For a dream to be "right," it must be in harmony with universal spiritual laws.

While Chapter Four makes a fairly thorough presentation of those laws, I will tell you now that when the master Law of Love is guiding your dreams you will experience the greatest personal enrichment from efforts to make your dreams come true. With this principle in mind, I'll leave it up to each of you to be your own judge about how much love your dream(s) contain. Right now, it's far more important for each one of you to ask yourself these questions about your dreams:

1. **How will this dream enrich my life?**
2. **How will this dream enrich the lives of others?**

Answering these questions is not as easy as it seems. For example, if one of your dreams is a material possession, you may find it hard to easily explain how this will enrich the lives of others. Yet, if you can not do this, your dream may not be "right" for you *at this time*. Here is why.

To make any dream come true, you will need the help and cooperation of other people. You will probably need the help and cooperation of lots of people. You absolutely must have the help and cooperation of your marriage partner. To get that help, you must persuade others that your dream is of some benefit to them. If you can't answer the second question above, you are not prepared to "sell" your dream to anyone.

If you can explain how your dream(s) will enrich the lives of other people, but discover over time that you are unsuccessful in persuading others to help or cooperate with you, this may not mean your dreams are "wrong," but it could mean this.

The final test of the "rightness" of your dream is your willingness to pursue it in the face of challenge, opposition and adversity.

But if you have difficulty gaining the cooperation and support of others for your dream, then it is wise to continue refining your answers to Question Number 2.

Deciding how a dream will enrich your life may seem like the easier question to handle. However, your answer(s) to this question could reveal extreme selfishness, a preoccupation with comfort, pleasure-seeking, or some other "wrong" desire. Remember, "wrong," as used here, simply means that what you want (your dream) is out of harmony with universal spiritual laws. For example, if your dream is to seek revenge on someone who has hurt you, then you are definitely in violation of a universal spiritual law. Such a dream can only bring more hurt to your life.

A dream that is based on envy is also "wrong." Envious dreams are those that come from wanting something someone else has. Envy is watching what others "get" in life and keeping score. This violation of spiritual law destroys appreciation for your own life, your own gifts, your own dreams.

When a dream is "right," then one of the benefits of making it come true will be a very special quality in your life called "joy."

Joy is more than an emotion or a feeling. It is a quality of life that brings deep and lasting satisfaction even when circumstances are challenging and difficult. More importantly, when a dream is "right," joy is present and available during the process of making dreams come true. Just striving for a "right" dream is a joy-filled experience. Joy means being yourself and liking yourself; it means being alive in the here and now; it means appreciating what you have while making your dreams come true; it means being in

touch with reality; it means living your life based on the principles of love and caring and cooperation with others and it means more—much more.

When a dream does not bring you joy, then it is not enriching your life. In that case, you will have to look again at your answer to the first question above. But, if just thinking about your dream brings you joy, and your heart is on fire when you talk about your dream with your marriage partner, you're probably on track and your dream is probably "right" for you.

If your marriage partner has a dream that, in your opinion, seems "wrong" based on this discussion, remember—everyone must decide for him/herself about the "rightness" of a dream. Be cautious about passing judgment on anyone's dreams, especially those of your marriage partner. It is fair to ask questions, seek clarification or understanding, and share observations when asked. Acting as judge and jury or playing "little tin god" can be especially destructive when it comes to dreams. Helping your partner answer the two questions above will do more good than anything else to examine in a loving and compassionate way whether a dream is "right" or "wrong."

What Is The Price of Making Your Dreams Come True? And Are You Willing To Pay It?

One of the realities of life is that there is a price to pay for everything. Some dreams have much larger price tags than others. Nevertheless, whether large or small, the price of making dreams come true is an important consideration. The price can present itself in many forms, such as time, energy, pain and sacrifice. When you consider your willingness to pay the price of making a dream come true, you should take all these factors into consideration. But the price I want you to think about now is the cost in terms of money.

Once again, go back to your first financial profile and compare the monetary cost of your dreams with your finances. Can you presently provide the money needed to pay for your dreams? If not, are you willing to learn all you can about how to be successful with money in order to afford to make your dreams come true? This is the easiest question to fool yourself about because it is so easy to say, "*Yes.*" A serious *"Yes"* means that you're prepared to read every chapter in this book and grow in knowledge and wisdom so that the money you need can one day be yours.

To test the seriousness of your commitment to make your dreams come true, see how well you do at completing the next exercise.

Changing Dreams Into Goals

During your talk about your dream lists, you may have found that some of your dreams were exactly the same. These dreams are called "shared dreams." Other dreams you discussed were totally individualistic. Take just a minute to go back to your dream lists and mark those that were exactly the same with a large "S." The "S" stands for "shared."

The next exercise is designed to help you begin to organize your dreams and to start making them come true. To begin making a dream come true, you simply change it into a goal.

A goal is nothing more than a dream with an attached time schedule.

You may have strong emotional feelings as you work on this next exercise, but whatever you do, don't let anything keep you from making the dream-to-goal changes! You may feel that doing such an exercise is useless because right now you can't see how in the world you could ever make those dreams come true. Don't bother with that feeling. We'll deal with it later. You may have all kinds of thoughts that will tend to slow or stop your progress. Do not give in to those thoughts. It has been said that when we give up our dreams, we give up our very lives and we begin to die. This is the absolute truth. It is just as true (and even more important to realize) that when we are able to make our dreams come true, we feel the true magic of being fully alive.

Arranging Your Dreams

The space below is for you to list your long-range dreams. Long-range dreams are those that you believe will take ten, fifteen, or twenty years, or even longer, to make come true. Identify the shared dreams with an "S." Mark those dreams that are individually yours with your initials.

Our Long-Range Dreams:

_____   Cost $ _____

_____   Cost $ _____

_____   Cost $ _____

_____   Cost $ _____

_____   Cost $ _____

_____   Cost $ _____

This second section is for listing your ambitious dreams. These dreams will take you several years to achieve—maybe five years or more.

Our Ambitious Dreams:

_____ Cost $ _____

_____ Cost $ _____

_____ Cost $ _____

_____ Cost $ _____

_____ Cost $ _____

_____ Cost $ _____

There may be some dreams on your list that you believe you can make come true in a relatively short period of time—anywhere from a year to three years. These are your immediate dreams.

Our Immediate Dreams:

_____ Cost $ _____

_____ Cost $ _____

_____ Cost $ _____

_____ Cost $ _____

_____ Cost $ _____

_____ Cost $ _____

Psychological Paychecks

As you work to make your dreams come true in these first three arrangements (Long-range, Ambitious, and Immediate), you should realize that during the weeks, months, and years of working, saving, and investing, there must be what I call "Psychological Paychecks."

Psychological Paychecks are the small rewards or special occasions that mark mileposts or checkpoints along your journey toward making dreams come true.

These "Paychecks" keep you motivated—hungry to complete the bigger goals of married life. They make you want to stand right up and say, "If we can make this small dream come true, we can make our bigger dreams come true, too!"

You will find those things that you listed under "Really Small (but important) Dreams" are a great way to identify Psychological Paychecks. The "Psychological Paycheck" list may have on it small reminders of caring.

For example, you may include on that list a gift of a single yellow rose every month, or a note now and then that says, "I love you" tucked into a coat pocket or a lunch sack. It may provide for a dinner once-in-a-while at a favorite restaurant or tickets to a special concert.

While you complete the exercise on the next page, it is important to communicate what *you* consider to be "Psychological Paychecks"—ones that will make *you* feel loved, appreciated, and motivated. The idea of sharing these thoughts is to help your partner succeed in communicating his or her love and encouragement by helping make these small dreams come true. Be sure to list things that you can do for yourself, too. You may make this list large, but keep the costs low—well within your ability to afford them.

Saying, "I love you" or "I love myself" doesn't have to be expensive. It only has to be said often in a meaningful way.

By the way, if you believe that sharing this kind of information takes the spontaneity out of saying, "I Love You," think again. There is nothing more loving than telling your partner how to communicate successfully. Often we expect our partner to read our mind. This can not be done, but couples often act as though it can. Don't make this mistake. If your partner knows what you like, then he or she can "*spontaneously*" help to provide it.

Our Psychological Paychecks:

Hers:

_____ Cost $ _____

_____ Cost $ _____

_____ Cost $ _____

_____ Cost $ _____

_____ Cost $ _____

His:

_____ Cost $ _____

_____ Cost $ _____

_____ Cost $ _____

_____ Cost $ _____

_____ Cost $ _____

Agreement Check:

1. Look back at the exercise you just completed (your Long-range, Ambitious, Immediate Dreams, and Psychological Paychecks). Make sure that your list of dreams in each arrangement includes at least one shared dream for both of you and at least one individual dream for each partner.

2. Talk over with each other why you picked the items on your lists and tell each other how excited you are to make the effort to reach these goals. Be sure to listen carefully to what your partner says about the importance of each goal. Stay in touch with your own excitement about helping your partner make these dreams come true.

3. Will reaching any of these goals require learning on your part? Identify any new skills or knowledge either of you will need to make these dreams come true. Talk openly about the ways you will try to get these skills or knowledge.

4. In each arrangement (Long-range, Ambitious and Immediate Dreams), did you include ways of caring for people outside your marriage? If you don't find any, go back to the "Lottery" exercise in this chapter and look at your list on caring for others. See if you are moved to add some goals for caring to your dream lists.

Arranging Your Dreams In Order of Importance

Very few couples can go to work on all of their dreams at once *financially*. This is the reality you need to work on next. You can do this by arranging your dreams in order of importance.

To help you do this, I suggest you concentrate on no more than one Long-range Dream, one Ambitious Dream, and two Immediate Dreams at this time. Selecting one of your dreams as most important may make you wonder if your other dreams will get put off forever. I can understand this concern. However, this is not really true. Here is why.

In the course of this book, you are going to learn how to be successful with money so you can make your dreams come true faster than you ever thought possible.

As this happens, you will be returning frequently to your dream lists to set new priorities. Some dreams that didn't make your first list of "most important" dreams will be on your next edition of that list.

The healthy way to do this exercise is to agree which dreams you will tackle first. Making that kind of decision may be entirely new for you. For this reason, I suggest in the beginning you identify a *shared dream* to work on in the first two categories (your Long-range and Ambitious Dreams). In the Immediate Dream category, you should each have at least one *personal* top priority goal that you will work on as a couple.

In the Psychological Paycheck category, you need to have as big a list as possible and make sure those dreams get worked on every day, every week, and every month.

By reading this book, you are also going to discover how to care for one another's world of dreams—all of them all of the time. And while sometimes it may be necessary to take turns making dreams come true, you must learn to keep *all of your dreams* pictured in your mind no matter which one(s) you are actually working on at the moment.

You will learn that by constantly encouraging the realization of one another's dreams, you will create tremendous confidence and respect in your marital partnership.

You see, you may not be able to work on all of your dreams at once *financially*, but you can work on all of your dreams at once *psychologically and emotionally*.

You will learn more about this in the next part of this chapter, but for now, talk each other through the following Agreement Check:

Agreement Check:

1. Look back at your dream lists once more. Identify one shared dream in each of the Big Dream and Medium Size Dream categories that you agree will be your top priority for now. Using a red pen, mark that one, "TOP PRIORITY."

2. In the Small Dream category, select two TOP PRIORITY dreams. One should be marked "HERS" and one "HIS." Mark these with a red pen, also.

3. With the same red pen, mark all of your Psychological Paychecks as TOP PRIORITY. These should be small enough to work into your financial life with no financial strain whatsoever. Remember, they are the love letters of your continuing commitment and promise to keep working on dreams together in the face of every possible obstacle.

4. As a final step, buy some 3" X 5" cards at the local drug store and write these TOP PRIORITY dreams down and carry them around with you wherever you go. Take them to work, tape them to your refrigerator, put a set in your visor in the car. Have a set by your bed so you can review them at night before you go to sleep and when you get up in the morning. To learn how to turn up the sound on this exercise in a way that will really boost your power to make dreams come true, read on.

Picturing Your Success

One of the most powerful ways known of making things happen is to concentrate on a picture in your mind of the goal you want to reach. This is a technique used by many successful people. In basketball, for example, in the seconds just before he shoots a free throw, a player imagines or "sees" a picture in his or her mind of the ball swishing through the hoop. Championship golfers "see" a picture of their golf ball in perfect flight toward the green. Dieters are often instructed to "see" a picture in their minds of how they will look after they lose their extra weight. An executive will "see" a picture in his or her mind of the end of a successful business deal.

You must "see" in your mind, in as much detail as possible, exactly what you want in order to have your mind, your spirit, and your body focused so that you can do the very most with them.

In **Appendix A** you will find forms to put in images or pictures of your dreams. This is so you can create (and use effectively) your own marriage Dream Book. Before starting this book, however, it is very important to go through one more step toward getting ready.

Mental Power Building

I want you to imagine that you have a movie projector or a VCR in your mind. Now, I want you to turn it on and play back a time or a scene in which you did a major job or performance or accomplishment that was very satisfying and rewarding for you. It may have been winning an award in school for good grades or making a sports team. You may have finished building or making something that gave you great pleasure and satisfaction. You may have learned a language, climbed a mountain, learned to swim, gotten a job you really wanted or earned a promotion. Remember every detail of that experience. How did you feel when you were working toward that goal? What did success look like? Remember the sounds of people telling you how great you were or what a great job you did. Remember how you told yourself that you were a success and how you agreed with all those other people. For just a few minutes, put yourself right there in that time and place. You know how hard you worked to reach that goal. You remember all the obstacles that were in your way but you overcame them—all of them. You were absolutely incredible in the way you kept trying to reach your goal—

and you did it!

Remember listening to your friends who helped you and encouraged you on the way to reaching your goal. What were some of the words they used that kept you going?

Play back the scene in your mind when you actually reached your goal. Remember every detail. Where were you? What time of year was it? How old were you? Who was there with you? Just for a few moments, relive that wonderful experience all over again.

Now, sit down with your marriage partner and tell him or her everything about this experience. Ask your partner to do the same thing with you. Most importantly, listen carefully to each other and take detailed notes of what was said.

The purpose of this exercise will be explained to you later in this chapter. The next four pages provide a place for each of you to record every detail of what your partner told you. This is an exercise in mental power building.

As with all of the written exercises, forget spelling and grammar. They are not important here. What is important is to listen and to record the ideas and feelings carefully.

Notes: A Major Success or Accomplishment From My Partner's Past—Hers:

What was the event or accomplishment?

_____

What things got in the way and had to be overcome?

_____

_____

_____

_____

_____

What did other people say or do to encourage my partner to be successful during that experience?

_____

_____

_____

_____

_____

How did my partner feel about that experience? What are some key words she used to describe it?

_____

_____

_____

_____

_____

What does my partner remember about the sights and sounds of that experience?

_____

_____

_____

_____

_____

_____

_____

What did I observe about my partner during the telling of this wonderfully successful experience?

_____

_____

_____

_____

_____

How did making this dream come true enrich my partner's life?

_____

_____

_____

_____

_____

_____

Notes: A Major Success or Accomplishment From My Partner's Past—His:

What was the event or accomplishment?

_____

What things got in the way and had to be overcome?

_____

_____

_____

_____

What did other people say or do to encourage my partner to be successful during that experience?

_____

_____

_____

_____

How did my partner feel about that experience? What are some key words he used to describe it?

_____

_____

_____

_____

What does my partner remember about the sights and sounds of that experience?

_____

_____

_____

_____

_____

_____

What did I observe about my partner during the telling of this wonderfully successful experience?

_____

_____

_____

_____

_____

How did making this dream come true enrich my partner's life?

_____

_____

_____

_____

_____

_____

Creating Your Marriage Dream Book

If you have gone through every step in the preceding pages, you are now ready to create a Dream Book for your marriage. You may wish to use the pages in **Appendix A**, or you may enjoy buying a scrap book so you can add or subtract pages to your Dream Book. Be sure to create a page in your Dream Book for all of your dreams, even if some of them are not on your "most important" dream list.

You'll find it's much more fun if you build your Dream Book together.

Begin by finding some old magazines or brochures to cut up. You need pictures that represent your dreams. Answer the questions that appear on the Dream Book pages about each dream. Remember, *this should be fun*. Don't rush. Don't feel you have to do it all at once. Work on it steadily. But most importantly, do it!

Visual Repetition (or, "Play It Again, Sam.")

Now that you have a way of visualizing your dreams as goals, you will benefit by looking at your Dream Book often. There is no formula for how often to do this. Some couples like to review their Dream Books several times a week; others set aside only an hour each month. The point is that repetition, looking over and over at the pictures that represent your dreams, works to back up your promise to make these dreams come true.

When you take time to review your Dream Book, follow these guidelines:

1. Always review your Dream Book together. Set aside a time when you will not be interrupted.

2. Begin by simply turning the pages of your Dream Book and looking at the pictures.

3. Go back through the book, page by page, and talk over how you feel about each dream and how important it is to continue to make progress toward making each dream come true.

4. Encourage each other about realizing every dream in your book. Celebrate any progress you have made—even in a small way.

5. If things have gotten in the way of any of your dreams, talk about them and find ways that you will work together to overcome them.

Overcoming Roadblocks

On the way to making your dreams come true in marriage, you are bound to run into roadblocks. Such roadblocks can either encourage you to work harder, or they can discourage you. (Someone once said that our challenge in making dreams come true is to turn stumbling blocks into stepping stones.) Whether you are successful in overcoming the roadblocks of life or whether you let them overcome you depends to a great extent on how you choose to look at them.

Roadblocks are really just a sign that you are alive and well and out there fighting to make dreams come true for your marriage.

If you weren't working toward reaching your goals, there would be nothing to block your way. The fun lies in pointing out those roadblocks in your path and planning ways to remove them. To help you win at overcoming roadblocks, I have given you a summary below of the main kinds of roadblocks you'll encounter and some of the general plans of action to help you remove them and keep your marriage moving ahead.

Roadblocks	Plans of Action
1. Not enough knowledge.	**1.** Get more knowledge (books, classes, advice from experts, etc.)
2. Not enough time.	**2.** Reset time schedule. Allow more time to complete goal.
3. Missed financial goal.	**3.** Reset goal.
4. Missed chance.	**4.** Move on to the next chance.
5. Change in goal.	**5.** Set new goal.

Dealing With Discouragement

From time to time, you may get discouraged.

We all get discouraged. It's a condition of being human. But when this happens, your biggest roadblock can be yourself.

When you become discouraged, return to the section on Mental Power Building. Take turns remembering your past successes. Go over every detail just as you did when you worked out the exercise originally. You may want to add more successful experiences to the list. That's fine. Just remember to go over every detail of *those* experiences as well. You will find that this powerful tool will help you to overcome the great majority of discouraging experiences.

I also suggest that you surround yourself with reading material that tells the stories of other people's successes in overcoming roadblocks and defeating discouragement.

In fact, I encourage you to make a hobby out of this activity. When you're discouraged, you can pick yourself back up fast by reading the stories of people who pursued in the face of adversity and conquered it.

In the next chapter, you'll discover how the values you choose to live by can give you the strength to overcome discouraging obstacles and circum-stances. But the secret of winning at anything in life has been known for centuries. That secret is this.

Roadblocks are no match for persistence. "Persistence" is the will to continue in the face of adversity, and to never, never, never give up. Nothing in the world can take the place of persistence. Talent will not; genius will not; education will not. Persistence and determination alone are all powerful.

When you struggle with adversity and win, you are made stronger in will and character. Whenever you overcome a roadblock or adversity, your own self-confidence goes up. By persisting against adversity, you discover you can win; you can succeed. What is really special in marriage is that you have your own cheerleader, someone who cares for you and about you, and who is there to encourage you when the going gets tough.

To help you remember this important secret to financial success in marriage, memorize the little statement below. You will find it can keep you strong in the face of even the most discouraging circumstances:

"The pursuit of excellence in the face of adversity is invariably matched by the glory of the result!!"

Celebrating Success

Measuring progress is always a personal matter. This chapter has been about helping you to identify your dreams and setting your goals for the financial side of marriage. However, the simple guidelines below are presented to help you experience the joy of success as you make progress toward making your dreams come true.

How To Measure Success

1. Always measure success in inches. The old saying goes, "Inch-by-inch is a cinch, but yard-by-yard is hard." Every little bit of progress should be recognized, celebrated, and enjoyed. Celebrate finding new knowledge about your dream. Celebrate when you overcome a roadblock. And, of course, celebrate any financial success toward making dreams come true.

2. Reinforce your successes in ways that have special meaning for you. It is best to work out your own ways to congratulate yourselves. It can be something as simple as a note taped to the refrigerator door that lists your successes. You can update it every week. However you celebrate, just make sure you both agree on how you will back up one another for the successes you are experiencing—then do it.

3. Use the mental power building techniques described in this chapter and other chapters of this book. If you repeat over and over again your determination to make dreams come true by using positive statements and positive picturing, the power of your mind will be let loose in ways that will amaze you.

In Summary

You may wonder at this point if this book is really about how to manage the financial dimension of married life. I can understand if you have that question in your mind. Perhaps it will help if you recall the definition I gave you for "Happily Ever After."

"Happily Ever After" is the process of working together to make one another's dreams come true, both the shared dreams of married life and the unique, individual dreams that are special to each partner.

There are many sides to financial planning and management that you will need to learn and to master to make dreams come true in your marriage. Identifying your dreams is the first step. Each of the remaining chapters will help you take one more step. But—unless you have a burning desire in your hearts to make dreams come true, the subjects in those chapters will probably not interest you. Financial planning and management are only ways to help you get to where you want to go. It is up to you to set your own goals. Pushed by your goals and the realization that dreams can come true, you will discover that learning the secrets to financial success in marriage is more than interesting—it is an exciting journey of learning and growth.

Suggested Additional Reading:

Maltz, Maxwell, M.D., F.I.C.S. *Psycho-cybernetics*. Englewood Cliffs: Prentice-Hall, Inc., 1960.

Peale, Norman Vincent. *The Power of Positive Imaging.* Old Tappan, New Jersey: Fleming H. Revel Company, n.d.

Gawain, Shakti. *Creative Visualization.* New York: Bantam Books, 1982.

Arterburn, Stephan and Carl Dreizler. *52 Simple Ways to Say "I Love You."* Nashville: Oliver Nelson, A Division of Thomas Nelson Publishers, 1991.

Agreement Check:

1. Complete the following statement:

> ## "We agree to set time aside for regular reviews of our Dream Book and to talk about our progress toward reaching our goals. We will review our Dream Book every_____."

2. We know there will be things that get in the way of making our dreams come true. When this happens, we will encourage each other by:

_____

_____

_____

_____

_____

_____

_____

_____

_____

_____

_____

_____

_____

_____

_____

_____

"Follow The Yellow Brick Road"

Chapter Four

"The destination is important,
but the journey determines the quality of a marriage."
Anonymous

Now that you've identified your dreams for marriage, your next challenge is to create a financial plan that will help you make dreams come true. Most married couples manage their finances on the basis of crises, moods, quick fixes and immediate gratification—not on a sound plan that they both agree to live by.

A carefully thought out financial plan will allow you to work as a team and take advantage of financial "synergy."

"Synergy" is the ultimate team experience for a married couple. What it means is that the power and strength created by joining forces produces a result that is greater than the sum of what both of you could produce by working alone.

You may be surprised to discover that the first step in creating a financial plan is to agree on a set of values to guide you on your way to reaching your dreams.

Without values (or with the wrong ones) to guide you, not only will team work and synergy be impossible, but your financial ship of life can easily crash on the shores of harsh consequences when the winds of financial challenge and change start howling.

With the right values, you'll have a guidebook for all your actions and decisions. Even when financial times are hard, right values can give you a sense of direction and maintain your sense of security, prosperity, and personal power. A sound set of values to guide your marital financial planning may be the most valuable asset you own.

The principles and values I teach in this chapter have been selected for their ability to encourage cooperation, team work, and synergy. By reading and applying these lessons, you will actually begin the team building process so essential for financial success in marriage. Don't attempt to bypass these lessons or to take a shortcut.

Unlike financial success as a single person, financial success as a married couple can *only* be achieved when you work and act as a team.

Even when you share right values, you'll experience occasional conflicts as you plan and work to make dreams come true. Conflict is a natural part of living in the real world. In this chapter, you'll learn ways to minimize and to manage conflict. If you've come from a family background where conflict was not managed constructively, then learning these lessons will be extremely important if you want to achieve financial success in your marriage. Even after you learn these lessons, your education about conflict (the roots of conflict and its effect on financial success in marriage) won't be complete without reading Chapter Five.

The Importance of Planning

Everyone who wants to make dreams come true needs a plan. Since your dreams will cost money, you have to develop a plan to acquire money. Does that sound too obvious? It's not.

Most married couples don't have a financial plan, and only a few ever get around to making one. In fact, most married couples find it hard to even talk about financial matters.

into detailed planning with professional financial advisors.

How important is a financial plan? To be honest, without one you won't make much financial progress and you'll never reach the city of your dreams. But with one that you both develop as a team, you'll see your income and your financial worth steadily increase—*and*, you'll grow closer together as a couple.

It's strange when you think about it, but people who share bedrooms and bathrooms tend to back off quickly when the subject they need to talk about has a price tag.

This is mostly because they haven't been taught how to talk about money.

The financial planning process provided in this book may be new to you, and it may even be challenging, but at least it will give you a way to discuss financial issues and ideas. Hopefully, by the time you're finished reading this book, you'll have (at the very least) a preliminary plan for your financial future that will prepare you to move

Think of putting your financial plan together as though you were going to take a dream vacation.

The first thing you would do is talk about the places you both want to go (*identifying your dreams for marriage*). Next, you would read about these places and learn everything you could about them (*visualizing your dreams and creating excitement and inspiration to reach them*). Then, you would learn all you could about travel arrangements and costs (*identifying the price of your dreams and the knowledge you need to help make your dreams come true*). Of course, you would also learn the laws that govern travel to these places (*learning about values that inspire cooperation and the laws that govern financial success*). Next, you would talk to travel agents to find an expert who could make arrangements in countries that you wanted to visit (*finding the right financial advisor(s) to help you apply your newly discovered knowledge*). Once you selected the right agent, and before making reservations, you would carefully check your knowledge with the agent and fill in the gaps in your planning so that no detail is left to chance (*gaining more knowledge from your advisor(s) before making final decisions*). Finally, you would allow your agent to book your travel arrangements and room accommodations (*making intelligent financial decisions and taking responsible financial actions*).

Now, with your trip well planned, you would be free to sit back and enjoy yourselves. Sure, some things might not work out exactly as you thought. But because of careful preparation, it's far more likely that you'll have a great trip.

To the extent that you're both willing to plan the financial trip to the great city of your dreams, you can expect a far more enjoyable ride than most married couples.

But postpone planning, or ignore it completely, and your dreams will eventually look like those abandoned cars stranded along freeways waiting to be carted off to a junk yard.

The Importance of Value-Centered Planning

Now that you know your destination (your dreams), it would help a great deal to have a map that tells you how to get where you're going. Unfortunately, there is no map that can tell you exactly how to get to the great city of your dreams.

As all explorers of new frontiers, you will have to draw your own map. But you don't have to do this without benefit of a moral "compass" to guide you.

The financial frontiers you face in life require a basic knowledge of direction. Your dreams *and* values are what will give you that direction. Your dreams tell you where you want to go. Your values tell you whether or not you're going in the right direction.

Just as great explorers had to fix on the North Star to determine south, east, and west, you must take an occasional fix on your values so you don't end up making unethical or immoral decisions. The best time to do this is at the beginning of your marriage.

Every man and woman comes to marriage with his or her own set of values. These values can easily be put into categories labeled "Yours, Mine and Ours." You inherit most of them from parents, family, church, and society. You do not consciously select them. We must learn values early in life in order to sort out what is important from what isn't important. Every day we are showered with information and events. Without values, we can't take it all in, decide what is important, and make decisions about how to respond. Values shape our behavior and set the direction for our lives. If our values are "right," they can be of enormous help in making dreams come true.

"Right" values are those that spark cooperative living and provide the following three qualities of life:

Inner Security: Security is a sense of feeling that you are O.K. and a good person no matter what opinions others have about you and no matter what your circumstances happen to be at the moment.

A Sense of Prosperity: Prosperity is living easily and happily in the world whether you have money or not. Prosperity means that you love life, appreciate what you have, and believe that your dreams deserve to come true.

Personal Power: Personal power is the belief that applying your efforts can and will bring about a change in your circumstances (a change for the better) and allow you to overcome challenges on your way to making dreams come true. Married couples who combine the personal power they have as individuals have synergistic power. Synergistic power dramatically increases your ability to cause change.

While money and other financial assets can be taken away from you or drop in value, these three qualities above (and your dreams) can never be taken from you once you learn how to get them. And with them, you will discover a secret that has often escaped even the most clever financial geniuses. That secret is this:

True wealth is created only when the acquisition of money is combined with inner security, a sense of prosperity and personal power. Many couples believe that getting money and becoming wealthy will somehow give them these qualities of life, but this is not true. Actually, it works the other way around.

When, as a result of living with "right" values, you have inner security, a sense of prosperity, as well as personal and synergistic power, you can be far more successful with money.

For a married couple to have these life qualities, they not only need "right" values, they must both adopt the same ones. Conflicting values often lead to major communication problems. If you can't communicate effectively, cooperation, teamwork and synergy become impossible. Without committing to live by "right" values, any financial progress you make will be empty and meaningless because you won't really be together. At best, without sharing "right" values, your relationship may become a marriage of convenience in which you stay together to save face, or "for the children." At worst, your marriage will

become a hot bed of emotional warfare and could end in divorce.

It may seem odd and even a little frustrating to learn that the values you choose to live by could have such an impact on your financial success in marriage.

Some of you may quickly point out that people with wishy-washy or even evil values have done well financially. This may seem to be true on the surface, but the unhappy consequences of "wrong" values don't always show up immediately.

Frequently, they are invisible to the outside observer. But you can be sure that they show up eventually, if only as internal realities like guilt, fear, shame and loneliness.

That's why so much of this chapter is dedicated to helping you identify and adopt "right" values. By learning about these timeless, unchanging principles and by working through the exercises that follow, you can formulate a foundation of values that encourage cooperative living. You can have the added benefit of increasing your inner security, sense of prosperity and personal power. If you decide to adopt these principles as the value system for your marriage, they will keep you going in the right direction—no matter what circumstances or challenges you face in life.

A Closer Look at Cooperative Living

As used here, the word "cooperation" means the same as "team work" and "synergy." Most obviously, what you need for cooperation is a desire to join forces and work together for individual and shared objectives—like making dreams come true in marriage.

Because we live in a society that worships competition, cooperation is usually considered less important in our social value system.

As a result, the benefits of cooperative living are often overlooked. However, in marriage, cooperation is necessary to accomplish anything worthwhile. The possibility of truly important financial gains in marriage can *only* come about through cooperation. And when you think hard, it's easy to see that cooperation is a much higher form of civilized behavior than competition. Cooperation also offers many more benefits than competition.

Basically, cooperation is a willingness to work together to get something done.

When adopted as a lifestyle, cooperating with others will actually shorten the distance between you and your goals (dreams). Cooperation will also improve the quality of your journey to the great city of your dreams. Here is why.

Cooperation is a linking process that brings people together in a way that makes everyone feel appreciated for their unique qualities. We are all different and unique individuals, but in order to feel good about ourselves, we need to feel connected with others who love and appreciate us for our uniqueness. When this happens, we feel we belong. There is a sense of "We-ness." Cooperation links people together and provides this sense of belonging. Cooperation also creates an increase in resources to help accomplish a goal.

Cooperation is a creative process that allows you to share resources in a way that creates new resources. These new resources make it possible for you to deal with life's challenges and opportunities in creative ways that aren't available to you as individuals. The possibility of truly significant gains or significant improvement can take place only through cooperation. (*Imagine how far civilization would have come if humans had been unable to cooperate in any way.*)

Cooperation is an encouraging process that helps bring out each person's best by building self confidence, self esteem and feelings of self worth. Those who encourage us help us believe in our own abilities by becoming our cheerleaders. When we make mistakes, encouragement helps us accept and learn from our mistakes. This gives us the courage to face our imperfections, pick up the pieces of our mistakes and keep moving ahead.

Cooperation is a Win/Win process where everyone works together as friends in a way that assures that everyone will get some (and maybe all) of their wants and needs met. In marriage, the cooperative Win/Win process assures that all decision making is carried on in the spirit of *full respect* for the other person's feelings and point of view, and all decision making *benefits both* partners. The Win/Win process also *motivates and satisfies both* marriage partners.

Most couples bring a cooperative spirit with them to the start of married life. However, many meet early frustration in their cooperative ventures because they don't adopt a set of values that encourages cooperation and turn those values into guidelines for cooperative living.

Yet, once married couples actually experience cooperation in overcoming any challenge, their marriages are never quite the same. Once they taste the fruits of cooperation, they want more of these life and mind expanding experiences.

Just as inner security, a sense of prosperity and personal power result from "right" values, so do the benefits of cooperation, team work, and synergistic power.

When right values set the ground rules for all dealings between a husband and wife, cooperation becomes a real life experience that produces big rewards.

But no good will result if you are seeking a "quick" and "easy" technique to produce cooperation. Just as there is no such thing as "easy" when it comes to making dreams come true, there is no "quick" way to gain the lasting cooperation of others (especially a marriage partner). Because we live in a society that offers instant everything (and because there is a part of our mental makeup that hungers for instant gratification) it is more than a little unpleasant to accept this truth. But this, indeed, is the truth. There is no Shake 'n Bake formula for building a cooperative marriage relationship. If you want a microwave solution to building a lasting, loving marriage, you won't find it here. If, on the other hand, you're ready to build your marriage relationship on the challenging but productive principles presented in this chapter, you will soon find yourself on the super highway marked "cooperation."

I like to think of cooperation as the "yellow brick road" to the city of your dreams. Believe me, this road offers the smoothest ride and will bring you the greatest satisfaction.

So, if you're ready to learn about the principles, values and guidelines that produce cooperation, let's get started.

The Principle Behind Principles

The principles presented on the next few pages are expressions of universal laws that govern the way humans treat one another. Such laws are unlike man-made laws. Universal laws aren't here one day and gone the next. They are unchanging and timeless. Of course, humans violate these laws all the time, but not without consequences. Usually, the consequences are painful, sometimes tragically painful. History has clearly shown the high price to be paid for ignoring or violating these universal laws.

Knowing about these principles won't help you unless you bring your life into harmony and agreement with them.

When your values and strategies for dealing with life are in harmony with universal laws, it becomes a lot easier to make dreams come true in marriage. If your values are out of harmony with these laws, you will experience frustration and disappointment at every turn of the road.

Five chapters in this book are de-voted to presenting seven laws that govern financial success, but the next few pages present a brief summary of the laws that govern your success in getting along with others (cooperating). And believe me, that success is important. Why? Because...

...if you're not successful with people (especially the person you marry), then you won't be a success at living—no matter how much money you have.

Admittedly, life enriching principles exist that are not covered here. Don't let that stop you from finding them and applying them in your marriage. In fact, nothing I can think of will bring you inner security, a sense of prosperity and personal power faster than continuing to grow in awareness and wisdom through studying and living according to life's universal laws. Hopefully, you will devote a portion of every day to this study in order to gain values, guidelines and skills that will help you to cooperate with others and succeed in all your relationships.

How To Benefit Most From These Ideas

Each principle in the following pages is presented as a single statement. It is then interpreted as a value in an attempt to explain what the principle can mean when it is applied to your life and your marriage. At the bottom of each page are guidelines for cooperative living. These guidelines can expand your team building abilities in every aspect of married life if you adopt and live by them. This presentation is meant only to give you a starting point for your discussions about values. An agreement check follows each presentation along with a list of suggested readings. By working through the exercises and having the discussions I suggest, you will consciously choose (perhaps for the first time) those values that will guide your financial life and, hopefully, everything you do as a married couple.

Take your time reading through these pages. Don't feel you have to rush to complete this chapter. Work through one principle each night at bed time. That will give you plenty to think and talk about. To make these discussions about values a meaningful part of your financial life, you should revisit this chapter on a regular basis. Feel free to expand, redefine, change, or give new meaning to each value definition and the rules for cooperative living. Also feel free to add values and rules for cooperative living that you believe will strengthen your marriage.

Remember that the way you handle these discussions and decide on values is just as important as the end product.

If you approach these discussions in a spirit of openness and respect, express your different views and work together to create something you both believe in, then they will have deep and lasting meaning for your financial life. When the values you choose to live by are the product of shared thinking and discussion, they will strengthen the bond of love that I know you already share. By posting your values where you can see them every day, they will remind you to stop and think before you act. They can remind you that while "happily ever after" means working together to make dreams come true, the quality of your journey to the city of your dreams is what makes a really good marriage.

The Love Principle

Love is the source of all good things.

Love as a Value: The Love Principle is an expression of the master law of life. There probably is no simple or satisfactory definition of love. In Chapter Two, you were introduced to the Four Dimensions of Love as a way of helping you see that love is a process of growth. As humans, we grow from love of ourselves to appreciation of others. In the most mature stage of love, we go beyond appreciation of others to *attending to others*. One way to do this is by helping others (especially a loved one) to make love-filled dreams come true. The great teachings about the principle of love offer additional insights into how to be loving.

From the Bible we learn that:

"Love is patient, love is kind.
It does not envy, it does not boast,
it is not proud.
It is not rude, it is not self-seeking,
it is not easily angered;
it keeps no record of wrong doings.
It always protects, always trusts,
always hopes, always perseveres."

This biblical passage is intended to provide a standard against which all thoughts and acts of love can be measured. Of course, as humans, we frequently fall short of this standard, or "miss the target" in our thoughts and actions. Nevertheless, those who adopt the Love Principle as a value for their lives commit to an on-going attempt to reach this standard.

To be loving as humans, then, takes effort and courage. The effort of love is expressed by paying attention to others, becoming a good listener and encouraging others.

The courage of love is expressed in reaching beyond your comfort zone to make room for other people in your life. This means loving a person even when he or she may have some traits you might consider less than fully "lovable." In marriage, courage means commitment—the willingness to be there for one another in ways that really are important, not just in ways *you* think are important.

The courage of love also means being willing to confront one another honestly (and lovingly) about the need to grow or "grow up." This is the hardest part about adopting the Love Principle as a value. There are times when it is not loving to approve certain dreams, ambitions, and behaviors. To approve *all* behavior is impossible and not what the Love Principle requires of us.

The "real world" need to make moral decisions often creates a dynamic tension of acceptance and judgment of the people we care about most in life. Yet, if you choose love as a standard for your marriage you agree to act always in "loving" ways toward one another, even in trying moments when you must judge your partner's decisions.

Guidelines For Cooperative Living:

1. Never have a discussion in anger.

2. Make every effort to rid yourself of fear, guilt, jealousy, hatred and envy.

3. Touch each other tenderly every chance you get.

4. Use caution and compassion in exercising moral judgments.

Agreement Check:

1. What do you see in this principle that makes sense to you as individuals? As a married couple?

2. What do you see in this principle that does not fit with your own experience(s) or view(s) of how the world works?

3. What would you change in the interpretation of this principle to make it a value that you can embrace for your marriage?

4. In what way might adopting this principle as a value help you to make your dreams come true?

5. How might you benefit from bringing your personal and married life into harmony with this principle? Try to give specific examples.

6. What might be the consequences of ignoring this principle and living a life out of harmony with it? Try to give specific examples.

7. Are you willing to adopt this principle as a value for your married life?

8. How can you make this principle come alive in your marriage? How can you blend it into your financial plan?

9. Do the Guidelines for Cooperative Living make sense to you?

10. How would you change them or what guidelines would you add?

11. Are you willing to adopt the Guidelines for Cooperative Living (and/or the ones you modified) for your marriage?

12. How can you make these guidelines come alive in your marriage? How can you merge them into your management of money?

Suggested Additional Reading:

Buber, Martin. *I and Thou*. New York: Charles Scribner's Sons, 1970.

Peck, Scott, M.D. *The Road Less Traveled*. New York: Simon & Schuster, Inc, 1978.

Howard, Alice and Walden. *Exploring the Road Less Traveled*. New York: Simon & Schuster, Inc., 1985.

The Truth Principle

The love of truth is the beginning of wisdom

Truth as a value: "Truth," as used here means honesty, and it also means love. Both honesty and love must be combined to set one on the path of wisdom.

"Honesty" means to seek understanding and knowledge. The understanding and knowledge one seeks, however, must be focused on (1) learning how things work (as opposed to how one wishes things worked) *and* (2) developing a full understanding about one's self (intellectually, emotionally, spiritually, and socially). With *only* an understanding of how things work and *without* a knowledge of one's self, one is not fully informed and cannot be fully honest. For example, if you know *how* to drive a car but do not know *how you* will drive it in traffic (given that you are free to drive it carefully or recklessly), then the half truth you know will not assist you in making wise decisions.

You might well wonder if knowing yourself in relation to every truth is important. The answer is "Yes." Another fair question is, "Will you (or anyone else) *always* put forth the effort to combine knowledge of yourself with knowledge about how things work?" The answer is probably "No." Living honestly is a difficult task and humans have a tendency to be fairly lazy about the "knowing yourself" part of it. But understanding yourself *is necessary* for those who love the truth. When one does not love the truth, one may simply rely on others to "tell" them what is true and what is not true, or they may quickly and easily make their own "knee-jerk" judgments without deep thought. Both tendencies have unhappy consequences and usually result in lesser or greater degrees of dishonesty.

Even when one is fully honest, if his or her judgments are not tempered with love, they can (and usually do) make very unwise decisions. This is the second half of what it means to be truthful. With full understanding of the facts (and of yourself), your decisions, speech and behavior are less than truthful if the beacon for your interaction with others is not love. For example, you may know that theft is one course of action that can secure money, and you may know that you are financially desperate. But if your final decision is to take action that violates the Law of Love, you don't really love the truth and you are not very wise.

When a married couple loves truth, they have to manage three views of honesty and love. Both of them must manage their own personal view, and together they must manage their "couple perception." Sharing right values helps with this challenge. So does learning and mastering good communication skills.

Guidelines for Cooperative Living:

1. Always be honest in your dealings with one another and with others. Never lie, steal, cheat or seek to deceive in any way.

2. Continue your education in every way possible. Seek to expand your knowledge of your world and your self. Willingly and quickly give up your beliefs and understandings when they have been proven incorrect—but never give up your commitment to live by "right" values.

86

Agreement Check:

1. What do you see in this principle that makes sense to you as individuals? As a married couple?

2. What do you see in this principle that does not fit with your own experience(s) or view(s) of how the world works?

3. What would you change in the interpretation of this principle to make it a value that you can embrace for your marriage?

4. In what way might adopting this principle as a value help you to make your dreams come true?

5. How might you benefit from bringing your personal and married life into harmony with this principle? Try to give specific examples.

6. What might be the consequences of ignoring this principle and living a life out of harmony with it? Try to give specific examples.

7. Are you willing to adopt this principle as a value for your married life?

8. How can you make this principle come alive in your marriage? How can you blend it into your financial plan?

9. Do the Guidelines for Cooperative Living make sense to you?

10. How would you change them or what guidelines would you add?

11. Are you willing to adopt the Guidelines for Cooperative Living (and/or the ones you modified) for your marriage?

12. How can you make these guidelines come alive in your marriage? How can you merge them into your management of money?

Suggested Additional Reading:

Schutz, Will. *The Truth Option*. Berkeley: Ten Speed Press, 1984.

Peck, Scott M., M.D. *People of the Lie: The Hope for Healing Human Evil*. New York: Simon & Schuster, Inc., 1983.

The Abundance Principle

Everything you need or want in life already exists in abundant supply.

Abundance as a Value: Some people behave as though there isn't enough to go around—not enough time, food, money, love or whatever. Such behavior goes against the facts and violates this important law of life. Nevertheless, these people think and act in fear that unless they rush to grab all they can for themselves ("the one who dies with the most toys wins"), they will lose out.

Although everything you want or need already exists in abundant supply, there may be a problem with distribution. There also may be a temporary shortage of ideas about how to redistribute the supply so you can make your dreams come true. If you behave as though this momentary lack of ideas is just reason to break the Law of Love or other universal laws, then you condemn yourself to a mind set of "scarcity." As a result, you will always feel anxious that you don't have "enough."

Attracting your supply begins with tuning in to what you *really* need or want and measuring that against the Master Law of Life (the Law of Love). How love-filled are your dreams? The more love in you and in your dreams, the easier it becomes to attract your supply.

The next step in attracting your supply is to focus your attention, in order to resonate with your dreams. You begin to resonate with your dreams by creating your marriage Dream Book. But you can't stop there. You must constantly refine your thinking about how your dreams will enrich your life and the lives of others. In this way, your mind, your spirit and your body can work in harmony during the process of making dreams come true.

Another important step in attracting your supply is to believe in yourself— that you are the right one (with the help of your marriage partner) to make your dream(s) come true. This means that no matter what any person may think or believe about you, *you* believe that you are good and valuable and that your life is part of a great plan to bring more and more love into the world. Working to make your dreams come true (no matter how great or small) simply helps to fulfill this plan.

Those who believe in the Abundance Principle also believe in and encourage other people's dreams because they know that there is ample supply to fulfill every "right" or love-filled dream. By encouraging the dreams of others, you soon find that you are surrounded with supporters and friends who create cells of cooperation and synergy to assist you to make your own dreams come true. In this way, your *belief* in limitless supply is reinforced by the real-life *experience* of limitless supply.

Guidelines For Cooperative Living:

1. Agree never to act as though there existed a scarcity of supply.

2. Accept one another as part of the great supply, and an increase to your own supply. Frequently praise and give credit to the good in each other.

3. When scarcity seems real, believe that a way can be found for both of you to get what you want.

Agreement Check:

1. What do you see in this principle that makes sense to you as individuals? As a married couple?

2. What do you see in this principle that does not fit with your own experience(s) or view(s) of how the world works?

3. What would you change in the interpretation of this principle to make it a value that you can embrace for your marriage?

4. In what way might adopting this principle as a value help you to make your dreams come true?

5. How might you benefit from bringing your personal and married life into harmony with this principle? Try to give specific examples.

6. What might be the consequences of ignoring this principle and living a life out of harmony with it? Try to give specific examples.

7. Are you willing to adopt this principle as a value for your married life?

8. How can you make this principle come alive in your marriage? How can you blend it into your financial plan?

9. Do the Guidelines for Cooperative Living make sense to you?

10. How would you change them or what guidelines would you add?

11. Are you willing to adopt the Guidelines for Cooperative Living (and/or the ones you modified) for your marriage?

12. How can you make these guidelines come alive in your marriage? How can you merge them into your management of money?

Suggested Additional Reading:

Dyer, Dr. Wayne W. "Abundance." In *You'll See It When You Believe It*. New York, William Morrow and Company, Inc., 1989.

The Time/Patience Principle

There is a time for every purpose.

Patience as a Value: One of the realities we live with as humans is the reality of time. It is said that the dimension of time is what keeps everything from happening at once. Often, as humans, we resent this. We all tend to want what we want (or what we need) immediately. It seems that the younger we are, the more intensely we want our wants and needs met as soon as we're in touch with them. However, the dimension of time almost always stands between us and our desire to have or obtain what we want and need.

Time also limits the measure of what we can experience as humans. What this means is that because of time we have to accept the limitation that while we can have *whatever* we want from life, we can't have *everything* we want. This is why it is so important to choose (very carefully) what it is that we want. Because once humans focus in on what they want, and devote all of their time (and energy) to getting it, they can usually (over time) obtain it. If what you choose to bring into your life is not designed to fulfill the Law of Love, then the fruits of your labor may not be as fulfilling as you had anticipated, and may even leave you feeling empty or as though you had wasted your time.

Time and again you will be confronted by the limitations of time, forcing you to deal with the measure of time it will take to make your dreams come true. For this, you need patience.

Patience is more than calm endurance. Patience is the ability to flow with the unexpected events that temporarily interrupt your drive towards making dreams come true and never to take your eye off of the prize as you continue preparing yourself for your next move toward your goal.

When the unexpected occurs, the patient person attempts to discover the opportunity in those events. When the schedule is interrupted, the patient person simply reschedules. When resources don't materialize on schedule, the patient person uses creative thinking to find new ways to generate resources. When normal emotions like anger and frustration emerge, the patient person accepts those feelings and converts the energy from such feelings into constructive action that takes him or her one step closer to making dreams come true.

The patient person also recognizes that the universe has its own timing which is known as the "fullness of time." This timing is like an invisible door in time which will open only for those who constantly prepare and work very hard at making dreams come true. Those who are patient can be alert to the special moments in time when all of their work and preparation suddenly stands before this invisible door (often referred to as "opportunity"). Then, and only then, can their dreams become realities. Then, and only then, can they enter the "fullness of time" and understand completely that "there is a time for every purpose."

Guidelines for Cooperative Living:

1. As you work and prepare to make your dreams come true, develop the quality of patient persistence. Be patient with yourself, one another, and with the universe itself. But never, never, never give up your dreams.

Agreement Check:

1. What do you see in this principle that makes sense to you as individuals? As a married couple?

2. What do you see in this principle that does not fit with your own experience(s) or view(s) of how the world works?

3. What would you change in the interpretation of this principle to make it a value that you can embrace for your marriage?

4. In what way might adopting this principle as a value help you to make your dreams come true?

5. How might you benefit from bringing your personal and married life into harmony with this principle? Try to give specific examples.

6. What might be the consequences of ignoring this principle and living a life out of harmony with it? Try to give specific examples.

7. Are you willing to adopt this principle as a value for your married life?

8. How can you make this principle come alive in your marriage? How can you blend it into your financial plan?

9. Do the Guidelines for Cooperative Living make sense to you?

10. How would you change them or what guidelines would you add?

11. Are you willing to adopt the Guidelines for Cooperative Living (and/or the ones you modified) for your marriage?

12. How can you make these guidelines come alive in your marriage? How can you merge them into your management of money?

Suggested Additional Reading:

Schuller, Robert H. *Tough Times Never Last, But Tough People Do.* New York: Bantam Books, 1987.

The Appreciation Principle

A grateful heart is a magnet for all good things.

Appreciation as a Value: Once you grasp the truth that everything you want or need to make dreams come true exists in plentiful supply, you are free to stop focusing on what you don't have and start to focus on attracting your supply. One view is negative and the other is positive. Only when you no longer concentrate on what is missing in your life will you be free to allow the power of your dreams to make you a magnet for the supply necessary to make them come true.

Living the Appreciation Principle as a value is simple but powerful. Begin by taking inventory of all your assets—your health, your youth, your love for one another, your family and friends, your dreams and your finances—and express gratitude for these blessings every day. This exercise cannot be shallow. To magnetize what you already have and to help attract your supply, your expression of appreciation must be deeply sincere. I urge you to use the beginning of each day *and* the moments just before you go to sleep at night to do this.

The second step in living appreciation as a value is to concentrate on the master principle of love. After giving thanks, read the passage quoted on Page 84 or other teachings on love that hold great meaning for you. Attune yourself to the Love Principle. Get in touch with and feel those feelings that come from harmonizing or being one with that principle. In this state of mind, you are super magnetized to attract your supply.

The final step is to be quiet, *very* quiet—and still, *very* still. Then listen, *just listen*. With your spirit glowing with appreciation and your heart filled with the power of love, you become like a radio receiver. Any ideas that come to you while in this state of mind will help you determine what to do next in your quest to make love-filled dreams come true. By the way, don't expect to hear voices or anything like that. Listen for positive, constructive, loving ideas. They may be little ideas that come to you like whispers. Or, you may have a very deep insight that nearly knocks you over. In any case, share these ideas with one another and discuss them (lovingly). If you feel the need, test your new idea or insight by repeating this appreciation exercise for several days. Then, if it still seems right, act on it. If your idea and your actions truly come from gratitude and love, they will be "right" and they will be "good."

Guidelines for Cooperative Living:

1. Give thanks everyday for your life, one another, and all your blessings. Never take each other, anyone, or anything, for granted.

2. Have the courage to act on ideas inspired by love.

Agreement Check:

1. What do you see in this principle that makes sense to you as individuals? As a married couple?

2. What do you see in this principle that does not fit with your own experience(s) or view(s) of how the world works?

3. What would you change in the interpretation of this principle to make it a value that you can embrace for your marriage?

4. In what way might adopting this principle as a value help you to make your dreams come true?

5. How might you benefit from bringing your personal and married life into harmony with this principle? Try to give specific examples.

6. What might be the consequences of ignoring this principle and living a life out of harmony with it? Try to give specific examples.

7. Are you willing to adopt this principle as a value for your married life?

8. How can you make this principle come alive in your marriage? How can you blend it into your financial plan?

9. Do the Guidelines for Cooperative Living make sense to you?

10. How would you change them or what guidelines would you add?

11. Are you willing to adopt the Guidelines for Cooperative Living (and/or the ones you modified) for your marriage?

12. How can you make these guidelines come alive in your marriage? How can you merge them into your management of money?

Suggested Additional Reading:

Hill, Napoleon. *Think and Grow Rich [Including Action Manual]*. New York: Hawthorne/Dutton, 1982

The Unity Principle

Every person is a part of the whole.

Unity as a Value: Because of our limited vision caused by our limited viewing point in the Universe, it is difficult to see how we are connected to the whole of humanity *and* the whole of existence. Our culture makes a fetish of our independence, our individuality, our separateness. This only makes it more difficult to see and believe in the Unity Principle, our "connectedness" to the whole.

However, when we observe a colony of bees, we are much better at seeing the "whole" and how each individual bee going about its own business is, at the same time, a unit or element of the hive. We like to think that we are different—that we aren't like that. Yet, we selectively "connect" with others all the time. We like to associate with heroes, movie stars, great athletes, and great leaders (known as "winners"). When we see suffering or hardship in other humans, we tend to think that this has nothing to do with us.

The power to choose our "connections" does not contradict the Unity Principle. Like all universal principles, if it is ignored, the road to the city of your dreams can get very bumpy. Take an issue such as the environment. You may choose to believe that environmental issues have nothing to do with you. Then, you learn that the air you breathe makes you sick. Suddenly, your connection to the environment (which always existed) becomes painfully obvious.

Those who adopt the Unity Principle as a Value accept that when any part of the whole is ill, in pain or suffering, we are all affected. Realizing that we can't directly impact everything and everyone, those who value the Unity Principle create positive loving environments in their personal relationships. They do this by seeking ways for everyone to win, (Win/Win—which means everyone's wants, needs and feelings are important and everyone gets some, and maybe all, of what he or she wants and needs). To deny others, especially marriage partners, their right to get what they want (their love-filled dreams), to fail to help them, or (even worse) to stand in the way of their dreams, is self-destructive. By encouraging anything less than a Win/Win lifestyle, we pollute the river from which we ourselves must drink—the "river of life." On the other hand, by dedicating our energy to creating Win/Win environments, we enrich the "river of life."

Guidelines For Cooperative Living:

1. Agree that you and your marriage partner have equal rights to being satisfied and that you are equally involved and equally responsible for finding Win/Win solutions to every problem, challenge, or conflict in your life.

2. Say "I Love You" often and always think "Win/Win."

Agreement Check:

1. What do you see in this principle that makes sense to you as individuals? As a married couple?

2. What do you see in this principle that does not fit with your own experience(s) or view(s) of how the world works?

3. What would you change in the interpretation of this principle to make it a value that you can embrace for your marriage?

4. In what way might adopting this principle as a value help you to make your dreams come true?

5. How might you benefit from bringing your personal and married life into harmony with this principle? Try to give specific examples.

6. What might be the consequences of ignoring this principle and living a life out of harmony with it? Try to give specific examples.

7. Are you willing to adopt this principle as a value for your married life?

8. How can you make this principle come alive in your marriage? How can you blend it into your financial plan?

9. Do the Guidelines for Cooperative Living make sense to you?

10. How would you change them or what guidelines would you add?

11. Are you willing to adopt the Guidelines for Cooperative Living (and/or the ones you modified) for your marriage?

12. How can you make these guidelines come alive in your marriage? How can you merge them into your management of money?

Suggested Additional Reading:

Dyer, Dr. Wayne W. "Oneness" In *You'll See It When You Believe It*. New York, William Morrow and Company, Inc., 1989.

The Diversity Principle

Within the whole, everything and everyone is unique.

Diversity as a Value: While it's true that everyone and everything is connected to the whole, it's also true that everyone and everything is unique, different, special. Sometimes we fail to fully appreciate our differences. You don't need to be weak, wishy-washy, or permissive to appreciate the uniqueness of each person you meet. You can debate, negotiate, set limits, advise and even plead with others. But when you adopt the Diversity Principle as a value, you become *accepting* of differences.

Accepting differences means you are willing to spend the time and energy needed to understand the people in your life and never manipulate or use power plays to get what you want. When we give understanding to someone, we honor them. Honoring another person is a way of acknowledging their right to exist *and their importance* in the larger scheme of life. Understanding helps others feel safe, secure, and accepted. This makes it easier for them to want to participate in the cooperative process.

When power plays or manipulation are used to get what you want, the cooperative process breaks down. Manipulation and power plays reflect an "I Win—You Lose" strategy for life. Such a strategy is another form of competition.

Applied to a marriage, the Diversity Principle becomes a value when you agree to devote the majority of your human relations energy to understanding your partner. This is vastly more difficult than trying to understand hundreds or thousands of people. Understanding a spouse requires a new decision every day to listen, learn, accept and even appreciate one another's differences. It also means speaking your thoughts clearly so that your spouse has a fair chance to understand you. Unless both of you agree to share 100% of who you are with one another, the cooperative process breaks down.

Guidelines for Cooperative Living:

1. Talk with each other every day. When you talk, work as hard to understand as you work to be understood.

2. Say 100% of what you want and what you need, and don't expect your partner (or anyone else) to read your mind or rescue you if you fail to express yourself fully.

3. Agree never to use power plays or manipulation to get what you want.

4. Make understanding unconditional by remaining open to revisit any topic, issue or decision at any time.

Agreement Check:

1. What do you see in this principle that makes sense to you as individuals? As a married couple?

2. What do you see in this principle that does not fit with your own experience(s) or view(s) of how the world works?

3. What would you change in the interpretation of this principle to make it a value that you can embrace for your marriage?

4. In what way might adopting this principle as a value help you to make your dreams come true?

5. How might you benefit from bringing your personal and married life into harmony with this principle? Try to give specific examples.

6. What might be the consequences of ignoring this principle and living a life out of harmony with it? Try to give specific examples.

7. Are you willing to adopt this principle as a value for your married life?

8. How can you make this principle come alive in your marriage? How can you blend it into your financial plan?

9. Do the Guidelines for Cooperative Living make sense to you?

10. How would you change them or what guidelines would you add?

11. Are you willing to adopt the Guidelines for Cooperative Living (and/or the ones you modified) for your marriage?

12. How can you make these guidelines come alive in your marriage? How can you merge them into your management of money?

Suggested Additional Reading:

Paul, Jordan, Ph.D. and Margaret Paul, Ph.D. *Do I have to Give Up Me To Be Loved By You?* **Minneapolis: Compcare Publications, 1983.**

Durst, Michael Gary, Ph.D. *Napkin Notes: On the Art of Living*. **Evanston: The Center for the Art of Living, 1982.**

Dyer, Wayne, W. *Your Erroneous Zones*. **New York: Avon Books, 1977.**

The Stewardship Principle

You are the treasure, and your life is a sacred gift.

Stewardship as a Value: Personal growth is a very important part of living this principle as a value. But personal growth is not the same as self improvement. Self improvement is an obsession in our American culture that begins with a belief that we are flawed and imperfect. With that belief as a starting point, no amount of "change" or "improvement" will provide a sense of being whole. The Stewardship Principle teaches us that we are already whole. "Your life, your personality, your talents, skills, and abilities are a treasure," this principle says, and you are a gift of life that is fully loved and fully lovable from the moment you are born. According to this principle, you are a precious treasurer just because you exist.

When married couples adopt this principle as a value, they see their marriage partner as fully lovable (in spite of differences) *and* they recognize that the health, happiness and personal growth of the individual in marriage is just as important as cooperation, team work and synergy.

This principle acknowledges that every man and woman has been given unique gifts of intelligence, talent, and ability. These gifts are *personal treasures*. These treasures (including the treasure of life itself) are a trust. Each of us has been trusted to make the most of our gifts (to act as stewards) during the course of our lives. Through personal growth, we develop our treasures. If we also use them to bring more love into the world, then we can be sure we have lived the Stewardship Principle to the fullest.

Those who fail to make the most of what they have find that their marriages suffer and often fail. This is because every act of loving is also an act of giving. We are only able to give to the extent that we have established a storehouse of energy from which to give. This storehouse of energy increases when we invest our personal treasures and make the most of ourselves. Those who fail to do this usually look to their partners for much of their strength. This creates a dependent relationship. All marriage partners depend on one another to a degree. But too much dependence in a relationship destroys a marriage.

Remember, being married does not mean that you *become one*. It means that you are one *plus* one, and through the magic of cooperation, team work and synergy you can produce the energy, strength, and power of three, five, seven, or ten. But you can do this only if you both make the most of your life through careful stewardship of your personal treasures.

Guidelines For Cooperative Living:

1. Be all that you can be and encourage your partner to be all that he or she can be.

2. Love and treat each other as equals in every way, in every situation.

Agreement Check:

1. What do you see in this principle that makes sense to you as individuals? As a married couple?

2. What do you see in this principle that does not fit with your own experience(s) or view(s) of how the world works?

3. What would you change in the interpretation of this principle to make it a value that you can embrace for your marriage?

4. In what way might adopting this principle as a value help you to make your dreams come true?

5. How might you benefit from bringing your personal and married life into harmony with this principle? Try to give specific examples.

6. What might be the consequences of ignoring this principle and living a life out of harmony with it? Try to give specific examples.

7. Are you willing to adopt this principle as a value for your married life?

8. How can you make this principle come alive in your marriage? How can you blend it into your financial plan?

9. Do the Guidelines for Cooperative Living make sense to you?

10. How would you change them or what guidelines would you add?

11. Are you willing to adopt the Guidelines for Cooperative Living (and/or the ones you modified) for your marriage?

12. How can you make these guidelines come alive in your marriage? How can you merge them into your management of money?

Suggested Additional Reading:

Mandino, Og. *The Greatest Salesman in the World*. New York: Bantam Books, 1967.

Mandino, Og. *The Greatest Salesman in the World-Part II: The End of the Story*. New York: Bantam Books, 1988.

Lair, Jess, Ph.D. *I Ain't Much, Baby—But I'm All I Got*. New York: Fawcett Crest, 1972.

The Generosity Principle

Give until it "hearts."

Giving as a Value: If every act of loving is an act of giving, then every act of giving should be an act of loving. Of course, we know that this is not so. Some people use giving to manipulate and give only with a specific return in mind. When we give with a specific, hoped-for return, then we are investing, not giving. There is nothing wrong with investing when it is done openly and honestly, but that is not what the Generosity Principle is all about.

The Generosity Principle tells us that nothing contributes more to mankind's violation of the Love Principle than the hardening of our hearts. When the pursuit of money for its own sake is a goal, then there is no need to take into consideration the effects that our decisions might have on others. By not considering the human consequences of our decisions, our hearts quickly and easily become hardened. A hardened heart is one without compassion or concern for the rest of humanity.

Even when couples dedicate themselves to making love-filled dreams come true in marriage, unless they constantly share their "riches" and find ways to "enrich" others, they violate the Generosity Principle.

The Generosity Principle, when adopted as a value, teaches us that true giving occurs only when we share our abundance unselfishly, without a specific, expected reward in mind. When we give without looking to gain anything from anyone, we soften our hearts, *and* we plant seeds of love. These seeds may or may not fall on fertile soil. But this does not reduce the benefit to the human heart. Truly unselfish giving always increases our ability to harmonize with the master law of life (the Law of Love) and improves our ability to live according to all of the other laws. And when our giving does fall on fertile soil, then love on earth expands, thus fulfilling the master law of the universe.

Of course, giving begins at home, but it must not stay at home. How much you give back to the human race and to the planet on which we live is a decision each must make for himself or herself. The form of your giving is also completely in your hands. You can give time, service, understanding, encouragement and money. Every gift counts. But definitely and without reservation, give until it "hearts."

Guidelines For Cooperative Living:

1. Give generously and often to each other. Pay special attention to those items on the "Psychological Paychecks" lists from Chapter Three.

2. Find some way to give of yourself to your community. Pay special attention to the needs of the less fortunate. Give the gift of a smile to everyone you meet.

Agreement Check:

1. What do you see in this principle that makes sense to you as individuals? As a married couple?

2. What do you see in this principle that does not fit with your own experience(s) or view(s) of how the world works?

3. What would you change in the interpretation of this principle to make it a value that you can embrace for your marriage?

4. In what way might adopting this principle as a value help you to make your dreams come true?

5. How might you benefit from bringing your personal and married life into harmony with this principle? Try to give specific examples.

6. What might be the consequences of ignoring this principle and living a life out of harmony with it? Try to give specific examples.

7. Are you willing to adopt this principle as a value for your married life?

8. How can you make this principle come alive in your marriage? How can you blend it into your financial plan?

9. Do the Guidelines for Cooperative Living make sense to you?

10. How would you change them or what guidelines would you add?

11. Are you willing to adopt the Guidelines for Cooperative Living (and/or the ones you modified) for your marriage?

12. How can you make these guidelines come alive in your marriage? How can you merge them into your management of money?

Suggested Additional Reading:

Hyde, Lewis. *The Gift: Imagination and the Erotic Life of Property*. New York: Vintage Books, 1983.

The Discovery/Courage Principle

Life is full of surprises

Courage as a Value: As you move along the road of life, you will encounter many surprises. This is true even if you live by "right" values. Because the mystery of life is too complex to be grasped by the power of our rational minds, we are very frequently surprised when events occur that we didn't anticipate. This can be just as frustrating as encountering the limitations of time.

The surprises you encounter will come from two sources. First will be the surprises of events and people. Second will be the surprises that come from within yourself. Surprises tend to come in two forms: as nuggets of gold or stumbling blocks. Nuggets of gold are those happy surprises that speed us on our journey and have pleasing consequences. Stumbling blocks may be pebbles in our shoes, or huge boulders that are there to teach us an important lesson, make us stronger, and prepare us for the next stage of our journey.

You will encounter surprising events and people every day of your life. Each surprise will require you to make decisions. How will you respond? What will you do? When you encounter a stumbling block, running away won't help. You must face each one courageously.

Courage is the quality of spirit to face the moment with self-possession and confidence.

True courage is a form of personal power and is one of the benefits gained from living by "right values." True courage means inviting each surprise into your life as an honored guest, while reviewing your values carefully and thoughtfully to determine how each new event or person fits into your dreams and harmonizes with your values. Ultimately, courage means taking action. But the action of a courageous person is always taken in the spirit of love and at a pace that allows one to maintain inner peace and tranquility.

How about the surprises that come from within? Inner discovery is as rich and as full of surprises as the outer world. No one has ever found the ultimate boundaries of the human psyche. These surprises may come to you in the form of dreams, or as powerful feelings that won't go away. Some of you will attempt to run away from these discoveries, but you will miss an important part of your life's journey if you do this. If you face the surprises of your inner life with courage, there is no need to be afraid or to lose your inner peace.

Remember, for those who accept the definition I have given for "Happily Ever After," life is a journey and an adventure in making love-filled dreams come true. Adventures imply surprises. But courage is the quality of life that absorbs the shock of surprises and allows one to maintain balance. Courage alone will keep you moving ahead with your journey when others (those without a commitment to love-filled dreams and those who choose to live without "right" values) give up and end the process of discovery.

Guidelines for Cooperative Living:

1. Promise each other to face each surprise in life with courage by anticipating the unexpected, celebrating surprises as gifts, and joining forces to incorporate surprises into your personal and shared quest to make love-filled dreams come true.

Agreement Check:

1. What do you see in this principle that makes sense to you as individuals? As a married couple?

2. What do you see in this principle that does not fit with your own experience(s) or view(s) of how the world works?

3. What would you change in the interpretation of this principle to make it a value that you can embrace for your marriage?

4. In what way might adopting this principle as a value help you to make your dreams come true?

5. How might you benefit from bringing your personal and married life into harmony with this principle? Try to give specific examples.

6. What might be the consequences of ignoring this principle and living a life out of harmony with it? Try to give specific examples.

7. Are you willing to adopt this principle as a value for your married life?

8. How can you make this principle come alive in your marriage? How can you blend it into your financial plan?

9. Do the Guidelines for Cooperative Living make sense to you?

10. How would you change them or what guidelines would you add?

11. Are you willing to adopt the Guidelines for Cooperative Living (and/or the ones you modified) for your marriage?

12. How can you make these guidelines come alive in your marriage? How can you merge them into your management of money?

Suggested Additional Reading:

Sheehy, Gail. *PATHFINDERS*. New York: William Morrow and Company, Inc., 1981.

The Forgiveness Principle

The path marked "forgiveness" is the way to inner peace.

Forgiveness as a Value: One of the great stumbling blocks to making dreams come true is the tendency to blame other people for our circumstances and our feelings. The way we talk actually reinforces this. For example, we say things such as:

> "If it weren't for (_____),
>   my life would be great."

> "If only I had (_____),
>   I would be rich."

These blaming statements are faulty ways to look at the facts. Blaming keeps us looking at everyone but ourselves for responsibility for our lives. The more we blame, the less responsible we feel. Blaming is the first step in a downward spiral of negative thinking that slowly undermines inner security, a sense of prosperity, and personal power. Blaming is also an obstacle to cooperative living—within or outside of marriage.

Forgiveness is the positive, constructive process of giving up blame, anger, hatred, and the desire to get revenge. If you have been wronged, truly wronged, it is because the wrongdoer is living outside the Law of Love. Such people pollute the river of life from which we all must drink; but if you join them, come down to their level and live the way they live, you *also* pollute the river of life. Furthermore, you trade your inner peace for inner confusion and turmoil. This is too high a price to pay.

Inner confusion and turmoil are also caused by a failure to forgive *yourself.* Forgiveness must always include forgiveness of yourself for the emotions and behaviors that usually come with the hurts you sense from others. Angry feelings and angry behavior are natural and everyone must learn constructive ways to deal with them. Failure to do so leads to guilt. Guilt saps your ability to love as much as anger does. Forgiveness of yourself means saying "goodbye" to guilt.

Forgiveness is not an easy principle to accept as a value. It requires great spiritual and emotional maturity. However, learning to forgive will make an enormous contribution to cooperative living, your sense of inner security, prosperity and personal power. When you become good at forgiving, you will find it much easier to harmonize with the other universal principles discussed in this chapter.

Guidelines for Cooperative Living:

1. Learn about and practice forgiveness, compassion and self-forgiveness.

2. Never blame one another (or anyone else) for your feelings or your circumstances. Blaming, being judgmental and critical, muddy the emotional environment of a marriage and make cooperation impossible.

Agreement Check:

1. What do you see in this principle that makes sense to you as individuals? As a married couple?

2. What do you see in this principle that does not fit with your own experience(s) or view(s) of how the world works?

3. What would you change in the interpretation of this principle to make it a value that you can embrace for your marriage?

4. In what way might adopting this principle as a value help you to make your dreams come true?

5. How might you benefit from bringing your personal and married life into harmony with this principle? Try to give specific examples.

6. What might be the consequences of ignoring this principle and living a life out of harmony with it? Try to give specific examples.

7. Are you willing to adopt this principle as a value for your married life?

8. How can you make this principle come alive in your marriage? How can you blend it into your financial plan?

9. Do the Guidelines for Cooperative Living make sense to you?

10. How would you change them or what guidelines would you add?

11. Are you willing to adopt the Guidelines for Cooperative Living (and/or the ones you modified) for your marriage?

12. How can you make these guidelines come alive in your marriage? How can you merge them into your management of money?

Suggested Additional Reading:

Dyer, Dr. Wayne W. "Forgiveness." In *You'll See It When You Believe It*. New York: William Morrow and Company, Inc., 1989.

Murphy, Dr. Joseph. *The Power of Your Subconscious Mind.* New York: Bantam Books, 1985.

The Justice Principle

Take anything you want from life, but be prepared to pay the price.

Justice as a Value: Your success in life, just as your success with money, will result from a series of events, all of which will come to pass as a result of your decisions—decisions you will make every day. There won't be any grand slam home run that will assure you of success on your entire journey. Whether you were born to money or whether you earn it, you will never be wealthy without trying to make love-filled dreams come true. You will also need to acquire inner security, a sense of prosperity and personal power. There is no way to do this without bringing your life into harmony with the principles just presented. There is also no way to avoid the consequences of living a life out of harmony with these principles. There *is* a price to pay for every decision you make.

This price is never restricted to and should never be measured *strictly by* human reactions to your decisions. The scales of universal justice are far more sensitive than that. Human reaction is only one measure of justice and it is often unreliable. Sometimes human reaction sends an innocent man or woman to prison. Entire social systems can be unjust as was evident in Hitler's Germany. So to search for evidence of the Justice Principle only on the playing field of human behavior is not sufficient and could lead to wrong conclusions.

The justice of the universe is seen most clearly by the price that is paid by the human soul for living outside of these universal principles. What this means is that the light inside your life can grow stronger or darker (and even go out) based on the values by which you live. Even those who have been battered by difficult circumstances can have a glow of "rightness" about them because they live by "right" values. Over time, right values make a life—and a marriage. To see this fact takes the vision to see things that are truly invisible. I hope you have that kind of vision, and I hope you will see that the values discussed in this chapter can set in motion powerful forces that will pull you steadily toward positive outcomes. But even if every outcome doesn't happen just as you had hoped, by living with this set of values as your moral compass, your journey will be joyful and you will always have the strength to face the next challenge and keep moving in the direction of the great city of your dreams. When you know you are right, nothing can stop you, and your inner glow will never be extinguished.

Guidelines for Cooperative Living:

1. Take full responsibility for your life and the consequences of your decisions.

Agreement Check:

1. What do you see in this principle that makes sense to you as individuals? As a married couple?

2. What do you see in this principle that does not fit with your own experience(s) or view(s) of how the world works?

3. What would you change in the interpretation of this principle to make it a value that you can embrace for your marriage?

4. In what way might adopting this principle as a value help you to make your dreams come true?

5. How might you benefit from bringing your personal and married life into harmony with this principle? Try to give specific examples.

6. What might be the consequences of ignoring this principle and living a life out of harmony with it? Try to give specific examples.

7. Are you willing to adopt this principle as a value for your married life?

8. How can you make this principle come alive in your marriage? How can you blend it into your financial plan?

9. Do the Guidelines for Cooperative Living make sense to you?

10. How would you change them or what guidelines would you add?

11. Are you willing to adopt the Guidelines for Cooperative Living (and/or the ones you modified) for your marriage?

12. How can you make these guidelines come alive in your marriage? How can you merge them into your management of money?

Suggested Additional Reading:

Frankl, Victor E. *Man's Search For Meaning*. New York: Simon & Schuster, Inc., 1984.

Ziglar, Zig. *See You at the Top*. Gretna: Pelican Publishing Company, 1982.

Conflict and Cooperation

There is no doubt that couples who are looking for a way to build a successful financial life together will be more successful if they adopt and live by the principles, values, and guidelines for cooperative living I have just presented. But a plan to build a cooperative relationship would not be complete without being prepared for conflict. Even the most cooperative couples face conflict in their marriages, especially in the financial arena. Two of the most common sources of conflict are anger and mistrust. Let's take a closer look at both of these feelings.

Anger as a Source of Conflict

In our culture, anger is a real problem because we often think it is the same as violence, either physical or verbal. Anger is really just a feeling—and a natural one at that. It *may* become an action, and that action *could* be violent, but it could also be constructive. If you hold anger in, that is not a constructive act. If anger isn't released, it becomes self destructive. If it is expressed in the form of an attack, it can hurt others (which is also a way of hurting yourself). But anger can also be released by simply stating it as a fact. For example:

"I'm really feeling angry about..."

"I'm feeling irritated because..."

"When you...I feel...Because..."

Once anger is expressed and brought out in the open, it is immediately less harmful. Choosing the time and place to express anger is also important. Instead of expressing anger directly and immediately, it often helps to set a time aside to get things off your mind—time that is considered "safe" and established just for this purpose.

A weekly conference for "clearing the air" or "blowing off steam" is a very constructive way for married couples to express anger, especially little irritations that may build up. These sessions should always have peacemaking as an ultimate objective. These sessions should not take place on the same day that you hold your financial planning sessions—nor should they be held in your bedroom or the room where you work on financial matters. Here are some simple guidelines for handling this kind of "anger releasing/peacemaking" session.

1. Always express your angry feelings as a statement of fact. You don't have to attack or "live" your anger. A statement of fact tends to invite a solution to conflicts.

2. Take responsibility for your anger and don't talk as though your partner is making you mad or is responsible for your feelings. Use statements that start with "I feel..." rather than "You make me feel..." If your anger is a reaction to something your partner said or did, that same behavior may have been funny or entertaining to someone else. Your anger is an expression of your unique emotional make-up and your partner can't control that. So own up and begin by examining the source of your feeling interpretations.

3. Be ready with constructive ideas about how to do something positive that will put your anger to rest. The major benefit of expressing anger is the discovery of peacemaking action. Something has to be done. But that something has got to be a Win/Win idea. Scolding and punishing are not part of the Win/Win process. A changed behavior might be desirable. Perhaps you can find a way to re-interpret or understand more fully something that was said or done. Whatever your Win/Win solution is, remember that you are both on the same team. Don't ever act as if you aren't. And don't ever give up seeking a solution until you both feel good about it and have made peace with one another. Pool your mental and emotional resources and brainstorm until you are mutually satisfied and mutually motivated to put your solution into practice—together.

Anger can get out of hand, and in some cases, it can become a source of mental illness. These simple guidelines won't take care of deep, sick disturbances. But they will help manage conflict resulting from ordinary, "garden variety" anger that can sometimes surprise young married couples.

If practiced from the beginning of your marriage, these guidelines for anger management will enhance your cooperative efforts and may even help avoid the more sick behaviors that develop when things have gone too far.

Mistrust as a Source of Conflict

Trust is the cornerstone of all successful communications. If you don't trust someone, or if they don't trust you, nothing they or you say is heard. Trust is the feeling of safeness you have when you're with another person. The ability to work together is also largely determined by the degree of trust that exists. Your cooperative efforts as a married couple (and your ability to communicate about money) will be especially dependent on how much you trust each other.

Since trust is another of those "invisible" qualities of life, it may help to think of trust in marriage in the same way you think about a savings account at the bank. With your savings account, you put money in, and you take it out (hopefully to make good investments). The more you put in, the more you have to take out.

In marriage, from Day One, you have a "trust account" which can also grow or decrease over time. While the balance in your "trust account" won't be recorded in a handy little book, you'll certainly know when you've made a deposit or withdrawal.

You'll feel it; you'll hear it—in the tone of your partner's voice, and you'll see it in his or her eyes. If your trust account gets too low, you have mistrust. It's really that simple.

Committing to live by right values will go a long way toward building trust in marriage. But this, in itself, will not be enough. Trust will grow only if you *live* by right values ("Don't snow me, show me!"). If you only talk a good life without living one, then what you are speaks so loudly that no one can hear a word you say.

It's hard to trust someone who isn't reliable in living what they say they believe.

Of course, since we are all human (which means we're imperfect), there needs to be room for forgiveness when we make mistakes. But that's exactly why you have to work so hard at living your values every day. There are many forces at work trying to sabotage your efforts to live by right values, and it takes tremendous self-discipline to stay on course. However, when you do, you are considered trustworthy. When people can count on you to stay the course, it's a lot easier to forgive occasional mistakes (trust withdrawals) and keep working with you in cooperative ways.

In marriage you are both 100% responsible for building trust.

Trust building fails if you try for a 50-50 arrangement, because if your partner falls down, you have to pay a price, too. It's no good to say, "Well, I did my 50%, where's hers or where's his?" You both have to give 100% to get cooperation, team work, synergy. That's the only way you get results.

If either of you do something that is seen by the other as a break in trust, you both have 100% responsibility to do something about it.
Little withdrawals, or even big ones, need to be balanced by trust account deposits.

Otherwise, you "set-up" yourself, your partner, and the marriage for poor communication—and that means conflict. Your trust account never gets to the mistrust level without both partners participating, sharing the responsibility, and sabotaging the relationship.

If you find this hard to accept, look at it this way. At the start of marriage, when you trust each other very much, your trust account is very full. (If you deny this, then you admit you entered marriage without trust, which is completely self-destructive.) If you want your dreams to come true, and you know trust is important for this to happen, you can create a plan to build trust. You cooperate, collaborate, team up and strategize to win (to build strong trust). Anything short of that is to admit from the outset that you didn't want

things to work out.

If you really want trust to build, complete the exercise on pages 112 and 113. That exercise suggests ways to make trust account deposits and withdrawals. Look them over and then add your own suggestions. Make these lists as large as you possibly can. Tape them to the front of your refrigerator door. Hang them over your bed. Paste them to the inside front cover of your Dream Book. This list is your key to succeeding at the challenge of trust building. Make it work. Find creative ways to make the deposits. Avoid withdrawals. But when you make a withdrawl, take the steps suggested at the end of the next chapter to do something about it.

Remember, if your trust account balance dips down into the mistrust level, nothing else you learn from this book will work. Absolutely nothing.

While sharing right values will launch you down the "yellow brick road" of cooperation, it takes trust (lots of it) to keep you on that road and moving steadily toward the city of your dreams.

Our Marital Trust Building System

Deposits	**Withdrawals**
1. Share common values.	1. Fail to share common values.
2. Encourage one another.	2. Criticize, scold, lecture or put each other down.
3. Share feelings.	3. Ignore feelings.
4. Build on each other's strengths.	4. Dwell on weaknesses.
5. Laugh at and learn from the mistakes you make together.	5. Laugh at your partner's mistakes, and never laugh at yourself.
6. Speak softly. Ask for what you want lovingly.	6. Yell, scream and demand what you want.
7. Always be truthful.	7. Lie.
8. Keep your promises.	8. Break your promises.
9. Spend time with each other.	9. Be too busy to spend time together.
10. Give one another Psychological Paychecks.	10. Ignore these paychecks.

Your Suggestions:

Managing Conflict Constructively

Even with your best efforts to manage anger and to build trust, there are going to be moments of conflict. Negotiating conflicts constructively is part of the success formula in any marriage, and it's especially important in managing marital finances successfully.

In the first few months of marriage, negotiating differences will be a major task. After all, this is when you're really discovering the most about one another and yourselves.

This is when you'll come face-to-face with your financial strategies and your financial styles (the ones that you inherited from your parents). Rather than relying on love and luck to get you through this critical time, try using the negotiating process outlined on the next few pages. While these guidelines won't work *every time*, using them *will* give you a framework for making rational decisions together.

Successful Negotiating Strategies

Step No. 1. Define The Problem— This may seem easy, but this is the hardest step. If emotions are the cause of a conflict, they may be hard to identify. If the conflict is a matter of different wants or needs, those have to be stated clearly, and put on the table so you each understand the other person. Remember that stating a want is not the same as making a demand. In this step you're just sorting things out. So, go slowly. Take your time with this step and be sure you really understand one another's wants before you move on.

Step No. 2. Agree to Negotiate— Successful negotiating occurs only when both parties agree to negotiate—to find a way for both parties to get what they want and need. Agreeing to negotiate means you won't use power plays or manipulate in any way. You're committed to use rational processes and fair play to find workable solutions. If you do nothing else, just reassure one another that negotiating is how you want to solve this conflict.

Step No. 3. Set the Stage— When you set the stage, you agree on a time and place to have your talk. Some couples can stop almost anytime and "set the stage" because their marital trust account is so full they have no fears. They trust themselves and their partners to shut out all other considerations and talk things out rationally and gracefully. But in the beginning of marriage, while trust is still building, it really helps to set aside a time and place for important negotiations. This gives a feeling of safeness that helps build trust gradually.

Step No. 4. Brainstorm— With this strategy, you begin by assuming you want a Win/Win solution, one where you both get what you want and need. To brainstorm you simply run through (and make a list of) every solution you can imagine—no matter how wild it sounds. Your goal is to find a new and original solution that will suit you both. You may have to abandon any "old think" solutions that helped create the conflict, but that's OK if you both get to Win in the end. The bigger the menu of ideas, the better the chances that you'll find one that is Win/Win. Don't stop brainstorming until neither one of you can think of another thing. Then, eliminate those ideas that you both dislike. Keep right on weeding out ideas until you have only one left, the one you both like—or like the most.

Step No. 5. Seek Mutual Agreement— When you find a Win/Win solution, you are both motivated to implement it. This is the best of all worlds. Sometimes it takes several brainstorming sessions to reach mutual agreement. Don't quit if after the first session you still don't have the Win/Win solution you're looking for. Stop, take a break, and reset the stage for another session. Of course, sometimes the perfect solution isn't found. In that case, and if you both agree to it, go to the next strategy.

Step No. 6. Compromise— "Compromise" means accepting a solution that works, but it means neither one of you gets everything you want. It's OK to compromise. There's nothing immoral about it. And if it's done after you've exhausted your efforts to find a Win/Win solution, you shouldn't feel bad. A good compromise is still better than conflict. Besides, compromising now and then is not abandoning your commitment to Win/Win. Compromise can be a real Win for both of you if you learn something from it. Go inside yourself and see what you learned about your emotions and your wants. Share your insights with one another and reaffirm your commitment to cooperation as a way of life. Whatever you do, don't let a less than perfect solution deter you from your overall sense of purpose—your commitment to make dreams come true in marriage.

Step No. 7. Make Concessions— Sometimes it may help to take turns winning. This is called "concession." Although this is the least desirable solution to a conflict, it may be the only way from time to time. There may be an issue that one of you feels so strongly about that a Win/Win solution or a compromise just isn't possible. If the other spouse doesn't care that much, conceding can be an OK solution. However, a concession is a gift; it shouldn't be taken for granted. As long as it doesn't become a pattern, where one partner always makes the concessions, it can be a sensible way to keep your marriage on the cooperation trail.

Step No. 8. Confirm the Decision and Act— For clarity, restate the decision before you end your negotiations. This is important because confusion about the solution can get you right back into a conflict. Simply say, "OK, we buy growth stocks instead of that high risk oil and gas deal, but we won't just leave our money in a savings account, either. Is that our agreement?"

"Yeah, that's it." Now you have an agreement and the conflict should be solved. Congratulate yourselves, in whatever way you find appropriate—a hug, a touch, or whatever. If you can't express affection at this point, you probably don't have a solution and you may have to start over. Cool down for a couple of days and then get back to the negotiating process. Use the in-between time to get in touch with your feelings so you can define the problem when you start over. However, if you're both O.K. with your solution, implement it.

Using these negotiating strategies may take some practice. No one comes to marriage having mastered them all. You *will* make mistakes. Don't be discouraged by that. Just pick yourselves up and go back to step one and work through the entire process as many times as necessary. An occasional conflict is not a sign that your marriage is in trouble.

Don't let conflict or a bad negotiating experience undermine your love for one another. Keep your commitment to cooperation and love open and responsive. Don't withdraw from one another or give up. Genuine love is a decision to keep trying to reach one another even in the face of conflict.

Suggested Additional Reading:

Dinkmeyer, Don and Lewis E. Losoncy. *The Encouragement Book*. New York: Prentice Hall, 1987.

Augsburger, David. *Caring Enough To Confront*. Scottsdale: Herald Press, 1973.

Fisher, Roger and Scott Brown. *Getting Together: Building Relationships As We Negotiate*. New York: Penguin Books, 1989.

Fisher, Roger and Scott Brown. *Getting To Yes: Negotiating Agreement Without Giving In.* New York: Penguin Books, 1983.

Scott, Gini Graham, Ph.D. *Resolving Conflict —With Others and Within Yourself*. Oakland: New Harbinger Publications, Inc., 1990.

Notes

Out of the Cave and Into a Partnership

Chapter Five

*"We have met the enemy
and he is us."*

Pogo

The last chapter focused on the values you need to live by to achieve financial success in marriage. You learned that you can launch your financial ship of life down the road marked "cooperation" only by adopting "right" values and guidelines for cooperative living. You also learned that managing anger and conflict constructively and developing trust in one another is the only way to keep your marriage on that road and moving steadily toward the great city of your dreams.

In this chapter, you will learn about another major secret to financial success in marriage—the power of partnership. Partnership is a way of living and working together that transcends cooperation. Partnership is the highest level of cooperative living.

A partnership relationship has the ability to tap the greatest strengths of both husband and wife to produce the most desirable outcomes for a marriage—both financially and otherwise. A partnership marriage is the most empowering, the most unifying and the most exciting way to travel to the great city of your dreams.

A partnership marriage is also the most challenging way to live because it completely violates a set of rules for male-female relationships that are planted deep inside every human brain. To fully understand and appreciate what a partnership marriage can accomplish, you first need to appreciate the primitive side of human nature and see how "dynamics of the cave" are still very much with us and are expressed almost everywhere in modern married life. Hopefully, by contrasting the dynamics of primitive relationships with partnership dynamics, you will see that the way things *are* does not represent the way things *could and should be*.

In this chapter, we will also answer questions such as, "Where have we been?" and "Where are we going?" The answers will give you a way to gain perspective about how the first five chapters relate to the rest of this book. This perspective should help motivate you to keep putting one foot in front of the other as you work through each new lesson and have the conversations so important to your financial growth and success.

Before this chapter ends, you will be asked to make an important decision about your willingness to live by the partnership principles that are discussed. Partnerships thrive on commitment, and if the partnership model for marriage is to have deep and lasting meaning for you, you will need to make a commitment to live by a set of standards that may be quite different from your current "style" of relating (Don't panic at this seemingly radical statement; I'll explain its meaning soon).

At the end of this chapter, I'm going to give you some suggestions about how to manage trust account withdrawals when they occur—something I mentioned in the last chapter.

Even when a couple is committed to live by partnership principles, they will occasionally slip and act in a way that violates trust. It's a good idea to have a plan ready to handle those painful moments—especially if you're going to avoid entrapment by your more primitive instincts.

The agreement check that concludes this chapter is very important. The discussions you have regarding financial roles will give you a chance to apply partnership principles and test your commitment to partnership living. Of course, this won't be your last test. Every day of your life will test this commitment because, as you'll soon discover, there is a primitive, Neanderthal, caveman-cave woman living inside of your brain ready to assume control of your life at a moment's notice. In spite of this, I believe that any married couple can stay on course and manage the financial side of their lives successfully if they understand why they think and feel and behave in certain ways, and if they understand what success looks like and will invest the energy to move steadily in the direction of success.

I sincerely hope that the following discussions will provide a constructive way for you to think about and understand why certain behaviors and emotions seem to crop up consistently when married couples try to manage their finances—even married couples who have learned and applied every idea discussed in the first four chapters of this book. More importantly, I hope these ideas will help you to stay on course and spot danger signals in your own behavior. Getting to the city of your dreams isn't a matter of missing every bump in the road, it's more a matter of staying on the right road and not ending up in a ditch or on some detour or at a dead end. Above all else, I hope you will learn once and for all that when the road gets really bumpy, or when you get sidetracked, it's because of your own careless driving. I think this chapter will help you see clearly what Pogo meant when he said, "We have met the enemy and he is us."

Awareness, Choice, and Self-Control

It has been said that the greatest gift that can be given to another human being is the gift of choice. To take advantage of choices, we first have to be aware that they exist. When completely absorbed in the daily routine of managing our lives, it is hard to think about choices—why we do the things we do and why we say the things we say. We just act. Becoming aware of our choices requires that we look at ourselves objectively and get creative about our actions. Once we do that, we can discover new solutions to old problems, and new solutions lead to constructive outcomes. This is particularly important in human relationships.

Without thinking about how we act (and interact), we may believe that we have only one choice. The truth is, we almost always have many choices about how to behave toward one another.

In the last chapter, I stressed the importance of cooperation as a way for married couples to make their dreams come true. Cooperation was presented as an alternative to competition, which is the primary model for relating in our society. Now, I want to help you understand why competition is so highly prized as a model for human relations and why competitive tendencies constantly trip up cooperative efforts in marriage.

By learning the source of our primitive, competitive nature, you will gain great insight about why one minute you can act in a cooperative way with your marriage partner, yet seem totally competitive and even irrational the next minute.

Many couples are confused by this. Why, they want to know, after agreeing to adopt right values and rational guidelines for cooperative living, do they experience moments of apparent insanity and resort to primitive (selfish) behavior to get what they want? How can human beings go from calm, logical, and business-like behavior, to irrational, emotional, and stubborn behavior in the wink of an eye? Why?

The answer is not complicated. The truth is, for all of our evolutionary development, we haven't come that far from the cave. In fact, inside the brain cavity of every one of us there exists the brain structure of our caveman and cave woman ancestors with its own built-in, primitive rules for how to relate and behave in every situation. This primitive brain colors everything we do, and can be especially influential in the area of money management. The rules of the primitive brain are called "instincts." These primitive brain instincts made survival more possible millions of years ago when Neanderthal cavemen and cave women settled their differences with stones, clubs, and axes. By contrast, this chapter offers a new model for marital relating called "partnership." This model is the product of higher thought processes which have evolved over the last million years. These higher thought processes are the source of my belief that humans are not destined to go through time acting towards one another like their Neanderthal ancestors. Examining the differences between the "partnership" and "Neanderthal" models of marriage should allow you to see that you really do have choices for how to behave that can dramatically influence your success with money in marriage. Perhaps more importantly, your awareness of these choices can lead to greater self control.

As you will come to understand, self control, or making civilized choices, is a critical factor in achieving financial success in marriage.

Have fun exploring the ideas of this chapter. While you may find it humorous, I hope you will see what a serious and revealing chapter this is. In addition, I hope you have the foresight and commitment to apply what you learn and thereby gain from these insights. Since these explanations of human behavior are fundamental to understanding many other lessons in this book, take your time with this chapter. You may wish to read it over two or three times to help fix its message in your mind.

The Unruly Ancestor That Lives Inside Our Head

Consider the caveman.

His days were filled with hunting for food, defeating his enemies and finding a mate. Success was based on "survival of the fittest." Everyday was a challenge to eat or be eaten.

Consider the cave woman.

Her days were filled with hunting and gathering, finding a caveman to protect her from enemies and mating. Since she was less muscular than her caveman counterpart, she relied heavily on him to keep saber-toothed tigers away from the cave entrance.

Both the caveman and cave woman were controlled by a primitive brain. This brain was rather small (about the size of a man's fist) and came completely programmed (something like a computer). It knew everything it needed to know by instinct—a set of rules that controlled behavior and emotions from birth. Some of these rules were:

1. Survival. The first order of primitive life was to survive at all costs. Survival was constantly in question. Every action of primitive men and women was measured against this rule. Truly, the law of the jungle prevailed. It was kill or be killed every day.

2. Perpetuate the Species. The second order of business was to produce new life, and the primitive brain that regulated the production of sex drive hormones saw to it that life was produced in abundance. There was no such thing as family planning. Since most children died at birth, the species was far more likely to perpetuate itself by producing as many children as possible as fast as possible.

3. Immediate Gratification. "Get it now," was another very important rule,

whether that meant getting a mate, getting food, or getting a new club. Who knew when there would be another chance to "get it?" The primitive brain did not understand patience, self-discipline, or delayed gratification.

4. Fight or Flight. Whenever frightened or threatened, even if only a suspected threat, the primitive brain would trigger one of two responses—stay and fight or run away. The sense of danger that triggered this fight or flight response could be caused simply by someone or something coming too close, crossing an invisible territorial boundary or even appearing to be different in some way.

5. Dominance or Submission. The primitive brain insisted that someone must be in control and, in mating, the other partner must be submissive. The dominance-submission instinct also created tribal hierarchies, with the chief at the top, followed by warriors, then gatherers, children, the elderly, the sick and then women.

6. Might Makes Right. Whoever was strongest was granted special rights and privileges according to primitive brain rules. Strength was measured purely by physical skill or ability. The weakest were granted fewest privileges. The strong were "right" and the weak were "wrong." There were no moral standards or values against which to measure human behavior. Those who were "mighty" were also in control—of themselves, other people and (to some degree) their destinies.

Sometime during the last million years, our primitive ancestors began to leave the cave. Unfortunately, the caveman-cave woman brain came along for the ride.

The caveman-cave woman brain (called the "Neanderthal brain" during the rest of this discussion) is that part of our brain which controls our emotions and these instinctive rules.

The Neanderthal brain is located at the base of our skull and continues to play a very influential role in determining our actions and reactions to every event in life.

However, the human brain has also changed a lot during the last million years. Those parts of the brain that control thinking and logic (called the "modern brain" during the rest of this discussion) have expanded—stacked right on top of the Neanderthal brain. We call this part of our brain the "cerebral cortex." It is this part of our brain that makes us uniquely human—more than simple animals operating strictly by instinct.

It is the modern brain that allows us to choose our values, for example, and to negotiate our differences without resorting to clubs and spears.

That the modern brain has developed extensively during the last million years is a scientific fact clearly established by a branch of science called "physical anthropology." We like to think that our modern brain has now become the one in control of our lives. However, the Neanderthal brain, with its primitive rules, often overpowers the modern

brain and regains control of our behavior.

Proof that the Neanderthal brain often dominates is a fact you can easily observe in daily life. Anytime people are angry, frightened, fighting, or mating (having sex), their Neanderthal brains are in control. Of course, these are the obvious examples of the Neanderthal brain in action. Not so obvious, but very important examples of Neanderthal brain behavior are competition, manipulation, power plays, blaming, criticizing, courting and moodiness.

It's easier to look objectively at Neanderthal brain behavior while observing others. It can even be comical. Everyone has watched couples engaged in public displays of kissing and petting, deep in the grasp of their hormones, totally oblivious to the world around them. This pre-mating behavior might be embarrassing to them if they could step back and look at themselves rationally. Unfortunately, when the Neanderthal brain is in control, all rational thinking stops. This is especially true in the financial arena.

Almost every financial action and interaction is influenced to some degree by the Neanderthal brain *and* in a variety of ways. Consider the couple who are having some hard times. In a fit of self-pity and indulgence, a woman goes on a shopping spree and buys $400 worth of new clothes. When her husband finds out, he goes into a towering rage, stalks out of the house, and buys an $18,000 fishing boat. That's the Neanderthal brain at work! More subtle examples of the Neanderthal brain at work can often be seen in the financial "styles" and "strategies" men and women adopt early in life and bring with them to marriage. However, this is not always true. As you will learn, some financial styles and strategies are the products of higher brain functions and are in harmony with the laws that govern financial success. Nevertheless...

...*your* financial "style" may be nothing more than a modern day example of the caveman-woman's club which is wielded to help you survive, perpetuate the species, meet your needs for gratification, fight or run from your enemies, dominate or submit or be "right" (which means being in control).

Neanderthal financial styles and strategies quickly become "war clubs" (although they are often thinly disguised weapons in the hands of a modern day Neanderthal). Unless you rise above your Neanderthal instincts and use your modern brain to guide your financial life, you will never achieve the goal of financial success in marriage. Let's look more closely, then, at the function and potential of the modern brain.

The modern brain is the source of our reasoning, organizing, and analyzing abilities. While it has been developing for more than a million years, the modern brain is little more than a Johnny-come-lately to the brain business. Furthermore, there is something about the gene pool that sprinkles modern brain capabilities unevenly throughout the population. Everyone on the playing field of modern brain intelligence is not an Albert Einstein. However, Mother Nature has given the vast majority of humans enough reasoning abilities to grasp fundamental realities—including moral and financial

realities. (I'm counting on the fact that my readers have at least average reasoning abilities, and most will be above average—so don't let me down.)

When you are calm, relaxed, and can look objectively at a problem, you can be sure that your modern brain is in charge of things. The potential of the modern brain is that it alone can lead humans to organize and re-organize reality and find creative alternatives to managing the challenges of life—including the challenge of how to get along with one another. Some of the achievements of the modern brain, especially in the last few hundred years, have been very impressive. It has allowed us to develop ever more complex tools, invent ways to dramatically improve food production, and to improve our health and health care so that average life expectancy is now about three times longer than our Neanderthal relatives (at least in the United States). Yet, we still haven't been able to end war, hunger, and basic social inequities. We pollute our environment based on the immediate gratification instinct, over-populate our planet as if the species were going to die out any day, and commit unthinkable crimes against one another based on the instincts of survival and fight-flight. In marriage, we still struggle to overcome the dominance-submission instinct and live together in cooperation, love, and kindness.

How dependable is the modern brain to lead us further away from the cave? The jury is out on that question, but frankly it appears to be our only hope. Furthermore, the eventual outcome appears to heavily depend on the effort we're willing to invest in our struggle to overcome Neanderthal instincts and invent a better life.

In other words, becoming a more loving, caring species is hard work. And the central focus of this work is our personal, moment-to-moment struggle between the appeal for control by the Neanderthal brain and our modern brain.

In a way, this struggle is like having two trial attorneys living inside of our heads, each one arguing unceasingly for her or his case each time we face a decision. One of those attorneys is an unruly, primitive ancestor who just won't leave. The other one is a civilized, caring, and calm creature who chooses to live by values, morals and ethics. The arguments between these two produce a lot of stress, too. And while I personally think that this struggle is due to some kind of design flaw which is slowly being corrected over time, I'm also convinced that the modern brain has evolved far enough that it can win the lion's share of these struggles and produce a winning formula for how to succeed in marriage,

including how to succeed in the financial arena. But let me say it once again—the key ingredient for those who want to become more loving, caring human beings is effort (actually it's choice, first, and effort, second).

The Neanderthal brain is going to be with us for a long time to come and it will exert an enormous influence on our personal (and interpersonal) behavior. But the enormous, primeval force of the Neanderthal brain can be harnessed and put to constructive use if you are willing to really work at it. It also helps to start early in life. As newlyweds, starting early means your modern brains will have a chance to set the rules for financial behavior before your Neanderthal brains launch you down the road marked "Bad Habits." Bad financial habits are especially hard to break. So, let's take the next step down the "yellow brick" road of cooperation by becoming more familiar with the primitive drama of Neanderthal life. The purpose? To show you how *not* to behave. Pay special attention to how this primitive drama still influences the dynamics of financial management in many modern marriages.

Financial Management—Caveman Style

Imagine this drama.

Caveman meets cave woman. Caveman snarls, jumps up and down and displays his dominance. He parades in front of cave woman, preening and puffing. He watches carefully to see if she likes what she sees. If he sees the slightest show of interest, he clubs her, grabs her by the hair and drags her off to his cave.

After mating, he brings his newfound woman gifts of food, tools to make her work easier and animals skins to keep her warm. She accepts (although Prince Charming this guy is not).

In the morning, he wakes up early and chases down their breakfast—literally. When he brings it home, she prepares it and they eat.

During the remainder of the day, he hunts for supper, and she hunts for berries. The berries are to eat, but also to make dyes to adorn herself—so she'll "look good."

As long as he keeps bringing home food, she'll prepare it, store some for hard times, and make clothing and blankets. As long as she "looks good" to him and keeps his cave in good order, he'll probably not trade her in for a younger, more attractive mate (but there are no guarantees).

If while hunting, instead of bringing home food, he becomes food, she's got some hunting to do herself—for a new mate. If while hunting, her caveman becomes badly injured, he's considered damaged goods, which also means she must find another mate. Even worse, if a caveman knocks at her door who has bigger muscles than her current mate, a bigger club, and more food, she will leave and live with him.

We often fail to appreciate just how much our thoughts and behaviors are affected by this primitive drama after millions of years of living this way. The Neanderthal brain model for how to behave is imprinted deeply in our thoughts and is still displayed in ways that are only slightly different from the behavior of our primitive ancestors. To demonstrate that this is true, I'm going to tell another story that could have been the story of hundreds of thousands of "modern" couples by just taking the theme and changing it a little in each case.

Imagine *this* drama.

It's one million years later. **Andrea and Jack** meet while in college. He is a promising law student who is known on campus for his party personality. She is an attractive coed with an active interest in campus social life. Neither one really thinks their campus romance will lead to marriage. But somehow, even before graduation, those wedding bells ring and they're walking down the aisle together.

Since Andrea came from a fairly well-to-do family, Jack gets the message quickly that he has some big financial hurdles to jump in order to keep Andrea happy. There will be no apartment living for Andrea. She wants a house in a prestigious neighborhood. They borrow money from Jack's parents for a down-payment, and during law school, he works as a law clerk to make the house payments.

Since Andrea doesn't work, she finds herself always in a position of having to ask Jack for money. It irritates her that Jack seems to be a "squirreler" (which is his financial style). She likes to spend, and she enjoys shopping (which is her financial style). She is fascinated, however, by how Jack seems to have a keen ability to take his small "squirreled"

127

savings and make little investments that turn a nice profit. She has no idea how much Jack is saving, and he won't tell her. She knows even less about his investments. All she knows is that when she asks for money, after a ritual of resisting, he gives in for some amount that she decides she can "live with."

Twenty years seemed to fly by. It is now three children later, and this "modern couple" find themselves living in Scottsdale, Arizona. He has become a successful lawyer and has continued to make smart investments. She has learned to become a bit of a "squirrel" herself, and has managed to "stash" funds from the account Jack set up for her to manage household expenses. Their financial situation has changed. They have low debt, a high income, and their net worth places them in the upper five percent of the population.

Two years ago, Andrea decided that she wanted a career and became the director of a local arts organization. Jack never sees her income, and this irritates him—more than he will admit. Jack's party personality has developed an interesting twist, at least according to Andrea. Jack now drinks a bit too much. Andrea had noticed over the years that Jack seemed to spend more hours at the office than most men, but never questioned it or complained because the money kept flowing in and the investments kept piling up. But lately, Jack misses work occasionally because he doesn't feel well after a big party. She says that's one of the reasons she decided to become employed—she is worried about Jack's health and could imagine him being unable to work full-time.

When I met Jack and Andrea (not their real names), it was to interview them for an article to be published in a well known national magazine for women. They became increasingly uncomfortable when I asked them to discuss their individual and shared dreams. Neither could name a single thing they did together for fun. "We need to be less brainy," Jack said to break the silence.

"I think everyone should work in the garden," she countered quickly.

Nor could they name a single dream each had helped make come true for the other, although both were vocal about what they wanted the marriage to provide. Andrea said she's waited all these years to live in a large and lovely home. Jack said all he wanted to do was cut back on his work and do some serious golfing and fishing.

I gave them the "lottery exercise" that you completed in Chapter Three. When they traded papers to see how each imagined the other spending the winnings, they could barely hide their hostilities.

"We're $400,000 apart on what we think a 'nice' house costs," Jack said, smiling thinly. "And there's no way to broker this decision because if we do, we both lose."

Jack and Andrea were expecting a major amount of money within the year because their home had been condemned by the city in order to develop a major commercial park. Their settlement with the city was to be more than $500,000. "When we get down to it, we'll probably do—like we always do—just what Jack wants," Andrea retorted.

If you were to look at their marriage in terms of their net worth, they would appear to be economically healthy. But their ability to work together as a team (cooperate toward making dreams come true) had evaporated, and their marital "trust account" was bankrupt.

It was clear to me that Jack and Andrea were confused and angry about dreams coming true in their marriage.

"I feel rode-hard and put-up-wet," Jack confessed.

"I've put my dreams on hold—for his—for 22 years," Andrea said.

Jack and Andrea never learned how to talk to each other about their dreams and include each other as they set their priorities. In my mind, they seemed to be operating much like their Neanderthal ancestors. Only their clothing, the size and furnishings of their cave, and their war clubs had changed.

Within two years of my interview with them, Jack and Andrea were divorced and out hunting for new mates.

The bottom line is that common goals keep partners invested and involved in a relationship. A marriage without shared dreams (and I don't mean identical dreams) is in the end, meaningless. A married couple who have lost the ability to cooperate and trust each other is a divorce in search of a lawyer.

Neanderthal Brain Courtship and Marriage

For the caveman and cave woman, decisions about courtship, marriage, and managing wealth were easy, but also brutal. Their Neanderthal brains made all the decisions based on the rules that were discussed earlier. Of course, these rules were expressed in the form of a drama played out in five acts that went something like this:

1. **Get a Mate**
2. **Man's Work-Woman's Work**
3. **Survival is Everything**
4. **Might Makes Right**
5. **My Way or the Highway**

Let's look more closely at each act in this drama.

The curtain rises on "Get a Mate." The Neanderthal brain rule to continue the species was and still is expressed through the human sex drive. That's good. Without that very basic drive, you and I would not be here today. But this basic drive also tends to blind us to other considerations. When the caveman sees a cave woman who "looks good," the Neanderthal brain sends an overriding signal to "get" her. A cave woman responds in similar fashion. If she likes what she sees from a cave woman perspective, her Neanderthal brain just takes over. She sends back unmistakable signals to her caveman that she's interested.

Think about it. Have you seen this behavior in modern life? How about your own behavior towards the opposite sex? I refer to couples in this state of mind as hormone driven. The modern brain functions are definitely not in control at this point, although don't try to tell that to a couple when this rule is operating in their lives.

Once the mate has been "gotten,"

Act Two (Man's work-Woman's Work) begins with the Dominance-Submission rule taking center stage. This rule becomes obvious when men and women define their marriage roles based on sex and power. This Neanderthal brain rule insists that a man's work is to hunt, "bring home the bacon," make the important financial decisions, etc. Women, when ruled by their Neanderthal brains, are designated (and they accept) roles such as home management, managing the checkbook, buying the family's clothes, etc. In a caveman's world, there is no negotiation of these roles. A "real man" (i.e., a caveman) wouldn't dream of doing woman's work. A "real woman" (cave woman) wouldn't allow herself to stick her nose in her man's business—at least not directly. Once again, the modern brain functions are bypassed. The opportunity to pool mental resources and ideas, to create the most productive outcome, is completely missed.

Of course, productive outcomes are measured against only one standard by the Neanderthal brain—survival.

In caveman days, people lived only to eat and to survive. There was little concern for tomorrow. Many couples still live this way. They spend everything they earn. They don't plan for the future. At the end of each month, they complain that they run out of money before they run out of month. Couples whose lives are driven by financial survival are the paycheck-to-paycheck wage earners who never seem to go anywhere, financially. Eventually, their ability to earn a living is diminished by old age, if nothing else, and then they find out that survival itself may not be possible. Usually, things get desperate long before old age settles in. Sometimes a married couple discovers during their first year that money doesn't "stretch" to cover all of their living expenses. Saving money is out of the question. This mindless life-style applies to people who earn very high incomes as well as those of modest means. These are the couples who fight constantly about money. They fight because their survival needs are the only thing on their minds. They fight because they are fearful and angry that their dreams will never come true. They fight because they are totally focused on themselves. But what rule do you think determines how those fights occur? You guessed it—"Might Makes Right."

Might is no longer purely physical in modern life. In our time, we substitute other symbols of strength for the caveman's club. During courtship, good looks, a muscular body, the way he dresses, the car he drives, his education and his ability to earn a living are examples of male strength and attractiveness. You can probably think of other symbols for men. For modern women in courtship, the primary symbol of power is still her outer appearance. If she "looks good" and shows interest in a man, she has the power to trigger almost any man's Neanderthal brain and start the mating game.

But once a couple is married, the symbols of power change. Almost without exception, the one with the larger income or more property uses that fact as a war club. In these cases, money is used as a means of control.

Such displays of financial might are often answered by an angry partner with primitive brain behavior such as overspending, acting helpless, running up credit purchases, lying, etc. These behaviors are also modern day "war clubs." When a couple relates to one another primarily from their Neanderthal brains, they are in a constant power struggle. Power struggles are usually settled in a caveman way, by some form of domination by one mate over the other. The results can be ugly. Have you ever seen modern couples display this type of behavior? You may already have guessed that the final act of this play begins sooner or later in all marriages where "might makes right" is the standard way of relating.

"My Way or the Highway" expresses the ultimate power play and the final act in this drama. Both cavemen and cave women had the freedom to find another mate when things didn't go their way. (This is still true.) The failure of a caveman to "measure up" in the hunt for food, the provision of animal skins, or the sheltering of his cave woman signaled that it was time for her to find a new mate. On the other hand, a cave woman was on the way out if she failed to produce children (preferably males who could be taught to hunt and defend the cave), prepare food, "look good," and display the proper submissive behavior. With modern couples, the divorce courts are the stage where this expression of Neanderthal brain activity is played out financially. Ask any divorce attorney about the primitive displays of modern couples locked in mortal combat over money and property rights. You'll hear ample testimony to the fact that the Neanderthal brain is still very much with us and often in total control of human behavior.

When the modern brain, the thinking, logical and intuitive part of the brain assumes control, it becomes clear that there ought to be a better way to manage the financial side of a marital relationship. Well, there *is* a better way. It's called "forming a partnership."

What Does a Partnership Look Like?

Now that you know how *not* to achieve financial success in marriage, a contrast can be drawn between the Neanderthal model for relationships and a marriage partnership. One of the greatest challenges to writing this book is that most couples who read it will not have had good examples to imitate. Very few of your parents will have understood the idea of "partnership" as presented here. More likely than not, they will have lived out some variation on the Neanderthal brain theme that has already been described. This observation is not meant to be judgmental in any way. It is a simple statement about the way things are, but that doesn't mean *you* have to live this way.

If the following discussion about partnership living seems far removed from your own experience and more like a good theory than anything else, please don't be put off. Weigh the merits of the partnership way by its attractiveness as a model for the way you want your own marriage relationship to unfold. Then keep this simple thought in mind. Whenever we seek to grow as human beings, good ideas precede exploration. Exploration leads to discovery. Through discovery we gain understanding.

The partnership way of living and relating is one of the truly great secrets to financial success in marriage, and the best way I know to create more human, more loving and more caring behavior between men and women.

In addition to presenting an overview of the partnership way in the next few pages, I'll also try to answer the questions, "Where have we been?" and "Where are we going?" (a promise I made at the outset of this chapter).

Forming a partnership is a modern brain activity that opens up possibilities the caveman and cave woman never had. The word "partnership" is usually associated with a business arrangement. However, as used here, a partnership is a way of relating as a married couple that results in practical, business-like behavior to manage the financial side of married life—and it means more. A marriage partnership also requires creating and nurturing a deep and lasting bond—an invisible connection between a married couple that is spiritual in nature. This bond can only be created by using the reasoning, thinking and intuitive functions of the cerebral cortex (your modern brain). This means that if you want a partnership marriage, you will have to make a fundamental choice between modern brain and Neanderthal brain dominance. My hope is that you'll choose the partnership model for relating and that you'll do this at the beginning of your life together. Financial success in marriage is too important to let your Neanderthal instincts run the show.

Let's examine these two aspects of partnership—business-like behavior and bonding—separately.

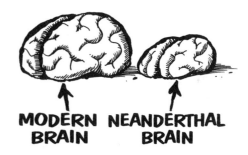

MODERN BRAIN   NEANDERTHAL BRAIN

The Business Side of a Marriage Partnership

My readers who are in business for themselves or who are business managers will recognize many successful business ideas contained in the following description of a marriage partnership. Those who have read and completed the Agreement Checks in the first four chapters of this book will now discover that they have already implemented two of the most important partnership principles.

Partnerships don't have rules, they have principles. The word "rules" implies rigid thinking, and it is the rigid, mindless rules of the primitive brain that undermine a successful partnership. Partnership principles are very different from the principles that express universal laws. As used here, a "principle" is a guideline for success in some particular endeavor—a way to get results. In this case, the endeavor is financial success in marriage. You can choose to adopt or ignore these guidelines for success, just as any business can choose to adopt or ignore proven success principles. There are no moral or ethical implications in making this kind of choice. What is clear is that if you don't adopt these principles, you won't get results. Let's examine successful partnership principles more closely.

The principles for the business side of a partnership are:

1. **Create a Vision**
2. **Adopt "Right" Values**
3. **Obey the Financial Laws of Success**

Let's review these principles one by one.

The first principle **(Create a Vision)** is the most important and the most fun to accomplish. A vision for your marriage is critical to success because it defines exactly what you want out of life. The caveman and cave woman didn't need a vision for their way of living because their every action was based on survival. But modern couples tend to want a lot more than to meet their survival needs—they want to make dreams come true. To make dreams come true requires an ability to visualize a future outcome—a goal. In Chapter Three, you created a vision when you completed your marriage Dream Book. Let's review the fundamental requirements of a vision for your marriage:

To Make A Vision Work For You:

1. You must reach deep within yourselves, and, trusting your partner, share your dreams with one another.

2. You must accept the fact that dreams cost money; your dreams have price tags.

3. You must be willing to throw aside those dreams that are merely fantasies, and keep only those that you are willing to go after with all your might.

4. You must set dates for the achievement of your dreams, thereby converting them into goals.

5. You must create a Dream Book, with pictures, and review it together often to help strengthen the belief that your dreams actually can and will come true.

In the business world, the importance of having a vision statement is now fully accepted. A business that doesn't know what it wants to look like in five, ten or fifteen years is on its way out of business. This can also be said for marriages that don't have a vision. Most couples, of course, don't share their dreams, and don't create dream books.

These couples get caught up in just making it through one tedious day or week or month after another. There is never any sense that they are going anywhere. Their marriages just drift, and eventually the people in them tend to drift apart.

Your marriage can be different because you have already created a vision of your future. You have already taken the first step out of the cave and into a partnership.

How about partnership principle Number Two—(**Adopt "Right" Values**)? In Chapter Four, you discovered that wealth in marriage is created only when money and other financial assets are combined with inner security, a sense of prosperity and personal power (synergistic power in marriage). You were introduced to a set of values and guidelines for cooperative living that can provide these important life qualities *and* launch your marriage down the yellow brick road marked "cooperation." Those values and guidelines for cooperative living are very much like a code of business ethics and personnel policies. Their purpose is to establish ground rules for business operations so everyone knows how the game will be played. As in any business, these values will be helpful only if you are truly committed to them. So, momentarily, I'm going to ask you to make a formal declaration of this commitment.

Making this commitment is very important because you each need to know you can count on "fair play" from each other to create a partnership environment. Making this commitment will also help elevate your love for one another into the Fourth Dimension of Loving that was described in Chapter Two, **"In your happiness, I find my happiness."** Let's review the fundamentals of that fourth dimension of love.

"In Your Happiness, I Find My Happiness" means:

1. We have taken the time to share our dreams and we will give the very best of ourselves to helping each other make dreams come true.

2. We both have arrived at this level of caring and support for one another—even while recognizing that we are very unique and quite imperfect human beings.

3. We both will maintain a healthy commitment to self-love, but the health of our partnership is our top priority.

4. We will manage our behavior in a way that will foster cooperation and build trust and confidence in one another.

5. When we make mistakes, we will be slow to judge, seek ways to avoid the same mistakes, and be quick to forgive one another.

The ideas expressed by the Fourth Dimension of Loving are complete opposites of Neanderthal brain instincts and represent the second step out of the cave and into a partnership. When a married couple enters this dimension of loving, they also set the stage for creating the invisible, spiritual partnership bond that is needed to achieve financial success in marriage. Creating and nurturing that bond requires constant attention and really never ends, but it *begins* with making a commitment to a set of values and rules that encourage cooperative living.

Well, that should answer the question, "Where have we been?" How about answering the question, "Where are we going?"

In Chapters Six through Ten you will be introduced to seven universal laws that govern success with money (called "Rules of the Financial Road"). Learning about these laws, and how to work *with* them, is critical to developing a financial plan that will produce impressive financial gains.

Learning about these laws is a lot like taking a driver's education course before you get your driver's license. Every step you take to bring your life into harmony with these laws will take you further from the cave and deeper into a marriage partnership. But remember, obeying these laws is possible only if your modern brains are in charge of your actions. Your Neanderthal brains have no interest in learning the "rules of the financial road" and care even less about obeying them. Since your present financial styles may be little more than bad financial habits created by your Neanderthal brains, they too must be controlled and given a back seat on the trip to the great city of your dreams.

Getting the modern brain to consistently override the Neanderthal brain's selfishness and obey the rules of the financial road is not always easy. In fact, everyone slips up now and then. But, if you commit to live by these rules and practice them as a form of self-discipline one day at a time, you will be far more successful than couples who don't make the effort. If, while managing your marital finances, you find yourself feeling Neanderthal emotions or slipping into Neanderthal behavior—stop. There is always time between every stimulus and response to think. When you think, you automatically shift gears from your Neanderthal brain to your cerebral cortex. Once your cortex is back in control, remember what you have learned from this chapter. Then, remember the purpose of money in marriage and the values and guidelines for cooperative living. Choose your next move carefully. Make sure it is one that will help you move in the direction of making your dreams come true.

Partnership Bonding:
The Spiritual Side of Partnership

The three principles just discussed reflect the "how tos" for successfully building the business side of a marriage partnership. These are the exterior secrets to financial success in marriage. Knowing these secrets and putting them to use in your marriage is absolutely critical to being successful at making dreams come true. But there is an inside dimension of a marriage partnership that is just as important (actually it's more important). I'm talking about the bond of togetherness, trust, love and synergy that, while invisible, is evident only in those couples who have that special something that makes it possible for them to really work "two-gether." I call this something special "partnership bonding."

Just for a minute, think back to the stories of Mark and Cathy-John and Melanie in Chapter One. Although you probably can't find a word or name for it, you can certainly tell that something has gone very wrong *between* Mark and Cathy. Of course, now you know that they are heavily into Neanderthal brain behavior. What you also sense is that the bond between them is weakening by means of a process I call "negative synergy." One Neanderthal reaction leads to another, and each one represents a trust account withdrawal. If not stopped, a downward spiral of withdrawals will lead to the complete evaporation of marriage trust. On the other hand, you sense that something very right is happening *between* John and Melanie. They are experiencing "positive synergy." If positive synergy continues, their marital "trust account" will grow richer every day.

A marriage partnership is never fully developed until the invisible bond of trust and love between a married couple becomes abundantly rich. The question is, "How can this invisible bond be strengthened to achieve a true marriage partnership?"

The answer is: through value integration and the development of "super trust."

"Value integration" sounds complicated, but it is really a simple idea. What it means is that the values you choose to live by become so much a part of you, that people can always count on you to act according to your values.

Even under the most stressful conditions, someone who is value integrated does not resort to Neanderthal brain behavior. They are steady at the wheel, and you always feel safe with them. If you claim for yourself the values that I presented in Chapter Four, the ones that will encourage cooperation and provide the life qualities of inner security, a sense of prosperity and personal power, then the very center of your value system is love. Every day your partner will ask, "How well does my spouse practice what she or he claims to believe?" Your answer will be expressed in your behavior. If you consistently adhere to your values by means of action, eventually you will become value integrated. Through practice, your values become habits; through more practice, habits become integrity (dependable, value centered behavior).

136

The consistent practice of your values makes steady deposits to your marital trust account. In time, you reach a point where you have "super trust."

There is no way for me to tell you exactly how long it takes to reach this stage of relationship strength, but I can give you some hints about how to tell when you have arrived.

The first thing you notice is how the quality of **companionship** dominates your marriage. Companionship means that your marriage partner has become your best friend, someone you can rely on to always be there, and who is fun to be with. With a companion, you always feel co-equal, not as if one of you is top dog. Also, there is no competition between you (although occasional conflict *is* a part of your reality). You feel absolutely free to be yourself because you know that you are always accepted. And because the trust between you is so strong, you know you won't be quickly judged if you don't express yourself perfectly the first time or if you innocently step over an invisible line or on a sensitive toe. Companions know instantly when that has happened and are just as quick to apologize, forgive and make course corrections.

The second quality is **collaboration**. Instead of just cooperating, you and your spouse have an ability to easily divide responsibilities, play complementary roles, and shift roles. Instead of resorting to Neanderthal tendencies to assign responsibilities based on sex and-or power, you assess strengths and weaknesses and assign responsibilities and roles based on present circumstances to form the most powerful and effective team to produce the most favorable results. This is only possible when you have a sense that you and your spouse are *fully committed* to making each other's dreams come true. As a result of this commitment, you are *always* going for Win-Win. Even when there is conflict, the way you negotiate assures that you both will get what you want and need. And while this means you often come up with creative solutions that are different from what either one of you originally envisioned, there is always consensus—a feeling that you both want to implement the winning solution. Collaborators feel a sense of "two-getherness" that allows them to synergize more frequently and more fully than other couples.

The third quality is **communication**. When a couple has super trust in their marriage, they find communicating much easier. They also communicate on many levels *and* with tremendous ease. Sometimes just a wink, a touch on the hand or a certain body movement is all it takes to signal their partners and be completely understood. This gives them enormous advantages in dealing with others. Their rapport allows them to carry on a private dialogue, even in the presence of other people. But much more indicative of their communication strength is their willingness and ability to communicate feelings. Nothing clogs up the arteries of a marriage faster than the inability to share and explore feelings. Yet, unless you can rely on your spouse to always act in loving ways, you *won't* share feelings. So, now we come full circle. To share and explore feelings and keep the energy of a relationship flowing freely, you must start with right values. And the most important value of all is love because love creates the best environment for trust building.

Of course, no married couple achieves perfection in their spiritual bonding. Real life is full of what Anne

Morrow Lindbergh calls "intermittencies," which is her way of describing the movement in and out of those intense moments of closeness that partners experience. A good partnership relationship, in her words, "has a pattern like a dance and is built on some of the same rules. The partners do not need to hold on tightly, because they move confidently in the same pattern… now arm-in-arm, now face-to-face, now back-to-back—it does not matter which. Because they know they are partners moving to the same rhythm, creating a pattern together, and being invisibly nourished by it." There are even moments when the dancers make missteps, lose their timing or dance to different beats. Whether caused by fear, doubt or the hesitation of not fully understanding one another, these moments create trust account withdrawals. To move from these awkward moments and return to the partnership dance with ease and grace requires a skill of its own.

In Chapter Four, I said that because we are all human, and that means imperfect, we all make trust account withdrawals. This means that getting to the "super trust" level doesn't happen quickly. Sometimes it takes years; other couples reach this level of trust in a relatively short time. However, it seems never to happen for some couples because they don't know what to do or how to respond when a trust account withdrawal is made. As a result, they quickly resort to Neanderthal brain behavior. It helps enormously to be prepared for this and have a plan ready to manage it. Let's discuss that topic next.

Managing Trust Account Withdrawals or, "Ouch, that hurts!"

Some trust account withdrawals can break a marriage, but that rarely happens. Most withdrawals are innocent and small in nature. Still, they hurt. Sometimes one hurt can lead to a sharp reaction that becomes another withdrawal. If not stopped, one reaction can lead to another, and another and another—creating a downward spiral of withdrawals (negative synergy). For this reason, it's critical to have a plan ready to handle these situations. The suggestions that follow are basic and fundamental to manage marital trust account withdrawals successfully. Add to them or change them in any way you wish. Just be sure you adopt some guidelines and stick to them. I assure you, you'll be glad you did.

1. When you feel that your partner has done something to violate your trust, express your concern within 24 hours of the violation. Don't "stuff" or "gunny sack" your feelings and mull over the offense for several days or weeks. Agree with your partner on a non-verbal signal to indicate your need to talk (although a verbal signal is O.K., too). Something as simple as a "time-out" signal, forming a "T" with your left and right hands, works well. However, postpone the discussion until each partner is calm enough to discuss the problem.

2. Set the stage for this talk with care. Make sure the TV is off, and that neither one of you is involved in some activity that will be distracting—such as reading the newspaper. It also helps to make physical contact. Going for a walk and holding hands while you talk can be most effective. Find a nice park where you can be surrounded by nature. Use eye contact frequently during your talk as a way of showing openness and sincerity.

3. When you express your concern, use a soft voice. The partner with a "complaint" should state the problem fully as he or she sees it, using "I feel..." expressions. If you have difficulty controlling your Neanderthal emotions, write out your "I feel" expressions and ask your partner to read them. Be sure to talk straight. Don't beat around the bush, use double talk or use expressions that blur your meaning. Be especially careful to avoid the use of accusations or sarcasm—even humorous sarcasm is hurtful.

4. The person listening (or reading) should assume that his or her partner is telling the truth about his or her feelings or concerns. This doesn't mean you should automatically accept what is said, but it does mean you are willing to maintain an open-minded approach to communication. Sometimes people say things from their points of view that don't make any sense from yours. Ask questions and allow them to make their feelings clear. Be a considerate listener. Try to understand what has happened and the feelings that are being expressed. See if you can repeat your partner's point of view without judgment. If you feel defensive, don't be surprised. That's just your Neanderthal brain at work. Keep your modern brain with its higher brain functions firmly in control.

**5. Before responding, allow some time to pass in order to absorb and

process your own feelings and thoughts. When you do respond, ask first for clarifications about anything that remains unclear. Both of you should assume that the other is trying to communicate something important and is also trying to understand your communication. The truth is that most people prefer to have situations resolved in a friendly way, and would like to avoid Neanderthal behavior. Try to confirm your partner's view if at all possible by saying words such as, "Yes, I see what you mean," or "I can understand why you feel that way," or "I hear you. You've helped me understand."

6. During your discussion, express your feelings, but don't relive them. You only need to name them. While either one is talking, don't interrupt. If one of you becomes heated or angry during the discussion, take time out, but come back to the discussion at an agreed upon time. (This may seem difficult to do, but when discussions get emotionally "hot," productive communication stops.) Neither of you should: bring in past events or other people; berate, call names or resort to controlling behavior like crying, frowning, etc.; attack by bringing in sensitive material not pertinent to the discussion; leave the discussion without a tentative solution.

7. If the break in trust has occurred because of a misunderstanding, treat the other person as if he or she were from another country and spoke a completely different language. Men and women often see, hear, feel and understand the same events in vastly different ways. Assume that the miscommunication is not an attempt to belittle or manipulate, but is a genuinely different way of interpreting events, based on differences alone.

8. When a partner asks for time to express a concern about trust in a sincere way, rationalizing or minimizing the offense is a big mistake. It will only make a bigger "trust account" withdrawal. If the break in trust is due to some action that could or should have been avoided, whether the action was intended to break trust or not, apologize immediately. A sincere apology can make an immediate deposit to your marital trust account. (A half-hearted apology can be a disaster.) There is immediate healing power in words such as:

"I was wrong."

"That wasn't kind of me."

"That wasn't respectful, and I'm deeply sorry."

"I didn't honor the trust you gave me, and I should have been more considerate."

9. Forgive. We all make mistakes. In the best of marriages, there are misunderstandings and miscommunications. Forgiveness is very healing. By fully forgiving one another, you can get on with trust building. But if you carry anger around with you, it will create a steady withdrawal of trust from your marriage. In addition to forgiveness, exchange a few sincere, specific compliments. Let each other know that all is not darkness.

10. Learn from this talk. Learn about your partner and what does and does not make him or her feel trust. Then, change your behavior if that will help. Learn about yourself. Discover how your way of seeing things is probably not the only way. This can be a humbling experience, but a little humility about ourselves can go a long way to improve communications.

11. Complete your discussion about any trust withdrawal within 48 hours. This will avoid festering.

Festering is what happens to an open sore when it is infected (it gets red and angry looking) and nothing is done to clean and heal it. Remember, too, your bedroom is off limits for these discussions.

12. End these kinds of discussions by thanking your partner. Communicating a broken trust takes courage, just as responding in a calm and caring manner takes courage. If trust account withdrawals are handled well, you will have each made a gift to the other. Paying someone careful attention, honestly trying to hear what that person has to say and trying to find out who she or he is, is a very precious gift. Even a partner who doesn't fully understand when he or she really tried to understand, deserves a "Thank you!"

To end this discussion about partnership bonding, I'm going to give you a chance to make a commitment to right values and rules for cooperative living—something that I know will strengthen your resolve to live and work as partners in the management of your financial life. The declaration on the next page is a statement of understandings and promises that reflects a desire to use the reasoning capabilities of your modern brain to direct your financial life. By reading and signing it, you commit to a common direction for your marriage partnership. If you don't like the wording, write your own. You may find that changing this declaration to reflect your own needs is an even more rewarding experience.

141

A Declaration and Commitment

**Because We Know We Have Choices About How To Behave
Toward One Another,
We Acknowledge And Accept Full Responsibility For
The Choices We Make.
When We Act Toward One Another In Any Way That Is
Less Than Fully Loving,
We Vow To Abide By The Following Affirmation:**

1. We are in this world to love each other, and we are dedicated to build a marriage partnership based on right values and the principles of cooperation.

2. We fully acknowledge that we are each capable of acting in primitive, reactive and destructive ways that can undermine our marriage partnership.

3. We will let each other know lovingly and honestly when we feel that a trust or the rules for cooperative living have been broken. We will be slow to accuse the other, asking first about his or her motives and expected outcomes. We will withhold judgment and control our reactions until we fully understand.

4. We will sincerely apologize when we have violated a trust or act in any way that is contrary to our loving commitment to cooperative living. We will be quick to forgive completely, so we can move forward without carrying a burden of anger or guilt.

5. We accept and respect that there are financial success laws that we must understand and obey in order to make dreams come true. We promise to grow in knowledge, skill and ability and to share equally the financial responsibilities of our marriage, so we can realize as many of our dreams as possible in the course of our life together.

Signed:

_____

_____

Date _____

Agreement Check:

1. Everyone comes to marriage with his or her own styles and strategies for thinking and behaving financially. If those styles and strategies are Neanderthal in nature, they become war clubs and the goal of financial success in marriage becomes impossible. In a marriage partnership, you lay down your Neanderthal clubs, axes and spears and agree to live by the principles, values and guidelines for cooperative living presented in Chapter Four *and* by the universal laws that govern financial success (rules of the financial road—which you will learn about in the second half of this book). In the space below, I want you to become more fully aware of your current financial styles. There is no need to pass judgment in this exercise. The goal is to be descriptive *only* at this time.

   A. How would you describe your financial style? A few adjectives have been provided to help you think about your answer to this question. Each of you should check the ones that you think help describe your style. If none of these adjectives are appropriate, pick some of your own.

Well Informed	Competent
Good Provider	Disorganized
Nurturer	Spendthrift
Intuitive	Shopper
Experienced	Controlling
Harebrained	Fair
Generous	Squirreler
Organized	Honest
Incompetent	Prudent
Confidential	Miserly
Objective	Impulsive
Saver	Investor
Charitable	Manipulative
Others:	

   _____   _____

   _____   _____

   _____   _____

   B. Once you both complete this exercise, set aside some time to explain why you picked those adjectives that you believe describe your financial style. While one partner is talking, the other should carefully listen without judging. Keep firmly in mind that what you have been does not have to represent what you will be. If your style is compatible with the rules of the financial road (the laws that govern success with money), then little change in your style is required. (You can check out the compatibility of your current financial style with the rules of the financial road by reading the next five chapters). But if your financial style would cause you to break one or more of those rules on a regular basis, you will have to change your Neanderthal habits or face harsh consequences.

2. A very important part of your financial plan is role playing. There are a variety of roles that must be filled in managing your trip to the great city of your dreams. In a marriage partnership, these roles can be negotiated and renegotiated to meet changing needs and circumstances. A presentation of these roles appears below (and on the following pages) along with some questions to answer to help you make role assignments. Go through this exercise now, and then revisit it after reading each of the chapters that follow. See if your roles change after reviewing the material in the rest of this book. Remember, assigning a role to one partner does not mean that the other partner can wash his or her hands of responsibility in that financial area. You are both 100% responsible for everything that happens in your financial life. However, you should take advantage of strengths to create the best possible team to play all the financial roles in marriage.

☐ **Role No. 1: Providing Income**

☐ **Role No. 2: Financial Records Management**

☐ **Role No. 3: Cash Flow Management**

☐ **Role No. 4: Debt Management**

☐ **Role No. 5: Investment Management**

☐ **Role No. 6: Insurance Planning**

☐ **Role No. 7: Tax Planning**

☐ **Role No. 8: Estate Distribution**

☐ **Role No. 9: Annual Net Worth Calculation**

☐ **Role No. 10: Coordination of Continuing Education**

Role No. 1: Providing Income.

This includes earning your primary income(s), the development of a second income stream (to be discussed in Chapter Seven), and contributions to income from other *existing* income sources such as trusts, investments, etc.

Who will play this role in your marriage? Will you share this role?

What is expected of the person(s) who play this role? (Be very specific.)

Why did you assign this role in this way? What financial strengths or special qualifications are you taking advantage of by assigning this role in this way?

How will the supporting partner participate in the fulfillment of this responsibility? (Be very specific.)

How often will you hold partnership meetings to review your progress in this area of financial responsibility? How will you share information with each other and be supportive of one another in this financial area in between those partnership meetings? (Be very specific.)

Notes

_____

_____

_____

_____

_____

_____

_____

_____

_____

_____

_____

Role No. 2: Financial Records Management.

This task is fairly well defined in Appendix B on pages B-1 through B-6. Establishing a financial record keeping system and carefully maintaining it is one of the most overlooked financial responsibilities in marriage. Like it or not, good record keeping is the cornerstone of all other financial management tasks.

Who will play this role in your marriage? Will you share this role?

What is expected of the person(s) who play this role? (Be very specific.)

Why did you assign this role in this way? What financial strengths or special qualifications are you taking advantage of by assigning this role in this way?

How will the supporting partner participate in the fulfillment of this responsibility? (Be very specific.)

How often will you hold partnership meetings to review your progress in this area of financial responsibility? How will you share information with each other and be supportive of one another in this financial area in between those partnership meetings? (Be very specific.)

Notes

_____

_____

_____

_____

_____

_____

_____

_____

_____

_____

Role No. 3: Cash Flow Management.

This task (covered in Chapter Six) includes preparing your monthly Spending Plans _and_ management of your savings programs.

Who will play this role in your marriage? Will you share this role?

What is expected of the person(s) who play this role? (Be very specific.)

Why did you assign this role in this way? What financial strengths or special qualifications are you taking advantage of by assigning this role in this way?

How will the supporting partner participate in the fulfillment of this responsibility? (Be very specific.)

How often will you hold partnership meetings to review your progress in this area of financial responsibility? How will you share information with each other and be supportive of one another in this financial area in between those partnership meetings? (Be very specific.)

Notes

_____

_____

_____

_____

_____

_____

_____

_____

_____

_____

_____

_____

Role No. 4: Debt Management.

This task (covered in Chapter Six) includes managing all strategies for debt reduction and debt ceiling management, learning everything possible about how to use debt responsibly and becoming expert on all subjects related to borrowing money.

Who will play this role in your marriage? Will you share this role?

What is expected of the person(s) who play this role? (Be very specific.)

Why did you assign this role in this way? What financial strengths or special qualifications are you taking advantage of by assigning this role in this way?

How will the supporting partner participate in the fulfillment of this responsibility? (Be very specific.)

How often will you hold partnership meetings to review your progress in this area of financial responsibility? How will you share information with each other and be supportive of one another in this financial area in between those partnership meetings? (Be very specific.)

Notes

_____

_____

_____

_____

_____

_____

_____

_____

_____

_____

_____

_____

Role No. 5: Investment Management.

This task (covered in Chapter Eight) includes learning everything possible about investments, development of an investment plan, selecting investment advisors, developing a partnership approach to making investment decisions and managing investments.

Who will play this role in your marriage? Will you share this role?

What is expected of the person(s) who play this role? (Be very specific.)

Why did you assign this role in this way? What financial strengths or special qualifications are you taking advantage of by assigning this role in this way?

How will the supporting partner participate in the fulfillment of this responsibility? (Be very specific.)

How often will you hold partnership meetings to review your progress in this area of financial responsibility? How will you share information with each other and be supportive of one another in this financial area in between those partnership meetings? (Be very specific.)

Notes

_____

_____

_____

_____

_____

_____

_____

_____

_____

_____

_____

Role No. 6: Insurance Planning.

This task (discussed more fully in Chapter Nine) includes learning everything possible about the various forms of insurance coverage necessary to protect your marriage from financial disaster, selecting insurance advisors, reviewing insurance proposals and making the best possible insurance decisions.

Who will play this role in your marriage? Will you share this role?

What is expected of the person(s) who play this role? (Be very specific.)

Why did you assign this role in this way? What financial strengths or special qualifications are you taking advantage of by assigning this role in this way?

How will the supporting partner participate in the fulfillment of this responsibility? (Be very specific.)

How often will you hold partnership meetings to review your progress in this area of financial responsibility? How will you share information with each other and be supportive of one another in this financial area in between those partnership meetings? (Be very specific.)

Notes

_____

_____

_____

_____

_____

_____

_____

_____

_____

Role No. 7: Tax Planning.

This task includes reading at least one book about taxes and tax return preparation each year, preparing an estimate of your tax liability at the beginning of each year (complete with tax reduction strategies), holding quarterly partnership meetings to make adjustments to your plan, making sure the right amount of withholding or estimated taxes are being paid and working with tax advisors to prepare and file your annual tax returns. (See Appendix C, pages C-1 through C-5.)

Who will play this role in your marriage? Will you share this role?

What is expected of the person(s) who play this role? (Be very specific.)

Why did you assign this role in this way? What financial strengths or special qualifications are you taking advantage of by assigning this role in this way?

How will the supporting partner participate in the fulfillment of this responsibility? (Be very specific.)

How often will you hold partnership meetings to review your progress in this area of financial responsibility? How will you share information with each other and be supportive of one another in this financial area in between those partnership meetings? (Be very specific.)

Notes

_____

_____

_____

_____

_____

_____

_____

_____

_____

Role No. 8: Estate Distribution.

This task (covered in Chapter Ten) includes making sure you both have up-to-date and properly drafted wills, learning everything possible about the process of estate distribution and settlement, planning for the use of trusts to protect children that might be born to your marriage (also to make the passage of assets to a surviving spouse as easy and inexpensive as possible) and holding an annual review of your estate distribution plan.

Who will play this role in your marriage? Will you share this role?

What is expected of the person(s) who play this role? (Be very specific.)

Why did you assign this role in this way? What financial strengths or special qualifications are you taking advantage of by assigning this role in this way?

How will the supporting partner participate in the fulfillment of this responsibility? (Be very specific.)

How often will you hold partnership meetings to review your progress in this area of financial responsibility? How will you share information with each other and be supportive of one another in this financial area in between those partnership meetings? (Be very specific.)

Notes

_____

_____

_____

_____

_____

_____

_____

_____

_____

_____

Role No. 9: Annual Net Worth Calculation.

This task includes the annual appraisal of your assets and liabilities and then subtracting your liabilities from your assets to determine your net worth. How to do this will be more fully explained in the transition between this chapter and Chapter Six.

Who will play this role in your marriage? Will you share this role?

What is expected of the person(s) who play this role? (Be very specific.)

Why did you assign this role in this way? What financial strengths or special qualifications are you taking advantage of by assigning this role in this way?
How will the supporting partner participate in the fulfillment of this responsibility? (Be very specific.)

How often will you hold partnership meetings to review your progress in this area of financial responsibility? How will you share information with each other and be supportive of one another in this financial area in between those partnership meetings? (Be very specific.)

Notes

_____

_____

_____

_____

_____

_____

_____

_____

_____

_____

_____

Role No. 10: Coordination of Continuing Education.

This task includes developing a plan to strengthen your financial planning and financial management skills through reading, formal classroom training, correspondence courses, etc. It also includes monitoring your educational progress on a regular basis and making sure your financial partnership is surrounded with excellent financial advisors.

Who will play this role in your marriage? Will you share this role?

What is expected of the person(s) who play this role? (Be very specific.)

Why did you assign this role in this way? What financial strengths or special qualifications are you taking advantage of by assigning this role in this way?

How will the supporting partner participate in the fulfillment of this responsibility? (Be very specific.)

How often will you hold partnership meetings to review your progress in this area of financial responsibility? How will you share information with each other and be supportive of one another in this financial area in between those partnership meetings? (Be very specific.)

Notes

_____

_____

_____

_____

_____

_____

_____

_____

_____

_____

_____

Suggested Additional Reading:

Eisler, Riane. *The Chalice & The Blade*. San Francisco: Harper & Row, 1988.

Eisler, Riane and David Loye. *The Partnership Way*. New York: Harper Collins, 1990.

Tanenbaum, Joe. *Male & Female Realities: Understanding The Opposite Sex*. Sugar Land: Candle Publishing Company, 1989.

Tannen, Deborah, Ph.D. *You Just Don't Understand: Women and Men In Conversation*. New York: William Morrow and Company, Inc., 1990.

Lindbergh, Anne Morrow. *Gift From The Sea.* New York: Pantheon Books, 1975.

Notes

When You Get Married

The end of Chapter Five signals a transition away from the philosophical and psychological secrets to financial success in marriage. As you begin Chapter Six, the emphasis will be on the laws that govern the practical dimension of managing money successfully as a married couple. I hope and expect that you will go slowly through each of these chapters, perhaps reading one chapter each week or taking a couple of weeks with some chapters. However, there are some financial tasks that should be taken care of almost immediately when you get married. The following check list will help you get started.

1. If there is a name change, then:

☐ Change your driver's license. There is a time period (different in each state) set by law within which you are required to do this.

☐ Change your credit cards to reflect your new name(s).

☐ Change all other identification.

☐ Contact current and former employers and let them know your new name(s) and ask them to place a notice in your personnel file.

☐ Contact the Social Security Administration by telephoning your local office. Your social security numbers won't change. However, by notifying the SSA, your social security account will be properly credited when you pay social security taxes.

2. Name each other as beneficiary of all:

☐ Company pension and profit-sharing plans.

☐ Individual Retirement Accounts (IRAs).

☐ Keogh H.R. (10) plans.

☐ Life insurance policies.

3. Have new wills drafted. Both of you need wills that are up-to-date in every respect. If you doubt this, read Chapter Ten.

4. Make appropriate adjustments in your federal income tax withholding allowances with your employer. If you're not sure whether to increase or decrease your withholding, you probably need to have a tax planning session with a C.P.A. immediately.

5. Review your health insurance coverage by meeting with your insurance agent and/or your employee benefits coordinator. If you both work, make sure your coverage doesn't overlap, and that you have adequate maternity coverage.

6. Review your life insurance coverage and have the conversations about life insurance that are suggested in Chapter Nine.

7. Review your automobile insurance coverage and have the conversations about auto insurance that are suggested in Chapter Nine. Your auto insurance costs may drop significantly now that you are married.

8. Review your homeowner's or renter's insurance. Be sure you are adequately covered—that there are no gaps in coverage that could bring you unhappy surprises later on. Make a photo inventory of all your possessions.

9. Go to a bank and establish checking and savings accounts. You decide if they will be joint or separate accounts, but start a relationship with a bank right away. Open up a safe deposit box with the bank and store the following documents there:

Birth certificates	Copies of your wills
Marriage licenses	Copies of insurance policies
Military discharge papers	Title to property you own
The photo inventory of	including deeds, mortgages, leases,
your possessions	stock and bond certificates and
Expensive jewelry	other securities
Stamp collections	Coin collections
Other valuables that	Other important papers and
may not be covered	documents.
by homeowner's	
insurance.	

10. Set up a financial record keeping system. See **Appendix B** for suggestions about how to do this.

Getting started on the right foot is important in anything you do in life. This simple check list will help you do that financially. So will completing the net worth assessment presented in **Appendix D** and then reading each of the next five chapters in this book. Don't put it off. Start now to learn the practical secrets to financial success in marriage.

Where Are You Financially?

The first five Chapters of this book were devoted to (1) helping you identify your dreams, (2) selecting values to serve as a moral compass as you work to make dreams come true, and (3) starting you in the direction of becoming financial partners. You have also been given some important guidelines for managing ordinary, garden variety conflicts, and for rebuilding trust when occasional trust violations occur. Now, before learning the rules of the financial road, it's important to check the fuel in your financial gas tank. In answering the question, "Where are you financially?" your response should be "At the beginning." It's always best and easiest to start there. As newlyweds, starting at the beginning will give you many advantages. Your biggest advantage is that you don't have a lifetime of bad experiences and memories to overcome. And if you choose to live by the principles and values presented in Chapters One through Five you can keep that advantage. Getting off on the right foot, with a knowledge of the "rules of the financial road," is another big advantage. You will learn about these financial rules by reading Chapters Six through Ten. However, two notes of caution are in order before you begin reading those chapters.

Caution No. 1: The trip to the city of your dreams is not going to be a weekend drive in the country. To get where you want to go, you must be patient, very patient, with yourself and with each other. So what if you don't have enough financial fuel to make all your dreams come true at the start of married life! Who does? Very few couples start out with vast financial resources. Even when they do, unless they go through the process of planning and learning to live by the rules that determine financial success, their trip is so rough and bumpy that they usually break down along the way. Remember, no matter where you start, you aren't really making progress unless your planning efforts produce cooperation, team work, synergy. So keep working through these pages together—**and be patient.**

Caution No. 2: Just because you're married doesn't mean that everything you own is "Ours." This can be a very delicate subject, but let's get it on the table. Just as the values you bring to marriage can be divided into "Yours, Mine, and Ours" so can your possessions. You each have an "idea of ownership" which is your personal idea of who owns what. These "ideas of ownership" may be very different from how ownership is considered under the law. The next financial planning exercise I want you to complete is the net worth inventory in **Appendix D**. As you complete that inventory, it's a good idea to identify and clarify who owns what, both legally and in terms of your "ideas of ownership." This will be a great help to your trust building efforts because a large part of building trust is knowing where your partner's boundaries are and showing respect for those boundaries.

If one of you is coming to marriage with substantial assets, then you may want to formalize your understanding of who owns what in a prenuptial agreement. A prenuptial agreement is a legal document that takes precedent over state laws in the event of divorce or death. While prenuptial agreements are seldom needed by most married couples, they *are* a part of the real world (financially speaking) and you can learn more about them by reading **Appendix G**. However, if you're already married, or even if you're still engaged, your education about "Yours, Mine and Ours" should focus on "Where do we go from here?" Let's look more closely at what the law says about ownership before you turn to **Appendix D**.

"Yours, Mine, and Ours" and Property Ownership

Human beings learned a long time ago that recording the ownership of property on paper tends to keep us from defending our property rights with caveman clubs. We call this simple practice "title." Titling property has evolved and is now a well accepted, but complicated, part of our legal system. Legal ownership (title) provides it's own definition of who owns what (as opposed to personal opinion), and determines the rights that go along with ownership. Most married couples don't know how they hold title to their property, but they should know. For this reason, I'm going to give you a quick course in the standard forms of legal title. Here they are:

Sole and Separate Property: Any property titled in the name of only one person. You usually acquire such property when you are single, then bring it with you to marriage. When you get married, title to your sole and separate property does not change. At death, sole and separate property passes to a surviving spouse only if there is a valid will that specifically directs the property. Your spouse does not automatically inherit it.

Joint Tenancy with Rights of Survivorship: Two or more owners are needed to title property in this way. What it means is that each person owns a whole or undivided interest in the property, sharing all income from the property and all money received from the sale of the property. If one joint tenant dies, her/his share passes automatically to the surviving joint tenant.

Tenancy in Common: This form of title is similar to joint tenancy but there are important differences. Tenants in common have an equal right to manage the property they own together and to benefit from that property during their lifetimes. If that property is sold, each tenant shares in the profits according to his or her percentage of ownership. This form of title is often used to hold investment property. When one investor dies, the surviving investors do not automatically inherit. In other words, a valid will is needed to determine who should inherit.

Community Property: Only married people can acquire community property, and only in the eight states that have community property laws (Arizona, California, Idaho, Louisiana, Nevada, New Mexico, Texas and Washington). Community property is equally owned by husband and wife. When one spouse dies, the survivor does not automatically inherit it. If you want your share of community property to go to your spouse, you must say so in your will.

Equitable Title: The four forms of title above provide property owners with both the rights to enjoy property *and* the responsibilities for managing that property. Equitable title only gives a person the rights to enjoy property. An example would be one's right to the income from a trust (I'll discuss trusts in Chapter Ten). The important thing to remember is that when you have equitable title, you do not have responsibility for property management.

These definitions *do not* represent everything you need to know about legal title. However, they will help you complete the estate inventory that appears in **Appendix D**. In addition, they should help you think carefully about the way you title new property as your estate grows. I urge you to broaden your understanding of title and to pay careful attention to how you title every asset you acquire. Pay particular attention to how your choices will affect your partner's rights to inherit your estate. If ever you have doubts about these subjects, please consult an attorney. Much of your effort to create a marital estate can be destroyed by not knowing how you hold title to your property.

Since I've used the term "estate" so liberally in this discussion (without defining it), let's see exactly what it means.

Estate: Everything That You Own; Everything That You Owe

The word "estate" has a kind of high dollar sound to most people. Some think of an estate as being a big mansion on wooded grounds, surrounded by a high brick wall. That's just one meaning of the term. Surprising as it may seem, everyone has an estate—not just the very wealthy. *You* have an estate. "Estate" simply means ownership of assets, including any property or personal possessions. These assets can range from owning a home, a car, a few bonds, perhaps some stocks and an insurance policy, down to personal items like the family silverware, weddings gifts and your wristwatch.

All estates are made up of two parts: your assets and your liabilities. **Assets** are those things you own that have value outside of their value to you. **Liabilities** represent what you owe to someone else. When you subtract what you owe from the value of what you own, the difference is called your "net worth."

The Annual Estate Inventory: Keeping Track of Changes In Your Net Worth

One way to measure your progress towards financial success in marriage is to know your net worth now; then chart changes in your net worth each year to see if you are doing well, just OK, or need to make some changes. This measure of progress is well accepted and helpful, but it won't tell you if things like trust, cooperation, inner security, your sense of prosperity and personal and synergistic power are growing. So, if you look only at your growing net worth, you won't have a true picture of how well your marriage is doing. In spite of this drawback, you still should develop the habit of taking an annual estate inventory of your assets and liabilities to determine your net worth. Think of it as checking the level of fuel in your financial gas tank. It may be only one step in preparing to take a trip, but *it is* an important one.

161

To help determine your current net worth, estate inventory forms have been provided in **Appendix D** that will allow you to complete your first, thorough estate inventory *together*. Complete this exercise before going on to the next chapter. Be sure to identify your ideas of ownership for both assets and liabilities, and the legal form of title to major property items if you know it. If you don't know, find out and then fill in the blanks.

If, after completing your inventory, you feel that your present net worth is very small, just remember that this is only a starting point. By learning and obeying the "rules of the financial road," and by making an investment of hard work, you are going to see a dramatic improvement in your net worth in years to come.

If, after completing your estate inventory, you have a sense of being financially secure, you may be in great danger. Why? Because financial security can too easily be taken for granted. Money does not take care of itself. Financial security is possible only through careful planning, attentive management and the generous investment of your labor. So don't stop here and assume you've got it made.

OK, it's time to complete your first thorough inventory. Take as much time as you need, but do it— **together**.

The Rules of The Financial Road:

Part I

Chapter Six

"Money is governed today by the same laws which controlled it when prosperous men thronged the streets of Babylon, six thousand years ago."
George S. Clason

In 1926, George S. Clason wrote a book entitled, *The Richest Man In Babylon*. In his book, he tells wonderful stories of how one man, who lived six thousand years ago, learned the laws that govern success with money. Mr. Clason claimed that Babylon became the wealthiest city of the ancient world. He claims that its citizens were the richest people of their time because they appreciated the value of money. They practiced sound financial principles in getting money, keeping money and making their money earn more money.

Mr. Clason's parables are based on the fundamental principle that there are universal laws which govern success with money. The reality of such laws has become abundantly clear to me, and I think they become obvious to anyone who thinks deeply and examines the lives of those who have been financially successful. But most of the time, we are so involved in making money that there is little time to stop and "tune the engine"—to learn these basic laws and apply them to married life.

By taking the time to read and learn the lessons in this and the following chapters, you will be "tuning the engine" of knowledge so your financial trip to the city of your dreams can be as safe and sane as possible.

I hope the learning experience created for you in the following pages will give you a new perspective on how to achieve financial success in marriage and that you will come to see that by working in harmony with universal financial laws, your dreams *can* and actually *will* come true.

The financial laws that Mr. Clason believed in and taught are included and expanded upon here. You will discover that they are not complicated or mysterious. In fact, they are easy to grasp and quite straightforward in their simplicity. These laws have a reality that exists outside of you or me. They govern your chances of success with money, no matter what you think or believe about them. It makes no difference whether you are dominated by your Neanderthal brain or your modern brain, or if you have no brain at all—these laws operate and control financial success in all cases. It is as though they seem to exist as part of the human condition itself, and deep down, most of us have a consciousness about them regardless of our formal financial education.

You will soon learn that harmonizing with these laws requires adopting specific *financial strategies*.

Therefore, I'm not only going to introduce you to the "rules of the financial road," I will also provide suggestions about financial strategies to help you harmonize with them. Adopting these strategies will indeed give you great power to make your dreams come true. But if you ignore these strategies, you will only experience frustration and disappointment at every turn of the financial road.

Let me give you an example that demonstrates how knowledge about financial laws (and the strategies that harmonize with them) can change the way a married couple relates.

Financial strategies are goal oriented guidelines that build communication and management skills and allow you to capture the power of the laws that govern financial success.

The Story of Carl and Susan

Susan and Carl were not a typical young married couple. Carl grew up in a wealthy family. His family often used money and the possessions it could buy as an emblem of achievement and social acceptance (his financial style). Susan, on the other hand, was raised by parents who were very practical. She bought things she needed rather than things she desired (her financial style). In spite of these differences in background, Carl and Susan shared many "right" values and agreed that they wanted to use money to help make their dreams come true. They developed a marriage Dream Book and started out on their financial trip through life.

However, they discovered during the first few months of marriage that they were ending each month a little deeper in debt. Although they sensed that taking on debt was probably not a good idea, they had been swamped with offers of easy credit because they both had high-paying jobs. The increasing debt didn't bother them at first because they were able to pay all their bills. Carl found that debt was an easy way to buy expensive presents for Susan, a practice he engaged in without her agreement.

Soon they began to notice that the amount of money needed to pay creditors was eating a larger share of their monthly income. They also become more irritable with one another when they held their weekly money-planning sessions. After one session turned into a real clash, Susan confronted Carl with two concerns. First, she told him, she was actually annoyed that he wouldn't stop buying her expensive presents on a whim. She wanted their commitment to making dreams come true to be a shared experience, and she didn't want debt to be the way that they financed their dreams. Second, she expressed concern that going deeper and deeper in debt broke a fundamental financial law. If debt were to be used at all, she felt they had better learn more about the subject, and set up some guidelines for debt management. Most important of all, she believed that all decisions about debt should be made together—not independently.

Carl was hurt, and unwilling at first to accept this new reality. But when Susan showed him a notice from the bank complaining that Carl had exceeded one of his new credit card limits by several hundred dollars and demanding immediate payment down to the approved limit, reality began to sink in. The confrontation was hard for him. For the first time, he realized that having a common goal was not enough. There were financial realities that had to be faced. Going into debt was probably a bad way to finance dreams, he conceded. And if they didn't develop some new habits for thinking about and managing debt, Carl knew that their marriage was headed for troubled times. For the first time, he realized that being married meant giving up some of his independence, and developing communication and decision making practices that hadn't been necessary in a family in which money was always abundant.

Although Carl and Susan shared values and had a financial goal, they didn't yet have a full understanding of the financial laws that would govern their success with money. They were already breaking a primary rule of the financial road, and as a result, they were breaking themselves against that rule.

They hadn't yet learned how important it is for young married couples to avoid debt, even though they *sensed* that going into debt was a big mistake. Their ignorance of this rule was compounded by their lack of financial strategies relating to the rule. They had no guidelines for communicating about and managing debt—therefore no way to capture the power of this law. Once the pain of breaking this law about debt began to create problems in their marriage, Carl and Susan were ready to learn more about this subject.

Can a married couple experience financial success without harmonizing with the rules of the financial road (the laws that govern success with money)? The answer is clearly, "NO."

Don't even think about it. Learn and apply these rules to your financial life now. Otherwise, you will be forced to learn them the hard way—by attending the School of Hard Knocks. Let me assure you, the tuition at that school is very high. You can dramatically lower the cost of your financial education by reading everything in the pages that follow, and then continuing your education by reading the books suggested at the end of each section.

On your trip to the city of your dreams, there will be many temptations to break some of these financial laws, even after you learn about them. Believe me, there is a price to pay for every financial act you commit. Yet, unlike the city streets and highways you travel in your car, you won't see warning signs along your financial roadway. There won't be any financial police, either. Just consequences—most of them unhappy and painful.

Each time you break a financial law, you will find yourself falling farther and farther behind on the road to making your dreams come true.

Some couples break so many financial laws so often that they become mired down along the financial road of life, unable to get going again. This is always tragic. However, this does not have to happen to you.

Many married couples have taken decades to learn these financial road rules. If they could talk to you, they would say that you owe it to yourselves to avoid the high cost of learning them the way they did. They would urge you to master the material that follows, and avoid any temptation to break these rules. But their advice would probably not motivate you.

166

I'm counting on the fact that you *will* be motivated to learn these lessons because you love each other and because you do have dreams that you want to see come true in the course of your life together. I'm counting on the fact that you have the intelligence and good judgment to see the wisdom of learning from other people's experiences.

And if I'm right, if you really do love each other, and are willing to renew your commitment to making dreams come true each and every day of your married life, then I know you *will* learn these lessons, and you *will* reach the city of your dreams—sooner, rather than later. So, let's get started.

"Lucky" is a word often used to describe the financial success of people we don't like. In truth, however, financial success in marriage is always the result of learning the rules of the financial road, and then developing sound communication and management skills (financial strategies) that allow these rules to work *for* you. This approach to financial success is not a "get rich quick" approach. The path I offer involves a lifelong learning process and a tremendous commitment. But it has the homely virtue that it really works.

167

Financial Law No. 1:
Spend Less Than You Earn

The first rule of the financial road is that **you must spend less than you earn**. This is one of the first lessons of Mr. Clason's book, *The Richest Man in Babylon*. This law recognizes that earning money is a universal aspect of being alive. Work is the birthright of almost everyone except the few who are born "with silver spoons in their mouths." You, as many others, may wish that you could be one of those born to wealth and that work was not your birthright. But even if that wish came true, you would discover that inherited wealth brings with it problems you never imagined. And ultimately, you would learn that even with great wealth, you can not break this first law and remain wealthy.

This first law also acknowledges that spending the earnings you gain by your work is a behavior not easily controlled. Look deeply within yourself. How powerful is the desire to spend and buy? In the advertising business, this human trait is exploited in every possible way. But as you discovered in Chapter Three, unless what you buy with money is a dream for which you are willing to work and sacrifice, and unless your dream will enrich your life and the lives of other people, you are only buying a burden.

"Spend less than you earn." Think about what it means. It certainly means that you will have to think very carefully about what you want *now* as compared to what you want later.

This implies that you will have to sacrifice and to go without some of those things that seem so attractive now. This idea may seem more than a little painful to think about, and some of my readers will stop right here and say, "No, thank you." However, let's look at what obeying this law offers as a benefit.

The Quest for Financial Independence

If you are like most young couples, you are thrilled with your new adult rights and privileges. It feels so good to go where you want to go and do what you want to do without your parents, or some parental figure, overseeing your every move. But how independent are you financially? In most cases you are like a newborn infant, totally dependent on others. You can't decide some morning not to get up and go to work. You *have* to work *and* earn in order to pay for the basics of life. Food, shelter, and clothing, all of which used to be provided by your parents, are now fully *your* responsibility.

Many of my readers have very limited choices about what kind of work they can do to make the money they need for survival. And most who read this book have no way of nurturing or sustaining themselves financially without the jobs provided by their employers. Think about what would happen if you lost your job suddenly. How long could you last financially without finding a new job?

> **"Financial dependence" is defined as a state of being so heavily dependent on your immediate income for meeting basic needs that the loss of income would create serious anxiety and a desperate search for employment.**

I'm not saying that financial dependence is inherently bad, but total financial dependence is terribly restrictive and a lot like being a child in an adult world. By harmonizing with the first rule of the financial road, you can begin moving away from total financial dependence and begin to develop some financial independence. Eventually, by harmonizing with the rest of the rules of the financial road presented in this book, you can gain tremendous financial independence.

> **"Financial independence" is defined as a state of being in which you are able to meet all of your basic survival needs from your own financial resources, so that employment becomes a way to enrich your life through making dreams come true.**

Financial independence opens up your life so your energy can be invested in self-actualizing behavior—behavior that allows you to emphasize life enrichment as your primary goal.

I won't lie and try to make you believe that there is such a thing as *total* financial independence. Even multimillionaires discover that we are all interdependent in some way. We all need each other to drive the great financial machine called our economy. But there is greater and lesser financial dependence and independence. The question is, will you move towards financial independence, or will you remain financially dependent the rest of your married life?

Those who remain financially dependent throughout marriage discover that very few of their dreams come true. They discover that work is not only their birthright, but it becomes their

169

burden. When you spend everything you earn, this burden becomes heavier every year. Eventually, it will weigh you down and break you down and escort you to your grave.

Financially dependent people must look for everyone else to take care of them. They always require an employer to hire them, to come through with raises for them, to provide basic life benefits for them. And most important of all, financially dependent people never have the ability to make dreams come true. Financially independent people, on the other hand, have choices. They are self-reliant, they are responsible, they can make things happen financially. They may need a source of income, but they have a greater number of choices about how they will obtain that income. When hard times come, financially independent people have the financial resources to get them through until things are better.

And when financial opportunity comes knocking, financially independent people can open the door because they haven't spent everything they earned— they have cash or investments to take advantage of opportunities.

In marriage, financial independence is gained through financial interdependence or cooperation. The freedom of financial independence is gained only through working together as a team.

As you learned in Chapter Five, the highest form of cooperation is a marriage partnership. Couples who form a partnership have a "we can do it" master strategy for their financial lives.

Financial Strategies for Harmonizing with Financial Law No. 1: Creating a Spending Plan

As a financial team, you will have to obey this first rule of the financial road by adopting a **financial strategy** that allows you to do this successfully. Traditionally, this practice has been called "living on a budget," but I prefer to call it "winning with a Spending Plan." Budgeting brings to mind an image of couples who are deprived or living in fear. The word "budget" derives from the French *bougette* and means small purse. The implication is that you can't put much money in a small purse—that those who live on a budget are restricted and have no choices. If *"spending less than you earn"* means this to you, then you will feel resentment and anger toward this financial law and will repeatedly break it.

> **A married couple doesn't get to the city of their dreams by budgeting their trip, they *plan* their trip. There is a world of difference in meaning between the words *"plan"* and *"budget."***

Budgets constrain and limit. Plans give you choices and options. Budgets are rigid. Plans are flexible. Budgets demand going without. Plans encourage taking control and finding creative ways to help you get what you want out of life.

If your plan is well designed, it will do the following things for you:

1. It will paint a clear picture of where your cash comes from and where it goes.

2. It will give you control over spending decisions.

3. It will help you build a monthly profit that can be directed toward savings and investments.

If you work your plan, your monthly profit will steadily increase from a trickle to a river of cash that can be invested for even greater profit. If you don't create a small profit with your spending plan during the first month of your marriage, don't be surprised. But don't let it happen over and over again. If you spend everything you earn each and every month, you will quickly discover that you are forced to violate other rules of the financial road.

To help you create your spending plan and make it work effectively, I have provided some simple forms you can use (see **Appendix E**, Pages E-1 through E-7). Let's explore how these forms can help you provide the three benefits outlined above.

1. Where does our money come from and where does it go? The first form tracks your monthly income. This includes money from wages and salaries, plus income from investments and other possible sources. You will also see a special place for "second income stream" earnings. I'll explain the purpose of this income category in Chapter Seven. Just leave it blank for now.

The second form tracks expenses. There are three columns: one to fill in your projected expenses, one to identify your actual expenses, and one to record the difference between the two. If you have trouble staying within projected expenses, this three column method will help you find the problem. If you know the problem, instead of resorting to Neanderthal behavior, you can look at the situation rationally. Then you can make intelligent decisions together about how to change the situation.

2. How can we control and redirect our spending? Spending is that part of your plan over which you want to gain control. Spending decisions can always be redirected, *if you plan ahead.* However, some decisions are easier to change than others. It's hard to change payments for rent, mortgage payments, payments on outstanding debts and insurance premiums. But decisions about food, clothing, entertainment and recreation are easy to change. You must be realistic, of course. There's little to be gained in understating likely expenses. But you do have enormous power to manage your spending decisions when you sit down each month and develop a plan. And unless you form a habit of doing this, you won't be able to harmonize with the other rules of the financial road.

3. Where will the money come from for savings? Managing marital finances is a lot like managing a business. Unless a business generates a profit, there is never any money to invest in the future. In the course of your marriage, more than $2 million (on average) will pass through your hands. Some couples will have more, and others less. Most of this will go towards providing for your survival needs (such as food, shelter, and clothing). But unless you generate a steady profit and manage this profit wisely, there won't be any money to help make dreams come true. Your spending plan is designed to help you *track* your profits. But your spending plan won't *create* the savings you want. You'll have to obey other financial road rules to get that result.

By using the Spending Plan forms in **Appendix E**, along with the guidelines that follow on the next page, you will dramatically increase your success in obeying the first rule of the financial road.

How To Make Your Spending Plan Work

The Immediate Gratification instinct of your Neanderthal brain won't appreciate your efforts to develop a spending plan. That's why teamwork is so important in winning with this strategy. Working together, you can encourage each other and help one another *think* as you carry out your plan. No matter how carefully you plan, be prepared to face temptation and beat it. By following the guidelines below, you'll discover that you can win—you *can* control spending, and you *can* redirect income to savings and investments. Give these guidelines a try.

1. Always prepare your spending plans together. Doing so will build a deeper sense of partnership.

2. Have a specific, agreed upon time for these planning sessions. When that time arrives, if either one of you is tired or irritable, reschedule. Make sure you are relaxed, rested, and that you won't be disturbed during these planning sessions.

3. Don't dictate to one another. No matter who earns the money or the most money in your partnership, dictating how spending decisions are going to be handled is an abuse of power and will threaten and frighten your partner. Neither of you will like the results.

4. Remember those "Psychological Paychecks" you identified earlier? They must be included in your plan.

5. At the end of each planning session, set the date and time for your next one.

6. As you receive actual income and spend it, record each transaction on a daily basis.

7. Make a change in your spending plan only after you both have discussed it thoroughly and have spent at least 24 hours between the impulse to spend and the act of spending. (Of course, this does not apply to medical emergencies).

8. Stay away from situations that might influence you to violate your plan. Avoid the malls. Never go shopping if you're feeling down or depressed. If you have credit cards, leave them at home in a desk drawer when you go shopping.

9. When you experience success in spending less than you earn, praise one another. Find a way to celebrate your success without spending money.

10. Be honest. When you violate your plan, don't make excuses. Don't be discouraged if you end a month spending all that you earn or even more than you earn. Return to the next planning session with greater determination, realizing that you don't want to pay the price of breaking the first rule of the financial road.

Agreement Check:

1. Answer the following questions apart from each other. Then talk about your answers together:

A. I have used a spending plan before:

☐ Never ☐ Occasionally ☐ Always

B. I like working with a spending plan:

☐ Yes ☐ No

C. I am good at working with a spending plan:

☐ Yes ☐ No

D. I am willing to try working with a spending plan:

☐ Yes ☐ No ☐ Maybe

E. The greatest temptation to spend money happens to me when:

_____

_____

_____

_____

_____

_____

_____

_____

_____

_____

_____

_____

2. A spending plan should allow each of you freedom to make some individual spending decisions. The following questions are designed to help you reach agreement about how to do this:

A. The money for individual decisions within our spending plan will be provided by:

☐ The individual income we each earn that is not needed to cover our shared expenses.

☐ A specific amount of money that will be set aside for this purpose from our pooled income(s).

☐ A specific amount of money that will be set aside for this purpose from the sole source of income for our marriage.

☐ Some other way as described below:

_____

_____

_____

_____

_____

_____

_____

_____

_____

_____

_____

_____

_____

_____

3. To help create a source of cash for individual spending decisions, it helps to answer the following questions:

    A. Will you have separate checking accounts for use in making personal spending decisions?

        ☐ Yes   ☐ No

    B. Will you have a joint checking account for shared spending decisions?

        ☐ Yes   ☐ No

A Suggestion

Many married couples find it helps to set up one special checking account from which all monthly bills are paid. The check book they use for this account is a large, "three-up" style that cannot be carried around in a purse or pocket. Then, every two weeks, both husband and wife sit down and pay all their bills from this account. Both husband and wife are signatories (both must sign the checks) on this account. This allows both partners to have a separate account if they wish. With separate accounts, they can each have a share of the money earned to use as they wish. Generally, with this type of arrangement, the husband is the signatory on his account, and the wife is the signatory on her account.

4. Return to the last chapter and revisit your discussion about financial roles. This time, only discuss the role of cash management. This role should include the preparation of your spending plans. See if your answers are any different after reading about this first rule of the financial road.

Suggested Additional Reading:

Clason, George S. *The Richest Man In Babylon*. New York: Signet, 1988.

Suggested Computer Software Programs:

***WealthStarter*. Produced by Reality Technologies, 3624 Market Street, Philadelphia, PA. 19104, (215) 387-6005.**

***Managing Your Money* by Andrew Tobias. MECA Software, Inc. P.O. Box 907, Westport, CT. 06881.**

***Quicken*. Produced by Intuit, P.O. Box 3014, 66 Willow Place, Menlo Park, CA. 94025-3687 or call 1-800-624-8742.**

Financial Law No. 2: Avoid Debt

The second rule of the financial road is—**Avoid Debt**.

Young couples starting out married life should not get into debt. Getting into debt is like wading in quicksand. It may not look dangerous in the beginning, but it can suck you down, no matter how hard you struggle. And unless you get out of debt, the outcome is certain.

It makes no difference whether you earn $150,000 a year or $15,000 a year—debt can ruin the quality of your married life. If you start out in debt, you will spend most of every paycheck just paying creditors. If you go more deeply in debt after marriage, worry and tension will mount and you will soon find there are bills you can't pay each month. Then you may start to dread receiving the mail—fearing that you'll find more bills in your mail box. Even answering your telephone becomes a source of fear when you are deeply in debt. The next call may be from an angry creditor demanding payment.

These fears put pressure and strain on your marriage relationship. The joy and pleasure which should be yours as a married couple start to die, and you may find that you are often emotionally and physically exhausted.

Couples deeply in debt often argue and fight about money. These arguments are usually expressions of anger, frustration and hopelessness caused by their financial situation.
If no changes are made, the arguments become more personal and bitter.

Is all debt bad? No, it isn't! Debt can be used in some situations to make your financial life better, and in this chapter you'll learn how. But all debt puts some pressure on your marriage. Therefore, debt should be kept as low as possible, and unless debt is used in the ways prescribed in this book, it should be avoided.

Listen, Deadbeat—
I want this bill paid **now!!**

Financial Strategies for Harmonizing with Financial Law No. 2: Learning Debt Management

When you are first married, there are many temptations to buy on credit. That temptation may come in the form of pre-approved credit cards. If you really want to be tempted (which will almost certainly lead to credit problems), just start accepting such offers. It always seems so easy to buy things on credit at the moment you buy them. Buying on credit makes you feel more wealthy than you really are. Some people even get a high when they buy things on credit. However, for every high, there is a corresponding low. One of the lows about credit purchases is that they are always more expensive than they seem. Interest charges drive the price of your purchases higher than you can possibly imagine. For this reason, every credit decision should be managed within two debt management guidelines. These guidelines are expressed as two fundamental questions that you should ask (and answer) before you make any debt decision:

1. How will this debt decision help establish and/or maintain our credit record?

2. Will the goods and/or services we purchase with this debt help pay off the loan?

Let's explore these two debt management guidelines individually.

Establishing and Maintaining a Credit Record

You need to establish a credit record or credit history soon after you are married. Having credit allows you to obtain goods, services, or cash on your promise to pay for them later. Credit is basically a privilege—not a right. There is nearly always a cost for this privilege called *interest* or *finance charges*. Interest always increases the cost of anything you buy on credit. Never forget this. And try never to buy anything on credit without knowing how much more it will cost after interest has been included.

The importance of having credit in marriage is to be able to borrow money to take advantage of investment opportunities—not to make everyday consumer purchases.

An investment opportunity does not have to be limited to stocks or real estate or a business transaction. But when opportunity knocks, if you don't have credit and can't obtain a loan, you may very easily miss an important opportunity to increase your net worth. I'll have more to say about this later, but for now, let's look at how to establish a credit record or credit history so you'll have credit when you really need it.

Establishing credit means establishing trust with a bank, or some other lending institution. The decision to loan you money (to trust you) is never made in a vacuum. It is based on an assessment of an assortment of facts, both financial and non-financial in nature. Most important in the process of securing credit is to convince a lender that you can and will pay back the loan. A sincere smile

and an honest face won't be your tickets to credit worthiness.

Most credit granting organizations share information with one another by means of credit bureaus. These records are kept about every person who has ever used commercial credit. They contain information collected by the bureaus from banks and other lending institutions, from stores you deal with and from public records and other sources. Any time you apply for credit in any form, including credit cards, the prospective lender will secure a credit report on you from the credit bureau. This report will contain a detailed history of your borrowing and repayment patterns. A credit record tells creditors how they can expect you to act when you have a debt to pay.

Creditors rate you on what is known as the "three Cs": Character, Capacity, and Capital.

"Character" is judged primarily by how you pay your debts. If you pay your debts on time and live within your means, that is a very important measure of your financial character. In most cases, that is all anyone will see. But some creditors (especially bankers) will look at how you dress and how much thought you put into making your case for a loan. When applying for a bank loan, it's up to you to convince your bankers that you're the type of person who deserves to be trusted.

"Capacity" refers to the stability of your employment and your ability to absorb and pay off debt. When judging capacity, a potential creditor will look at your income and your ability to make the monthly payments on a new debt and still pay all your other obligations. The greater your income, the more capacity you have to pay back a loan if it is granted.

"Capital" refers to the collateral that may exist to secure a new debt. Collateral is property that is pledged to the creditor until the loan is paid off. If you have savings or investments, a lender could ask for the right to take these assets in the event you fail to make your payments. Or, if you're buying a car or a house, the lender will ask for the right to repossess them if you fail to pay. When you grant this right, you give the creditor a *lien* on your property. Some loans are unsecured, which means you don't need collateral. A good example is a credit card. With unsecured credit cards and other unsecured loans, you are trusted 100% to pay back what you borrow.

Creditors weigh the "three Cs" differently. Points are assigned subjectively to help determine your credit worthiness. This is called "loan scoring." If you're turned down by one creditor, another may accept you because points are assigned in a different way.

When you get married, your credit record, assuming you have one, does not change. Therefore, if one of you has had a pattern of not paying your debts on time, this could be a problem.

Of course, there may be a perfectly good explanation for a missed or late payment, but that explanation won't appear on your credit record; unless, of course, you have filed an official explanation with the credit bureau, which you are allowed to do. If you've never seen a copy of your credit report, I urge you to do so. It will cost you about $10

to $20. The federal Fair Credit Reporting Act requires credit bureaus and credit reporting agencies to provide you with either a copy or a summary of your report on request. Some make you visit their offices and review your report there. Occasionally, there will be an error on your report. If so, you should take swift action to correct it. The credit bureau will tell you how to do this.

There are more than 2,000 credit bureaus across the country, and one or two of them are located in or near your community. If you have already established credit, your records are on file with one of these agencies. To find out which bureau has your records, look in the Yellow Pages under "credit reporting agencies." Just call until you find one that has your file. If you want to be very aggressive, call all of the credit reporting agencies in your community and get a copy of your file from any that have it.

The credit bureau makes no judgment about you. It is the prospective lender who will make a judgment as to whether or not you are a good credit risk.

There is no credit rating on your credit bureau report. If you are turned down, the Equal Credit Opportunity Act says that the creditor must let you know in writing. You must also be given the reason for the rejection or be told that you can request the reason. You also have the right to know which credit report was used (there may be more than one credit reporting agency in your community). If you know why you were turned down, you may be able to take steps to improve your credit rating. If the turn down is the result of a mistake on your credit report, you might re-apply and be approved, or you might simply want to apply somewhere else.

Take any rational steps to remedy a turn down, but never call up the potential creditor and act irrationally.

If you have been used to talking your parents or other people out of their subjective decisions, don't count on this approach with your creditors. Some creditors will listen to a personal appeal, but rarely.

If one or both of you already have a credit record, and if it is not a good one, or if you have no credit record at all, you may need to have someone co-sign (guarantee) your first loan as a married couple. Your parents, a close family member, or a friend may be willing to do this for you. However, serving as a co-signer is not something one takes lightly or does without careful consideration. To be a co-signer, one must have an excellent credit record and be willing to take on a tremendous responsibility. What it really amounts to is that a co-signer trusts you to make the loan payments. If you don't make the payments, he or she is required by law to pay the loan for you. So don't be disappointed if someone turns you down when you ask them to co-sign for a loan.

Even though you're married, you each have a right to apply for and to receive credit as individuals.

Under the Equal Credit Opportunity Act, a man or a woman can apply for and receive credit in his or her own name. The law prohibits creditors from asking questions that are clearly discriminatory (such as questions about your use of birth control and child-bearing plans). I believe that you both should maintain a credit history as individuals and as a married couple. However, I also believe that all debt decisions should be made together, including individual debt decisions. To begin incurring debt without telling your partner is a tremendous breach of trust.

It should be clear from these comments that credit is something you need to take great care to protect. When credit is granted and you receive a loan, you must make each and every credit payment on time. This is the only way to establish and maintain an excellent credit record.

How To Get That First Loan

Remember, the rule is: "Avoid Debt." However, to establish a credit record as a married couple, you must borrow money. The suggestions that follow are intended to help you get that first loan. Here's how to go about it:

1. Make a visit to your bank, the one where you have established (or are going to establish) a checking and savings account. Introduce yourselves and let the bank officer know that you are newly married and want to establish a credit record.

2. Ask your banker to suggest the best loan product to help you establish credit. A credit card may be suggested, or a regular loan, depending on the policies of the bank and your unique financial situation. If necessary, offer your savings account as "collateral" or "security" for the loan. Giving your savings account as security or collateral means that if you fail to make your loan payments, the bank can take the money out of your savings account to repay your loan. Also keep this fact in mind; when you use your savings as security, you probably won't have the use of your savings until the loan is repaid.

3. Repay the loan, or pay monthly on your credit card, making each and every payment on time.

By paying back this first loan, and taking at least six months to do so, you will establish a credit record with the bank. While there will be a slight interest cost for doing this, it will be worth it to have a credit rating and a credit record. You can then use the bank as a credit reference if you decide to open other credit accounts. However, the purpose of paying off your first bank loan is to be able to make a second loan at that bank—one that you really need and one that will help you start your marriage investment program.

By taking out a second loan, you will be asking for more trust. It isn't likely that your banker will move you from a secured loan to an unsecured line of credit, but if you have a good reason to make your second loan, assuming you have faithfully repaid your first, you'll probably get it.

Keep in mind that your banker is looking for answers to five questions when evaluating each loan. They are:

1. How much money do you need?
2. What is the purpose of this loan?
3. What is your ability to repay this loan?
4. What collateral do you have to secure this loan?
5. How long do you need to repay this loan?

As your trust with your banker increases, you will be able to borrow more money, and you will also be able to borrow money in different ways.

Your first real loan (not your first credit card) will almost certainly be what is known as an "installment loan." An installment loan is made for many reasons, but it is always tailored to a

182

monthly payment schedule based on your current income. As you move up the scale of your banker's trust, you will eventually be able to qualify for an unsecured line of credit. This is the highest form of trust extended by bankers. It is reserved almost exclusively for those who are considered to be financially prosperous. A line of credit commits the bank to make funds available at any time the lender requests it up to a specified maximum amount. The repayment schedule is not a rigid monthly amount. You know when you have arrived at the top of the bank's credit pyramid when you can obtain an unsecured line of credit.

However, over time, if you are careful to work *with* your banker and slowly build your credit rating, you will discover that you *can* obtain loans when you really need them.

I have purposely avoided a lengthy presentation about credit cards, department store charge accounts, gas credit cards and many other subjects relating to borrowing and loans. If you want to broaden your education about the subject of credit, I urge you to read the publications suggested in the bibliography at the end of this section. However, before you do that, you need to become familiar with a second guideline for managing debt.

Making your way to the top of a bank's credit pyramid will take time. There is no point in trying to rush this process because that in itself would cause you to violate the second rule of the financial road.

CONGRATULATIONS! We only give these to our most trusted customers!

Borrowing for Things That Help Pay for Themselves

Some things you buy actually help pay for themselves. Some of what you buy will appreciate, or increase in value. Other purchases will make it possible for you to earn more money (increase your income). The problem is that often it is difficult to know which goods and services will appreciate in value or increase your earning potential. So, I've listed some examples below:

A. Your home—the purchase of a home has many tax advantages, and is an investment that normally will grow in value.

B. Your education—borrowing for educational or career opportunities can increase your personal value tremendously.

C. Yourself—investing in yourself could mean having your teeth straightened to improve your appearance and your self-confidence. When this kind of investment leads to better job performance and promotions, it can be one of the best uses of borrowed money.

D. Your car—you must have transportation to work, and buying an automobile on credit may be your only choice if there is no public transportation available.

E. Investments—some investments can be made to your advantage and profit by borrowing money. When you make the right investment decisions, the cost of your loan can be paid for by the increased value of the investment.

In truth, all of these examples represent investments. Each one of them could help make it possible for you to repay your loan. However, one question remains: When and how much should you borrow for these purposes?

Only you as a married couple can make this decision, but a good rule of thumb is to limit debt, excluding your home mortgage, to 15% or less of your annual, after-tax income. A better rule of thumb is: If there is any doubt in your mind about the reason for going into debt, don't do it! Otherwise, keep your debts as low as possible.

...and best of all, I can earn you money!

FOR SALE

184

How to Make Debt Management Work

Are there communication skills for helping you harmonize with this second rule of the financial road? Yes, there are! By screening all your debt decisions through the following set of questions, you will force a communication discipline on your marital debt decision making. By taking time to answer each question together, you will soon find all debt decisions fitting very comfortably within the two guidelines I've just given you for managing debt reasonably.

1. Is this item something we really need now? What do we mean by the word "need?" Will this purchase help pay for itself? How?

2. What is the real cost of this purchase when the finance charge (interest) is added on?

3. Can we really make each and every monthly payment on time? Where is the money going to come from to make the payments?

4. Even if we can make every payment on time, will we find that the monthly payments make it impossible for us to reach some of our other financial goals?

5. Before signing a credit contract, are we willing to take a couple of days or even a couple of weeks to cool down and think about our desire to purchase on credit—then make a final decision?

Earlier, I said that decisions about debt should always be shared decisions, even if you have separate credit accounts. This recommendation about sharing decisions is offered as a way to strengthen your financial partnership.

Even if you agree to disagree about a debt decision, you show how important your partnership is when you sit down and talk through your decisions to use credit. If you ignore this important recommendation, you can be sure that your partner will be offended. When one partner creates debt without the participation of the other, the message is sent that the partnership is not very important. Of course, if you are both independently wealthy, this rule isn't as critical. But when you are just starting out, your incomes will almost certainly be limited, and debt can threaten your ability to keep a roof over your head and food on your table. So get in the habit of sharing decisions about debt and build strength into your partnership.

Before you start on the next Agreement Check, read the simple facts about debt that appear on the following page. Remember them! Post them on your bulletin board! They are extremely important and may serve to help you *avoid debt.*

Facts About Debt

Over the years, I have come to see that there are certain facts about debt that are undeniable. These facts are summarized below. I suggest you memorize them. If you don't want to do that, then promise one another to read them out loud before you make any debt decision. Just by reviewing them together, you will stimulate higher brain functions that may keep you from making a "get it now," Neanderthal debt decision.

1. Debt must be paid off. It just doesn't magically disappear. It almost never is forgiven. Your payments on debt must be paid each and every month—without exception.

2. Putting off borrowing (a way of spending) is often the best way to avoid spending.

3. When you want to buy something that does not promise to pay for itself,

just remember—you probably can't afford to buy it *unless you have cash in hand to make the purchase.* (Because of this fact, I suggest that you never buy any of your everyday needs on credit. Example: Don't buy groceries or gasoline with a credit card.)

4. Not all lenders charge the same amount for using their money. Therefore, when you make a decision to borrow money, shop around for the loan just as you would shop around for a pair of jeans.

5. Those who set a ceiling on how much debt they will incur are much more successful at avoiding debt. Therefore, keep excellent records of all of your credit purchases and review your credit purchases together every month to make sure you don't exceed debt limits that you negotiate for your marriage.

Agreement Check:

1. Briefly list below any problems either of you have had in managing debt in the past. If you've had credit problems, list the names of the creditors with whom you have had these problems. By making this list, there won't be any surprises later on when you first apply for credit as a married couple. Remember, your credit history follows you right into marriage, so it's best to discuss your credit history now.

Problems I Have Had With Credit and Creditors in the Past: His

_____

_____

_____

_____

_____

_____

_____

Problems I Have Had With Credit and Creditors in the Past: Hers

_____

_____

_____

_____

_____

_____

_____

2. What credit cards and accounts do you currently have open? List the names of the creditors, the account numbers, and any balances owed.

Credit Accounts Now Open: His

Creditor	Account No.	Balance

Credit Accounts Now Open: Hers

Creditor	Account No.	Balance

3. What agreements are you able to make with each other now in order to pay off any of these debts? Write down any agreements you are able to reach here.

_____

_____

_____

_____

_____

_____

_____

_____

_____

_____

_____

_____

_____

4. What agreements can you make with each other about taking on additional debt?

We won't take on any more debt until:

_____

_____

_____

We will limit our use of credit by:

_____

_____

_____

_____

Additional agreements we have reached about the use of credit:

_____

_____

_____

_____

_____

_____

_____

_____

_____

_____

_____

_____

_____

_____

_____

_____

_____

_____

_____

_____

_____

_____

_____

5. Do you want to keep individual, separate credit accounts—at least with some creditors?

☐ Yes   ☐ No

If your answer is YES, with which creditors will you maintain separate credit accounts?

Creditor	His or Hers	Credit Limit

6. Whose income do you expect to use to make the payments on these separate credit accounts or loans?

Loan or Credit Account _____

His/Hers_____   Balance_____

Monthly Payments_____

To Be Paid In The Following Manner:

_____

_____

_____

Loan or Credit Account _____

His/Hers_____   Balance_____

Monthly Payments_____

To Be Paid In The Following Manner:

_____

_____

_____

Loan or Credit Account _____

His/Hers_____   Balance_____

Monthly Payments_____

To Be Paid In The Following Manner:

_____

_____

_____

Loan or Credit Account _____

His/Hers_____   Balance_____

Monthly Payments_____

To Be Paid In The Following Manner:

_____

_____

_____

Loan or Credit Account _____

His/Hers_____   Balance_____

Monthly Payments_____

To Be Paid In The Following Manner:

_____

_____

_____

Loan or Credit Account _____

His/Hers_____   Balance_____

Monthly Payments_____

To Be Paid In The Following Manner:

_____

_____

_____

7. Return to the last chapter and revisit your discussion about financial roles. This time, discuss only the role of debt management. See if your answers are any different.

Suggested Additional Reading:

Corrigan, Arnold and Phyllis C. Kaufman, *How to Use Credit and Credit Cards*. Stamford: Longmeadow Press, 1987. *(This book is carried in most Waldenbooks and can also be ordered by calling toll free 1-800-322-2000).*

Brown, Charlene B., *The Consumer Guide to Credit: Everything You Need to Know to Get or Repair Credit (without an M.B.A., C.P.A. or BMW)*. Irvine: United Resource Press, 1991.

Pollan, Stephen M. and Ronald E. Roel and Raymond A. Roel. *How To Borrow Money*. New York: Simon & Schuster, Inc., 1983.

Financial Law No. 3: Keep A Part of All That You Earn

Benjamin Franklin is still the most frequently quoted sage on the importance of saving money. Nearly everyone is familiar with his famous saying, "A penny saved is a penny earned." He also said, "Money makes money, and the money money makes, makes more money." Saving money is the way you fill your financial gas tank so you can travel to the city of your dreams. Without forming the savings habit, you won't be *going* anywhere.

What is baffling and very strange is that citizens of the United States are, generally speaking, very poor at saving their money. Personal savings have always been important, but they are more important now than ever before. Why? Because the Great American Dream (not to be confused with your personal dreams) of financial security (guaranteed employment, economic stability and ample pension and Social Security benefits for retirement) is quickly evaporating. Our federal and state governments have broken the first two rules of the financial road so many times that they have seriously compromised our nation's economic strength. This means you can't rely on the government to provide anything as far as your financial future is concerned. The government is so deeply in debt that the interest on debt eats up the largest share of our nation's taxes each year. Periodically, the government tries for a quick fix to solve its financial problems, including offering special saving incentives to taxpayers, but these are rapidly reduced or taken away when their true cost is realized. A part of all that you earn is yours to keep, but only after taxes and inflation have taken their toll.

I want to state very clearly what is meant by keeping a part of all you earn.

You are not keeping a part of all that you earn when you simply buy some item you need for half price, or end the month with a small profit. Keeping a part of all you earn means more—much more.

It means acknowledging that your dreams are important and that you are important. It means showing through action that you believe your dreams *can* come true and *will* come true. It means setting goals for saving that may be extraordinary by other people's standards. It means always paying yourself first and it means taking maximum advantage of the opportunities available to earn interest on your savings.

The sooner you start harmonizing with this financial law, the sooner the habit of saving will become a way of life. Sooner is definitely better when it comes to keeping a part of all you earn.

There is never a convenient time to start saving money. When couples are in their twenties, they usually make excuses for not saving such as:

"We can't save now, we're buying furniture and a house. We're young; there's plenty of time."

As the years go by, the excuses change, but the balance in the savings account doesn't change. As a result, the idea of making dreams come true gets left for the "romantics." Let's get one thing straight; the time to start saving (and making dreams come true) is right now, at the beginning of your marriage. When you start saving early, *you* can be the "romantics" and have a real romance with life.

Financial Strategies for Harmonizing with Financial Law No. 3: Becoming Disciplined Savers

Assuming you are committed to keeping a part of all that you earn, let me give you three strategies for becoming disciplined savers. In the next chapter, I'll give you some ideas on how to provide more money for your savings program, but first, read and remember these strategies:

To Become a Disciplined Saver:

A. Set specific goals for your savings program. (Saving 10% of all you earn is a minimum goal that every couple should shoot for. Those who are serious about making dreams come true should aim for 15%—20%—or 25%.)

B. Always pay yourself first—before paying your living and other expenses.

C. Always place your savings where they will earn interest.

Let's examine these strategies more carefully by looking at guidelines for implementing them.

EXPENSES   SAVINGS

Set Goals for Saving

When you state in writing, very specifically, how much you are going to save over a set period of time, you have a superb chance of hitting your goal. Too many couples set no goal at all, and they reach it. It's far better to have a specific lofty goal and come up short, than to aim at nothing and hit it.

When you set your saving objectives, it's wise to make saving for an **Emergency Fund** your first priority. This fund is your lifeline when the unexpected occurs. You may have medical problems, major car repairs or household emergencies. These events may represent more than minor interruptions in your financial life. Even worse would be the sudden loss of your income. That would certainly be an emergency. Unemployment is a possibility for everyone these days, and it can happen for all sorts of reasons. There is nothing that can completely take the place of cash in your hand to pay the bills when emergencies strike. I recommend that you set aside at least enough money in your emergency fund to pay all your bills for 3 months. Some couples may wish to have as much as 6 or even 9 months of protection.

Once you have an emergency fund in place, you should be saving for other purposes. Saving for vacations, birthdays, and important holidays will probably be high on your list—and they

should be. But you also need savings that will provide money for investing.

Saving for investing may be your first real challenge on the financial road of married life. Most couples I know can relate to setting up an emergency fund and saving for special occasions. But few have ever had experience with saving money for investment purposes.

Yet, unless you want to spend the rest of your life financially dependent and working for everyone but yourself, you will absolutely have to save *and* invest. It is only through combining these two financial disciplines that you can get to the city of your dreams.

Furthermore, your investment savings goals will have to be progressively larger each year. For example, if you set aside $2,000 for investment savings during the first year of marriage, you should save at least $3,000 for investing during the second year. A five year savings program might look like the one on the chart on the next page.

FIRST YEAR $2000.⁰⁰

THIRTIETH YEAR $1,000,000

	Year	Amount Saved	Progressive Increase Over Previous Year
	1	$2,000	50%
	2	$3,000	50%
	3	$4,500	50%
	4	$6,750	50%
	5	$10,125	50%
Total		**$26,375**	

You're probably wondering how you can save for all these objectives (emergency fund, savings for special occasions, and investment savings) at once. It would be unfair to put this third financial law in front of you and not give you some way to develop the savings you need. I'll do that as promised, in the next chapter, after you make the decision that you *will* save; that you *will* set aside at least 10% of all your income each time you receive a pay check; that you *will* pay yourself first.

Always Pay Yourself First

[If you believe in tithing, I acknowledge that your first obligation is to share 10% of your income with others through giving to your church or in some other way. You should assume that the following discussion is not intended to offend you or in any way persuade you to abandon your religious beliefs and values.]

Most couples create a spending plan that pays everyone except themselves. In fact, the first check you write when paying your bills should be the one for deposit to your savings account. After all, you worked hard for that money. Does it make sense that you should be the only ones who don't get paid? That's what a savings program is—it's your payment to yourself for hard work that will someday make it possible for you not to work so hard *and* to make

dreams come true.

The sooner you get in the habit of paying yourself, the faster you will make financial progress. To help make this point abundantly clear, look at the chart below. Here is a comparison of financial progress between those who start saving early and those who start later. In this example, the early savers put away $2,000 a year for just ten years at 8 percent—and save *nothing more* for the next *thirty* years. The couple that starts saving later in life spends all of their money during the first ten years of marriage, then starts saving $2,000 a year. As you can see, the late saver couple will need *almost 30 years* to catch up with the couple who start saving early, and, this will be possible *only* if they save $2,000 each and every year.

Year	Couple A: Early Savers Depositing $2,000 a yr. @ 8%	Couple B: Late Savers Depositing Nothing
1	$2,186	0
5	$13,316	0
10	$34,646	0
	Couple A: Early Savers Depositing Nothing But Building @ 8%	**Couple B: Late Savers Depositing $2,000 a yr. @ 8%**
11	$37,854	$2,186
20	$61,501	$34,646
30	$102,768	$92,539
40	$171,725	$189,279

The amount of money you pay yourselves may seem very small at first, but as the old saying goes, "From little acorns, mighty oak trees grow." What makes your savings grow, of course, is interest.

Always Place Your Savings at Interest

The third strategic guideline for saving is to make sure your money is working as hard as possible. Many people will tell you that interest is no longer a significant factor because of taxes and inflation. While it is true that interest from savings in any one year is not significant, over many years, interest can add up to a lot of money.

Whether your savings dollars are going to be used for your emergency fund or ultimately to help you make an investment, they should be earning interest—lots of interest. Interest is the money paid to you for "loaning" your savings to a financial institution. "Compounded interest" is interest paid on interest (what Ben Franklin was talking about when he said that "…the money money makes, makes more money"). How important is it to receive the highest interest possible on your money? Look at the following example:

Comparative Interest Rates Over Time				
		Capital Accumulated		
Annual Investment	Compound Growth Rate	10 Years	20 Years	30 Years
$10,000	5%	$132,068	$347,193	$697,608
$10,000	8%	$156,455	$494,229	$1,223,459
$10,000	10%	$175,312	$630,025	$1,809,434

This simple example does not reflect the effects of taxes and inflation. Its only purpose is to show you how higher interest can lead to tremendously different outcomes. Compounding at higher rates (paying interest on top of interest) makes the outcome even more dramatic. And, as you can see, time is also a very important factor.

The Interest Rate Obstacle Course

When you shop for the highest interest rates, you will find the experience is like making your way through an obstacle course. It can be very confusing. There are so many places to park your savings while looking for the right investment opportunity. Consider this list of choices:

Bank Accounts—including pass book savings accounts, money market accounts, and certificates of deposit.

Treasury Bills—a type of government security that matures in 90 days, 180 days, or one year.

Treasury notes—which offer a fixed rate of interest from one year to 10 years.

U.S. Savings Bonds—which offer tax-deferred interest, but you must pay the taxes on interest when the bond(s) mature and you must hold them for a minimum of five years.

Taxable money market mutual funds—which tend to offer higher interest rates than a bank, but are rarely insured and a little more risky.

Tax exempt money market mutual funds—which offer a better overall yield for savers in high income tax brackets, but are also uninsured.

Taxable and tax-exempt short-term bond funds—which squeeze out a little higher interest rate because they invest your savings in an investment that has a little higher risk.

In addition to the confusion of so many choices, advertisements by banks and savings institutions are also confusing. Every financial institution wants your money and they are willing to appeal to your Neanderthal brain to get it (another obstacle). Your job is to make your way through all these obstacles by sorting out the good deals from the bad ones. A few guidelines to help you do it successfully are presented on the following page.

How To Select a Savings Plan

When you receive an appeal for your savings, you need to have a set of questions to help separate the type from the hype. That's why this section is included. The financial environment is always changing, and the appeals will come from many kinds of financial institutions, but if you ask the right questions, you can make your way safely through the interest rate obstacle course.

If you read advertisements as a way of shopping for a savings account, read all the wording in the ad. The ads feature the rate of return in bold type, while far more important information is buried in the fine print. Your Neanderthal brain, with its desire for immediate gratification, will tend to focus in on the big type—the interest rate. Use your modern brain to read the small print and footnotes.

After reading all the copy in the ad for a high interest rate, if you're still interested, make a telephone call or meet with a representative of the savings institution and ask these questions:

1. How long is the advertised rate good for? Sometimes the rate is good for only a couple of weeks, and then it drops like a rock.

2. What is the minimum to open the account? You may have $500 or $1,000 to invest shortly after your wedding, but high interest rate accounts may require you to open the account with an outlandishly huge balance—such as $25,000 or $50,000. If your balance falls below a set amount, the interest rate drops, too. Be careful.

3. Must we have our checking account here or do anything else (other than open the savings ac-count) to get the advertised rate?
A savings institution may want your checking account as well as your savings. This may not be a problem, but other requirements could be. For example, the high interest rate may not be available unless you keep a minimum balance in your checking account *as well as* your savings account. That *could be* a problem. If you try to go along with this requirement, and your balance dips below the minimum, your high interest rate will disappear.

4. Is the rate fixed or variable?
Fixed rates don't change, but variable rates can change frequently. These changes may be tied to some economic indicator that is outside the control of the savings institution. In these cases, an interest rate "floor" is usually available, meaning that the rate can't fall below a set amount. Find out what that floor is. If it is too low, shop elsewhere.

5. How long do we have to leave our money with you to get this rate?
If you need your savings for emergencies or to take advantage of an investment opportunity, you don't want your savings in an account that penalizes you for taking your money out. Some savings plans will tie your money up for several months or even several years. Is this what you want? Ask for a complete explanation of all penalties for early withdrawal.

6. Is there a fee for this savings program? Some savings programs charge a fee, a small amount to buy the savings vehicle. Fees reduce your profits from interest. Of course, if the interest rate is very high and if you can leave your money in a savings account long enough, it may be worthwhile to pay the fee. But you must calculate carefully (do the arithmetic) to be sure.

7. How financially strong is this institution? Making sure your money is safe is very important. This is something you can no longer take for granted. Many savings institutions have gone under in recent years. Smart savers have to be very careful and investigate thoroughly in order to protect their money. Ask for a copy of their financial statement. Look to see if they have had steady profits for at least the last three years. For a modest fee, Veribanc, Inc., will send you a financial evaluation of any bank or savings and loan. Contact Veribanc, Inc., at P.O. Box 461, Wakefield, MA 01880; 617-245-8370.

8. Are our savings insured? Don't assume that all financial institutions are insured. Some are insured but the insurance isn't adequate. Ask how the insurance works. The best insurance is the Federal Deposit Insurance Corporation because with this plan, Uncle Sam has pledged to protect your savings up to certain limits. The best insurance programs have pamphlets that can be obtained by writing for them or asking for them at the insured institution.

9. Is this firm reputable? This is a fair question for any savings institution.

However, it is an extremely important question for those that are uninsured. For example, money market mutual funds are rarely insured. In this case you have to rely on the firm's reputation for integrity and performance. A higher rate isn't worth the possibility of losing your savings or your sleep. So check carefully and know to whom you are giving your money. Everyone likes higher interest rates, but make sure the firm offering these rates is well managed by people with superior money management skills who are not betting your savings on high-yielding but very risky investments.

10. How is the interest rate compounded? Remember, the more often the compounding the better. Most compounding will be expressed in terms of time, such as annually, semi-annually, quarterly, monthly, and daily. The best compounding is daily or continuous compounding.

Some savings officers won't answer all your questions. If you don't get straight answers quickly, shop elsewhere. You may find the savings officer will have a change of heart when he or she sees you walking out the door. Even then, be cautious. That's the only way to get through the interest rate obstacle course safely.

203

A Final Word About The Importance of Saving Money

When you become a disciplined saver, many opportunities will present themselves for making more money. The fact that you have savings in the bank will give you great bargaining power, freedom to make choices and peace of mind. J.P. Morgan once said that he would rather lend a million dollars to a man of sound character who had formed the habit of saving, than he would a thousand dollars to a man without character who was a spendthrift. So bite the bullet now, at the beginning of your married life. Adopt the principle that at least 10% of the money flowing into your marriage is for saving; that this 10% will be your first obligation every time you get paid; and that you will wisely invest your savings in interest-bearing bank accounts. Once that decision is made, you're ready to learn about Financial Law No. 4.

Agreement Check:

1. With regard to savings, you both have had some opportunity to save in the past. How do you rate yourself as a saver of money?

My Evaluation of My Saving Habits: Hers

☐ Excellent   ☐ Good   ☐ Fair   ☐ Poor

Explain your reasons for giving yourself this rating:

_____

_____

_____

_____

_____

_____

_____

_____

_____

My Evaluation of My Saving Habits: His

☐ Excellent   ☐ Good   ☐ Fair   ☐ Poor

Explain your reasons for giving yourself this rating:

_____

_____

_____

_____

_____

_____

_____

_____

_____

_____

_____

2. Write down one experience from your past when you were able to successfully save money for something you really wanted. Do this independently (on a separate sheet of notebook paper) and then share these experiences with one another.

_____

_____

_____

_____

_____

_____

_____

_____

3. How important is saving to you now? Each of you complete the following statement.

His Answer:

I Consider Saving To Be:
- ☐ Extremely important
- ☐ Important
- ☐ Something to consider
- ☐ Not very important

My Reasons Are:

_____

_____

_____

_____

_____

_____

_____

Her Answer:

I Consider Saving To Be:
- ☐ Extremely important
- ☐ Important
- ☐ Something to consider
- ☐ Not very important

My Reasons Are:

_____

_____

_____

_____

_____

_____

_____

4. Before going to the next chapter, each of you should write down what you believe is a challenging but achievable savings goal for the first year of marriage.

His Answer:

I Believe That A Challenging Savings Goal Would Be:

_____ percent of our annual income.

My Reasons Are:

_____

_____

_____

_____

_____

Her Answer:

I Believe That A Challenging Savings Goal Would Be:

_____ percent of our annual income.

My Reasons Are:

_____

_____

_____

_____

_____

5. Now use the negotiating guidelines I gave you in Chapter Four to reach agreement on a percentage of your annual income that you are both willing to adopt as a challenging but achievable savings goal.

Our Answer:

We Believe That A Challenging Savings Goal Would Be:

_____ percent of our monthly income.

6. What annual savings goals can you negotiate for the next five years? Use your answer from the above agreement check to establish a first year dollar goal. Then, build a five year plan with progressively larger goals. There is no magic formula for completing this exercise. If saving 50% more each year seems too hard for you, negotiate an annual increase that is achievable but challenging.

We Believe That Challenging Savings Goals for the Next Five Years Would Be:

Year	Savings
19_____	$_____
19_____	$_____
19_____	$_____
19_____	$_____
19_____	$_____

Our Reasons for Choosing These Goals Are:

_____

_____

_____

_____

_____

7. The money you need to meet your savings goals has to come from some income source(s). What will that income source(s) be? Talk about this first, and then write your answer here:

_____

_____

_____

_____

_____

_____

8. Return to your Spending Plan forms in **Appendix E**. Notice that the first expense category is "SAVINGS." Even if you don't yet know exactly how you will reach your savings goals, I want you to divide each of your annual savings goals by twelve. Your answer will tell you how much you need to save monthly to reach your goals. When you hold your monthly Spending Plan planning sessions, put this monthly savings amount in the "projected" column, even if you don't yet know how to reach your goal.

9. If there is not enough income at this time to make it possible for you to save or to reach your savings goals, and assuming you are committed to a savings program, list some ideas you have for how you might change the situation to make savings possible. This list should include every idea you can possibly think of. You can develop your best ideas further by reading the next chapter.

_____

_____

_____

_____

_____

_____

10. Return to the last chapter and revisit your discussion about financial roles. This time, discuss where you will assign the responsibility for overseeing your savings program. Look at both the record keeping and the cash management roles to see if some portion of the savings program responsibility belongs to each role. Remember, you are both 100 percent responsible for meeting your savings goals.

Suggested Additional Reading:

Heller, Warren G. *Is Your Money Safe?—How To Protect Your Savings in The Current Banking Crisis*. New York: Berkley Books, 1990.

Sherman, Michael, Ph.D. *Comprehensive Compound Interest Tables: Newly Revised and Updated Edition*. Chicago: Contemporary Books, Inc., 1986.

Notes

The Rules of The Financial Road:

Part II

Chapter Seven

Financial Law No. 4: Earn More Than You Spend

"Whatever you do, do with all your might!"
P.T. Barnum

Who was P.T. Barnum? He was a fascinating character who is usually remembered as the producer of one of the world's great circuses—Ringling Brothers, Barnum, and Bailey. He also wrote a famous essay titled, "The Art of Money Getting." Included in his advice about how to be successful with money, Mr. Barnum encouraged all-out dedication and hard work in order to be financially rewarded. He spoke clearly and often his belief that "ambition, energy, industry, and perseverance…" should result in "…financial success." By this he meant that the investment of hard work should result in a good income. That sounds reasonable enough, doesn't it? Then why isn't every hard-working married couple making a good income?

One reason is that every married couple does not have the same talents, skills and education.

We may live in a country where all men and women are created equal, but we are not all the same. We may admire doctors, lawyers and corporate chief executives, but we can't all become one of these professionals.

This doesn't mean, however, that we have to settle for a life of poverty. In fact, this chapter is dedicated to the idea that there is more than one way to provide income to help you make your dreams come true, even if you weren't born with great talent or genius. Of course, to be financially successful, you'll have to make the most of what God gave you, but even if you do that, you may still need some help to increase your income. I believe you'll find some of that help here.

The Need for a Second Income Stream

The second reason hard work alone doesn't produce ample income is because of a well-kept economic secret that I call "the 30% rule."

The 30% rule states that an employer must keep the cost of labor to 30% or less of the cost of any product in order to compete successfully in the marketplace.

When the cost of labor forces an employer to break this rule, the employer usually looks in a foreign country to find cheaper labor. As a result, the 30% rule keeps the lid on what most people can earn by their labor alone.

The 30% rule was not developed out of disrespect for labor. The 30% rule simply reflects an economic fact: It is impossible for most businesses to make a profit if they pay more than 30% for labor to produce a product.

This means that it is highly unlikely that you will ever become wealthy if you depend entirely on your employer for all of your income.

Besides, as you will learn in this chapter, labor alone is not what makes free enterprise the greatest economic force in the world. It is *labor* plus *ingenuity* plus *selling* that makes free enterprise such a fantastic way of life, filled with opportunity. I'll elaborate on

this formula as we go through the discussions in this chapter.

By the way, the personal service industries (sales professionals, physicians, lawyers, accountants or any other industry that does not manufacture products) are not bound by this 30% rule, but they have their own limitations that make it impossible to become financially successful by way of service labor alone.

The medical profession and a few other professions may be exceptions, but those who believe that they fall into the "exception" category may still benefit from the ideas in this chapter.

As a young married couple, you will face many financial challenges. The first and most obvious challenge is how to bring income into your life. I'm sure at least one of you is employed. But beyond that, I don't know much about you. However, I do know about the world in which you live and work. I know that even if you live within a carefully controlled spending plan, you will find it hard to reach your savings goals. I know that your current income is under attack from taxes and inflation. I know that even if you avoid debt and use credit wisely, you will still need to find ways to increase the flow of income to your marriage in order to make your dreams come true.

Perhaps most importantly, I know that almost all of you will end up living a paycheck to paycheck lifestyle unless you develop a "second income stream."

In this chapter, we will review and judge time-tested financial strategies to create that second income stream. You will also learn how to make your primary source of income more productive. The title of this chapter may sound like a simple restatement of Financial Law No. 1: *Spend less than you earn.* I assure you that this is not the case. Unlike Financial Law No. 1, which focuses attention on *income management*, Financial Law No. 4 focuses attention on *income production.* Financial Law No. 1 requires communication and management skills to help you control spending.

Financial Law No. 4 requires communication and management skills to help increase your income so there is plenty of cash to create the savings you will need for investing.

Believe me, married couples who manage money successfully give just as much attention to income planning as they do to careful spending. I hope this will be true of you, too.

As you review the financial strategies for earning more than you spend, keep in mind that these ideas are worthless unless you put them into practice. There is no free lunch for those who want ample income. You will have to work very hard, especially in the beginning of your marriage. But, if you're willing to do that, *"with all your might,"* then the income you want and need is definitely within your reach.

213

Financial Strategy No. 1 for Harmonizing with Financial Law No. 4: Know what you are doing; love what you are doing.

[The following discussion is dedicated to my personal mentor, Mr. Cavett Robert, whose teachings about success with people have served as reliable guideposts throughout my adult life. Mr. Robert is the founder of the National Speakers Association and the Number One speaker in America on human engineering and motivation. If you have never heard him speak, you have missed a real treat. Since his formal retirement eighteen years ago, he has addressed more than 3500 audiences. While you may never have the privilege of meeting him personally, you can still gain from his down-to-earth humor and teachings by reading his book, Success with People Through Human Engineering and Motivation. *You can obtain his book from Parker Publishing Company in Chicago, Illinois.]*

There is no way for me to know what you are doing to earn money right now. It may be something you enjoy very much. It may be your life's work. However, it may be "just a job." Yet, you almost certainly need that job to provide your primary source of income. Your primary income provides cash for the basics—food, shelter and clothing—your survival needs. You will also begin your savings program by setting aside at least 10% of everything you earn from your primary income. That means that the cash that flows into your marriage from salaries and wages is very important. Therefore, it seems fitting to share with you two fundamental principles about how to make the most of your work life and to assure yourself the greatest possible return on the investment you make to produce your primary income. If you apply the following principles to whatever you do to earn your living, I know you will enjoy your work more and you will prosper from whatever you do.

Do you know what you are doing?

Principle Number One: Know What You Are Doing

To really make the most out of your job, career or profession, it is critical to know how to do what you do better than anyone else. The rewards of income go first to the man or woman who **knows** **what he or she is doing**. In addition, those who constantly prepare to do better are likewise going to receive the first fruits of income.

Abraham Lincoln once said, "The older I get, the more I realize that there is but one wealth, one security on this earth and that is found in the ability of a person to perform a task well." But he didn't stop there. He went on to say, "And first and foremost that ability must start with knowledge."

Sketchy knowledge is not enough. In our modern, fast-moving economy, school never lets out for those who want to earn a higher income. By dedicating yourself at the beginning of marriage to a course of constant learning, you are certain to make important financial progress. But remember, the educational process itself must never end. If you grow tired or lazy along the way, the world will pass you by.

Knowing what you are doing means getting the education, training or apprenticeship necessary to be considered a skilled person. But that is only the first reach of this first principle. Knowing what you are doing also has two other dimensions. Let's explore them.

To know what you are doing also requires a knowledge of how your work is *valued* by others.

To make money in a free enterprise economy, you must provide a product or service that other people want or need and for which they are willing to pay money. Bernard Baruch was one of the great business leaders of this century. He was an elder statesman, a financial genius and an advisor to U.S. presidents. As a man who was financially successful by anyone's standards, he was once asked about his secret to success in business. His answer? "Find out what people want and give it to them." Let's look at two examples to see what this means for a married couple.

Example One: A few months after Mike and Mary were married, it became obvious that they could not survive financially on Mike's salary as a messenger for a law firm. Mary was pregnant and most of the available jobs in the community would require long hours on her feet—something her obstetrician felt she should avoid. Mary came from a large family, loved children, and had years of experience caring for them. She decided to provide day care for children of well-to-do mothers who would like to spend all or part of the day in activities such as tennis, golf or volunteer work. Mary reasoned that these mothers could afford to pay her well for her services. After fielding calls from several mothers who responded to her ads, however, Mary found that the marketplace for such services was totally different from what she expected. Those mothers considered such services as simple "baby-sitting," and were unwilling to pay more than the going rate for this service. Furthermore, they were unwilling to bring their children to Mary's home. Mary quickly decided to find a different marketplace. She found it in working for a local tennis club that wanted to offer child care as an additional attraction to its members.

Example Two: Rob had been very fortunate. Through his father's connections, he had gotten a job as a construction laborer. The pay was great, and he and Sue had done very well in the first year of their marriage. Rob had paid cash for an older car but had fixed it up with detailing and upholstery of his own design. Then, the bottom dropped out. A management error caused a major layoff. Rob had very low seniority in the union and was one of the first to go. Fortunately, Rob and Sue had a small savings account. It wasn't anything special, but it helped get them over the first few weeks of zero income. In trying to decide what to do, Rob suddenly realized how many admiring looks and outright compliments he had received for the customizing work he had done on his car. In two weeks, Rob had set up his own car customizing shop in their garage. Friends helped spread the word, and within a month, Rob had all the work he could handle at very good pay. He had provided a desired service for people who were willing to pay well for it.

In both examples, income was increased by identifying an interest, a talent, or skill and changing these into a service or product that other people wanted or needed. "Knowing what you are doing" includes staying aware of the value of your talents and services in today's marketplace. Without this knowledge, you may not have any buyers for your products or services— no customers. Without customers, you're out of business.

Knowing what you are doing also means having knowledge of how your work *performance* is seen by others.

I once heard a story that illustrates how one person gained this kind of knowledge in a unique but effective way:

A pharmacist overheard a young man making a telephone call. The young man dialed a number and said, "Hello, is this 555-9373? I want to apply for a job as a gardener. Oh, you have a gardener! Is he a good gardener? Is he doing a good job for you? You have no plans to change? Well, thank you anyway."

As the young man was leaving the store, the druggist approached him and said, "Don't be discouraged. Just keep trying. You'll get a job."

"Who's looking for a job?" was the young man's question.

The pharmacist, rather surprised, replied, "I thought I overheard you asking for a job as a gardener."

"Oh, no," said the young man, a little embarrassed, "I am the gardener. I just call every now-and-then to check up on myself and see how well I'm doing."

How do you check your performance in the eyes of the people you work for? Do they see you as keeping pace, giving your best, going all-out? Or are you about to be replaced by someone who knows more than you, works harder and is always willing to go the extra mile?

The average person will change jobs at least five times in the course of a lifetime. I hope that each time you change jobs, it's because someone thinks you are so knowledgeable *and* valuable that they want you to be a part of their organization. I hope it's not because you *had* to find a new job after you were let go by someone who saw that you didn't invest in knowledge, grow with your job and pay the price of giving your best each and every day you came to work.

216

Of course, you may say, "I don't really like what I am doing, so how can I be expected to go all out and give my very best?"

In reply to that kind of response, let me first congratulate you on recognizing that you may not like what you are doing to earn income at this time. If that is the case, I hope your not liking your job will soon turn into deep discontent and that you will begin looking for employment elsewhere. There is nothing more wonderful than young adults who are filled with the kind of discontent that keeps them looking for their life's work rather than just grinding out one day after another at a job they hate. But whether you like your job or not, you don't have to make yourself and your employer miserable. You can still project optimism and enthusiasm for life. And that is part of what it means to love what you are doing.

217

Principle Number Two: Love What You Are Doing

What does it mean to love what you are doing? It means that you believe thoroughly that what you are doing to earn your living is enriching your life and the lives of other people. Whether involved in producing a product or providing a service, the person who loves what he or she does feels a sense of involvement in and commitment to his or her work. Will Rogers expressed it perfectly when he said, "If there's nothing else you'd rather be doing, then it ain't work."

Why is it so important to love what you are doing?

Earning money is something you will do most of your working life. But if it is the wrong kind of work, or if you approach work with the wrong attitude, then your life will be spent like a person who walks around wearing size 8 shoes on size 10 feet. It will be painful.

However, to find the right work for your life—*your life's work*—may take some time, and you need to be earning a living *right now*. So before discussing how to find your life's work, let's look at one of your most important work-related assets—your attitudes toward life and work.

218

Get An Attitude! —But Get The Right One!

What is your attitude towards life? Do you love life so much that you are delighted to wake up in the morning? Are the first words you think of when you see the light of day, "Good morning, God!"? Or do you roll over, hit the alarm button, and mutter, "Good god! It's morning!"? Think about it. Have you ever noticed that some people spread mental body odor around everywhere they go? They have this air about them that stinks up the lives of everyone they come near. These are the people who brighten up a room just by leaving it. Don't you just hate being around this kind of person? Please, whatever you decide to do to earn your income, don't be like these people. Even if you don't like what you are doing right now, you do have a lot to be happy about. I hope you spread that happiness among everyone you meet.

Because you are a free person, you are Chairman of the Board of your attitudes toward life. If you think of your life attitudes as a product, produced by a company that you direct, it can really change your outlook about what you do with your attitudes.

How do you run yourself? Are you the producer of the greatest optimism, enthusiasm, and positive life force that the world has ever seen? Or does your company produce mental garbage? The most an employer can ever offer you is a job. Your employer can't offer you a positive life attitude. Only you can do that. *You can* produce optimism and enthusiasm for life even when your job is a pain. Furthermore, to be successful at earning an income, you will almost certainly have to be optimistic and enthusiastic.

The question you may ask is, "How?" The answer to that question could fill another book—maybe several of them. The good news is, those books have already been written, and reading them is the best way I know for you to answer your own question. Go read those books (I've given you a good list to choose from at the end of this chapter), and learn what the experts say about how to be a positive, optimistic and enthusiastic person. Yet, after reading all of those books, if you still can't produce positive attitudes toward life (and assuming that you aren't suffering from an emotional or psychological disorder), I suggest you fake it. That's right. If all else fails, fake it. Fake it every moment of every day. Fake it at work in the face of the miserable people who work around you and who supervise you. Fake it to your monster of a boss. Fake it when you pick up that lousy pay check that should be two or three times more than it is. Fake it right up to the day you find a new job, one that you like a whole lot more than the one you have now. And then keep on faking it as you move on to your next job.

Why fake it? Because when you practice expressing positive attitudes over and over every minute of every day, things change. First of all, *you* will change. You can not make progress on the outside and stand still on the inside. Your behaviors cause a change in your attitudes. And faking the proper life attitudes will change you inside—where your attitudes live. Second, even when you fake a positive, optimistic and enthusiastic attitude for life and everything in your life, people will be attracted to you. Of course, if you have been producing mental garbage for a while, this change won't happen immediately because people will think you're faking it—which you are. But if you stick to it and don't give up, people will begin to believe that you really have changed, and they will like being around you. As a by-product, you may soon find that your employer and fellow employees will begin treating you in new ways. In fact, if you're not careful, they may increase your pay and make it hard for you to want to leave. Wouldn't *that* be a problem?

Of course, you must be prepared for the possibility that the people around you won't change at all and you may still need to move on. Accept this. It is perfectly O.K. to find a new job, one that pays better and provides a more stimulating, rewarding and satisfying working environment. Take your new life attitudes and behaviors right with you—and take your work ethic, too. Having said that, let's take a look at your work ethic.

What? Me? Work?

I said at the beginning of this discussion that your attitudes toward life *and* work were important. Now that you've looked at your attitudes toward life, take a look at your attitudes toward work. What are they? Are you overjoyed to live in a country where you're free to pursue any line of business you please? Do you believe that work adds to human dignity? How does work fit into your value system? Can you see a way to define work so that it doesn't mean the same as the word "chore" but means something more like the word "play?" Your answers to these questions are very important because they are clues to your work ethic.

Every employer wants to hire people who have strong work ethics. This means they want employees who believe that work is a way to strengthen their human dignity, who like working, who give their very best to their work, who find work fun or make it fun.

People who believe that work supports human dignity would work even if they were rich. I'm not talking about people who are workaholics, either. That's something altogether different. No, people with a strong work ethic choose to work because work dignifies their lives, and through work they can express the meaning and value of their lives. These people work hard at doing a good job even when the job they do is not their life's work.

People with a weak work ethic just punch a clock. They go through their working day in a nearly unconscious state of mind. They live for the weekend, and celebrate Wednesday as "hump day"—meaning they are on the top of a huge hill they call work (a hill they didn't want to climb in the first place), and they see Thursday and Friday as the downhill slide into Saturday and Sunday (party time). At best, these people think about and act towards their jobs only as a means of keeping their responsibilities to creditors, of gaining some worldly goods, or of receiving status and recognition.

This is a deeply tragic way to look at work. I can't think of anything that is more sad than seeing work in this light considering that work takes so much of our lives. What should you do if your work has taken on this meaning?

First of all, be honest about it. If you don't love what you are doing, you're ruining your life. You won't find any happiness this way. In addition, work won't be any fun and you probably won't make much money—or at least the money you make won't mean as much to you.

Second, make a commitment to start honoring your self through work. This commitment must begin with the full recognition that you have a self to express, even if that self has been carefully hidden. Begin by getting in touch with that self. This may take some learning. Learning how to get in touch with your self means learning how to listen to your inner voice, and that may be easier for some than for others. Your inner voice will tell you how to set limits and clarify your needs so that through work you can find emotional, creative and spiritual satisfaction, as well as financial rewards. If you need career counseling to help you, then get some. Just remember, until you learn how to honor and express your self, you are only half alive.

Third, start your personal search to find your *life's work*. Your life's work is any work that allows you to express your self (thereby showing love for yourself) *and* to serve others. Begin your search by acknowledging that to discover and develop a life work will require a patient, disciplined, long-term investment of your self. When you seek your life's work, you no longer simply accept other people's definition of *success*. There is a great temptation in our society to accept blindly the popular image (or our parents' image) of success. By definition, those success images (the ones from our parents, the media or the corporation we may presently work for) don't come from *within us*. Furthermore, they usually glamorize overwork, earning money and an all-out race to get to the top of the heap, while minimizing the importance of self-fulfillment, family, community and one's own needs beyond work (including the need to make love-filled dreams come true). Those who chase the success goals of others end up depressed, dissatisfied and exhausted. Usually, they don't even know why.

When you seek a life work, you have to be honest about what kind of life and work *you* want for *yourself*. That is the *first* step in creating your own definition of success. But you can't stop there.

To find a life work, you must also see clearly and understand fully how your work will allow you the opportunity to serve others. One of life's great mysteries is that humans have been created in a way that requires service to others to feel whole, complete and good about themselves. Those who approach work selfishly, seeking only what it can do for them (or how much money they can make) never find true self-fulfillment through their work. In essence, they *never* find their life's work.

Please keep in mind that in seeking your life's work, your service to others doesn't require that you take on a huge project of humanitarian importance. The only requirement is that you approach your search honestly, seeking a way to provide others with a product or service that will in some way enrich *their* lives. Remember, any work you approach in the spirit of serving others is going to lead you one step closer to finding your life's work.

One clue that you have found your life's work is when you truly begin to believe in what you are doing and look forward with excitement and enthusiasm to going to work each day.

Another clue is found in leading a balanced, meaningful and joy-filled life that includes ample time and attention to family, community and to the emotional and spiritual dimensions of your own life. While a life work may be creative, fulfilling and intellectually challenging, it should *never* become the end all and be all of your life. Those people who truly discover their life's work find it much easier to experience the full range of life's treasures, including enjoyment of life qualities such as compassion, generosity, courage and love for others.

If you have started out in the wrong direction, finding your life's work may mean going back to school or serving an apprenticeship. Yet, over time, if you are faithful in your search, the rewards will far outweigh any early sacrifices you may have to make.

There is no employer who can offer you a life work. Your employer can offer you a work opportunity, but you have to find a way through that opportunity to express your inner self and serve others. Your employer can't offer you security, either. The person who constantly seeks job security usually has a terrible fear of losing his or her job. And the person who is fearful of losing his or her job does not have a job—the job has the person. Your job, what you do to earn your primary income, is just a tool. Hopefully, you will use that tool to express and honor your inner self. Then, if you lose your job, you don't have to lose your inner self, your positive life attitudes, your enthusiasm or your commitment to use work to enhance your dignity. These qualities are yours by simply claiming them. I encourage you to take them with you to work every day of your life.

The next time you walk in your employer's door, wear a smile. Look into the faces around you and watch that smile come back at you. As you approach the tasks of each working day, do more than what you believe is expected.

Put your talents, skills and attitudes into action and show through every task that you are more than just a Social Security number. If you can't fall in love with your job right now, at least fall in love with your life, and keep looking for the job that you can fall in love with.

But remember, while someone employs you in a job you may not enjoy, give that employer the gratitude and appreciation he or she deserves by knocking yourself out for him/her. Even if you don't like your employer, speak well of him or her and speak well of everyone who works with you. Remember this simple law of life: You will never receive appreciation (especially financial appreciation) from those for whom you work until you first give it and give it in abundance. And maybe what is even more important, you will never fully love what you do until you find a life work, one that will allow you to fully honor your self, serve others, and live a balanced, creative and spiritually enriching life.

Agreement Check:

1. How valuable are you in today's job market? Make a list of skills and talents you now sell to others for money. If you are presently unemployed, show what the marketplace would pay for your skills and talents if you were employed. Be as realistic as you can. Be conservative in your figures. Most importantly, be sure you both complete this exercise.

Skill and/or Talent   **Hourly Value $**

Hers:

_____

_____

_____

_____

_____

_____

_____

_____

Skill and/or Talent   **Hourly Value $**

His:

_____

_____

_____

_____

_____

_____

_____

_____

2. The inventory of your skills and talents reflects your *hourly value* in the marketplace. To fully appreciate what you are worth as an employed person, it is important that you have an idea of what your *lifetime capital value* is. The easiest way to figure that value is by completing this exercise.

    a. Determine the number of your future working years (for example, if you are now 20, you have 45 future working years).

        His Working Years_____
        Her Working Years_____

    b. Your working years (X) 2000 (approximate number of work hours in a year) = _____ (lifetime working hours)

    c. Your lifetime working hours (X) your present hourly rate of pay = $_____ **This amount is your lifetime capital value.**

    NOTE: The exercise you just completed does not take into account increases in your wages and salaries over a lifetime. It also does not take into account the effect of inflation on your income. The purpose of the exercise is simply to help you see clearly that you are a valuable person in today's marketplace and that the way you choose to spend your time could result in money in your pocket.

    3. Your training and education are extremely valuable and have contributed to increasing your lifetime capital value. To help you appreciate how much has been invested in your training and education, complete the following exercise. List all secondary education (high school and above) as well as any specialized training (courses or on-the-job training). All of these are definite assets to you. Be as thorough as possible.

Training and Education: His

_____

_____

_____

_____

_____

Training and Education: Hers

_____

_____

_____

_____

_____

4. Since the education and training you received in the past has increased your lifetime capital value, continuing your education and training in the future will make you even more valuable. You live in a society that puts tremendous importance on formal education and rewards education by paying more money to those who have it. It is critically important, then, to invest some of your time gaining more education. Use this exercise to state your own plans for continuing education in your chosen field or in a field that you would like to enter.

My Plans For Continuing Education: His

_____

_____

_____

_____

_____

_____

_____

_____

_____

_____

_____

My Plans For Continuing Education: Hers

_____

_____

_____

_____

_____

_____

_____

_____

_____

_____

_____

_____

Suggested Additional Reading:

Jones, Charles, T. *Life Is Tremendous.* Wheaton: Tyndale House Publishers, Inc., 1968.

Peale, Norman Vincent. *The Power of Positive Thinking*. New York: Fawcett Crest, 1990.

Peale, Norman Vincent. *You Can If You Think You Can.* New York: Prentice Hall, 1986.

Sinetar, Marsha. *Do What You Love, The Money Will Follow*. New York: Dell Publishing, 1987.

Paulus, Trina. *Hope for the Flowers.* New York: Paulist Press, 1972.

Robert, Cavett. *Success With People Through Human Engineering & Motivation*. Chicago: Parker Publishing Company, Inc., 1969.

Financial Strategy No. 2 for Harmonizing with Financial Law No. 4: Look to Your Hobbies as a Source of Income

Do you remember that at the beginning of this chapter I said that financial opportunity is a combination of *labor* plus *ingenuity* plus *selling?* I should have qualified that and said *successful selling*. Until someone sells a product or service to someone else, money doesn't change hands and no one prospers. However, before selling starts, labor must be invested in a product or service that is ingenious. Webster's dictionary says that "ingenious" means something that is made or done in a clever way. That definition is pretty narrow, but it will serve my purpose. While we explore this next income strategy, I'm going to focus on ingenuity as a part of the financial opportunity formula.

There is always a demand for an ingenious product or service. How many times have you heard stories of people who found financial success through inventing a new and clever product? It may have been a game that they invented, a computer software program or a household product. It may have been a consulting service or a service that filled a special spot that no one else had discovered. Often, the ideas these people had for their products or services came from a hobby or an existing special interest.

Your hobbies or special interests may also be a rich source of ingenious products or services waiting for *you* to discover *them*.

Assuming you give your best effort to your employer and receive the highest financial rewards available at this time, you may still find that you need more income. When you develop a hobby or special interest into an income source, you are creating a "second income stream." What does this mean? It means that in addition to the money you earn from your employer(s) to provide the river of cash for survival needs and to help create a small pool of savings, a second source of cash flow is created for swelling your savings and for creating a large pool of cash for investing.

Is this important? Can you get to the city of your dreams without a second income stream? Yes, of course you can—if you start out with a large inheritance or are capable of earning a high income from the first day of your marriage.

Since most couples don't start marriage with silver spoons in their mouths, and since few will earn large incomes at the start of married life, a second income stream is critical for creating enough savings to take advantage of investment opportunities.

Furthermore, when you are younger, you have more energy to invest in developing a second income stream. Couples in their forties, fifties and sixties often discover the value of a second income stream, but, by then, they seldom can find the energy to prime the second income stream pump.

Remember this. A second income stream doesn't have to begin as a gusher. It can begin as a trickle. The important thing is to guarantee that the money generated from this income source flows directly into your savings account. It should never become available to meet your day-to-day survival needs.

Some couples create a second income stream by living off one income from a two-income marriage. If you are both employed, this *can* work, but my experience has proven that it seldom does. Over the years, I have come to see that only those couples who consciously plan to create a second income stream from sources other than wages and salaries succeed in creating the dedicated flow of cash to successfully meet their savings goals. Will you be one of these couples? I hope so.

If you're interested, let's look more closely at your hobbies and special interests as a first strategy for creating *your* second income stream.

Hobbies and Special Interests Review

Many people have hobbies or special interests they consider really fun things to do, but have never considered such interests as a way to make money. The truth is that these hobbies and special interests sometimes offer a real opportunity for creating income, especially a second stream of income to supplement savings. Occasionally, hobbies and special interests can even become a way to find your life's work. Consider the example of Rob and his interest in auto detailing. He thought of it only as something fun to do until it occurred to him that it might be profitable. In this exercise, all you need to do is inventory your personal hobbies and special interests. In the section that follows, I'll help you explore how any of them could be used to increase your income.

Hobbies and Special Interests: Hers

_____

_____

_____

_____

_____

_____

_____

Hobbies and Special Interests: His

_____

_____

_____

_____

_____

_____

_____

Determining Whether Your Hobbies and Special Interests Can Increase Your Income

It's possible that your hobbies or special interests represent a valuable commodity. This is not always true, but it's worth looking at. By answering and discussing the questions that follow, you can begin to make this determination and explore your own interest in converting your hobby into a second income stream.

1. Do you believe that your hobby or special interest has the possibility of increasing your income?

    ☐ Yes   ☐ No

2. Do you have a real desire to use your hobby or interest to increase your income?

    ☐ Yes   ☐ No

3. Who might use (or purchase) the skills or products that you have developed (or would develop) from your hobby or special interest?

_____

_____

_____

_____

_____

_____

4. How much would these users pay for your skills or the products produced by your hobby?

_____

5. How much of your time are you willing to give up to provide products or services to a potential user?

_____

6. How much can you expect in yearly income from selling these products or services?

_____

7. Does the answer to Question 6 offset any trade-offs or disadvantages necessary on your part to start using your skills to increase your income?

☐ Yes ☐ No

It's very important to talk over your answers to these questions *together*. In all probability, it will be the hobby of one spouse that appears to have the greatest income producing ability. This means that the other spouse will need to play a supportive role in converting that hobby into a money-making enterprise.

Assuming you both are excited about the possibility of creating a second income stream from a hobby or special interest, be sure to consider the ideas presented in the next section.

Unless both of you are fully convinced that this is a good idea, it will be impossible to gain full cooperation of the reluctant partner and you will lose one of your great advantages as a married couple—the synergistic power of joining forces and working as a team.

Taking a Business Approach to Your Second Income Stream Enterprise

If you both agree that increasing your income through a hobby or special interest can be rewarding, the next step is to begin organizing your enterprise around business principles that will insure your success. When you take a business approach to creating a second income stream, you will discover many benefits. The first benefit is realized in the creation of a **business plan.**

Creating a business plan is the first success principle of any enterprise. A good plan answers the following questions:

1. How many customers might buy our products or services and how can we reach them?

2. Will our customers provide repeat business by buying frequently from us, or will we provide that once in a lifetime purchase?

3. What will it cost to produce our products or provide our services?

4. How much will we have to charge to make a profit?

5. How much capital (investment money) will we need to start our business?

6. What will be our annual budget for operating the business?

7. How much monthly or annual profit do we expect from our business?

After answering these questions, it should be possible to see if a new enterprise promises a few dollars a month or a few hundred dollars a month. Remember, if the investment doesn't promise enough extra income to motivate you, you certainly don't want to invest your extra time in it.

The second benefit from a business approach to creating a second income stream is found in **tax benefits.** If establishing a business enterprise is your choice, you'll have to learn about managing business finances. There are major tax advantages for those who take the time to learn about them and keep good business records. (The additional readings suggested at the end of this section will help you learn much about this and other aspects of starting a small business.)

The third benefit to be gained from a business approach to your enterprise is **time management.** Let's face it, you won't want to spend all of your extra time managing a second income stream business. You need to think through just how much time must be spent to succeed. This is another decision you must make together. Any time not sold to an employer is time you could be spending with one another. How you choose to use that time should be carefully negotiated. Once you decide exactly how many hours you will commit to creating a second income stream business, don't arbitrarily change your mind. Such changes should be made through thoughtful re-negotiation with one another.

Naturally, taking a business approach to converting a hobby or special interest into a second stream of income can only be decided after careful investigation and thorough discussion. To help you with those discussions, I suggest you answer the following questions:

233

1. Based on your answers to questions one through seven above, are you *still* excited about establishing a second income stream business?

☐ Yes   ☐ No

2. Are you *both* willing to use some of your evening or weekend time to develop this small business enterprise?

☐ Yes   ☐ No

3. Do you have a *burning desire* to do this?

☐ Yes   ☐ No

4. Are you willing to work hard and learn everything possible about the principles of operating a business successfully in order to make your business grow and succeed?

☐ Yes   ☐ No

If, after answering and discussing these four questions, you remain excited about converting your hobby or special interest into a small business, then it's time to begin your venture into free enterprise. I urge you to start by using the local library. Read books about setting up and managing a small business. Talk to others who have similar businesses. Ask them what mistakes they made that you can avoid. Then lay out your own step-by-step plan for setting up and operating *your* business. Do all of these things before you actually launch the business *and* do them together. Then, sit down and review the four questions above one more time to make your *final* decision about launching your business.

If after creating your business plan, you decide against starting a small business from a hobby or special interest, you still have other ways available to help you increase your income. Read on.

Suggested Additional Reading:

Ramsey, Dan. *101 Successful Ways To Turn Weekends Into Wealth*. West Nyak: Parker Publishing Company, Inc. 1982.

Levinson, Jay Conrad. *555 Ways to Earn Extra Money*. New York: Holt Rinehart and Winston, 1982.

Kahn, Steve. *How To Run A Business Out of Your Home*. Stamford: Longmeadow Press, 1987.

Arden, Lynie. *The Work At Home Sourcebook*. Boulder: Live Oak Publications. 1990.

Touchie, Roger D., B. Comm., M.B.A. *Preparing A Successful Business Plan: A Practical Guide for Small Business*. Bellingham: International Self-Counsel Press, Ltd., 1989.

Hynes, William G. *Start and Run A Profitable Craft Business*. Bellingham: International Self-Counsel Press, Ltd., 1990.

Financial Strategy No. 3 for Harmonizing with Financial Law No. 4: Increasing Your Income Through Someone Else's Business

When a hobby or special interest can not offer second income stream potential, the use of evening or weekend hours to increase your income may require you to piggyback on someone else's business. Sometimes this means taking a second job. If you both work, this may sound pretty challenging. However, if you both commit to working one weekend a month, and it is the same weekend, you can then take the other weekends for recreation. Remember the rule: Income from this additional weekend employment goes straight into your savings account.

Another choice is to join an already established business that allows you to participate as a full partner.

The way to do this is to take advantage of an entrepreneurial revolution that has become very popular and very profitable for many Americans called "network marketing" (sometimes called "direct sales" or "multi-level marketing").

For many young couples, a second income stream can only be created in this way. In this section, I'm going to focus exclusively on this strategy. Let's begin by defining what is meant by "network marketing." The best way to do this is to show the contrast between *traditional marketing* and *network marketing.*

Please keep in mind that all marketing is a way of providing the third dimension of financial opportunity that was identified at the beginning of this chapter—sales.

Traditional marketing takes a product and moves it through a network of middlemen from the manufacturer to the consumer. Each middleman pays a little higher price for the product. By the time the product reaches the consumer, it is usually marked up five times. That is to say, a product that costs $1.00 to manufacture will cost the consumer $5.00.

In network marketing, the network of middlemen is not eliminated but it is transformed into a direct selling network. Instead of a product passing through a long chain of middlemen who mark up the price several times before there is a direct sale to consumers, the middlemen become the distributors *and* sales representatives for the product. In this way the cost of distribution and sales is tremendously reduced and the profits that would normally go to the middlemen now go to the distributors-sales representatives. The distributors-sales representatives are ordinary men and women who are seeking a way to create a second income stream.

Many couples have discovered they can make $300, $500, or even $1,000 a month or more by joining a network marketing organization to sell products that can't be purchased in stores. Examples of such businesses are: Amway, Matol, J.R. Watkins Co., Avon, Mary Kay Cosmetics, Tupperware, etc.

Some of the advantages of increasing your income through one of these programs are listed below:

1. You do not have to invest much of your own money to get started.

2. Most of these businesses sell products that are used in everyday living and, therefore, repeat sales are built in.

3. Most of these businesses offer a high quality product that is sold at competitive prices.

4. All of these businesses allow you to profit by recruiting additional distributors. A portion of all that your new recruit sells benefits you.

5. Most of these businesses deal in cash, and therefore avoid the problem of collecting payment or the high cost of extending credit. In addition, your profits are almost immediate.

Unlike a second job, this approach offers you more flexibility. You may be able to devote as little as one weekend per month and one or two nights a week and still create a substantial second stream of income. In addition, this option may be more readily available than a weekend job. And, perhaps most important of all, this option allows couples to create their second income stream by working **together!!**

If you do join a network marketing business, you should follow some guidelines for successfully selecting and profiting from this second income stream strategy. Here is a quick summary of suggested guidelines to consider:

A. Find a business that is right for you—one that offers a valid product or service that you believe in.

B. Be sure that the company offers you training and consistent management. Check its track record in this regard by talking to others who work for them.

C. Be sure you understand how you will be paid, including payment of special sales incentives and bonuses.

D. Make sure you will be provided with top quality promotional and support material.

E. Make sure you will have a sponsor or coach within the company who is willing to work with you and help you become successful.

F. Make a commitment of at least one year to working with the company you choose.

G. Learn how to deal positively with discouragement and rejection.

H. Be enthusiastic.

I. Be determined.

To help you explore this option, I've listed the names, addresses, and telephone numbers of a large number of network marketing companies that are currently considered top-rated organizations offering these second income stream opportunities (see **Appendix F**, Pages F-1 through F-6). These players are not lightweights. Some are Fortune 500 and New York Stock Exchange companies. A simple telephone call can open up an important second income stream opportunity for you.

236

After exploring one, you may decide you want to learn about several others before making a decision. That's fine. But whatever you do, explore this option. It could open doors that you never dreamed were possible.

Suggested Additional Reading:

Scott, Gini Graham. *Get Rich Through Multi-Level Selling*. Bellingham: International Self-Counsel Press, Ltd., 1989.

Babener, Jeffrey, A. and David Stewart. *The Network Marketer's Guide To Success*. Scottsdale: The Forum For Network Marketing, 1990.

A Final Word About Increasing Your Income

If you have a burning desire to increase your income, you can succeed by (1) investing your time through education, (2) developing skills from a hobby or special interest or (3) by joining someone else's business organization. Any of these plans or strategies will work—as long as you work.

Developing a second income stream to increase your savings is more than just a good idea. Remember, increasing your income must be part of your overall planning to make your dreams come true.

Increasing your income by creating a second income stream or by increasing your primary source of income is not just a frantic exercise in chasing dollars. Earning a higher income requires giving true value in exchange for well deserved payment. When earning a higher income is combined with other financial management disciplines, you will end up with more money to save, and, finally, to invest. If your dreams represent what you want most in life, then take action now to start increasing your income. **You must take action to get results.** Working through this chapter should have stimulated several ideas about action you can take. If you aren't satisfied you have found the right idea

yet, go back to your Dream Book and look through it again. By flipping through the pages of your Dream Book, you may be surprised about additional ideas that will come to mind about how to increase your income. Write all of your ideas down. But don't stop there. Do something! In fact, do anything that will start the process of changing your ideas into action.

What if you try something and it doesn't work out? So what? There is no such thing as failure! "Failure" is a label that we put on actions that just didn't have the results we expected.

Winston Churchill, former Prime Minister of England, once said, "The key to success is to jump at your opportunities." Someone then asked him, "How do I know when I have an opportunity?" "Just keep jumping," was his reply.

Opportunity isn't only *knocking* in America. For those of you who want to increase your income, it's *beating down the door and it's calling your name!* You are surrounded by opportunity! But opportunity can't force you to take action. Only you can do that! Motivated by your own dreams and your love for one another, get started now!

Agreement Check:

1. List below every idea you can possibly think of for developing a second income stream. Try using the brainstorming technique that was discussed in Chapter Four under the topic heading "Successful Negotiating Strategies." Write down every idea that comes to mind. Don't try to analyze your ideas at this time. You can do that later. Remember, don't stop listing your ideas until you feel you've completely exhausted your creativity.

Notes

_____

_____

_____

_____

_____

_____

_____

_____

_____

_____

_____

_____

_____

2. Use the forms on the following pages to further refine your best ideas and to identify the action steps you would/could/should take to make these ideas become real. Complete this exercise for at least three (and preferably five) of your second income stream ideas. Then refine your thinking by prioritizing your ideas (best, second best, third best, etc.) Finally, choose the one that you are both excited about and start implementing it. Remember, if you find the first one doesn't open the door you want, go to your next idea. Keep taking action until you find the idea that really works for you.

Ideas For Increasing Our Income:

_____

_____

_____

Action Steps to Make This Happen:

Step 1: _____

_____

Step 2: _____

_____

Step 3: _____

_____

Step 4: _____

_____

Step 5: _____

_____

Step 6: _____

_____

Step 7: _____

_____

Step 8: _____

_____

Step 9: _____

_____

Step 10: _____

_____

Ideas For Increasing Our Income:

_____

_____

_____

Action Steps to Make This Happen:

Step 1: _____

_____

Step 2: _____

_____

Step 3: _____

_____

Step 4: _____

_____

Step 5: _____

_____

Step 6: _____

_____

Step 7: _____

_____

Step 8: _____

_____

Step 9: _____

_____

Step 10: _____

_____

Ideas For Increasing Our Income:

_____

_____

_____

Action Steps to Make This Happen:

Step 1: _____

_____

Step 2: _____

_____

Step 3: _____

_____

Step 4: _____

_____

Step 5: _____

_____

Step 6: _____

_____

Step 7: _____

_____

Step 8: _____

_____

Step 9: _____

_____

Step 10: _____

_____

Ideas For Increasing Our Income:

_____

_____

_____

Action Steps to Make This Happen:

Step 1: _____

_____

Step 2: _____

_____

Step 3: _____

_____

Step 4: _____

_____

Step 5: _____

_____

Step 6: _____

_____

Step 7: _____

_____

Step 8: _____

_____

Step 9: _____

_____

Step 10: _____

_____

Notes

The Rules of the Financial Road:

Part III

Chapter Eight

Financial Law No. 5:
Never Buy Diamonds From Bricklayers

"Give a man a fish, he eats for a day.
Teach a man to fish, he eats for a lifetime."
Ancient Chinese Proverb

In George S. Clason's book length parable, *The Richest Man in Babylon,* Arkad, the main character, discovers that saving ten percent of all he earns is not enough to give him financial independence. Saving a part of all that he earned was a good beginning; but, as he soon learns, savings must be wisely invested to provide a financial harvest rich enough to assure financial independence. Unfortunately, Arkad's first investment decision is to buy diamonds from a bricklayer. This bricklayer promises to increase dramatically Arkad's savings "by traveling over the far seas...to buy...the rare jewels of the Phoenicians." As you might guess, the result of this first decision is a disaster. The bricklayer returns with a bag of worthless glass that he was unable to tell from real jewels.

"Never buy diamonds from bricklayers" reflects Arkad's painful lesson. It also expresses the next rule of the financial road. It is a catchy little motto, and I urge you to memorize it. I hope it will remind you not to make the same mistake as you start your marriage investment program. As you will learn, avoiding bad investment decisions is not easy. Learning how to make good investment decisions is even harder. Learning how to invest money wisely will probably be one of your greatest challenges as a married couple. Why? First, most of you will have little or no investment experience. Second, if one of you has some experience, it is highly unlikely that the other has *any* experience. That brings us to the third reason that investing is so challenging for married couples.

To invest successfully, you must make investment decisions as a team. The days of male dominated investment decision-making in marriage are history. Not ancient history, I'll grant you. However, *investing* decisions must always be *shared* decisions for couples who commit to creating a financial partnership.

So, I have designed the financial strategies presented in this chapter to help you learn how to make thoughtful investment decisions together. By learning and using the decision-making model presented in the following pages, you really can develop a disciplined approach to this complex area of financial life. And disciplined thinking is absolutely required here. Every investment decision demands sound thinking and careful analysis (both of which are definitely modern brain functions). Even the most experienced investors sometimes use their Neanderthal brains to make their investment decisions. The results are almost always disappointing and sometimes tragic.

Some investors can't resist the temptation of immediate reward (get rich quick). This Neanderthal brain motive can be very powerful. How tempting (and foolish) it is to believe that money invested for a few days or a few weeks will return double or triple its original amount.

Yet, would-be investors continually fall for such promises. Another Neanderthal brain motive (closely associated with the attraction of immediate reward) is basic human greed. Greed is the belief in a "free lunch," the "something for nothing" fantasy left over from the days of our childhood. Believe me, there is no free lunch—anywhere! The idea of a free lunch in the world of investing is especially ridiculous. I hope that after reading this chapter you will never let these or any other Neanderthal brain motives lure you into ignoring your higher brain processes. Of course, you may think that investing is something married couples do only after several years of marriage, or only if they have plenty of money in the bank. Wrong! Couples who are successful with money start their marriage investment program as soon as they get married. While the lessons in this chapter may require that you read and learn slowly, I urge you to learn them now. Don't put off this fundamental education about how to be successful investors.

Successful investing, while usually overlooked as something for other people or for the super rich, is something *you* must learn about and apply at the *beginning* of married life to help make your dreams come true.

Before setting out on this next learning experience, take a few minutes to complete the Agreement Check on the next few pages. Share your investment experiences prior to marriage with one another and discuss how you feel about the subject of investing because of these experiences.

Agreement Check:

1. Investing may or may not be a new experience for you. Use the space below to write down your experiences with investing. Share these experiences with one another and discuss how you feel about the subject of investing because of these experiences.

My Experiences With Investing: His

_____

_____

_____

_____

_____

_____

_____

My Experiences With Investing: Hers

_____

_____

_____

_____

_____

_____

_____

2. The subject of investing requires training and education. In the space below, write down the training you have had on the subject of investing. Be sure to include any courses you have taken, books you have read or training you have been given by a parent, friend, teacher or employer.

My Training On The Subject Of Investing: His

_____

_____

_____

_____

_____

_____

_____

_____

My Training On The Subject Of Investing: Hers

_____

_____

_____

_____

_____

_____

_____

_____

3. Based on your completion of the last two exercises, how would you rate your preparation to invest your savings successfully? After rating your abilities, discuss your answers. Remember, there are no right or wrong answers.

My Evaluation Of Our Ability To Invest Successfully: His

☐ Excellent ☐ Good ☐ Fair ☐ Poor

Why did you select this rating?

_____

_____

_____

_____

_____

_____

_____

My Evaluation Of Our Ability To Invest Successfully: Hers

☐ Excellent ☐ Good ☐ Fair ☐ Poor

Why did you select this rating?

_____

_____

_____

_____

_____

_____

_____

Why Investing Is So Important: The Threats From Inflation And Taxes

Every married couple is caught in a two-way squeeze when it comes to making their money earn more money. From one direction, they're squeezed by taxes. From another direction, they're squeezed by inflation.

The old saying goes that "the only things certain in life are death and taxes." Yet, unlike death, taxes seem to grow more burdensome (and complicated) every time our lawmakers gather in Washington.

Taxes will probably eat up at least one-third of all you earn during your lifetime. Some of you may find that federal and state taxes will take as much as 50% of your earnings.

Your challenge is to keep your personal tax bill as low as possible—legally. I encourage you to work very hard at this by learning all you can about tax laws and working closely with tax advisors. But, taxes will always be a threat to your earnings, your savings and your investments.

The only way to win is to make enough money so that after taxes you still have plenty left for your needs—and your dreams.

[See **Appendix C** at the end of Chapter Ten entitled, "Tips for Preparing Your First Income Tax Return."]

Inflation is a silent tax. Inflation is a difficult idea to explain, but you always know what it means when you buy something. It means that the price has gone up.

Usually, the rate of inflation goes up faster than the rate your income increases. This means that the effective buying power of your income will always go down (unless you learn the lessons in this chapter). Let's see what this means for your financial future.

A dollar worth 100 cents today will be worth only 68 cents five years from now at an 8% inflation rate. In ten years, that same dollar at the same inflation rate will be worth about 46 cents. In fifteen years, it will be worth less than 32 cents. That is what it means to lose your buying power. Looking at it another way, let's say you need $3,000 a *month* to provide financial security today, and your cost of living is rising because of inflation by 8% each year. In five years, you will need $4,770 a *month* just to stay even. In ten years, you will need $6,480 a *month*. In twenty years, you will need $13,980.

To help you see this point even more clearly, let's see what inflation will do to your need for *annual income*. Assuming your income during the first year of marriage is a modest $25,000 and inflation remains at a modest 6% for the next thirty years, here is how much your income will have to grow just to stay even (to maintain your effective buying power).

How Inflation Erodes Your Effective Buying Power Your Need For Annual Income (Assuming a steady 6% inflation rate)				
Year 1	**Year 5**	**Year 10**	**Year 20**	**Year 30**
$25,000	$33,455	$44,771	$80,178	$143,587

With taxes and inflation as your financial enemies, how can you win? Every married couple looks for an answer to that question. The answer is clear, but putting it into operation is not simple. The only way to get ahead of the game (and to stay ahead of it) is to have a personal investment program that takes advantage of **compounding** and **leveraging** at the same time.

What Is Leveraging?
How Can It Work For You?

In Chapter Six, you learned about compounding (how money makes money, and the money that money makes, makes more money). Smart investors know that compounding produces even greater results when combined with the principle of leveraging.

A Greek mathematician by the name of Archimedes first described the principle of leveraging. Simply stated, he proved that a small force applied over a large distance could lift very large objects. "Give me a place to stand," he said, "and I will move the earth."

Just as a small force can lift large objects, small amounts of money can generate large profits, once you learn the trick.

Most of you will begin your investment program with small amounts of money. The trick is to use your small amount of money to unlock the door to someone else's large amount of investment money. Once you have a large amount of money and put it to work, then the magic of compounding can produce dramatic results. Here are several examples of how leveraging works in the world of investing.

Borrowing as Leveraging

The most traditional use of leveraging (opening the door to other people's money) is through borrowing. Here are two examples.

Example No. 1: You purchase your home with only a 10% down payment and the bank or mortgage company pays for the other 90% of the purchase price. As the years go by, the value of the home increases. But, the bank doesn't benefit from that increased value—you do. When you sell your home, its increased value (capital gain) is your profit. In addition, the interest portion of your monthly mortgage payments is income tax deductible, thus helping lower your annual tax bill.

Example No. 2: You use $5,000 of your savings to purchase common stocks through a stock broker. The value goes up to $15,000. You don't wish to sell, but you would like to invest more money in some additional stocks. You borrow against the value of your stocks or bonds to buy the additional stocks or bonds. In this way, you are able to own 50% to 75% more assets and your potential for profiting from your stock or bond investments is greatly increased.

[By the way, this is an example of leveraging that presents much greater risk than the first example. Nevertheless, this is a valid use of the leveraging concept, and knowledgeable investors use it often.]

Pooling as Leveraging

Another way to leverage is to pool your money with other people's money to secure benefits that might not be available to you as an individual with a small amount of money to invest.

Example No. 3: You use $5,000 of your savings to buy shares in a mutual fund that has $4 billion invested in stocks and bonds. This allows you to participate in a diversified and balanced investment portfolio with outstanding management—an advantage that is unavailable when you buy stocks and bonds as an individual investor. As a result of excellent performance, your mutual fund shares average a 24% annual return, compounded daily, during the next five years. During this same five year period, the stock market only grows by an average of 14% annually. As a result of pooling your investment funds with other investors in the mutual fund, you realize a much greater financial gain.

[Be sure to review the display on the next page about mutual funds.]

Example No. 4: You use $10,000 of your savings to invest in a real estate purchase that costs $250,000. You become a "limited partner." Others agree to do the same thing. They all pool their funds and become limited partners with you. There may be one "general partner" who has arranged the real estate purchase and is knowledgeable about the investment details of the real estate project. The general partner may or may not participate financially (invest money) in the project (but he will share in the profits and losses of the partnership). Together with the other limited partners, you become bankers by lending to each other, but you are also owners who stand to profit. Each year the value of the real estate goes up. When it sells, you share in the increased value (capital gain) to the extent that you shared in the ownership.

[Limited partnership investments generally have annual tax consequences, and these consequences should be thoroughly understood before making such an investment. In recent years, the tax laws have removed many tax benefits that were previously associated with limited partnership investments. Also, all limited partnerships are not of equal quality. The long-term economic benefits offered by a limited partnership should be substantial, and the quality of the investment should be very high before you decide to invest in one.]

253

What Are Mutual Funds?

Mutual funds are large holdings of stocks, bonds, real estate, and other investments that are purchased by many individual investors who pool their resources. Many types of mutual funds exist, and they all have different investment objectives. Mutual funds also differ in their degree of success in meeting their objectives. The reasons most investors give for investing in mutual funds are:

1. Investors can participate by investing small amounts of money.

2. Those who want to avoid paying sales commissions can do so by buying no-load mutual funds.

3. All mutual funds provide professional management and excellent record keeping services.

4. Diversification is available, thus allowing the small investor to keep from "putting all his eggs in one basket."

5. You can convert your shares into cash quickly, which means your investments are relatively liquid.

If you would like more information about mutual funds, contact the Investment Company Institute, 1600 M Street, N.W., Washington D.C. 20036 (202-293-7700). For more information about no-load mutual funds (mutual funds you can purchase without paying sales commissions) contact the Mutual Fund Education Alliance, 1900 Erie, Suite 120, Kansas City, MO 64116 (816) 471-1454.

Tax Shelters as Leveraging

When you can shelter your investments from taxation, you are also leveraging. The pool of funds you access with this form of leveraging is Uncle Sam's money. Tax sheltering can take several forms, including tax deductions, tax credits and tax deferrals. Limited partnership investments once provided the most advantageous form of tax sheltering, providing tax deductions equal to one, two, or even three times the amount originally invested. Current tax laws have largely eliminated these benefits. Now, tax deductible, tax deferred retirement plans are the dominant form of tax sheltering. Following are two examples of retirement plans that provide leveraging through sheltering your investments from taxation:

Example No. 5: In the first year of marriage, you establish an Individual Retirement Account in the name of each spouse. You put $1,125 in each account for a total of $2,250. This entire amount is income tax deductible, thus lowering your income taxes for that year. In addition, you earn 15% through investing your IRA funds in a mutual fund during that first year. The 15% increase in value is not taxable until you withdraw it at retirement. Therefore, the entire 15% increase is available to earn more money for you in future years. You continue to add more funds to your IRA accounts each year, thus saving on income taxes each year and allowing your investments to grow within your IRA without taxation.

Example No. 6: Your employer offers you an opportunity to participate in a 401(k) plan. Your contribution (which can not exceed a specified limit as determined by an indexing formula established by law) is matched by your employer up to 50% of the salary you defer. This means your actual contribution for the year will be 50% greater than what you set aside from your own salary. In addition, as money accumulates within the 401(k) account, it is free of current taxation. The ability to leverage your 401(k) savings to access matching contributions from your employer (and Uncle Sam's tax money) allows compounding to work much harder for you.

These are only two examples of how retirement plans use tax sheltering as leverage. See the summary of available tax deductible, tax deferred retirement plans on the next page.

There is another tax shelter available to every investor that should be mentioned now. I'm talking about the deferred tax on an investment's appreciation (increased value) which is also known as "capital gain." Simply stated, you don't pay any tax on the increased value of any investment until you actually sell the investment and realize your profit as cash. This tax shelter is one way our tax laws encourage ordinary citizens to invest, and I'm sure you'll benefit from this shelter many times in the years to come.

Note carefully that in each of the six examples above, investors were able to increase the value of their own investment cash by accessing more cash through borrowing, pooling or tax sheltering. Many investments will allow you to leverage by using all three of these techniques together. The point to remember is that through leveraging, it is possible to realize investment gains that are unavailable to an individual with only a small amount of money to invest. Also notice that in each example, the value of the investment went up. That is what all investors want, but that is not the way it always turns out.

An Overview of Tax Deductible, Tax Deferred Retirement Programs

Retirement is probably the last thing on your mind. However, as you consider your investment options, you should not overlook the enormous investment advantages that are available through tax deductible, tax deferred retirement programs. You may even wish to use more than one type of plan to help leverage your investment dollars. The following overview is designed to point to a few of those programs that deserve further study. This list is not comprehensive.

Individual Retirement Accounts (IRAs): Any married couple can establish and maintain IRAs. Deductions for your annual contributions are allowed within limits set by law. In addition, income taxes on the growth in value and reinvested earnings in these accounts are deferred until you make withdrawals. Be sure to become familiar with all current tax rules and regulations governing IRAs.

Keogh Plans: Self-employed individuals establish these plans. Keogh Plans are similar to IRAs except they offer more liberal income tax deductions for annual contributions.

SEP Plans: SEP stands for Simplified Employee Pension Plan. Some employers offer these plans, which allow the employer to make contributions directly to the employees' own Individual Retirement Accounts (IRA). In that case, if you should leave your employer, your retirement funds go right along with you.

401(k) Salary-Deferral Plans: When offered by an employer, these plans allow you to defer a portion of your compensation to the plan. The income tax is deferred on the amount directed by you to the plan and on any matching contribution by your employer. The income taxes on any earnings on the plan are also deferred until withdrawal.

403(b) Salary-Deferral Plans: These are similar to 401(k) plans. The difference is that they are for employees of non-profit, tax exempt employers. If you work for an educational institution, a hospital, a religious organization or any other organization that has charitable foundation status with the IRS, you may discover that your employer offers this benefit.

Corporate Pension and Profit Sharings Plans: There are several different kinds of pension and profit sharing plans that are offered by employers. Always study these plans carefully to make sure they are tax exempt by the Internal Revenue Service. Learn all you can about the type of plan offered. However, before you decide to use one of these plans as a means of leveraging your investment funds, be sure you plan to remain with your employer long enough to qualify for the right to take 100% of your pension and profit sharing benefits with you if you should leave. This is called "vesting." If you are not "vested," you may lose all or a major part of the funds that have been set aside in a pension and profit sharing plan.

How Do Investments Go Up In Value?

The main goal of investing is to end up far ahead of where you started financially. This means that your investments must grow faster than inflation, pay all required taxes and associated costs and still return a profit. Therefore, it is important to know how this can happen.

There are two ways your investments can go up in value: as current income and as appreciation. Current income may be received as interest, dividends or rent. Appreciation is received only when you find a buyer who is willing to purchase your investment for more than you paid for it. Let's look at some examples.

Income as Dividends, Interest and Rent

Some investments pay dividends, interest, or rent. All three are a form of current investment income.

Dividends are income paid out to those who hold stock in a successfully operating company. Owning stock in a company is a way of owning a small piece of it.

Public companies normally pay dividends directly to the investor or stockholder every three months. When an investment is doing well, the dividends will normally increase over time. On the contrary, when profits go down, a company reduces dividends. Dividends may be stopped entirely during a period of low profits and losses. Dividends paid to an investor are taxable as income in the year they are received.

[Note: Dividends you receive from an insurance company as a result of owning one of their insurance policies are not taxable income when they represent a refund for overpayment of insurance premiums.]

Sometimes businesses, governments, government agencies and not-for-profit institutions borrow money from investors. The traditional way for these entities to borrow money is to issue bonds. If you buy these bonds, you don't own a piece of the entity that issued the bonds, but you do earn interest from the loan you made to the issuer of the bonds.

The interest is generally (but not always) a fixed percentage of the original purchase price of the bonds. Interest on bonds is usually paid semi-annually. Investors often purchase bonds because they offer a dependable income at interest rates higher than can be secured through savings accounts or certificates of deposit. If you own a bond that pays a fixed interest of 8%, then it becomes more valuable if interest rates in the overall economy are at or fall below 8%. However, if interest rates in the overall economy rise above 8%, the value of your bonds will drop. Then, too, if the issuer of the bonds goes broke or is unable to pay the interest for other reasons, your bonds can become worth less than the paper on which they're printed. Remember, when buying bonds to make a profit, the bonds must provide a way to beat inflation, pay all required taxes and the cost of buying and selling them and still allow you to come out ahead financially. This is not as easy as it sounds, but this is the idea behind it.

When investors own real estate, they will often receive current income as rent. This is called "income producing" real estate.

When rent goes up, current income goes up, too. However, you must always subtract both management and maintenance costs from rent to measure its real value as current income.

When investors talk about current income from their investments, the two terms commonly used are "yield" and "return."

Very simply, **yield** is income expressed in percentages. For example, if you own stock that you purchased for $20 a share and you receive $1 a year in dividends, then your current income yield from that stock is 5% ($1 divided by $20 equals 5%). If you purchased stock for $40 and you receive $1 a year in dividends, then your current income yield is 2-1/2% ($1 divided by $40 equals 2-1/2%). If you own real estate that you purchased for $100,000 and your net rental income is $6,000 a year, then your current income yield is 6% ($6,000 divided by $100,000 equals 6%.)

[This last example assumes that your net cost is $100,000. You must always take into account your expenses on rental property to figure yield.]

Yield does not change with market swings. It is always based on investment return as a percentage of your original cost.

Return is current income expressed in dollars instead of percentages. Using the two examples above, the return on the stock would be $1 dollar a year. The return on the real estate would be $6,000 a year.

Future Income Through Appreciation

Some investments offer the possibility of appreciation. Investments that provide appreciation are called "growth investments" or "capital gain investments." Frequently, those investments with a high potential for appreciation provide little or no current income.

Capital gains represent the increased value of an investment over the original purchase price.

For example, if you buy one share of stock at the price of $10 and twelve months later it is worth $15, the capital gain is $5 (assuming you sell the stock at that time). If you hold the stock another eight months and it is then worth $20, the capital gain is $10 (assuming you sell the stock).

When an investment's value increases as capital gain, the gain in value is not taxable until a sale actually takes place. This means that your investment can continue to grow at a faster rate than it would if each year taxes reduced the gain. For example, if you purchase stock for $20 a share and in one year it becomes worth $30 a share, you don't owe any taxes unless you sell it. Assuming you don't sell, your stock might continue to grow and by the end of one more year be worth $45 a share. Even then, your profits would not be decreased by taxes unless you sold the stock. When you buy stocks (or bonds, or mutual funds, or limited partnerships or many other investments) and they increase in value, you only pay income taxes on the gain (capital gain taxes) when you sell them. Real estate sales often have special rules, however. For example, when you sell your home (assuming it is your principal residence), the capital gain tax may be deferred when you purchase another home of equal or greater value within a period of two years.

As you continue your education about capital gains, a term you should be familiar with is "equity." Equity is your value in an investment after subtracting any money you presently owe on it.

If you buy a home for $100,000 using $90,000 of borrowed money, your equity in your home is $10,000. If the home increases in value to $120,000, your equity is $30,000. Your equity in something you own can also increase because you have paid on the debt long enough to decrease your remaining liability. The important point to keep in mind is that "equity" is not the same thing as "capital gain."

Investors often express an investment's appreciation as "appreciation yield." This means they talk about it in terms of percentages, not dollars. An example is a stock that appreciated from $10 a share to $12 a share in one year. That stock's appreciation yield would be 20% ($2 of increased value divided by the original purchase price of $10 equals 20%).

Combining Appreciation and Current Income for Total Return

Which investments you choose for your marriage may be influenced to a large extent by whether you are looking for income (dividends or interest or rent) or capital appreciation as a major objective.

But, most investors combine the current income of an investment and its potential capital appreciation into a concept called "total return." The **total return** on an investment is simply the total of the current income *and* the capital appreciation.

Total return is usually expressed in percentages or yield. Total return expressed as yield is the sum you get by adding *current income yield to appreciation yield*. So, for example, if you own stock that pays a dividend equal to a 5% current income yield and that stock also has appreciation of 7% in the last year, then the total return (expressed as yield) is 12% for the year.

When investors look at potential total return, they always consider the effect of taxes. Once taxes are subtracted from total return, what you have left is *after-tax return*. An investment's after-tax return is a much more accurate measure of how valuable it really is. Even after taxes have been subtracted, the true measure of an investment's return is seen only when all costs associated with the investment *and* inflation have also been subtracted.

Let's look at an example to see how one investment by a young married couple combines leveraging and compounding. In this example, I'll also show how taxes, costs, and inflation affect the investment's total return.

The Story of Paul and Susan

*During their first year of marriage, **Paul and Susan** were able to save $15,000 to start their marriage investment program. They knew that the $850 they spent on rent each month was doing little more than providing a roof over their heads, so they had given serious thought to buying a house as their first investment.*

After searching for several weeks, they purchased a duplex for $195,000 in a nice neighborhood near an elementary school. They had to stretch to come up with the additional money for the down payment and closing costs, but they accomplished this by selling their new car and buying a reliable used one. This also lowered their annual car insurance expense. Although their monthly mortgage payment was $1,700 per month, they reasoned that they could live in one of the apartments and rent out the other one. The rental income would provide $750 each month in cash. They knew that the area was growing, so the value of their duplex could be expected to increase (appreciate). In addition, they were able to deduct the interest portion of their mortgage payments and all rental expenses from their gross income and thereby lower their income tax bill.

After two years of living in the duplex, they sold it for $268,000. When they added their capital gain to their tax savings and rental income, they had a total net return of $41,450. The actual computation to determine their total return required two pages of complicated calculations. However, a few of the significant items from that calculation are in the Table below.

Item 1	Gross Rental Income	$18,000
Item 2	Cash Payments (including mortgage payments for the period)	($44,750)
Item 3	Tax Savings at 28%	$9,200
Item 4	Net Cash Proceeds on Sale	$78,000
Item 5	Tax on Capital Gain at 28%	($19,000)
Item 6	Total Return	$41,450

A Closer Look at Paul and Susan's Investment

Paul and Susan started their investment program with $15,000 and in two years, they realized a profit (net total return) of $41,450 or an annual yield of 10.6% on a $195,000 investment. They did this by **leveraging** (using their limited resources to get an additional $180,000 from the mortgage company to buy the duplex). Yet, only Paul and Susan were entitled to the profits; the mortgage company received none of it.

Compounding was also working for Paul and Susan. Because real estate values were steadily going up, the paper gain on their original investment was compounding daily. Of course, the value of this compounding didn't come to them as cash until they sold their duplex. That's the bad news. The good news is that the magic of compounding affected both their original $15,000 investment and the $180,000 they borrowed from the bank. Both their little pool of money and the bank's larger pool were gaining value at compounded rates solely for Paul and Susan.

While this example shows how Paul and Susan gained from leveraging and compounding, this was a rather complex investment. Let's take it apart and see how complex it really was.

Inflation: At a modest inflation rate of 4%, Paul and Susan needed to make 6% each year on their original $15,000 just to keep even with inflation, and *preserve their effective buying power.* This is because state and federal income taxes on their 6% gain would have reduced their gain to 4%, and inflation would have taken away the rest of their gain. Our couple wanted to beat inflation. Real estate offered them a way to (1) *preserve* their buying power and (2) *increase* their buying power. An invest-ment that promises these two benefits is said to be a "hedge against inflation." When an investment delivers on this promise it is said to "outperform infla-tion." By investing in the duplex, their effective buying power over a two year period went from $15,000 to $41,450.

Risk: This young couple took several risks. Their first risk was finding a renter. Without renters, they would have faced a cash flow crunch because the full burden of the mortgage pay-ment would have fallen on their finan-cial shoulders. If they failed to make the mortgage payments, the bank could have foreclosed (reclaimed the prop-erty). If the bank had foreclosed, they would have sold the house as quickly as possible. Because real estate isn't highly liquid (not easy to turn into cash), the property might have sold for less than the loan balance. In that case, Paul and Susan would have been re-sponsible for paying off the loan bal-ance (another risk). They also were entering a field of investing in which they had no experience. The laws governing rentals and the applicable tax laws were all new to them. A major change in these laws, such as the pas-sage of strict rent-control laws, could have hurt them. Another risk was the housing demand. If the demand for housing had dropped during the two years they owned the property, they might have been required to sell for a much lower price.

Return: Both current income (rent) and future income (capital gain) were important to this couple. The rent was absolutley required to make the monthly mortgage payments. The capital gain (appreciation) was necessary to provide a profit when the duplex sold. They knew from the outset that they had to have both, so total return was an important objective. Current income without capital gain would have made this a poor investment for Paul and Susan.

Investment Costs: Because this investment was a rental, there were a variety of out-of-pocket expenses that Paul and Susan had to absorb during the two years they owned the property. These included property taxes; insurance premiums; and utility bills, including those for gas, electricity, water, sewer and garbage. There were also routine maintenance costs, such as painting, plumbing repairs and the replacement of a water heater. A portion of these costs were income tax deductible, but that didn't allow Paul and Susan to recapture the full costs of these expenses. They also had to pay a realtor 6% of the selling price ($16,080). (All of these costs were included in the calculation of total return.)

Taxes: Taxes were a very important consideration for our young couple. In this case income tax deductions allowed for maintenance and repairs and deductions for interest paid on the mortgage were *tax advantages* that helped increase profits. Without these tax advantages, Paul and Susan could not have

afforded this investment. However, our couple now faces *tax costs* on their appreciation (capital gain) of $19,000. If they turn their profit over in a home of equal or greater value within 24 months after the property is sold, they can defer a portion of this tax. This means they can use some of Uncle Sam's money a little longer to try to increase their net worth (another tax advantage).

Ease of Management: Managing this investment required attention nearly every day. In other words, it wasn't easy to manage. Paul and Susan had to be available to their renters at all times. They had to collect rents, make repairs, supervise the renter's behavior (within the limits of the rental contract), file special tax returns, etc. Every investment requires management, but some investments are harder to manage than others. This one was especially challenging.

While Paul and Susan had to consider all of these factors, their investment profit was very impressive. However, things don't always work out this way. While investments can go up, they can also go down. Because any investment can drop in value, let's look briefly at the primary reasons young couples make poor investment decisions.

The Down Side Of Investing—Why Investors Lose

When investments go down in value, you stand a good chance of losing some or even all of your invested savings. Both the current income and the market value of an investment can go down, and sometimes both happen at the same time. If you don't sell your investment at the right time, and if a downtrend is long and deep, you may have to sell and take a loss.

When you sell your investments at a loss, it is called a "capital loss." Because all real investing includes an element of risk, it is always possible to lose money through investing.

This is why you must never use your emergency fund for investing. Investment savings should be money that can be lost without threatening your family security and peace of mind. Of course, no one intentionally tries to lose money through investing, but it does happen and it could happen to you.

One of the most common reasons investors lose is because they take on too much risk.

"Risk" is defined as the chance or possibility of loss, of getting hurt. The higher the risk, the greater chance that you will lose some of your investment capital (your invested savings). Sometimes risk is so high that you can lose everything. For example, if you buy into an exploratory oil well and no oil is found, your investment is a total loss. But with most investments total loss isn't as likely to happen as losing 20 or 30 percent of your investment capital.

However, if you are prepared to accept greater risks, then you have a chance of receiving a higher return. Paul and Susan accepted a fairly high risk and realized a very high return. Without the promise of high return, it isn't likely that Paul and Susan would have bought that duplex.

The Investment Risk Pyramid on Page 265 shows many types of investments and their relative risk. Note that as you go up the pyramid, you increase your potential return through appreciation. As you come down the pyramid, you increase your potential return through current income.

Let's take a closer look at the idea of risk, by comparing investment risk with gambling. Those who approach investing as gamblers are usually big losers. A gambler is always after a quick profit; an investor knows and understands that the investment process takes time. A gambler has no way of knowing what outcome to expect. A gambler's risk is 100%. An investor, on the other hand, studies each investment before buying. Studying an investment may include seeking the advice of highly regarded professionals or digging out information entirely on your own. Either way, studying an investment should lower your risk and help you choose investments that have a much better chance of producing a profit.

Those who don't study their investments before making decisions are called "lambs." A lamb is also someone who makes investment decisions based on advice from promoters, con artists and uninformed sellers who work on commission and may not have the investor's best interests at heart. These people skin the lamb and line their pockets with the lamb's money. Someone who invests money based on rumors, tips, so-called "trends," and advice offered by equally unknowing investors is also a lamb. Together these lambs form a flock led to financial slaughter. You could be one of those lambs unless you use all of your modern brain intelligence to learn everything possible about the investments you make *before you make them.*

One other investing weakness that increases risk and creates big losers is laziness.

Sometimes the information is available to make one a winner at investing, but the drive to dig it out is missing. You have no sure protection from this weakness, but you must not give in to it. The consequences of laziness are the same as remaining ignorant.

One safeguard against laziness and ignorance is to know the right questions to ask when facing any investment decision. I have devoted a large part of this chapter to presenting a list of questions that you should ask (and answer) about every investment before you make it. I urge you to adopt these questions as a thinking discipline for your marriage partnership. Answering these questions won't guarantee success with your investments, but answering them will help you avoid the pain and agony of making careless decisions.

INVESTMENTS

An Investment Pyramid

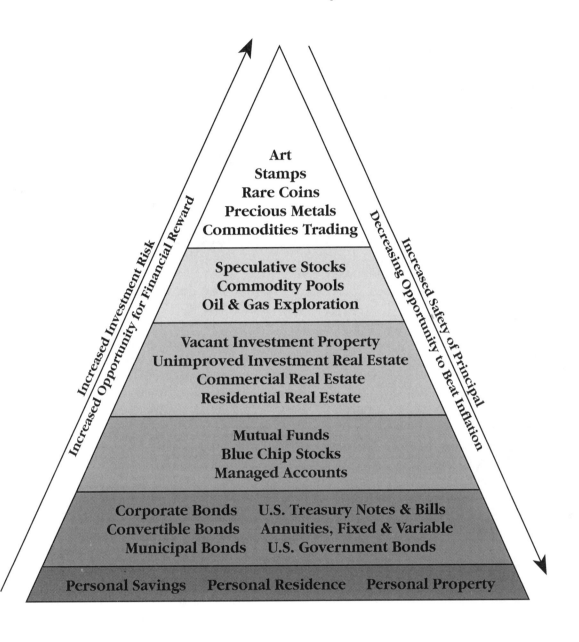

Art
Stamps
Rare Coins
Precious Metals
Commodities Trading

Speculative Stocks
Commodity Pools
Oil & Gas Exploration

Vacant Investment Property
Unimproved Investment Real Estate
Commercial Real Estate
Residential Real Estate

Mutual Funds
Blue Chip Stocks
Managed Accounts

Corporate Bonds   **U.S. Treasury Notes & Bills**
Convertible Bonds   **Annuities, Fixed & Variable**
Municipal Bonds   **U.S. Government Bonds**

Personal Savings   **Personal Residence**   **Personal Property**

Increased Investment Risk
Increased Opportunity for Financial Reward

Increased Safety of Principal
Decreasing Opportunity to Beat Inflation

265

What Qualifies As An Investment?

Before going any further, let's answer the question: What qualifies as an investment? Since the basic goal of investing is to make a profit after subtracting taxes, inflation, and investment costs, then any purchase capable of providing this result qualifies. Typical investments that offer such profits include stocks, bonds, real estate, business ownership, mutual funds, precious metals, gemstones, commodities, and collectibles such as art, antiques, stamps, coins, paintings, etc. Traditionally, all investments have been placed in only six categories. They are:

Cash and cash equivalents, such as money-market funds, checking accounts, passbook savings accounts and short-term certificates of deposit.

Fixed income vehicles, including tax exempt bonds, corporate bonds and long-term certificates of deposit.

Equities, including both domestic and international stocks.

Real estate, including your principal residence, income properties, raw land and real estate investment trusts.

Natural resources, including oil and gas.

Tangibles, such as gold and silver.

It is not within the scope of this book to give you even an overview of these investment modes. I offer several suggested resources at the end of this chapter to help you begin to understand and appreciate the hundreds of investment opportunities that exist in today's marketplace.

However, as you explore your investment opportunities, keep these principles in mind:

First, choose your investments very carefully. The promise of profit should never be taken at face value.

The only way to be certain your investments can be profitable is to put pencil to paper and do the required calculations. If you need help with this, seek professional advice. Never make your investment decisions without complete and accurate information about the investment itself and the potential net profit to be gained. After investigating, if you still feel uneasy, don't buy the investment.

Second, especially at this stage of your life, pick investments for the long term. Don't act like a Neanderthal couple and go for the big play, the grand slam home run. You're building an investment foundation. Start with putting a roof over your head if at all possible. Your home may be one of your very best investments. Then build your investments very conservatively.

Third, diversify. Don't put all your eggs in one basket. Once you buy a home, put your next investment savings dollars into a good mutual fund that will help you spread your risk by investing in a variety of assets that promise good returns based on current market conditions. Always build your investment holdings by allocating or spreading your investment risk, so you can profit from a good economy as well as a weak one.

Fourth, always leave something on the table. Don't feel you have to ride your investments to the very top of an up trend and get every last dollar. That's greedy. You'll be doing great if you can anticipate the trends and move in and out of investment markets before they top out and head down again.

Fifth, pay attention to your investments. Since every investment must be managed, be prepared to stay aware of all the things that are likely to affect your investments. When investment climates change, be prepared to sell.

Selling may also be appropriate when you see that you are too heavily invested in one type of asset or when you are no longer willing to take certain risks or carry the burden of managing certain investments.

Sixth, keep firmly in mind that there is no one "right" investment plan for every married couple. What is right for your marriage partnership may be wrong for another couple. But you must have a clear cut strategy for investing that helps you decide what to buy and what not to buy. That is why you will benefit in a big way from filtering all of your investment decisions through the ten questions presented in the next section of this chapter.

Seventh, remember that investing is not an end in itself. Investing is

simply a way of helping you make dreams come true in marriage. If you do it well, your savings will become the seeds for an investment harvest that will provide you with financial independence.

All investment decisions that you make as a team will strengthen your marriage partnership. Even if you make some mistakes, if you make them together and have used the decision-making model that follows, you will develop a stronger bond within your marriage.

267

Financial Strategies for Harmonizing with Financial Law No. 5

As you go about the business of making investment decisions, you should carefully answer each of the ten questions that follow. These questions and your answers to them should help you become very successful at team investing. If you don't think you need to examine each investment decision by answering these questions *before you buy,* then I suggest you forget about investing entirely. Unless you apply the disciplined decision-making process I give to you now, you may as well buy lottery tickets or go to Las Vegas or visit the local race track to try to get ahead financially. Are you serious about making dreams come true in your marriage? Are you willing to learn everything you can about your investment choices and opportunities? Are you willing to take time to develop a team approach to investing with your marriage partner? If you say "Yes," then answering these ten questions will help you make sound investment decisions and help you become a winner at the business of investing for profit.

By the way, it is highly likely that at least one of you will not have a talent for or interest in investing. But, you should not use that as an excuse for washing your hands of full responsibility for investment decisions in your marriage. If you walk away from sharing in the investment decision making process, you will still pay a price for poor decisions.

So accept the idea right now that being a full partner in marriage means reaching beyond your comfort zone and participating in every element of financial life.

Question No. 1
Is This A Decision We Are Making On Our Own, And Is It One We Are Making Together?

One of the three most often quoted rules of investing is: "The investing crowd is usually wrong." Following the crowd is never wise when it comes to making investment decisions. Above all, you must be sure that you have investigated each investment carefully and that you feel completely satisfied that this investment is something you both want to do.

I hope you will soon establish an investment plan with specific investment objectives, and that each investment decision will fit into its appropriate place within that plan.

If you have not done this, or don't feel capable of doing it alone, then it is wise to seek the guidance and counsel of a highly qualified professional advisor. Later in this chapter, you'll learn who your financial advisors are and what role each of them plays. You will discover in this discussion that there is a financial planning profession and those who practice this profession may be the best qualified to help you develop your investment plan. Their planning services will help you answer the following questions:

1. How important is investment liquidity? Are you ready to tie up some of your investment savings for a long period of time, or do you need most of your cash available for emergencies?

2. How important is safety of principal? If the market for your investment or the entire economy started to go into a deep economic downturn, how important would it be for you to sell your investment for about the price you paid for it?

3. How important is current income? Are you looking for cash returns from your investment this year?

4. How important is future income through appreciation (capital gain)? Are you more interested in keeping ahead of inflation and preserving your effective buying power than receiving immediate cash returns?

5. How important is it for you to get all the relief possible from the tax advantages of certain investments and what tax relief is available?

6. Are you prepared to borrow money to buy investments? What is your capacity to do this? Does borrowing make sense at this time in your life?

7. Is ease of management important? Are you willing to buy investments that require constant attention, or is your life arranged in a way that makes it hard for you to watch over your investments on a day-to-day basis?

8. How important is diversification at this time? Is this the time to make a major investment purchase like buying a home, or should you be spreading your risk?

9. What is your tolerance for risk, both financially and psychologically?

10. Based on assumptions for inflation for the next five year period, what is an appropriate total investment return to aim for if you are going to beat inflation?

11. Do you have any current investments that should be sold and reinvested for a higher return?

12. What annual amount of cash can you set aside from your current income(s) to devote to your investment program?

It is perfectly acceptable to buy guidance and counsel from professionals to help you answer these questions and to help you choose your investments—if you can afford it. Often, you will be doing this indirectly, anyway. For example, when you purchase an investment in a mutual fund, you buy advice. Professional advice costs money, so be prepared to ask in advance about what costs you will face and how they will be billed to you. Professional fees can be charged for developing an investment plan, helping you find your investments and for managing your investments. Sometimes, the fees are carefully hidden or given names that make them sound like something harmless, so ask questions until you are certain you know the full costs you will pay.

Always remember, no matter what you pay for advice, *you* should accept full responsibility for selecting and managing your investments. The motives of all the investment advisors of this world, when added together, won't begin to match *your* motivation to manage *your* investments successfully.

No one will ever care about your investment success as much as the two of you. In addition, no investment advisors can guarantee that their investment advice will produce a profit. This is true even if they have a highly successful track record. This means that while paying for advice, you must continue your education about investments. Accept the idea that your advisors are only hired help. Your marital partnership is where the investment decision-making buck stops.

Question No. 2
Do We Know How This
Investment Works?

Do you completely understand how this investment can make money for you? Of course, you're almost certainly counting on the value of the investment to go up. You also may count on current income. What will make this happen? Do you expect that most of your profit will be from current income? Or will it be capital gain that carries the heaviest responsibility for profit? Are you depending on both to happen in order to come out ahead?

Sometimes the increase in an investment's value is tied to a series of complex events. If any investment is dependent on a series of events outside your control, be sure you know what those events are.

Study the possibility of each event taking place. Don't kid yourself about what you can and can't count on. The more you know about these events, the better. Remember the old saying, "A chain is only as strong as its weakest link?" If there are many events in the chain, this only weakens your chances of success.

Be sure that one of the events needed to produce your profit is not that someone less informed than you will buy your investment at a higher price than you paid for it. Counting on someone else's ignorance to bail you out of a bad investment is itself a gamble. It is far better to understand the driving forces that normally affect marketability. Then, when you sell your investment, you know why an informed buyer might reasonably be expected to buy. There are several factors that determine marketability. Let's examine five of them.

Demand. If there are many buyers, the numbers will help assure that you can easily sell your investment. A large number of buyers means more demand. Therefore, you should try to understand the forces and conditions that would create large numbers of willing buyers.

Supply. It is also important to be sure that a monopoly or a few individuals or groups aren't controlling the market. A monopoly can control supply. Too much or too little supply will definitely change the marketability of your investment.

Fads. There are times when an investment is a fad, and many buyers invest in it for only a short time. Here, future marketability is in question because your investment might become unpopular. Remember the advice you were given about following the investment crowd?

Trends. A trend is different from a fad in this way: a trend is a new direction in the market that sets the tone for a period of many months or even a year or two. For example, a recession is a trend—a downtrend. The challenge is to spot a trend early and to take advantage of the investment opportunities it offers.

Affordability. When you sell, your investment must have a price tag that is within reach of those who are buying it. For example, lots of people want to buy houses, but can they afford the one you own? Can they afford your home after it increases in value over the next several years? Of course, you can't control the economic climate at the time you decide to sell your investment. Nevertheless, you haven't made a sound investment decision unless you have carefully considered whether or not your investment will be affordable in the future.

Just remember, there are many factors that can make buying your investment attractive or unattractive at a future time. Study those factors carefully as part of learning how your investment will actually work to provide your profit. If market conditions start to change dramatically, consider selling (or buying). But, don't count on the ignorance of others to bail you out.

Question No. 3
Are We Buying This Investment At The Best Possible Price?

All investments are priced differently. The first thing to understand is how the price is established for your investment. Then, do some comparative shopping in order to know that you are buying at the lowest current price. For example, stock prices are set daily by the forces in the stock market. You can check daily stock prices by purchasing a local newspaper and reviewing the stock price listings in the business section. Although you can't negotiate the price of a stock, you can purchase some stocks and bonds at a much lower cost by using a discount brokerage firm. Lower brokerage fees help keep your overall costs down. But, comparing brokerage fees is only one way to keep the purchase price of a stock low. Your challenge is to thoroughly understand *all* of the ways available to keep the purchase price of each investment you make as low as possible.

The most important concept to keep in mind when pricing an investment is "fair market value." The fair market value of any investment is usually considered to be what a willing buyer would pay to a willing seller, both being fully informed, and neither being under any pressure to act.

If you know the fair market value of a home, for example, you can then compare that value to the current price. If you can purchase a home for less than the fair market value, you may be on to an investment that is priced to your advantage. Any investment that can be purchased at less than fair market value is worth a second look. However, don't overlook other factors that may be influencing price.

The second most-often quoted rule of investing is, "Buy low and sell high." Everyone understands the importance of selling for the highest possible price. Too often, however, investors overlook the importance of buying low. Don't make this mistake. Shopping for the lowest price is an absolute must for careful investors. Otherwise, you can pay too much going in and this alone could change the profitability of your investment.

Question No. 4
What Are The Tax Advantages Of This Investment?

Every financial move has tax consequences. However, some financial moves have *tax advantages*. This means that current tax laws provide favorable tax benefits to investors that can increase the profitability of an investment. For example, an owner-occupied house has a double tax advantage as an investment. The interest you pay on the mortgage is tax deductible, so you pay a lower annual income tax. In addition, the capital gain or increased value of your home is protected from taxation until you actually sell it. Even then, you can turn your profit over in a new home and continue to defer the tax (as long as you do this within two years with a home costing as much or more than the adjusted selling price of your previous residence). Your personal residence can be one of your very best investments because of these tax advantages.

The term "tax advantaged," when applied to investments, can mean many things. It might mean that the current income is not taxed. An example would be tax-exempt bonds which provide an income free of federal income taxes. It might mean that you will be allowed certain tax deductions or credits that can be used to help lower your income taxes. An example would be certain limited partnership investments that provide special income tax credits in order to motivate investors to provide capital to select industries such as low-income housing. It could mean that growth in value (capital gain) and interest or dividends can build up within your investment, free of taxes until you retire and start to receive the income. This is called "tax deferral." Most pension and profit sharing programs, including Individual Retirement Accounts, Keogh H.R.10 programs, and 401(k) programs offer this benefit.

Just be sure you know what "tax advantaged" means when you make an investment. Also be sure you know that the tax advantages someone offers you are legal. Some tax advantages are legal but not available to all investors. Be sure you know when a tax advantage applies to you.

Because this subject of tax advantages can be complicated, I encourage you to seek the help of competent, professional tax advisors. You could spend a lifetime trying to become an expert on the tax laws. Just when you think you have mastered them, Congress will change them. The objective opinion of a tax expert, one not associated with the investment, will help put your mind at ease about any claims being made by anyone who offers an investment tax advantage.

Question No. 5
What Is Likely To Be The Net Profit Of This Investment, After Subtracting Costs, Taxes And The Impact Of Inflation?

If you are going to invest for real profit, you must take into account the effects of inflation and the cost of taxes on the growth in value of your investment. Do this *before* making your investment decision. This does not mean you have to be a fortune teller. It simply means you must make some educated guesses based on the best available information. Then, after you buy, watch what is happening with your investments to see if your "guesstimates" were right or wrong.

It's really not that hard to make reasonable predictions about inflation trends. **Inflation trends** are easily available and can usually be obtained by reading the local newspaper. Go to the public library and read recent articles on investing and you will pick up even more information about inflation trends. Finally, if you are still not certain, talk to an accountant. A good certified public accountant will usually be able to help you calculate the current rate of inflation and its impact on your potential investment.

Understanding the impact of **taxes** (i.e., the out of pocket cost for taxes) on your projected profits will take more study and *also* may require help from an accountant. For example, some investments, such as limited partnerships, have tax implications throughout their existence—not just when you sell. These tax implications can require complex tax calculations. Above all, be sure you know how your profits will be taxed when the investment is sold. If you haven't felt the sting of taxes beforehand, you will surely feel the sting of taxes when your investment sells!

I've already mentioned the importance of knowing the full **costs** that you'll pay for buying or selling an investment and the costs for management of an investment. These costs will lower your profits. Be sure to consider these costs as you complete your calculations.

After you take into account the impact of costs, taxes and inflation, ask yourself if the potential net profit seems impossibly large. If so, this should be a warning that you may not have investigated deeply enough. Be especially careful if the risks seem low while the profits seem high. A combination of both factors may indicate you are on your way to becoming a "lamb."

Question No. 6
In What Form And When Will We Receive Our Profits?

Timing is important in predicting your potential net profit. How long do you plan to stay with this investment in order to get the profits you expect? You may not know *exactly* how long to hold an investment to make your profit, but you should have some idea. In some investments, you can lose everything if you don't sell by a certain time. Other investments are very long-term, and you will have to hold on to them for years. In either case, you should be able to figure out and put in writing the *estimated holding period* necessary to make your investment produce a profit.

You have already learned that there are two fundamental ways to realize profit from your investments (as current income or capital gain). Ultimately, both income and capital gain must be turned into cash to be of real benefit.

However, there are some investments that produce only "phantom profits." Phantom profits are those anticipated by certain investments that can not become cash. Another term you should be familiar with is "phantom income." Phantom income is potential future tax income created by the current use of tax advantages (deductions and credits). An example would be a limited partnership that provides a $50,000 income tax credit in exchange for a $25,000 investment of your cash. However, when the limited partnership sells, there may be no cash profits. The law says, however, that you made a profit in the form of tax credits and you must now pay income taxes on those benefits. The problem? There is no cash to pay the taxes. Unless you know exactly how your profits will be turned into cash, you are open to investment schemes that may cost you everything. If you take time *before you invest* to predict when these profits should come due and what form they will take, then you have some yardstick by which to measure the success of your investment. The discipline of predicting when and in what form you will receive your profits is fundamental to all successful investing.

Question No. 7
What Is Our Degree Of Risk?

Knowing how much risk you are taking is first a question about what will happen in the future. Of course, no one can actually see into the future, so determining risk is, for the most part, based on looking at past performance and measuring it against present circumstances. Then you can predict an outcome based on trends, facts, and reasonable estimates.

The degree of risk among investments varies greatly. The degree of risk also tends to have a direct impact on the potential profit or loss from an investment. Generally, the higher the risk, the higher the possible reward. However, it is also true that a higher risk can mean a higher chance of loss.

If accepting high risk were the key to investing success, everyone would accept the gambler's risk.

Here are some questions to answer to help you determine the risk associated with *your* investments.

A. Regarding Safety of Principal and Liquidity Risk: If we place our savings with this investment, can we, at the very least, get our money back?

If your principal (the amount of savings you invest) is safe, and if you can easily get your money back when you want it, then you are not taking a big risk. Usually, certificates of deposit, federal savings bonds and Treasury securities are considered low financial risks because your principal is very secure and you know exactly when and how to get it back. If you buy stocks or

274

bonds, a drop in value could cause you to lose some of your principal. Therefore, these investments represent a higher risk. However, when stocks or bonds start to drop in value, there is usually, but not always, a way to quickly sell them and get out of the market before you lose everything. When you buy real estate, however, it may take many months to get your money out, but the property itself will not evaporate and will normally hold its value. (Occasionally, real estate will temporarily lose a portion of its market value in a depressed economy.) When you buy commodities, however, changes in value occur so fast that you may have lost everything before you are even aware you are in trouble. Commodity traders are considered high risk investors, and some experts consider them to be little more than poker table gamblers. Just remember that safety of principal and the ease with which you can get your money back are important considerations in determining your investment risk.

B. Regarding Purchasing Power Risk: Will inflation eat up our profit between the time we purchase this investment and the time we sell it?

If you invest $1,000 in a bond that pays 10% annually, you will end the year with $1,100. But if inflation has grown by 8%, you will only have a 2% profit after taking inflation into account. Instead of making $100, you will actually make only $20. If your bond pays you taxable income, then taxes will eat up as much as one-third of your $100 profit. Your investment could actually represent a loss ($100 minus $30 for taxes, minus the loss of purchasing power equal to $80, equals a loss). Unless an investment offers to reward you with returns that will beat inflation and taxes, it probably is not very risky. Most investors look for opportunities that will offer them a "hedge" or a defense against inflation. If

your investments can't beat inflation and taxes, then the effective buying power of your dollars will continue to evaporate.

C. Regarding Market Risk: What influences are marketplace changes likely to have on this investment?

There are many factors that cause changes in the marketplace. At times, these changes are so widespread that the entire market suffers a decline. Say you buy a valuable home and three years later your company wants to transfer you to another state. You want to sell your home. However, the economy of your entire region is in a slump. Your property is still valuable, but potential buyers are wary in general, so you drop the price by 15% just to bail out. These are the kinds of marketplace dynamics that can cause the value of an investment to plunge. Those investments that are relatively free from such marketplace influences are low risk investments. Government bonds, high-grade corporate bonds, and some securities present a lower risk because they are well protected from these dynamics. However, common stocks and real estate are two examples of investments that must be carefully rated for their possible responses to marketplace changes. Remember, the relative marketplace risk of any investment is always changing. For this reason, you will have to consider marketplace dynamics often when your investment is at risk from these forces.

D. Regarding Interest Rate Risk: What effect will changes in interest rates have on this investment?

Interest rates are always changing. When interest rates go up, your investment can go down in value. For example, if you own a bond that is paying 7% and interest rates for savings go to 8%, your bond won't be as valuable. Therefore, if you buy bonds because you want to concentrate on income as a way to make a profit, and if you believe you aren't at risk, think again. When it's time to sell those bonds, higher interest rates may have made your bonds less valuable, and your profits could disappear. On the other hand, if interest rates on savings have dropped to 6% or less, your bond (that pays 7%) could be quite valuable.

E. Regarding Business Risk: What are the chances that business competition will affect this investment?

Competition is always changing the value of some investments. Let's say you buy stock in a company that makes gasoline-powered engines. Then someone comes along and develops a car that runs on hydrogen extracted from sea water at half the price of gasoline. Suddenly, the earnings potential of your company drops like a rock. Or, say you buy a duplex like Paul and Susan, and shortly thereafter a large apartment complex is built just three blocks away. Suddenly, there is a glut of rental units on the market. That would make your rental less attractive and might lower the resale value of your duplex. The point is that competition can always reduce the expected return from certain investments and that means higher risk.

F. Regarding Leverage Risk: How will borrowing money to buy this investment increase our risk?

If you borrow money to buy an investment, you are taking on a higher risk. This is because an investment loss could mean that you lose your money and some or all of the bank's money. The bank still expects you to pay them, however. Therefore, always consider very carefully how much you will have to borrow to make an investment. If you borrow to buy a house, you make a secured loan, so there is not much chance of losing everything. The house will always be valuable. But if you borrow heavily to buy other kinds of investments, the loan may be unsecured, and any loss in the value of the investment could result in big personal losses for you. When you borrow money to buy an investment, and the investment goes up in value, everyone is happy and you appear to be a financial genius. But when things go the other way, then it's a disaster.

Risk also has an emotional dimension. As a married couple, you both will have different psychological tolerances for risk. Your job is to find a compromise when it is necessary to make sure that you stand together concerning the degree of risk you are willing to take.

Financial partners always honor each other's risk tolerance and seek a level of risk that is acceptable to both. Here are some considerations to help you measure if you are ready to take certain risks.

First, be sure you have an accurate assessment of "risk" as determined by answering the six questions above.

Second, be sure you know your financial objective in taking this risk. Be sure that the financial goal for this investment fits into your investment plan. Then, be sure the reward for taking this risk is promising enough to go ahead.

Third, review your income and your savings one more time to be sure those sides of your financial life are in order and will support taking the risk you are considering.

Finally, answer these questions: How serious a problem would it be for you if the investment fell in value or cuts its dividend for a year or two? Would a loss in the dividend or a loss in value of your investment wipe you out? What would total failure of the investment mean to you? Would major loss of value or failure of the investment cause you severe mental pain? What would such a loss do to your marriage? If you don't have the ability to stay with an investment through the ups and downs of the marketplace, then you may be taking a very big psychological risk. If both of you aren't prepared to deal with that psychological risk, then it's better to wait until you are prepared. As a final word of advice on this subject, remember this: if the risks and promised rewards of a potential investment are high, but you can't afford to lose 100% of your investment savings, then you should not make the investment—period.

There is nothing wrong with risk. All investments have some degree of risk. Just be sure that before you buy you have examined the outside risk factors that might affect your investment and your internal readiness to take those risks together.

Question No. 8
How Much Cash Will Be Required In Future Years To Stay In This Investment?

Be sure you know if your beginning commitment to an investment is your only commitment. Sometimes there are hidden costs that might require you to come up with additional cash in future years. Often, if you can't produce the additional money, you lose your entire investment. Some limited partnerships, for example, will permit you to participate initially for as little as $5,000. This amount of money may be readily available to you, and the tax advantages and

potential profit may be very attractive. But if there is an additional requirement that you commit cash to the partnership in future years, you may not be able to continue with the investment. Often such requirements are hidden. So be sure you know if you can possibly be assessed for additional contributions before you make your decision to invest.

Question No. 9
How Will Government Policies, Regulations, Or Laws Affect This Investment?

Admittedly, no one knows from year-to-year exactly how the government will change the laws of this country. But it is possible to identify trends in government policy and to predict with some degree of confidence how possible changes might affect your investments. Both your personal reading and your consultation with professional advisors can help you measure this important factor.

Changes in government policies or laws have been known to wipe out all profits from some investments. At other times, just the opposite is true.

The point is, if you don't consider this important factor, your investment risk may be much higher than you originally thought.

Closely associated with shifts in government policy is social change. Concerns about pollution or overpopulation are two good examples. As society becomes more aware and concerned about these and other issues, there will be dramatic shifts in consumer attitudes, product consumption, and the production or manufacture of products by corporations. By staying tuned in to what is happening in society, you can better anticipate trends that could possibly affect your investments.

Question No. 10
How Do We Go About Selling This Investment?

Don't ever buy an investment that you don't know how to sell. From time to time you *will* sell investments. You may want to take your profits (or losses), adjust your investment mix or take advantage of a more promising opportunity. It's amazing how rich the resources are that explain how to buy an asset, and how thin the resources are that educate about selling. Sometimes the selling process is simple, but costly. Somtimes investments are easy to buy but hard to sell because there are no organized resale markets. An example would be collectibles, such as antiques or gemstones.

In any event, before you buy any investment, write out a step-by-step procedure for how to sell it. Also write out the costs you should anticipate for selling, including penalties that might be tacked on for leaving an investment before a certain date.

There is always a cost for selling an investment, but when you sell in a hurry there are often penalties. The point is that exiting an investment is not something to take for granted. So, ask questions about how this process works and be sure you have the right answers.

These, then, are the ten basic questions you should ask about every investment you make. Does answering them seem like a chore? I assure you that compared to the consequences of making bad investment decisions, the effort to come up with the answers to these questions will be very worthwhile. Even after making a good investment decision, you will have to work at managing your investments. Some investments don't require much management to be successful. But if you look only at the profit opportunity and fail to recognize your responsibility to remain fully informed about your investments, you may be in for some unhappy surprises. School never lets out for the serious investor.

DIPLOMA
INVESTING 101

The third most frequently quoted rule of investing is, "Follow the 'smart money.'" Smart money is usually money invested by those who go against the crowd and the current trends. These investors believe that this strategy assures them of finding more investment opportunities. However, smart money people do make their decisions based on solid research. They dig deep for information and take very little risk with their investment programs. They may appear to be more fortunate than others. In fact, they just work harder at gathering information. My advice is that you become "Smart Money Investors."

Recognize now that learning and growing as an investor is a life-long task. Decide now to continue your own reading program, to attend courses and seminars and to learn everything you can about investing in every possible way.

One way to learn about investing is to surround yourself with the right professional advisors. When you find you need professional help (and you will need it), be humble and seek it out. With many financial decisions, opportunity won't afford you the luxury of waiting until you have gathered all necessary information yourself.

When you do seek professional advice, you will find selecting the right advisor can be as challenging as selecting the right investment. How to select professional advisors is the subject of our next discussion.

What Is The Role Of The Professional Advisor And How Do You Select One?

As you face the challenge of managing your financial future, you will undoubtedly need professional advice. The advisors you choose will have a major impact on your success. There simply isn't enough time in anyone's life to learn everything. We live in a world of specialization. If you surround yourself with competent advisors, you gain immediate access to expertise that may otherwise require months or years to get on your own. Therefore, the advisor selection process is critical. Don't put this task off thinking that "It can wait until we're rich." The selection of financial advisors is a task that should begin as soon as possible after your wedding. I hope that reading this next section will help you see why this is true.

Who Are The Players On Your Financial Team?

You are the captains of your financial advisory team. No one else should be given this responsibility. While advisors can play important roles in assisting you, they will never pay the consequences of poor decisions (but they can help keep you from making them). So accept the fact that while the players on your financial team are hired help, they are very important hired help.

Employing these professionals will often cost money (but not always). You probably can't afford to hire some of them at the beginning of your marriage, but you can interview all of them and identify the ones most qualfied to help you (a project that will only cost some of your time). Deciding which ones to hire means making choices about which

ones can do the most for you now—at the start of married life. The short descriptions of financial advisor roles on the next few pages will give you a brief idea of who is available to help you and what role each advisor plays. But deciding who you can afford and when to hire them is up to the two of you.

At the risk of sounding like a broken record let me remind you again: all of your financial decisions should be made together. While financial advisors should bring enlightenment to your decisions, they should never divide you as a team.

Once you become divided, your love for one another (which is one of your greatest assets in life) is unprotected. Use these advisors wisely, but always stand together as a financial partnership.

Your Banker

Probably the most important person on your financial team is your banker. Obviously, you need to establish a checking and savings account at a bank when you get married. Yet, bankers play a much more important role than providing these simple services. Your banker has access to other people's money and can make that money available for you to use in the form of loans. You can dramatically increase your borrowing power with a bank in two ways. The first way is to follow the guidelines in Chapter Six about establishing and maintaining a good credit rating. The second way is to establish a personal relationship with your banker.

Today it is common for banks to offer "personal banking services." Personal service banking is the bank's way of saying to its customers, "You are important." Intelligent married couples understand that it is wise to say, "You are important," to their banker. It has been my experience that if you can sincerely communicate to your banker that he or she is important, there is almost no end to the services that the bank will provide you in return. By the way, banks place a high value on stability and long-term relationships. If you are going to have a good banking relationship, concentrate on developing it with someone who is likely to continue in service with the bank. Be prepared to work on maintaining that relationship for as long as you need banking services. Remember, the higher your banker is within the banking organization, the more influence he or she will have to grant loans.

If you know the bank your employer uses, it is a good idea to make this your bank, too. Why? Your employer's business is probably very important to the bank, and the bank officers are probably willing to do a lot to hold on to that business. This means they may extend a little more consideration to you if you identify yourself as an employee of this important customer when you begin your banking relationship.

Try to arrange your first meeting by making an appointment with your bank's branch manager. Don't just drop in and expect to see him or her. By requesting an appointment, you send the message that you respect this person's time. Respecting someone's time is just another way to tell them how important you think they are.

Once you have a good relationship and credit rating with one bank, start working on developing a relationship with a second. You can start by depositing a small amount of money in a second checking account and applying for a small loan. Then, over time, by paying back your loans and building your credit, you strengthen your ability to borrow money. Even though I said it in Chapter Six, I want to repeat that borrowing should be used only to help you invest, not to make consumer purchases.

When it is time to make an investment and you need to borrow money, there is only one thing more valuable than a good credit rating. That is your personal relationship with your banker(s).

Your Bank Trust Officer

There are many services offered by your bank that may be new to you. The bank's trust department provides several of these services. The person who works for a bank trust department is called a "trust officer."

The primary service of a trust officer is management of trust agreements. However, trust officers provide other services that may be valuable to young married couples. Even after I describe some of them, you may doubt the value of this professional advisor. You may be right. But it won't take much time to visit your bank trust officer to ask questions about the services he or she offers. You will find that a bank trust officer will not charge you anything for an initial visit and he or she may give you your best orientation to subjects such as wills, trusts, and estate planning (again, all of this without charge). By making this visit *before* you see your attorney, (and by reading Chapter Ten of this book before visiting a trust officer), you'll be in the best possible position to gain the most from employing an attorney to help draft your wills and other estate planning documents. While the trust officer doesn't draft estate planning documents, he or she will review those drafted by your attorney and will send them back for corrections if they're wrong (Yes, attorneys do make mistakes).

Trust agreements (discussed in Chapter Ten) can be very important to you. A trust can be set up to save estate taxes (taxes that are paid to the federal and state governments when you die), provide financial management of your estate for the benefit of children and allow your estate to pass to heirs and beneficiaries more efficiently and less expensively.

The roles played by trust officers in managing trust agreements include:

1. Executor: the person responsible for settling your estate after you die.

2. Guardian: the person who manages your estate for the benefit of minor children when both parents die before the children reach adulthood.

3. Custodian: a record keeping service for investment transactions that are made by a trust.

You may wonder why anyone would use a bank trust officer to serve as executor. Couldn't your marriage partner or a close family member serve in this capacity? Good question. The reason for using a bank trust department is that, unlike human beings, they will not die, become disabled, divorce you or move away. Institutional trustees can also be counted upon to provide competent

professional services as executors. The legal requirements of this role are complicated. Your trust officer may have the best possible qualifications to be an executor. If you're not completely comfortable naming a bank trust department as executor, at least consider naming one to serve as co-executor with your spouse (I'll explain this strategy more fully in Chapter Ten).

Naming the executor of your estate is probably the last thing on your mind right now, but arranging to have a guardian for your children may be very important to you.

It may be that you already have a child or are planning a family. Although it is unpleasant to think about, you must consider the possibility that you may not live long enough to raise your children to adulthood. Occasionally, both parents die in a tragic accident. Planning for the guardianship of your children is one more side of being financially responsible adults. Many couples set up trust agreements funded with life insurance and then name a bank trust department to manage the trust for the benefit of their minor children. At the same time, they arrange for family members to finish raising the children. By separating the financial and emotional support of the children, there is less chance that any conflict of interest will develop and the children's welfare will be better protected.

Learning about the services of a trust officer is a part of your basic financial education in marriage. Take the time to do it. Then, take the steps that make sense to you to use this advisor in a way that is of greatest personal advantage.

Your Attorney

Your attorney is an expert in the field of law. Many people, however, look to their attorney for advice on nearly everything. This is a mistake. In fact, the legal profession is so complex and demanding these days that many attorneys are specialists, just like doctors.

As you look for an attorney to help with your financial affairs, it would make little sense for you to choose one who practices criminal law. More often than not, you should find one who specializes in tax law and estate planning.

The primary role of your attorney is to prepare legal documents for any financial transactions requiring them. Specific documents to be handled by your attorney include wills, trust agreements, real estate contracts, buy-sell agreements between business partners, incorporations and other contract documents. Your attorney should also review contracts that you plan to sign as part of an investment, *before you sign*. Your attorney will understand and explain the clauses in the contract, but should not be expected to give an opinion about the wisdom of the investment. If your attorney offers counsel on the advisability of an investment based on a particular clause in a contract, listen carefully. But the final decision to proceed or not to proceed with the investment rests with you. As long as you understand the legal consequences, you should be prepared to make your own investment decisions.

Checking the credentials of an attorney can be a thorny problem. All of them have attended college for six to eight years and are licensed to practice law by your state. However, having a license to practice law does not make an attorney an expert in areas of law that will help you get started in life. The price you pay for expert advice will be identical to what you pay for inexpert advice (except, of course, the mistakes of an inept attorney may be very costly). Most attorneys now advertise in the Yellow Pages of the telephone book and identify their specialties. In addition, the local bar association may provide an information service that identifies attorneys by specialty (check the telephone book for the number of the bar association and call their office). But to find the better ones, ask your bank trust officer. Bank trust officers know those attorneys who work constantly in areas of the law that will help you. After the trust officer makes his or her recommendations, check to see if any of those attorneys are on the bank's board of directors. While your attorney and trust officer need to work closely together, any "sweetheart" arrangements between the bank and your attorney may not be in your best interest.

Once you receive several recommendations from your bank trust officer, ask someone you know and trust to review the list and give his or her personal recommendation. A close family member or business associate who has used one of the attorneys on your list for similar services will add important knowledge to your search. If you can't get a personal recommendation (or even if you can), you should interview attorneys carefully before selecting one (see the discussion and read the publications suggested at the end of this chapter about how to do this). Make sure the one you select is willing to be a team player and will sit down periodically with your other advisors to brainstorm ideas and review your overall financial game plan.

Please keep in mind that a competent and honest attorney does not earn commissions. Attorneys who practice estate planning and provide investment counsel charge an hourly fee or a fixed fee. If you interview one who seems interested in anything other than serving you at a reasonable hourly or fixed fee, head for the door.

You should select an attorney as quickly as possible after your marriage. From the day you get married, you need to have wills prepared (see Chapter Ten). A competent attorney is the only one who can do this for you. Don't delay.

Your Accountant

Unlike attorneys, most accountants are generalists rather than specialists. While some certified public accountants do specialize in certain areas, this kind of accountant is not what you're seeking. What you want is someone who can help with record keeping, tax planning and preparation, financial and tax analysis of investments, and maybe even help with loan presentations. In general, it is advisable to deal only with CPAs, unless you know someone without these credentials who is well known for his or her highly professional work. More than likely, a CPA who has a small (1-5 person) office will give you the best service. You don't need the services of a national accounting firm for your marital finances. Interview and employ only someone with whom you feel confident and comfortable.

Like attorneys, accountants do *not* receive commissions. They are paid an hourly fee. Fee and billing expectations should be disclosed during your first meeting, and that meeting should be offered without charge. Your first meeting should also reveal exactly how an accountant can best help you. Let's review this advisor's role more closely.

Almost everyone knows that an accountant can help prepare your income tax return (be sure to study **Appendix C** at the back of this book). But accountants can do much more. Your accountant can help you prepare personal financial statements, make or review financial projections, and assist with loan presentations to lenders. Because your accountant does not have an investment product to sell, he or she can be very objective in analyzing investment opportunities.

When it comes to looking for investment tax advice, time spent with an accountant can be very rewarding.

Remember my advice earlier about the impossibility of learning everything yourself? A good accountant must keep up with tax laws. He or she can tell quickly whether a promised tax advantage applies to you and exactly how it applies. If, as a result of your accountant's investment tax advice, you select the right investment, your advisor will have saved you many times over the fee you pay.

When it comes to tax preparation, visiting your accountant once a year, at tax time, is not satisfactory. Your accountant should have a good overview of your entire financial situation long before the time arrives to prepare your income tax return. A meeting every three months is preferable. In this way, there is time to review financial changes and to make necessary adjustments before the tax year ends. Of course, in the early years of your marriage, you may feel that this is a luxury you can't afford. You decide. Just remember, your accountant can often save you much more than the fees he or she charges for tax planning advice.

Most accountants also provide a variety of bookkeeping and record keeping services. You may not want to pay an accountant to keep records for you. But it can be well worthwhile in the first year of marriage to have an accountant tell you how to keep your own records. If your records are in good form when you seek help to prepare your tax return, you can dramatically reduce the professional time spent working on this task. As a result, the cost of tax preparation will be lower and the preparation of your return will be much less stressful. (To help you get started with your financial recordkeeping, pay special attention to **Appendix B** at the back of this book.)

Your Stockbroker

Stockbrokers do not make investment decisions for you. Let's get that straight. You and you alone must make the decisions about investments you want to buy. Your stockbroker is the professional who can help you buy and sell those investments he or she represents. Your broker gets paid when you buy or sell an investment, and the way they get paid is by commission (more about this later).

Today, stockbrokers handle many types of investments. It is now common for them to represent real estate investments, oil and gas ventures, insurance, annuities, commodities, gold and silver, rare coins and even life insurance. Yes, they even sell stocks and bonds, including mutual funds.

When you are ready to make investments through a broker, it is important to find one who has considerable experience and one who has the respect of his or her professional peers. You don't want an order taker. By consulting with an experienced broker, you can explore many sides of the investment you are considering. Brokers can help you search out investments suited to your investment goals and can help you stay away from investments that, although attractive on the surface, may have hidden problems.

To be of greatest help, your broker should know you personally. It is important to let a broker in on how much you know about the market and why you are interested in a particular investment. Your broker also needs to know your financial and emotional tolerance for risk.

It is just as important for you to really know your broker. When you start your search for a broker, be sure you get good references. A reference from one or more of your close relatives or from trusted friends is a good place to start. Once you have these references, schedule face-to-face meetings with at least three brokers and see if you can find one whose style is compatible with yours. Try to find someone who has at least five years of experience and who has been through a good market (a bull market) and a bad market (a bear market).

Although the Securities and Exchange Commission (SEC) oversees the actions of all brokers, this doesn't mean all brokers are competent. You can learn a lot about a broker's competence by talking with three or four long-standing clients. These people won't lie about a broker's competence and may help you determine whether or not a broker can handle your specific needs.

When you interview brokers for the first time, ask many questions. Ask them to describe their typical clients in terms of age, income, portfolio size and types of investments. Find out if they specialize in specific financial areas. All of this information will help you to make a better decision about who will be the best broker for you.

Because brokers earn money only when a trade takes place, those who are unethical tend to "churn" the accounts of their clients (buying and selling just to generate commissions). You can help protect yourself against this unethical practice by keeping a journal that records clearly and accurately all of your brokerage transactions.

Your Life Insurance Underwriter

The role of the professional life insurance underwriter is often badly misunderstood. These people have an important job to do for you. Their primary role is to sell protection (in the form of life insurance) against life's most catastrophic event—death. Life insurance provides money for surviving marriage partners for a variety of purposes and needs (all of which will be fully discussed in Chapter Nine).

A professional life insurance underwriter helps you decide how much life insurance is enough to meet your special needs. To do this effectively, he or she must know your income capabilities, your financial goals, your short-term and long-term investment philosophies, and everything about what you

own and what you owe.

Once your life insurance needs are known, the life insurance underwriter helps you sort through the differences in life insurance products, answering every question you ask, and many questions you won't think to ask. If an underwriter isn't trying to force one type of product down your throat and allows you to make intelligent decisions based on sound and accurate information, you can be fairly certain that you are dealing with a qualified professional.

Because turnover in this field is very high, try to find an agent who has been in the business for a reasonable period of time. While life insurance may seem like a simple and straightforward subject, in truth it takes a substantial investment of time and energy to master the fundamental knowledge necessary to become a professional life insurance advisor. The title of Chartered Life Underwriter (CLU) is the highest professional credential in this field. To earn this title, an underwriter must pass a series of very difficult examinations.

Today, because life insurance professionals frequently represent a variety of products that combine insurance with investments, some underwriters have gained other professional credentials. Many have become Certified Financial Planners or are licensed with the National Association of Securities Dealers (NASD). This license allows your agent to sell a variety of investment products.

If you decide to purchase both life insurance and investments from your life insurance underwriter, then apply the same ten question analysis given to you earlier in this chapter to the investment products offered. While the practice of selling life insurance and investments isn't unethical, be cautious of those who claim expertise in more than one field of financial counsel. The body of knowledge to be mastered in any one of these fields is overwhelming.

Your Property And Casualty Insurance Agent

Your life insurance agent probably will not be your property insurance agent. Yet, property and casualty insurance are important to you, even in the beginning of married life. This advisor will sell you auto, home owner's and liability insurance. The purpose of these insurance plans is to protect you against sudden losses caused by theft, fire, burglary, natural disaster, lawsuits or other misfortunes.

Too often, people look on this professional advisor as an order taker. This just isn't true. The ability to properly advise you on these insurance plans requires an agent to master an impressive body of knowledge that includes study, tests and certification by your state. Those who reach the highest level of competency can write CPCU after their names. These initials stand for "Chartered Property Casualty Underwriter."

We live in a society of people who like to file law suits. We also live in a world where accidents happen and natural disasters strike. These things don't always happen to the other guy.

Without sound professional advice from a property and casualty insurance agent, you could someday discover that you are the other guy, who does not have adequate insurance coverage.

One of the more common disasters for a young married couple is to have their home or apartment burglarized. Any wedding gifts you received and your limited possessions for starting married life may represent your entire estate. If you don't have renter's or home owner's insurance, the loss from a burglary could be a real setback. In addition to properly insuring your property, it's a good idea to make an inventory of your belongings immediately. Etch identification numbers on them and photograph them. Place the photos and the inventory with ID numbers in a safe deposit box at the bank, or in someone's fireproof safe. Many police departments will loan you an engraving kit with which to etch ID numbers on your valuables. If you've got it, protect it.

Your Financial Planner

At the beginning of this chapter, I pointed out that it is important to develop an investment plan before starting your investment program. Hopefully, each investment you make will fit that plan in a way that will create the profits you seek. Most married couples need help with this job.

When you look for professional advice about creating an investment plan, you will probably turn to a financial planner. This advisor will begin by making an in-depth analysis of your present financial situation and will help you work through the twelve questions presented on Page 269. The next step will be to propose a plan in writing that meets your needs. The third step will be to help you put that plan into action by buying and selling investments. Financial planners are paid a fee for all three of these services.

The fees charged by financial planners to complete a financial analysis and develop a blueprint for your investment future vary widely. Your first meeting with a financial planner candidate should not cost you anything. At that time, the planner should tell you in clear terms the cost of developing an investment plan. You should also be told exactly what you will receive for this fee. If additional fees might be charged at some time in the future for services you do not now need, you should be told about these, too. A professional financial planner should give all of this to you in writing, probably in the form of a standard letter of intent or contract.

Some financial planners work only on a fee basis and some work only on commission. This makes comparing planners more difficult. To muddy the waters even more, you should know that some planners work on a combination of fees and commissions. Your best defense against confusion is to get a written statement of a planner's fee and commission policy.

Start your search for a financial planner by selecting at least three candidates. Your first step should be to check the credentials and reputation of each one.

Financial planning is a relatively new profession. The financial planner with an official "Certified Financial Planner" (CFP) title is one who has completed a series of correspondence courses and examinations from the College for Financial Planning in Denver. Those with a CFC title have a Chartered Financial Consultant diploma from The American College in Bryn Mawr, Pennsylvania. These titles should not be confused with college degrees, but they do demonstrate a special effort to develop knowledge and skill levels.

To assist in your search for the best financial planner candidates, call the Institute of Certified Financial Planners. They have a toll free number: (800) 282-

7526. On request, they will send you a list of the names of three financial planners in your area. This list will outline their education, licenses and registrations; how each is compensated; and how each practices. Also, I suggest you contact the International Association of Financial Planners, (800) 945-4237, and request a copy of their "Financial Planning Consumer Bill of Rights: a Consumer Guide to Financial Independence"; and a one-page, "pre-engagement," compensation disclosure form which you can take with you when you interview financial planner candidates. Most financial planners will give you a disclosure statement detailing their background. If they do not offer you such a statement, ask for one. I strongly urge you to choose a financial planner who has at least two to three years of experience.

Remember, being technically trained and having experience are just two qualities you should look for in seeking a competent financial planner. References will tell you much more. Be sure you ask for at least three professional references, such as attorneys, trust officers or CPAs in your community who can vouch for a planner's character and competence. Recommendations from friends and colleagues are also valuable. Talk to at least three current clients who presently receive services from each planner candidate. Finally, check with the Better Business Bureau to see if any complaints have been filed against any of the names on your list.

In addition to conducting financial analyses and developing formal financial plans, these professionals also sell a variety of investment products. It is almost certain that a Certified Financial Planner who completes a financial plan for you will want to sell you one or more investment products. However, you don't have to buy any investments from a Certified Financial Planner. You can buy investment products from anyone you choose.

Please keep this point firmly in mind—it is very difficult to be objective when selling both a financial planning service and an investment product.

Some investors prefer to buy investment products from professionals who have the professional title, "Registered Investment Advisor" in addition to Certified Financial Planner. Even more sophisticated investors insist that those who help them have the professional designation of "Chartered Financial Analyst." This last title is the most highly sought-after set of credentials. Anyone with this title has five years or more of financial management experience and has passed three difficult academic examinations.

Questions To Ask When Interviewing An Advisor

Unfortunately, too many couples rely on luck to lead them to competent financial advisors. There *is* a better way to make these decisions.

First of all, recognize that because each professional has mastered a complex body of knowledge, you will naturally have some feelings of inferiority. No one likes to feel inferior or to feel intimidated. But we all feel that way, to some degree, when we are in a dependent relationship with a professional advisor. If you acknowledge this fact, you will be better prepared to start the selection process.

Just because a prospective advisor has a degree or other credentials is no guarantee of competence. In fact, your task is to begin by questioning the competence and dedication of anyone being considered to be your advisor.

After all, it's your money and your dreams that you are asking them to share. And just because you are paying the bill does not mean the only fair question to ask is, "How much do you charge?"

Asking good questions is truly the key to selecting each of your professional advisors. By reading the books and articles suggested at the end of this chapter, you can better prepare yourself for an interview with any financial advisor. However, the purpose of this section is to give you a list of basic questions to ask yourself *after* each interview with an advisor candidate.

I encourage you to keep firmly in mind that you are entitled to ask any question you wish *during* the interview, including, "What color socks are you wearing?" There is no such thing as a stupid question. The only stupid question is the one you wanted to ask, but didn't.

However, I urge you to begin your advisor relationships in a way that will help you get to the great city of your dreams. Therefore, treat your prospective advisors with dignity. Expect and demand to be treated the same way in return.

In every case, final selection of a professional advisor should take into account his or her willingness to take the time required to treat you as a marriage partnership. Beware of those who seem rushed or hurried and can barely take five minutes to talk with you on the telephone. If you interview someone and feel they are angered by your questions, head for the door. On the other hand, give serious consideration to someone who asks about your hopes and dreams. Also give special consideration to those who ask for the names of your other advisors and who want to meet them personally or call them so a team effort can be established.

The questions on the next page are for you to ask yourself after each interview. Although this list is by no means exhaustive, answering these questions should help you put your thoughts in order before making a decision to sign a contract or letter of agreement with an advisor.

Questions To Ask After Interviewing A Prospective Advisor

1. Did this professional ask about our hopes and dreams for the future?

2. Were we asked about our financial background and our training and experience with the subjects on which this person will advise us?

3. Is the person we talked to the person who will handle our account? Who takes over if the advisor is unavailable, out of town or ill?

4. What are this person's credentials? Did he or she present us a résumé which spells out academic and professional training as well as experience and accomplishments? How long have they practiced in their field? What is their specialty? How long have they been with this firm?

5. Did we enjoy talking and dealing with this person?

6. Did we trust this person immediately? Did he or she appear to be moral and ethical?

7. How large is their firm? Are we more comfortable with a large or small firm? Why?

8. Is the advisor really going to be available to us when we need help? How was that communicated to us? Do we believe it?

9. What was the appearance of the office? Did everything look organized, neat and professional? How were we received by the secretarial staff?

10. Do we know how this person and/or his or her firm is doing financially? Is this information important and/or available to us?

11. Do we understand how this person gets paid? Do we fully understand his or her source of financial motivation to assist us? Does this person get a fee, or is he or she heavily dependent on commissions?

12. Did we receive a statement of his or her ethics or policies? Did we read it, and do we understand it? Does this statement clearly spell out any conflicts of interest he or she might have?

13. If it applies, did we receive a copy of his or her standard written agreement? Will we take time to read it carefully, asking questions if there is anything we don't fully understand?

14. Did we receive a list of other clients so we can call and ask them if they found working with this advisor a positive experience? Are we motivated to actually make these contacts and get this information?

15. Did we ask for the names of at least three professionals who are not clients of this advisor but who can serve as references? Are we motivated to call on these people before we enter into any business agreements with the advisor?

Welcome To The Investment Smorgasbord

You may have wondered why this chapter did not tell you exactly what to invest in to make your fortune. Even if this could have been done (which, by the way, no one can do) it would have been nothing more than giving you a financial fish. Hopefully, this chapter teaches you how to fish. Certainly the information is basic, but the basics are what often get overlooked.

The American marketplace is an ever-changing arena with a large variety of investment products to choose from. Every day there are new investment products and new investment conditions. That is what makes the free enterprise system unequaled in excitement and opportunity.

In countries where free enterprise is not allowed, the possibility of investing and profiting is limited to those who are born to wealth. In our nation, all who are willing to learn about free enterprise and follow the rules of the financial road can make rapid financial progress and acquire the wealth needed to make their dreams come true. This will be true for you, too, if you invest with intelligence.

However, to invest with intelligence, you must immediately begin the never-ending task of continuing your education about investing. Use the library, attend seminars, buy the books available at your local book store. Read, read, read and read some more.

Above all, remember that as a married couple, you are in the driver's seat. Use your advisors to help you draw your map to the great city of your dreams. But remember, where you end up financially depends on the choices and decisions that _you_ make. Don't allow anyone else to make those decisions for you. And most important, make your decisions _together_.

Agreement Check:

1. During the first year of marriage, it can be fun to try to add one member to your financial planning team each month. For example, during the first thirty days, concentrate on finding a banker. The next month, try to find an attorney, then a life insurance agent, etc. Read the articles and books suggested at the end of this chapter to better prepare yourself for each interview. Go at it as though you were the owner of a professional sports team. If it takes longer than thirty days to find the person you both feel is right, don't worry. Keep after this recruitment process until you both have identified all the players you need, even if you aren't ready to make big financial moves just yet. As you actually employ professional advisors, fill in the form on the next two pages so you have a list of their names, addresses and telephone numbers close at hand. Store a copy of this list in your safe deposit box at the bank. Send a copy of it to a close friend or family member in the event of an emergency, and make sure you provide the list to everyone on the list.

Our Financial Advisory Team

Name of Our Banker: _____

Address: _____

_____

Telephone: _____

Name of Our Bank Trust Officer: _____

Address: _____

_____

Telephone: _____

Name of Our Attorney: _____

Address: _____

_____

Telephone: _____

Name of Our Accountant: _____

Address: _____

_____

Telephone: _____

Name of Our Stock Broker: _____

Address: _____

_____

Telephone: _____

Name of Our Life Insurance Agent: _____

Address: _____

_____

Telephone: _____

**Name of Our Property
and Casualty Insurance Agent:** _____

Address: _____

_____

Telephone: _____

Name of Our Financial Planner: _____

Address: _____

_____

Telephone: _____

2. As soon as possible, it is important for the two of you to make some written commitments to continue your education about investing. Use the space below to set out your plans to do this.

This Year, We Will Definitely Take The Following Steps To Increase Our Knowledge About Investing:

_____

_____

_____

_____

_____

_____

_____

_____

_____

_____

_____

_____

_____

_____

Suggested Additional Reading:

Wurman, Richard Saul, Alan Siegel and Kenneth M. Morris, *The Wall Street Journal Guide to Understanding Money & Markets.* New York: Access Press, 1990.

Klott, Gary L., *The New York Times Complete Guide To Personal Investing*. New York: Times Books, 1987.

Scott, David, *Wall Street Words.* Boston: Houghton Mifflin Company, 1988.

Corrigan, Arnold and Phyllis C. Kaufman,
       Personal Banking: A User's Guide To Banking Services
       How To Choose a Lawyer
       How To Choose a Discount Broker
       Understanding Buying and Selling A Home
       How to Make Personal Financial Planning Work for You
       Understanding Treasury Bills & Government Securities
       Understanding Buying and Selling a House
       Understanding Condos and Co-ops
       Understanding the Stock Market
       Understanding Common Stocks
       Understanding Stock Options and Futures Markets
       Understanding Mutual Funds
       Understanding Money Market Funds
Stamford: Longmeadow Press, 1987 *(These books are carried in most Waldenbooks and can also be ordered by calling toll free 1-800-322-2000.)*

Dunnan, Nancy, *How to Invest $50-$5,000*. New York: Harper Perennial Publishers, 1991.

Grant, Anne R., *Keeping Your Stock Broker Honest*. Chicago, International Publishing Corporation, 1991.

Some sources for names of insurance agents:

National Association for Life Underwriters, 1922 F Street N.W., Washington, D.C. 20006

The Independent Insurance Agents Association of America, 100 Church Street, New York, N.Y. 10008

The National Association of Casualty and Surety Agents, 5454 Wisconsin Avenue, Chevy Chase, MD 20815

The Rules of The Financial Road:

Part IV

Chapter Nine

Financial Law No. 6:
If You've Got It, Protect It

*"The best laid plans of mice and men
often go awry."*
Robert Burns

One financial law that young married couples tend to ignore more than all others is this one—**"If you've got it, protect it."**

Right now you're probably feeling safe from harm and capable of conquering the world. When you're in love and newly married, or planning to marry, you may feel especially powerful. The feelings of strength and safety you have result from a trick played on you by your Neanderthal brain. The pituitary gland plays an important role in this trick. This peanut-sized gland is located deep in the Neanderthal brain. It is programmed to produce hormones that stimulate changes in your body and your mind when you reach your middle to late teens. From that point on, it just keeps manufacturing these hormones at a steady rate until about mid-life. These hormones carry the message, "I am (man/woman); hear me roar. I am

invincible, I can do anything."

As a result, men in their twenties and thirties feel like young warriors, and women at these ages feel similar emotions and express them in feminine ways. During these years, higher brain functions should keep you aware of how fragile life is. Instead, the modern brain takes a back seat to these very powerful hormonal messages from the Neanderthal brain.

The fact is, life is *very* fragile. It is filled with danger and risk. Even the caveman and cave woman understood the dangers.

In caveman days, the idea of the tribe grew out of recognition of life's dangers and risks (thanks to evolving higher

297

brain functions). By banding together, the primitive tribe was able to hunt more effectively and to provide food and shelter more dependably for all of its members. The tribe also provided protection against enemies. In essence, the tribe offered strength that was unavailable to an individual or to an individual family.

Within the tribe, the very young, the old and the sick or injured could be cared for. Those who were strong were most honored by the tribe, yet they also had needs that could only be met by working in harmony with other tribal members. However, as we all know from tribal stories, the very strong (dominated by their Neanderthal brains) often came to believe that they were invincible, unconquerable. Frequently, warriors and chieftains who were filled with pride and arrogance lorded over and demanded privileges from the tribe's weaker members—until some illness, accident, battle or old age brought them to their senses.

In truth, all social behavior is based on modern brain recognition that we need each other in order to survive as a species. In a word, humans are *interdependent* creatures.

The Neanderthal brain resists this fact. The Neanderthal in each of us argues for individualism and competi-

tion. The modern brain argues for cooperation and social harmony. Most human behavior is a mixture of these two themes. When the Neanderthal brain dominates, we act like our cave man and women ancestors. When the modern brain dominates, we work together and protect ourselves in much the same way as primitive tribes. However, today we have many more ways to provide protection. One way is through an idea called "insurance."

In this chapter, you will learn about insurance and why it is important to your marriage. For the reasons I've just discussed, learning insurance strategies to harmonize with this financial law requires great self-discipline, so the modern brain can dominate. Don't be surprised if your Neanderthal brain fights your efforts to learn these lessons. Most young couples tell me that the only financial task more tedious and boring than preparing their income tax returns is planning for their insurance needs. "Boring" is the message your Neanderthal brain will send every time you address this subject. But this doesn't have to be the case if you see insurance as an expression of love for one another.

Protection planning *is* a true expression of caring and love. As you will soon discover, you have a lot to protect.

There's No Such Thing As "Risk Free"

Insurance is based on the recognition that life is filled with risk. Most risks are not important from a financial standpoint. But, the risks that involve significant financial consequences are insurable. When you insure against financial catastrophe, you agree to pay money in exchange for a promise by an insurance company to cover your financial losses. The money you pay for this protection is called a **"premium."** Insurance premium rates are tied to the risk covered. Higher risks result in higher premiums. For example, before you reach twenty-six, most insurance companies charge a higher rate for automobile insurance. Statistics prove that drivers under that age have more accidents and are, therefore, at greater risk when they drive. There are professionals called **"actuaries"** who make their living by examining risks. Actuaries help insurance companies determine what their insurance rates should be in order to make a profit.

Of course, you don't need an actuary to tell you that you face significant financial risks as a young married couple. Let's list some of your major areas of financial vulnerability.

Finding yourself unemployed is a real possibility. If it happens, you will probably turn to your Emergency Fund to provide income support until you are employed again. Therefore, **your Emergency Fund is a form of self-insurance**. Yet, your Emergency Fund probably couldn't handle the cost of an automobile accident. Can you afford to be without automobile insurance? Definitely not. Can you assume that

because you are an excellent driver you will be spared from an auto accident? Again, the answer is "NO!" Hardly a day goes by that you don't read about someone in your community who had a serious automobile accident. Your vulnerability to an auto accident is so common that most states require you by law to protect yourself and the other driver with insurance.

How about property loss from theft or fire? Could that happen to you? Burglars don't ask their victims if they can afford a robbery. Many young married couples are devastated by a burglary because they have no insurance or are underinsured. These days it's unwise for anyone to leave a home or apartment unprotected against loss from theft or fire.

The deeper we get into this subject, the higher the stakes become. For example, a debilitating injury or illness which generates enormous medical bills could destroy the financial foundation of a young couple for years—unless they have health insurance. No one likes to think about that happening to them, but it happens—all too often. If such an injury or illness is serious enough, it might result in permanent disability. That could easily mean the loss of your income. Of course, this definitely won't happen to you, right? Wrong! It can happen to anyone. In fact, the chances that you will become disabled and unable to work are far greater than your chances of dying. Your Emergency Fund could probably handle a short period of disability. But anything longer than 90 days would probably be financially devastating.

Of course, death is the most unthinkable risk for young married couples. Life insurance isn't so important when you are single and have no dependents (no one who needs you to provide their financial support). But when you get married, you now have a partner to consider. If you want (or already have) children, their financial needs will also have to be considered. Here is an area of financial life where your thinking as a married person will have to change from those carefree days as a single.

This chapter will teach you some of the basics about various forms of insurance coverage. Each type of protection will be reviewed, and you will be provided questions to help you dig out the information required to make good decisions about insurance.

As each form of insurance is discussed, you will be given opportunities to talk with one another about important insurance topics. You will be encouraged to end those discussions by recording your decisions. These lessons are simple to learn and easy to understand. The benefits afforded by learning them will prove to be quite valuable. If you find yourself hesitating to continue with these lessons, just remember that you are probably fighting your Neanderthal brain. It wants you to believe that you are invulnerable and that you will be spared any of the disasters that I just mentioned. Armed with that knowledge and your love for one another, you have the power to overcome any tendency to put off learning these lessons. Remember, if you've got it (and right now you almost certainly do have life, health and earning capacity) for heaven's sake, protect it.

Financial Strategy No. 1 for Harmonizing with Financial Law No. 6: Revisiting Your Emergency Fund

A great deal of emphasis was placed on establishing your Emergency Fund in Chapter Six. Now, I want you to look at that Fund again—as a form of self-insurance.

Within the various forms of insurance coverage there is an idea called **"deductibility."**

The "deductible" portion of insurance is the amount of a financial loss *you* must pay before the insurance company starts to pay its share.

For example, when you have an auto accident, and you pay the first $250 in repair bills, that $250 is the deductible portion of your auto insurance. When you have medical bills, and you must pay the first $1,000 in annual medical expenses, that is the deductible portion of your medical insurance coverage. Where is the money supposed to come from to pay the deductible portion of your insurance coverage? If you plan well, there should be money available in your Emergency Fund.

When you set aside cash reserves to pay for these deductibles, you create your own insurance fund. That is what is meant by "self-insurance."

Basically, you pay an insurance company to cover the big portion of risk, and you agree to cover the little portion with your Emergency Fund. You and I know that the smaller portion of the risk is more likely to occur than the larger portion. Thank goodness! But that also means your Emergency Fund will be drawn on more frequently than your insurance policy benefits. Because your Emergency Fund (self-insurance program) will be called on frequently, Emergency Funds have to be kept liquid and immediately available.

If you've had any thoughts about not establishing an Emergency Fund, I hope this brief discussion turns that thought around quickly. You *can* purchase insurance coverage without deductibles, but the policy then becomes unaffordable for most married couples. Instead of paying prohibitively high insurance premiums for insurance without deductibles, you are better off to increase your deductibles, save the money you would have paid in higher premiums, and earn interest on your savings. (Just be sure you *do save* the money.)

301

Financial Strategy No. 2 for Harmonizing with Financial Law No. 6: Auto Insurance Coverage

Everyone who owns an automobile should have automobile insurance. Most states require minimum levels of auto insurance coverage by law. If your state legally requires you to carry auto insurance, and you don't have it, you are on a collision course with your state government and flirting with financial disaster. Believe me, you wouldn't like the consequences of colliding with the law. You would like even less the financial consequences of having an accident without coverage. Remember, all states require drivers to pay for losses they may cause others. Having insurance is the simplest way to comply. Furthermore, if you have to borrow money to buy a car, it is unlikely you will be able to take that car off the dealer's lot unless you have the necessary auto insurance coverage.

Many states have now enacted **no-fault car insurance laws.** Many people think this means that they only have to carry the minimum insurance required by law and that they can't be sued if they have an accident. While no-fault bypasses the complicated and often expensive task of finding out who is to blame for an automobile accident, it doesn't mean you can't be sued.

Most states with no-fault auto insurance laws allow you to take your case to court when costs from the accident exceed a certain minimum or if the accident results in personal injury or death.

If the person being sued has only the minimum coverage required by law, they're exposed to a financial disaster from which they may never recover. The point is, "no fault" doesn't mean "no risk." Cover yourself with ample protection or face harsh consequences.

Most auto insurance policies include at least two basic coverages. They are **"collision"** and **"public liability coverage."**

Collision coverage insures you against your own recklessness. That is, if you are responsible for damaging or destroying *your* car, collision coverage pays to repair your car or to replace your car.

Usually, this coverage is the most expensive part of your automobile insurance program. Many couples carry more collision coverage than is necessary because a large percentage of all claims against collision coverage are for low cost "fender bender" accidents. Most of us could bear the risk of a small loss and thus cut the cost of our insurance premiums appreciably by including a larger deductible in our collision coverage. How much deductible you are willing to assume for collision coverage depends on the degree of burden you are willing to place on your Emergency Fund in the event an accident does happen.

Many couples don't realize or never stop to think about the fact that their collision insurance premium does not automatically decrease in future years as their car grows older and less valuable (depreciates).

When you buy a new car, it's natural to feel that you should have excellent insurance coverage, because the cost of replacement is high. But as that car grows older, it depreciates in value. Five to seven years from now, after your car has depreciated significantly, it might be appropriate to consider reducing collision coverage or dropping it entirely. In any event, review the cost of collision coverage frequently to see if you still need the same amount of insurance.

The second major element of most auto policies is public liability coverage. Its purpose is to protect you financially by paying for losses you cause *others* while driving—also for your legal defense.

Time was when this coverage was relatively inexpensive. This just isn't true anymore. Liability insurance will tend to account for 40 to 45 percent of your annual auto insurance costs, and in some parts of the country, it will be more. Although the risk of such liability is fairly low, the cost of a lawsuit resulting from your carelessness could be catastrophically high. Many couples are significantly underinsured in this area. If you lost a lawsuit and were required to pay $100,000 or more in damages because of your carelessness, more than likely you couldn't pay the bill out of savings. For this reason, I advise you to take a long hard look at your auto liability coverage. It would be wise to carry as much as $300,000 in liability coverage, and in some cases, more may be needed. We live in a society that likes to sue. Don't become a victim of an auto accident lawsuit without liability coverage.

Auto insurance coverage also includes such things as **comprehensive coverage** (for wind, flood or fire damage, vandalism, theft and other problems *other than* collision damage, wear-and-tear and mechanical problems); **uninsured motorist coverage** (for your medical bills and the medical bills for occupants of your car, caused by someone else's negligence, who happens to be driving without liability coverage, and in some states when you are the victim of an underinsured motorist); **medical payments** (for injury sustained by you and your passengers when you are at fault); and **towing**. You can also buy **underinsured motorist coverage** (which makes up the difference between how much you can collect from an at-fault driver's liability coverage and your actual losses—up to your coverage limits) and **personal injury protection** (which pays for your passengers regardless of fault, for medical treatment and rehabilitation caused by accident injury).

What you pay for auto insurance varies by company and is influenced by several other factors.

If you buy all of the coverages listed above, you will increase your costs. Your costs will also be affected by how much each kind of coverage pays and by the deductible on each coverage.

What kind of vehicle you drive also affects cost since coverage of your car depends on its value. Generally, the more expensive the car, the more you pay. Insurance tends to cost more for certain types of cars, too, such as sports cars and off-road, four-wheel drive vehicles.

The final factor affecting cost is how you drive. Such factors as your driving record, where you drive, how much you drive, and your age, sex and marital status all impact the cost of auto insurance. As young married people, you may be surprised to find that you finally get a break because your auto insurance premiums will almost certainly be less than when you were single.

Shopping for insurance coverage is one way to cut costs. Hundreds of insurance companies will welcome you as a customer if your driving record is reasonably good. You're sure to save just by shopping for the lowest rates. If you select an agent who has the ability to sell policies for many companies, your shopping will be much easier. However, be sure to look at the service record of a potential auto insurance company, too. Price is important, but saving money won't mean much unless you get the service you need when you need it. Ask clients of a potential insurance agent how they are treated, especially when they have a claim. Find out how the company handles claims. Is the method convenient for you, no matter where you have an accident? Check out the company from an objective source. Your state department of insurance may keep a record of customer complaints. *Consumer Reports* periodically ranks insurance services, too.

Questions to Ask When Purchasing Auto Insurance:

1. What is an appropriate amount of insurance to carry? Is there a minimum amount prescribed by law in our state? What is recommended by our insurance agent? How much do we feel is enough?

2. Can we save money by increasing the amount of our insurance deductible (the amount we have to pay before the insurance company starts to pay)?

3. If our car is more than five to seven years old, and is worth less than $2,000, should we carry collision coverage?

4. Does our insurance company offer more favorable rates for (A) non-drinkers, (B) non-smokers?

5. Can we possibly save on insurance costs by shopping around and getting bids?

6. Have we notified our auto insurance agent about our marriage, so we can take advantage of the lower rates for married couples? If we were good students in school ("B" or better) and/or passed a Drivers' Training course, will these factors help us get lower auto insurance rates?

7. If we move to a new community, or even a different part of town, will our auto insurance rates go up or down?

8. If we drive fewer than a certain number of miles each year, can we receive a discount on our auto insurance rates? Would carpooling help to lower our costs?

9. Does either of our employers offer a group auto insurance plan? If so, is it possible that the rates would be lower than an individually purchased policy? How would the coverage compare to other policies?

10. If we already have health insurance, does our auto insurance have a duplicate health insurance rider, and do we really want or need it?

11. Does our insurance company charge lower rates for different occupations? Do either one or both of our occupations qualify for these lower rates?

12. If more than one car is to be insured, can we get a price break by putting all of our cars under the protection of one policy?

13. Is there a discount for paying our auto insurance premiums annually?

14. Because we can save money on auto insurance by purchasing a less expensive car, is that a strategy we should consider at this time?

15. Will our auto insurance policy cover us if we are involved in an accident caused by an uninsured or underinsured driver? If not, do we need to buy additional coverage?

16. Will our auto insurance cover us if someone files a lawsuit against us as a result of an accident that we caused?

17. Does our auto insurance cover us if either of us has an accident while driving someone else's car? If we lend our car to someone and he or she has an accident while driving, what coverage do we have in this case?

18. Does our auto insurance cover us if we are driving an additional car we own that isn't listed on our policy? What about a motorcycle or motor scooter we own?

19. Does our auto insurance cover us if we rent a car for either business or pleasure?

20. How will the filing of claims, small or large, affect our future insurance rates? Can our insurance be cancelled if we file a claim?

21. How would our insurance premiums be affected if we have an alarm on our car? Is there a savings and is the savings worth the cost of the alarm?

22. Can our insurance carrier give us current information about which cars are the most likely targets for theft so we can avoid purchasing those models?

23. Does our insurance carrier have the correct information about our driving records? (If your driving record has violations on it, they should be wiped from the slate after three years).

24. If our state has no-fault insurance, how does that affect our insurance coverage?

25. Will medical bills be paid promptly by our auto insurance carrier, regardless of who is at fault?

Agreement Check:

1. If you haven't already done so, share a complete driving history with one another. If you've been involved in traffic accidents or if you've received traffic tickets (including parking tickets), this is the time to share that information.

2. If you have changed your name, or if you are planning to change your name through marriage, what steps must be taken to change the information on your driver's license? Write your answer below:

_____

_____

_____

3. If you each own a car, what plans do you have to visit with your auto insurance agent(s) to make adjustments in your auto insurance coverage? Write your answer below:

_____

_____

_____

4. What is the total cost of auto insurance premiums you will pay during your first year of marriage if you do nothing to adjust your current coverage?

Annual Cost of Auto Insurance $_____

5. What can you do to lower these costs? Write your answers below:

_____

_____

_____

6. Complete the forms on the following two pages. Fill in these forms after you visit with your auto insurance agent(s).

Automobile Insurance: Her Car

Make _____ Year _____

Model _____ Insured Drivers _____

Insurance Company _____

Insurance Agent _____ Phone _____

Policy Number _____ Annual Premium _____ Date Due _____

Date Issued _____ Date Expires _____

Types of Coverage	Liability Limits	Cost
Liability		
Property Damage		
Bodily Injury		
Medical Payments		
Comprehensive		
Collision		
Towing		
Car Rental		
Uninsured Motorist		
Underinsured Motorist		
Other		

Automobile Insurance: His Car

Make   Year

Model   Insured Drivers

Insurance Company

Insurance Agent   Phone

Policy Number   Annual Premium   Date Due

Date Issued   Date Expires

Types of Coverage	Liability Limits	Cost
Liability		
Property Damage		
Bodily Injury		
Medical Payments		
Comprehensive		
Collision		
Towing		
Car Rental		
Uninsured Motorist		
Underinsured Motorist		
Other		

Financial Strategy No. 3 for Harmonizing with Financial Law No. 6: Homeowner's Insurance

Whether you own your home or rent it, you must protect yourself from potential losses with homeowner's insurance (it's called homeowner's insurance in either case, but sometimes the term "renters' insurance" is used). **Homeowner's insurance**, like auto insurance, is divided into two types. The first is insurance against damage or theft, fire and other disasters. The second type is liability coverage which protects you against law suits that accuse you of negligence.

Since many of my readers will begin married life by renting a home or apartment, let's look first at how homeowner's insurance protects renters.

Whatever possessions you bring to and store at your rental unit may represent everything you have in the world. Therefore, they should be covered by insurance for their **full-replacement value**. You can buy insurance that provides less coverage, but if there is a theft or fire, you may find that the insurance money (called a settlement) won't be nearly enough to replace your belongings. The owner of the apartment or home you rent will be responsible for insurance on replacement of the building, but that policy won't help replace *your* possessions.

Ask your insurance agent if the insurance you purchase covers the replacement value or the depreciated value of your possessions (replacement cost is the price to replace damaged property).

If only the depreciated value is covered, then a TV you bought for $800 might bring a settlement of as little as $200 by your insurance company in case of theft. You can insure the replacement value by paying a little more in premiums. When you have replacement value coverage, that $800 TV would be replaced at the current market cost, which might be more than what you originally paid for it. I say "might," because some items you own would cost less to replace than you originally paid for them.

Standard renter's policies have many exclusions (items you may own which are not covered).

Check these exclusions carefully. If you own valuables (like expensive furs, jewelry, gold, silver, guns, boats, trailers, stamp and coin collections, computers, computer software and business papers) you should probably buy policy riders (floaters) to cover them.

A policy rider is an additional insurance policy, or an addition to a policy you already own which covers items specifically not covered by a standard policy.

Riders can be purchased at a reasonable price, depending on what you consider to be reasonable. When you are first married, you may have very little extra cash for these insurance riders. If you can't afford insurance riders, consider another way of storing your valuables for safekeeping, especially items like jewelry, furs and cameras. For example, some couples store smaller items in a safe deposit box at their bank.

Once you move to your new residence, I urge you to photograph all your personal possessions and store the photos in a safe deposit box. Many police stations will lend you a special engraving pen so you can permanently mark or etch your valuables for identification. (Many hardware stores also sell these engraving pens.) It's smart to do so, then list the identification numbers for each item, and store this list with the photos.

Occasionally, when real disaster strikes, you may have to temporarily move out of your rental. While repairs are underway, you need to stay somewhere and you need to eat.

But that could cost more than you normally pay for these expenses. Renters should make sure that their coverage pays for the difference between these temporary expenses and normal living costs. There may be limits on this coverage, but ask your agent what benefits you might expect to receive.

If you are fortunate enough to start your married life as a homeowner, you will be required by your mortgage company (the lender who makes the loan to help you buy your home) to carry homeowner's insurance.

Today, young married couples find it necessary to borrow 90 to 95 percent of the cost of their first home (although in some parts of the country it's difficult to find mortgage companies willing to lend more than 80 to 85 percent of a home's value). You will find that the insurance industry has adopted a practice of insuring 100 percent of the replacement value of your home, unless you purchase a home that is more than twenty-five years old. The reason for this is that mortgage companies normally require such coverage. That's the bad news.

The good news is that because of this requirement, you will always collect enough to cover your damages. If your mortgage company doesn't require replacement value coverage, be sure you cover **your belongings** for 100 percent of their replacement value and **your home** for *at least* 80 percent of its replacement value. If you don't know what it would cost to replace your house, ask a local contractor or real estate agent for an appraisal (there is a fee for this service). Then sit down with your homeowner's insurance agent and ask about how to make sure you have enough coverage. Review your coverage at least every two years.

Homeowner's insurance policies don't cover every risk. For example, damage from an earthquake is never covered unless you specifically buy earthquake insurance.

When you meet with your insurance agent, ask for a clear explanation of what risks are and are not covered. The best coverage is "all risk" insurance. But even this coverage doesn't cover everything.

If you are going to live in a townhouse or condominium, you will need a special insurance policy. Usually your condominium or townhouse association buys a master policy that covers the building itself. But you need a policy that covers your belongings. You can also buy a rider to cover any fees assessed by your condo association for its uninsured losses. Once again, ask your insurance agent for advice.

To help keep your homeowner's insurance costs down, you can keep the deductible a little higher. Instead of a $250 deductible, you may want a $1,000 deductible. At least ask your insurance agent for the price difference between the two. Then, make the decision that is best for you.

I want to point out that in some parts of the country (Texas, California and the Gulf Coast States), there exist insurance practices that result in exceptions to these general rules. Your best defense against getting surprised is to ask questions—lots of questions.

Now let's look at **homeowner's liability insurance**.

It may be hard to believe that when someone comes to your home or walks onto your property a law suit could result that accuses you of carelessness. But just ask someone who has been in this situation how disastrous that can be.

Classic examples are a neighbor who slips on ice at your front door and then sues you, or your sweet tempered poodle suddenly takes a liking to the mailman's calf. The legal word for this problem is "tort." A tort is a wrongful act, accident or injury done willfully, negligently or under circumstances involving liability for which a civil suit can be brought against you. Liability insurance protects you against this eventuality. It is also fairly inexpensive. In fact, you can buy an umbrella liability insurance policy that covers your home, your car, your business and other liability actions against you for as little as $200 to $300 a year, giving you protection of up to $1,000,000. However, the cost of all liability insurance coverage is on the rise because of the tendency of people to file more and more lawsuits. This is all the more reason you should not take liability insurance lightly. In the long run, it may be more valuable than many other forms of insurance coverage.

If you rent, you still need liability insurance. The standard minimum liability coverage offered to renters is often only $100,000. This may not be enough in today's world. If your insurance company offers $200,000 or $300,000, you may have better protection, but you still may need more. Ask your agent to help you assess how much protection is needed.

Questions to Ask When Purchasing Homeowner's Insurance:

1. What is the appropriate amount of insurance to carry on our home and/or our personal possessions? What is recommended by our insurance agent? How much do we feel is enough?

2. Can we save money by increasing the amount of our insurance deductible (the amount we have to pay before the insurance starts to pay)?

3. Is this an all-risk policy? If not, what risks will our policy cover? (See the Risk Coverage Checklist below.)

Risk Coverage Checklist:

Hail
Explosion
Smoke
Riot
Flood
Theft
Earthquake
Riots and civil commotions
The weight of ice, snow
　or sleet
Power surges
Frozen plumbing, heating units,
　air-conditioning systems, and
　domestic appliances

Windstorm
Damage by Aircraft and
　Vehicles
Fire
Vandalism and malicious mischief
Lightning
Glass breakage
Comprehensive
Personal liability
Falling objects
The collapse of buildings
Accidental discharge or overflow of
　water or steam

Other coverage as determined by discussion with our insurance agent:

_____

_____

_____

_____

_____

_____

4. What types of risk are excluded from our policy?

- [ ] Earthquakes
- [ ] Floods
- [ ] Termites
- [ ] Landslides
- [ ] Wars
- [ ] Tidal waves
- [ ] Nuclear accidents

5. Will this policy cover the *depreciated* value or the *replacement* value of our personal possessions?

6. Do we require special insurance riders for extra protection on the valuables we own? If we are collectors, do we need special insurance for those possessions? Are we required to have appraisals of certain valuables or collectibles before we can take out personal property riders on them? Do the riders provide full replacement coverage, or could we end up with less than the full cost in case of fire or theft?

7. Does this policy cover us for personal belongings stolen or lost away from home? For example, if our car is broken into, and our clothing, suitcases or other belongings are stolen, will our homeowner's policy cover us? Is there a limit on this coverage?

8. Does this policy guarantee the replacement cost of our home?

9. Does this policy automatically adjust the replacement value as the market value of our home increases, or will we have to work with our insurance agent to adjust the policy each year?

10. Does this policy have a "Loss-of-Use" provision that covers living expenses incurred while our home is being repaired? What is the extent of this coverage?

11. What is the liability protection we need at this time in our lives? Does the policy we're purchasing provide us that liability protection?

12. What is this insurance company's reputation for handling claims? (You can get this information from *Consumer Reports.*)

Martha—could you check to see if we are covered against angry dinosaurs?

Agreement Check:

1. Do you have an up-to-date inventory of your personal property? (If your answer is "No," be sure to complete the inventory in **Appendix B**.)

2. Does your personal property inventory include photographs and identification numbers properly engraved on those items? Where is your inventory stored for safekeeping?

_____

_____

_____

3. What is the cost of homeowner's insurance that you will be paying during your first year of marriage?

Annual Cost of Homeowner's Insurance $_____

4. What are some of the best ways to save money on homeowner's insurance?

- ☐ Increase the deductible?
- ☐ Install dead-bolt locks?
- ☐ Install smoke detectors?
- ☐ Place fire extinguishers in our home?
- ☐ Install a burglar alarm?
- ☐ Install fire alarms?
- ☐ Apply for non-smoker status?
- ☐ Review our policy coverage frequently?
- ☐ Store valuables in a safe deposit box?
- ☐ Work with an insurance broker who may be able to get us discounts?

Other Ideas:

_____

_____

_____

5. Complete the form on the following two pages. Fill in this form after you visit with your homeowner's insurance agent.

Property Insurance

Name of Insured

Insurance Company   Insurance Agent

Address   Phone

Location of Property Inventory   Amount of Coverage

Policy Number   Annual Premium   Annual Deductible

Date Due   Date Issued   Date expires

Location of Policy

Coverage	Liability Limits	Cost

Homeowner's
   House
   Other Structures
   Personal Property
   Liability		

Fire or Lightning		
Windstorm or Hail		
Explosion		
Riot or Civil Disturbance		
Damage From an Aircraft		
Damage From Vehicles		
Smoke Damage		
Vandalism		
Theft		
Glass Breakage		
Volcanic Eruption		
Falling Objects		
Weight of Ice or Snow		

Property Insurance (Continued)

Coverage	Liability Limits	Cost
Freezing of Plumbing, Heating or Air Conditioning Systems		
Accidental Discharge or Overflow of Water from a Plumbing, Heating or Air Conditioning System		
Sudden and Accidental Discharge from an Artificially Generated Electrical Current		
Sudden and Accidental Tearing Apart, Cracking, Burning or Bulging of a Heating, Air Conditioning or Sprinkler System		
All Risk Coverage		
Personal Property Endorsements		
Protection for Loss of Use		
Incidental Property Coverage		
Liability Coverages Including:		
Personal Liability Protection		
Medical Payments to Others		
Damage to Others' Property		
Other		

Financial Strategy No. 4 for Harmonizing with Financial Law No. 6: Health Insurance

One of the greatest catastrophes that can hit a young married couple is illness—especially a major illness. Health insurance is your protection against the enormous costs of illness.

Today, more can be done to save lives and restore health than at any other time in history. But there is a price to pay for the miraculous medical technology that makes this possible—a very big price.

For the last thirty years, the rising cost of medical care has far outgrown both inflation and incomes. Today, even a short hospital stay can prove a substantial drain on the finances of a couple who is uninsured or under-insured. A long illness can prove to be a financial disaster.

Since the health insurance industry seems to have a language of its own, I'm going to give you a short glossary of terms that will help make this short discussion about health insurance easy to understand.

Deductibles—The amount of out-of-pocket expense *you* must pay before your medical policy pays any benefits. Health insurance has several types of deductibles:

Calendar Year Deductible—Runs from January 1st to December 31st of each year. That means each year you must meet your deductible before any benefits are paid. Some plans have a carryover provision that will give you credit for any expenses incurred during the months of October, November, or December. These expenses will then be carried over and used to help meet your next year's deductible.

Per Cause Deductible—Means that a deductible must be met for *each* illness or accident.

Family Deductible—The maximum number of deductibles a family must meet in each calendar year; usually two or three.

Co-insurance—The percentage of each medical bill that *you* are responsible for paying.

Stop Loss—The point at which you are no longer responsible for a percentage of your medical bills. In other words, the insurance plan now pays 100 percent of your eligible medical expenses, usually for the balance of the calendar year.

Lifetime Maximum—The maximum amount the insurance company will pay for medical expenses in your lifetime.

Pre-existing Conditions—Any illness, disease or injury for which treatment or consultation was rendered prior to the effective date of coverage.

Pre-certification—The process whereby the insured must notify the insurance plan prior to admittance to a hospital or before a surgical procedure.

Coordination of Benefits—The method used to determine who pays first when there are two or more medical insurance plans in force.

Health Maintenance Organization (HMO)—A medical insurance plan where the focus is on preventive care and tighter control of costs. Usually set up as a clinic with doctors from all specialities included, the insured selects a physician from within the clinic and pays a nominal fee ($5.00 to $10.00) for each visit. Normally, the insurance plan has a contract with a hospital or hospitals for that level of care, and the hospital(s) provide care at discounts to the HMO in exchange for their admissions.

IPA (Independent Physician Association) or PPO (Preferred Provider Organization)—Similar in concept to a Health Maintenance Organization but you are free to choose a physician or hospital from a list of physicians and hospitals that belong to that association. You see each physician at his or her own office, not at a clinic. A nominal fee (co-payment) is paid for each visit or procedure.

Health insurance today is almost always offered in the form of major medical coverage. This type of policy covers both your inpatient (in-hospital) and outpatient (out-of-hospital expenses).

Policies that provide coverage for in-hospital services only (usually referred to as Basic Hospitalization plans) are not as common today. The exception is some areas of the country where Blue Cross has a strong influence. In this instance, Blue Cross is written as the basic hospitalization coverage and then a major medical policy is written for the outpatient benefits. This type of plan is called a "wrap-around plan."

Because of the high cost of medical insurance premiums, you won't find many health insurance policies that provide "first dollar" coverage anymore. The insurance companies are now offering larger deductibles and greater co-insurance payments.

Health insurance deductibles are built around either a calendar year deductible or a per cause deductible. You don't have to worry that your policy will require both types of deductible.

A **calendar year deductible** runs from January 1st to December 31st of each year. Depending on your policy, you may have to pay anywhere from $100 up to $2,500 of your medical expenses before the insurance company will start to pay its share. The average for most policies is a $250 deductible. So, for example, if in January you break your leg while skiing and the total inpatient and outpatient medical expenses are $2,500, then, if your policy has a calendar year deductible of $250, you can expect help from your insurance company with $2,250 of this expense. You pay the first $250; then the insurance company will help with the rest.

Each health insurance policy differs in how much it will pay for **eligible medical expenses**. Some will pay as little as 70 percent, and others as much as 100 percent. The higher the percentage that *they* pay, the more *you* can expect to pay in annual health insurance premiums. The portion of eligible expenses you must pay is called the **co-insurance requirement**. Returning to our example above (assuming a calendar year deductible of $250), an insurance company paying only 70 percent of eligible expenses would then pay approximately $1,575 of the remaining $2,250 health care bill for repairing your broken leg. You would pay the difference of $675 as your co-insurance payment.

Now let's assume that you have a policy that requires a **per cause deductible** instead of a calendar year deductible. Now if you broke your leg, and for every injury or illness thereafter, you would be responsible for a deductible *each time* you filed a claim. These differences in deductibles (calendar year versus per cause) make it challenging to compare the cost of different policies. Furthermore, and just to make policy comparisons a little harder, to accurately determine just how much you might have to pay in annual health insurance deductibles, you need to examine the policy's "stop loss" provision.

Most of today's major medical policies have a **"stop loss" provision**. The stop loss provision is the point where the insurance company says, "O.K., you've paid out enough this year, we'll pick up the rest of your bills for the balance of the calendar year or benefit period (subject to policy limitations)." After the stop loss provision kicks in, major medical coverage *usually* provides 100 percent of the cost for the *really serious* health care problems you might face (like organ transplants, major surgery or other hospitalizations). With really serious health care problems, major medical providers protect themselves by placing a **lifetime maximum** on these benefits. Some policies have a lifetime maximum benefit of as little as $250,000 and others run as high as $5,000,000. Only in rare cases is the

maximum lifetime benefit unlimited. As you can see, it's super important to study these policy features *before you buy* insurance.

Most married couples will have the opportunity to purchase medical care coverage through an employer's group health insurance plan.

These group plans may offer a wide base of benefits that often include dental or vision programs and a prescription drug card. Some plans even provide psychiatric care. The best health insurance arrangements encourage the practice of preventive medicine through periodic and thorough checkups aimed at early diagnosis of potential problems. Of course, *you* should think prevention, too. If you stop smoking, take part in aerobics workshops and eat right, you probably won't get sick as often. Some employers creatively reward prevention activities because healthy employees mean lower medical costs *for them*. However, *you* should do this simply because of the good feelings that come with maintaining good health.

With health care costs rising so fast, most employers have experienced a dramatic rise in their health care insurance premiums. As a result, they are trying to find ways to limit or cut those costs. Most employers do this by providing less coverage than in the past, or by requiring you to pay a larger part of the monthly health insurance premiums.

319

Some employers have dramatically raised the deductible on their health insurance policies, and have even introduced deductibles based on a fixed percentage of your salary. Almost all employer policies require pre-certification before hospitalization or before surgery is performed to make sure that the treatment is medically necessary. In some cases, the pre-certification process will require that you secure a second opinion. Sit down with a health insurance representative at work and ask him or her to help you fully understand your policy's pre-certification requirements.

If you both work and both have insurance coverage through your employers you should make a thorough review of both plans and their respective premiums. Most plans have what is called a **"coordination of benefits" provision.** This provision outlines the guidelines for payment when an individual is covered under two group insurance plans. These guidelines determine which insurance plan is the primary plan and which is the secondary plan. When the benefits of two insurance plans are coordinated, you can't make money by collecting from both policies for the same health care services. However, both plans may offer benefits for the same illness with the primary plan paying first, and the secondary plan picking up where the primary plan leaves off. Ask your insurance representatives at work to thoroughly explain how the coordination of benefits provisions of your policies work.

When you get married, don't be tempted to drop one of your policies automatically if you both work. Carefully think through these issues first:

1. Job security—Which partner has the most job security and which employer is the most financially stable? Remember, if you work for a small to medium sized employer, there may be a chance your medical benefits could be terminated or changed if your employer gets a high premium increase or suffers a financial setback.

2. Pre-existing conditions—If there are any pre-existing health problems and one of you change jobs, would you be able to get back on another medical plan or qualify for new insurance?

3. Maternity—Are you planning to have children? If so, how soon? Will the mother go back to work after the baby is born? Does either of your employer-sponsored health care plans have maternity coverage? If so, is there a waiting period for the maternity benefit? How long is that waiting period and are you already qualified or not? If the wife's current policy covers maternity, and she decides *not* to return to work after the baby is born, would the husband's employer-sponsored policy insure her and the baby? If not, could she qualify for private insurance coverage?

Rather than choosing one employer to cover both of you, see if you can coordinate your own benefits. Many employers now allow you to pick and choose your coverage to meet your specific needs. Often referred to as **"cafeteria plans,"** these approaches allow an employee to customize his/her own benefit package. See if this option is available to you. Perhaps in this way you can pick up benefits that are available at one company but not at the other. Maybe a dental plan or a vision program will be available from one employer's plan but not available from the other one. The "cafeteria" approach to selecting benefits may give you the strongest and best coverage of all.

Some employers have introduced a **"health-care reimbursement account."** This plan allows you to pay for uncovered medical expenses with pre-tax dollars. With good planning, this can be an excellent way to lower your overall health care bill. The requirement is that you calculate in advance how much you will spend on uncovered medical expenses. Your employer will then withhold this amount from your wages or salary and create a fund to pay these medical expenses. If you don't use it, you lose it, but that shouldn't stop you from using this strategy. Remember, the development of planning skills is what this book is all about.

If you leave your employer, ask about **continued coverage**. Federal law now requires employers who have twenty or more employees to offer them an opportunity to continue their health insurance coverage even after termination. The cost for continued coverage is more expensive than paying premiums as part of a group and this extended coverage only has to be available for eighteen months, but you still have protection.

If you can't purchase health insurance through your employer, you may have to find an individual plan.

Be sure you look into Health Maintenance Organizations (HMOs) as one of your options. Health Maintenance Organizations have strong economic advantages and also offer time-saving convenience. Yes, you often give up other features traditionally associated with medical care when you join an HMO. In many cases, you can't select your own physician. The clinics may be crowded and plainly furnished. But this is not always the case. Some HMOs are "without walls," meaning they allow you to choose from a list of subscribing physicians and hospitals. These are called Independent Practice Associations (IPAs) or Preferred Provider Organizations (PPOs).

Many employers now offer HMOs as an alternative to their own health care plan. If you select an HMO, and then discover you don't like it, you can switch to your employer's plan during the annual enrollment period. An important consideration in selecting an HMO today is its likelihood of staying in business. While your employer will already have investigated the financial strength of any HMO offered to its employees, it's still your responsibility to make sure you don't get surprised and lose your coverage. Ask for copies of the HMO's financial statements for the last few years and look carefully at their ratio of assets to liabilities before joining. If they look weak financially, don't join the plan.

If you are going into business for yourself, you may find that you can't handle the financial burden of full coverage.

In that event, at least make sure you have **catastrophic medical coverage**. You get catastrophic medical coverage simply by purchasing a major medical health insurance policy with a very high deductible (anywhere from $1,000 to $5,000). This means *you* will handle the cost of most medical problems, but the serious illness that can cause catastrophic financial loss will be covered by the insurance company. By the way, don't just assume you and the insurance company have the same definition of the term "castastrophic coverage." Try to avoid policies that limit the number of days for hospital confinement and the amount that is paid per day of confinement. Also, policies that limit the amount of days in coronary or intensive care units are a problem. These are the areas that can cause financial setbacks and deplete your reserves. Examine very carefully what limitations your prospective insurer places on this type of coverage. Then, be sure you can live with those limitations.

One of the features of health insurance policies to watch out for is a clause in the insurance contract that prohibits payment for **pre-existing health care problems**, problems you had (or even problems you had consultation or symptoms for) before you joined the insurance plan. Ask about and read carefully any clauses relating to pre-existing conditions. Don't allow yourselves to be surprised by the exclusions to coverage created by such a clause.

Also be sure any health insurance plan you join is **guaranteed renewable**. This feature assures that your coverage won't be canceled as long as you continue to pay the premiums on time. Just remember, however, that your premiums can always be raised as long as the insurance company raises everyone's premiums at the same time.

Finally, watch out for and avoid health insurance policies that offer **specific illness coverage** only. Cancer policies are a good example. These policies usually duplicate insurance you already have through your group insurance at work or your own major medical policy.

Health insurance is regulated by both the federal and state governments. Since each state has its own mandatory provisions for health care policies, I urge you to find a local insurance agent who specializes in health insurance to help you review what is available and what is advisable to give you the very best coverage possible.

Questions to Ask When Purchasing Health Insurance:

1. How much coverage do we need? Do we need a policy that will cover everything, or is a major medical policy enough right now?

2. Can we purchase health insurance through a group insurance plan with our employer, union, or association?

3. If the plan under consideration is a basic policy which generally covers hospital and surgical expenses, what are the limits of that coverage? Do any of those limits make our coverage inadequate?

4. What types of coverage are specifically not included in the plan we are considering?

5. Are maternity costs covered? What are the limits of this coverage?

6. If any member of our family must be hospitalized, what percentage of the daily room rate is covered? How does this compare with the actual cost of a hospital room in our community?

7. How does the plan pay benefits? Is payment based on "usual, customary and reasonable" charges, or on full costs? (This seemingly small difference can make a *big* difference to you. Ask your agent or insurance representative at work about this.)

8. Does this policy provide any incentives for practicing preventive health care?

9. Does this policy have any clauses for a pre-existing illness or health care condition? Will this affect us?

10. If the pre-existing illness or health care condition clause will affect us, will that condition be covered later?

11. Are there any waiting periods we should know about?

12. Does this policy cover psychiatric problems, including treatment for alcoholism and drug addiction? If so, what actually is covered and what is not covered? (Generally, inpatient and outpatient benefits differ, so ask for a full explanation.)

13. Does this policy provide us major medical coverage? If so, what are the limits? Is this enough in today's world where catastrophic illness can be so expensive?

14. Does this policy cover home health care?

15. Can our premiums go up under this policy? How and to what extent?

16. Can our health insurance be cancelled for any reason? If so, what steps, if any, can we take to correct this problem?

17. How much is the annual or per cause deductible under this policy? Is there a limit on the deductible for the family? What expenses can be applied toward the deductible? Is there also a co-insurance charge with this policy (a portion of each bill that we have to pay even after the deductible has been paid)? Is there a stop-loss provision (the point at which our share of the coinsur-ance is no longer required)? What is the duration of the stop-loss provision (the point at which we will again have to pay deductibles)?

18. Does this policy duplicate any other health insurance coverage we have? What should we do about this if the answer is "yes"?

19. If we had a child, would our insurance cover that child from birth? What coverage would mother and child have in case of a problem pregnancy? Does the policy cover ordinary charges of pregnancy and delivery? Does it cover well-baby care in the hospital?

20. If we terminate our employment and we have health insurance coverage under our employer's group health plan, what are our rights to convert to a private policy? Would we lose any coverage benefits through such a conversion?

21. Does this policy cover organ transplants? If so, is there a limitation on the dollar amount or type of transplant covered? Does the transplant have to be from a live donor?

22. Does this policy provide dental coverage, and if so, do we pay extra for it? What limits are there on dental coverage if it is available?

23. Can we see any doctor we choose under our health care plan? If not, what restrictions are placed on us?

24. Are second opinions required before we have needed surgery or other specialized treatments?

25. Is pre-certification required for surgery or hospital admission? What are the requirements for emergency care?

323

Agreement Check:

1. Do either of you have any pre-existing health care problems that you may not yet have discussed? If you haven't already done so, this is the time to share a complete medical history with one another.

2. Who are your personal physicians?

Physician's Name _____

Address _____

_____

Telephone number _____

Physician's Name _____

Address _____

_____

Telephone number _____

3. What is the cost of health insurance that you will be paying during your first year of marriage?

Annual Cost of Health Insurance $_____

4. When you need to file a health insurance claim, what steps must you go through to do this?

_____

_____

_____

_____

5. Complete the forms on the following two pages. Fill in these forms after you make your decisions about the best way to provide health care protection.

Health Insurance: Hers

Name(s) of Insured
_____

Policy Owner
_____

Insurance Company
_____

Insurance Agent or
Employer Insurance Representative   Phone
_____

Policy Number   Annual Premium   Date Due
_____

Date Issued   Date Expires   Location
                                                     of Policy
_____

Terms of Calendar Year or
Per Clause Deductible
_____

Provisions of Coverage
_____
_____

Pre-existing Conditions Not Covered
_____

Coverage Exclusions
_____

Pre-Certification Requirements
_____

Lifetime Maximum
_____

Stop-Loss Provision
_____

Coordination of Benefits Provision
_____

Maternity Benefits
_____

Other Coverage Benefits
_____

_____

_____

_____

_____

_____

_____

Health Insurance: His

Name(s) of Insured

Policy Owner

Insurance Company

Insurance Agent or
Employer Insurance Representative   Phone

Policy Number   Annual Premium   Date Due

Date Issued   Date Expires   Location
                                                   of Policy

Terms of Calendar Year or
Per Clause Deductible

Provisions of Coverage

Pre-existing Conditions Not Covered

Coverage Exclusions

Pre-Certification Requirements

Lifetime Maximum

Stop-Loss Provision

Coordination of Benefits Provision

Maternity Benefits

Other Coverage Benefits

Financial Strategy No. 5 for Harmonizing with Financial Law No. 6: Disability Insurance

Disability insurance is really income protection insurance. As a married couple, you really should consider buying some form of disability insurance. Why? Because your chances of being incapacitated and unable to work are much higher than the probability of death. How high? At age 22, you are 7.5 times more likely to be seriously disabled for three months than you are to die during the year. For those between the ages of 30 and 65, six times as many people will become disabled as will die. Right now, 6% of adult Americans are classified as disabled.

Since young married couples are almost completely dependent on their income from salaries and wages, the loss of income for more than a few weeks would be disastrous. Disability insurance coverage is an important "safety net" for any financial plan.

Insurance companies have several definitions of disability which you should fully understand because they directly affect the type of insurance policy you buy and the cost of the policy. First, there is disability in which you are confined to a bed and totally incapacitated. Second, is the type of disability where you are not confined to a bed, but you are unable to work at any occupation at all. Third, is the type of disability where you are unable to work at a specific occupation. Buying

coverage for the third type of disability is the most desirable, but it is also the most expensive. Let's look at some of the important features of all disability insurance policies:

Elimination Period—Most disability insurance policies have a waiting period (elimination period) before income payments begin. The longer the waiting period, the smaller the cost of the insurance. The sooner income payments begin, the more expensive the insurance. I recommend a waiting period of no longer than three months if you buy your own policy. Why? For one thing, if the waiting period is three months, your first disability paycheck won't arrive until the end of the fourth month because insurance companies always pay claims at the end of the month, not at the beginning of the month. Most young couples could not wait longer than four months for the first disability income check to arrive. Another reason to choose a 90 day elimination period is because most insurance companies *won't provide coverage with a shorter waiting period if a wife's income is to be included in the coverage* (and this will be the case with many couples, because today a wife's income is often essential to financial survival). Insurance companies have taken this position because pregnancy is now treated as any other illness for purposes of applying for disability benefits. Most women take three or four months off work and apply for disability benefits after delivering their babies. Insurance companies *will pay*, but to reduce their losses, most have chosen to require a ninety day elimination period for coverage on a working woman in the child-bearing years. Besides, in terms of cost savings, the largest price break for extending the waiting period is usually between thirty days and sixty days. So the questions you have to answer are: (1) How much do we save if we increase the waiting period beyond three months and (2) Is the increased cost of a waiting period of less than three months really worth it? Because disability insurance coverage can be very expensive, many couples may not be able to afford it at all unless they choose a policy with a *one year elimination period*. If the only way you can afford coverage is to buy a policy with a one year elimination period, then do it. It's far better to have limited protection than go completely without it. *[Often a young couple can turn to family members for financial help or even secure a short-term loan when there is a serious disability. But this kind of help for more than one year isn't likely. If disability payments start after twelve months, you'll be able to stand on your own feet financially and even pay back a loan or reimburse family members.]*

Length of Coverage—How long payments last also influences the cost of disability insurance. The longer the period of coverage, the more expensive the policy. Most people who own disability policies have coverage that lasts two to five years. The average person has disability coverage that would pay them for five years. Coverage that lasts until age 65 or for life is the best. If you can afford this coverage, buy it. But if you can't afford it, buy a plan that pays benefits for as long as possible based on your ability to buy coverage.

Income Benefits—Usually the income benefits paid are stated as a percentage of your base salary or wages. Most policies won't provide more than 60 to 80 percent of your base pay. This is because the insurance company and your employer want you to have a strong incentive to go back to work and also because they don't want anyone to actually make money on a disability insurance claim. Disability income payments are often non-taxable, too (more on this later). Some policies offer income benefits that are indexed to inflation. When the income payments are indexed to inflation, that means your income will increase as the cost of living goes up.

Partial Disability—The facts indicate that a partial disability is much more likely than complete or total disability. Therefore, your disability insurance plan should definitely cover partial disability. Remember, you're insuring against risk, the kind of event that is *most* likely to happen. Since partial disability income benefits are paid differently from total disability benefits, be sure you have a full understanding of what your benefits would be under any plan you consider. *(Partial disability income benefits are expressed either as **residual** or **proportionate** benefits. Ask for a full explanation of these concepts from your agent or employer insurance representative.)*

One way to secure disability insurance is through a group insurance plan sponsored by your employer. When you are first married, this may be the only type of disability insurance you can afford.

There are two basic kinds of plans offered by most employers. They are **short-term plans** and **long-term plans**. Short-term plans usually have a short waiting period before benefits begin (a few days, for example, as compared to a few months for long-term plans). However, the income payments from a short-term plan last only for a period of weeks, perhaps 26 to 52 weeks. The income payments are usually modest, and they don't approximate your salary or wages. Short-term disability insurance plans simply don't attempt to meet the need for protection against more serious, prolonged disabilities that can be financially catastrophic. I don't recommend you participate in such a plan unless it is provided by your employer at no cost to you.

One form of short-term disability insurance you *should* examine is **mortgage disability insurance**. Mortgage disability insurance can be valuable because there may be times when all you need to get you through a short-term disability is money to pay your house payment each month. Nearly 50% of the mortgage foreclosures in recent years resulted from the loss of income due to disability. This type of disability insurance won't be offered by your employer. Most homeowner's insurance agents can give you competitive bids on this type of short-term disability policy. Banks and other lending institutions who make mortgage loans are also a source for mortgage disability insurance.

Long-term group disability insurance programs are designed to take care of the more serious long-term disability problems. A waiting period of ninety days to six months is almost always required before income benefits begin with these policies. Long-term group disability policies often pay to age 65, but not always. An employer-sponsored plan may limit your coverage to five or ten years. Be sure you know what benefits you have. The option is usually available to buy protection for life, but there is a little higher cost for this coverage.

Although disability insurance benefits won't equal your gross earnings, they may come close to your net, after-tax earnings.

If your insurance plan is purchased with money out of your own pocket, these benefits are *not taxable*. In that case, 60 to 80% of your gross income would almost equal your take home pay. However, if your employer provides your disability coverage, the benefits *are taxable*. Therefore, in the event your employer offers disability insurance as part of a total benefits package, you might ask if you can choose a benefit other than disability coverage and buy a disability policy on your own. If that choice isn't available (which it rarely is), then look at the benefits offered by your employer's plan and see if they are sufficient. If not, add to your coverage with a personal, supplemental plan.

If you buy a disability insurance policy that supplements the one provided by your employer, remember this fact: there is no such thing as double coverage with disability insurance.

You won't be able to collect disability insurance benefits from two policies. And no insurance company will pay a claim for disability insurance that exceeds 80% of your insurable income. However, the supplemental coverage you purchase on your own can *coordinate* with your group disability plan so that you receive an income when your employee benefits stop. That is not the same thing as double coverage. So before you buy a supplemental disability policy, make sure you know exactly how it coordinates with your employer-sponsored policy *and* make sure that you are not buying more insurance than your net earnings will allow.

If you leave an employer and your group policy can be extended or in any way converted to an individual, private policy, be sure to consider this option. Before you automatically cancel such a policy, see if the policy has provisions that would be hard to duplicate elsewhere. Sit down with your insurance agent and make this decision together.

If a group disability insurance policy is not available through your employer, your union or some other organization to which you belong, then you will have to look for an individual policy.

Of course, this is much more expensive. To keep the cost down, try extending the waiting period to at least one full year before payments begin. Selecting a longer waiting period may be the only way you can afford coverage as a young married couple.

Some insurance companies offer a "step-rate premium." If cash is tight, a step-rate premium can provide the policy at a lower cost to begin with, but the cost increases as you grow older. The assumption is that you will earn more as you grow older, and, therefore, you will be able to pay the higher premium later on.

Many insurance companies are now offering a new version of disability insurance called **"Annually Renewable Disability Insurance."** Under these plans, the premium is adjusted upward each year. Usually, the coverage for the first year or two is quite affordable, but

the cost in future years is *very* high. These plans have been designed to provide coverage to those who can't afford other plans and who anticipate *major* increases in their income. Try to stay away from these policies unless this is the only coverage you can afford. Even then, if you buy one of these policies, be sure that you can convert it to a level premium policy at a later date. (With a level premium policy, your premiums remain the same year after year.)

As your income increases, be sure to work closely with your insurance agent to make sure your coverage has also been increased. A disability insurance policy that covers 60 to 80 percent of your base pay should cover your current income, not what your income was several years ago.

When you buy a disability insurance policy, make sure that it is guaranteed renewable (that you can't be turned down for coverage at some arbitrary time because circumstances have changed).

Also, remember this important advice. Any disability insurance policy you buy should state clearly that the policy is **non-cancellable.** This will keep the insurance company from arbitrarily cancelling the policy and substituting it with one with much higher premiums. To be very specific about these two features (guaranteed renewable and non-cancellable), ask your agent to show you the exact wording in your disability insurance policy that provides this assurance.

If you become disabled, chances are very good that you will recover and be able to return to work. But you may not be able to handle full-time work at first.

For this reason, some policies offer **"transition benefits."** Transition benefits usually pay the difference between your actual income and what you would be earning if full employment were possible. At least that is the general idea. Keep in mind, however, that each insurance company defines transition benefits differently. Some companies won't pay transition benefits unless certain, very specific requirements are met. Ask for a full explanation of this benefit as it is defined in any policy you consider. Without transition benefits, you may find that any return to work may cause your disability income payments to stop completely.

You are also entitled to disability insurance protection under Social Security if you pay Social Security taxes.

But the benefits you might receive from this insurance are quite small. Usually, only those who are totally disabled ever receive such benefits. To get them you must have a physical or mental condition that prevents you from doing any gainful work, and the impairment must last at least 6 months or be expected to result in death. Disability payments usually start with the sixth full month of disability (although you can apply for benefits as soon as you become disabled). It pays the same amount you would get upon retirement at age 65. This may not even come close to your current income. You don't have to pay Social Security taxes very long to become eligible for disability benefits. If you are under 24, you qualify by having worked for 18 of the previous 36 months. The work time expands with age, reaching five years (20 calendar quarters) for people age 31 through 42. The longest anyone has to work to collect benefits is 10 years.

Call your local Social Security Administration office (or SSA's nationwide toll-free number 1-800-772-1213) for the latest information on benefits available. [By the way, if you haven't yet notified the Social Security Administration about your marriage, do that at the same time. Failing to do so could result in the loss of important benefits for a surviving spouse.]

Sometimes a disability insurance policy will pay a reduced income benefit when Social Security disability income starts paying. Check your insurance policy carefully to see if this is the case. It will cost more money to have coverage that is not reduced by Social Security payments. Nevertheless, the cost may be worth it.

Another form of disability insurance comes in the form of **Worker's Compensation benefits**. For those who are injured on the job, some coverage is usually provided under Worker's Compensation laws. These laws (while different in each state) are intended to provide benefits only for work-related injuries and diseases. Check with your employer to find out what your coverage includes. Also check to see if any disability insurance policies you own (private or group policies) offset against (subtract) Worker's Compensation payments from your disability insurance benefits because this could substantially lower what you receive from these policies. Whatever your Worker's Compensation coverage may be, don't rely on Worker's Compensation benefits as your only source of protection. As a young married couple, your ability to earn a living is your greatest financial asset. Take steps now to make sure you have sufficient coverage.

Questions to Ask When Purchasing Disability Insurance:

1. How long could we get by without our income if either one or both of us were disabled?

2. What other sources of income could we turn to if a disability should cut off our income(s)?

3. Do we have Worker's Compensation benefits in the event of disability? What are they and how do they offset any disability insurance policies we own or are considering?

4. What are the current Social Security benefits we would receive in the event of disability?

5. How much "sick pay" does our employer provide and how much "sick pay" credit have we built up with our employer(s)?

6. Does our employer provide a disability insurance program?

7. If the answer to No. 6 is "Yes," is the plan offered a short-term plan or a long-term plan?

8. What is the waiting period (elimination period) before income payments begin under this plan?

9. Does this plan cover disabilities caused by both accident and illness?

10. What is the definition of "disabled" under this policy?

11. Is partial disability covered under this plan? In order to qualify for partial disability benefits, do we have to be totally disabled first?

12. What are the monthly income benefits under this plan? Are these income payments taxable?

13. How long or until what age will we receive benefits?

14. Would our benefits stop if the one disabled were able to work in a limited capacity? Would payment of benefits be reduced if for any reason earnings continue to be received by the one disabled?

15. What will happen to our disability income protection if we change jobs? Can we take this coverage with us?

16. If there is no plan offered by our employer(s) or if the plan offered is not adequate, should we look for an individual policy to cover any income shortfall?

17. Does our disability policy provide special benefits in the event of the loss of a limb or eyesight, or death? Do we want and/or need these extra benefits?

18. Can the insurance company cancel our plan or raise our insurance premiums for any reason?

19. Is there a discount on the cost of disability insurance if we are non-smokers?

20. Will our coverage increase as our income goes up?

21. Do the benefits go up with inflation (before a disability occurs) (after a disability occurs)?

22. Are the premiums step rate or fixed? Are the premiums changed every year? (Some insurance companies offer Annually Renewable Disability Insurance policies that have very low premiums in the first year or two. After that, the premiums go up very rapidly. Before you buy one of these policies, discuss with your agent how you might be expected to pay the higher premiums in future years.)

23. What will it cost to have benefits payable for life?

24. How much more will it cost us to buy disability insurance if we wait a few years?

25. Where are our policies placed for safe keeping? Did we ask our employer for a copy of our disability insurance policy and did we actually get one? (If you don't ask for a copy of your employer's policy, you probably won't be given one.)

26. Did we request a copy of our disability insurance application, and have we reviewed it carefully to make sure it is accurate?

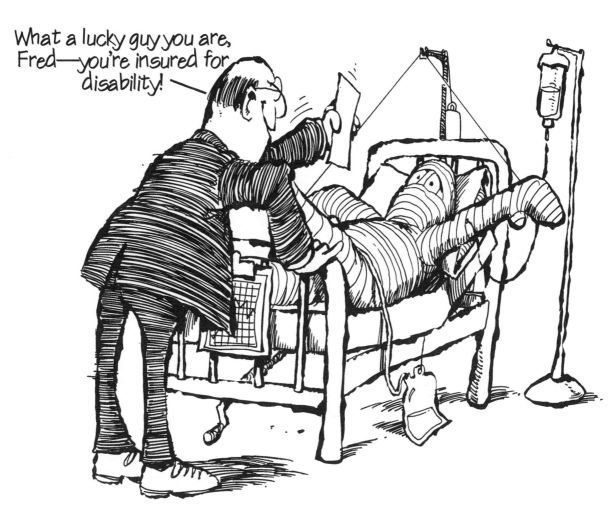

Agreement Check:

1. Do you feel that one or both of your incomes should be protected with disability insurance? Do you presently have some coverage? Should you increase your coverage? How can you do this most economically?

2. If you have disability insurance, what is the waiting period before you could begin to collect from your disability insurance policy? Write the answer below:

_____

3. How long would these benefits last?

4. What percentage of your annual income would be provided under your current coverage if either one of you became disabled?

% of Her Income_____

% of His Income_____

5. Are the benefits you would receive taxable? If so, how much would this reduce the value of the income benefits?_____

6. What is the annual cost that you will be paying for disability insurance during your first year of marriage?

Annual Cost of Disability Insurance $_____

7. How would you apply for benefits if you were disabled?

_____

_____

_____

_____

8. Complete the forms on the following two pages. Fill in these forms after completing a formal review of your disability insurance needs.

Disability Insurance: Hers

Name of Insured

_____

Policy Owner

_____

Insurance Company

_____

Insurance Agent or
Employer Insurance Representative   Phone

_____

Policy Number   Annual Premium   Date Due

_____

Date Issued   Date Expires   Location
                                                of Policy

_____

Definition of Disability
Under this Policy (Total & Partial)

_____

Provisions of Coverage

_____

Waiting Period

_____

Length of Benefit (5 Year, to Age 65, etc.?)

_____

Monthly Benefits

_____

Partial Disability Benefits

_____

Taxability of Benefits

_____

Transition Benefits (Included? Definition?)

_____

Guaranteed Renewability Provision

_____

Non-cancellable Provision

_____

Fixed Premium

_____

Indexing Benefit

_____

Exclusions (Permanent or Removable?)

_____

Dividends (When Payable?)

_____

Waiver of Premium (For How Long?)

_____

Other

_____

Disability Insurance: His

Name of Insured
_____

Policy Owner
_____

Insurance Company
_____

Insurance Agent or
Employer Insurance Representative _____ Phone _____

Policy Number _____ Annual Premium _____ Date Due _____

Date Issued _____ Date Expires _____ Location of Policy _____

Definition of Disability
Under this Policy (Total & Partial)
_____

Provisions of Coverage
_____

Waiting Period
_____

Length of Benefit (5 Year, to Age 65, etc.?)
_____

Monthly Benefits
_____

Partial Disability Benefits
_____

Taxability of Benefits
_____

Transition Benefits (Included? Definition?)
_____

Guaranteed Renewability Provision
_____

Non-cancellable Provision
_____

Fixed Premium
_____

Indexing Benefit
_____

Exclusions (Permanent or Removable?)
_____

Dividends (When Payable?)
_____

Waiver of Premium (For How Long?)
_____

Other
_____

Financial Strategy No. 6 for Harmonizing with Financial Law No. 6: Life Insurance

"Life insurance" is the ultimate euphemism. A "euphemism" is a word or a phrase used in place of another that is considered too unpleasant. Life insurance is a great example. Life insurance is really a contradiction in terms. It would be more accurate to call it "death insurance." Let's face it, the financial catastrophe you are insured against is death. You may not enjoy discussing this subject, but being married means caring enough to protect your partner against the consequences of an early death.

The fact is, "none of us are going to get out of this life alive." Death doesn't send an invitation, it just shows up at your doorstep. Usually one partner dies and one survives. The marriage partner left behind still has to carry on.

Life insurance provides an instant source of money to the surviving spouse. How much money will be needed? That's not an easy question to answer. Formulas have been developed to try to answer it. But in the long run, the two of you will have to sit down and answer this question for yourselves. Some of the factors to consider are:

Funeral Expenses—There is a high cost to dying. $10,000 will just about do it. If you want to go out in style, plan to spend a lot more.

Uninsured Medical Expenses—Remember, medical insurance for catastrophic illnesses will probably cover only 80%. The remaining 20% could be a lot of money.

Family Expenses—For at least two years (and preferably much longer), your surviving spouse will need money to carry on without you. There needs to be ample cash for all the normal expenses. How much will that be?

Emergency Fund—Every surviving spouse should have an emergency fund. As much as $25,000 to $50,000 may be adequate, but more could be needed.

Child-Care Fund—If there are children, no matter which parent dies, the survivor will face enormous child-care expenses. This is just one reason there should be life insurance coverage on both your lives.

Education Fund—The cost of education for a child should be considered, but so should the education and training of a surviving spouse. The cost of education is always going up, so you will have to assess and reassess this need every year.

Repayment of Debts—Adequate insurance coverage will pay off all your outstanding debts. This amount will be different for every married couple, and here, too, you will need to evaluate your coverage at least once a year.

When you are first married, you will probably see life insurance as a way of providing money for an adjustment period for the survivor. Later on, if you have children, you'll have other considerations. Their education *and* support will represent sizeable expenses. Even later in your marriage, life insurance can serve other purposes, such as paying for federal and state death taxes and other costs associated with settling your estate.

What type of life insurance should you buy? Young married couples should buy the most inexpensive form of life insurance available. That happens to be **Annual Renewable Term Insurance**. There are two types of life insurance, **permanent insurance** and **term insurance**. Permanent insurance combines life insurance with savings and/or investments. Permanent insurance is also known as whole life and/or cash value insurance. Term insurance is pure insurance. Term insurance is much less expensive than permanent insurance. That's why pure term life insurance is what is needed for the first few years of marriage.

How much will term insurance cost? You should be able to buy $100,000 worth of annual renewable term life insurance for less than $200 a year (assuming you are 20 to 35 years old, in good health and a non-smoker). Your premiums will go up a little each year, however. This is because as you grow older, your risk of dying increases. Since it is this risk that you're insuring against, the annual cost increase makes sense.

Your insurance agent will be able to show you how much your premiums will rise each year. If the projected increase is a ***guaranteed premium***, then there won't be any surprises. However, today most insurance companies are avoiding guaranteed premiums. This means that the projected increases

in the cost of your insurance might be *approximations*. With approximations, if the cost of providing insurance coverage goes up, the insurance company passes those costs on to you through higher premiums. Your challenge is (1) to select a company that will offer guaranteed premiums, *and* (2) to buy insurance from a company that is financially very strong. Stay far away from life insurance companies who also sell health insurance, because health insurance companies are going to face tremendous cost increases in the future. Those cost increases will be passed on to *all* of their policyholders. In all cases, ask your insurance agent to provide you with ratings from A.M. Best, Moody's and Standard and Poor's *before you buy any life insurance policy* (see footnote at the end of this chapter about these rating services).

Some term life insurance is "convertible." This means you can trade your term policy for permanent insurance later on if that makes sense.

One terrific way to keep your life insurance costs down is to be a non-smoker. Remember, the insurance company wants you to live and pay premiums as long as possible. Smoking increases your chances of dying early. If you have smoked in the past, but have stopped, you must usually have stopped for a full twelve months before an insurance company will consider you a non-smoker.

Where should you go to buy life insurance? Start with your employer. Most employers offer very inexpensive group life insurance policies as part of a fringe benefit package. If not available through your employer, you can buy individual policies from any life insurance agent. However, the life insurance industry is very competitive, so shop carefully.

When you fill out an application for life insurance, ask to be given a copy of the application from your agent. Why? Because you need to double and triple check that every piece of information on that application is true and accurate. If it is not, the life insurance company may never have to pay. False or fraudulent information on an application can easily result in letting the insurance company off the hook, even if you've been paying your insurance premiums. Also remember this piece of advice: when you apply for an individual life insurance policy, you will be asked questions about your medical history, your vocation, your avocations (hobbies), and your morals. Most insurance companies will take steps to verify this information. They can do this by asking your employers, neighbors and creditors (including the credit bureau) all about you. You can request that these background checks be waived and that all such information be gathered by way of a direct interview with you. If they refuse to do this, then be sure you request a copy of all information that is gathered so you can review and correct it. Why? Because your insurance company will file a report with what is known as the Medical Information Bureau. This is a national clearinghouse used by all insurance companies. If incomplete or inaccurate information gets into that file, it will stay there for several years and you may know nothing about it. Such inaccurate information could keep you from *ever* getting insurance.

Whose life should be insured?
Both of you should have some life insurance which names your marriage partner as the beneficiary. The beneficiary is the surviving partner who receives the life insurance benefits when death occurs. If you have children, having life insurance on both husband and wife is extremely important. The difference is, you'll need more of it.

If you already have a life insurance policy, the first thing you should do is contact your insurance agent and make sure your marriage partner is the beneficiary. Don't delay. If your policy is provided by your employer, go to the employment benefits office and make the change in beneficiary. Make sure your marriage partner is the beneficiary of any other forms of insurance you have as well.

Once this is done, sit down together with your agent or insurance representative and talk about how the life insurance benefits will be paid out when death occurs. Why? Because there are many options available, and only one of those options will provide the insurance benefits income tax free. It can be a terrible shock to a surviving spouse to discover that an insurance payout option has been selected that makes the insurance benefits taxable, or in some other way that imposes a hardship.

What about life insurance that combines insurance with a savings program and/or as a way to invest? Only permanent life insurance policies provide these benefits.

These policies go by many names. Some of the more familiar are **permanent insurance**, **whole life**, **endowment life**, **universal life** and **variable life**. You should take time to learn about all of them as you continue to expand your knowledge about money and finance, but whether you choose to use them will depend heavily on your saving habits and your investment objectives. If you have poor saving habits, then the discipline of combining insurance coverage with savings may be of help to you. However, the truth is that you will always pay a price for making this choice. Administration costs and other restrictions with such policies always reduce your saving benefits.

When you use life insurance to save *and* invest, study the insurance policy and the insurance company very carefully, applying the Ten Question Test I gave you on investing in Chapter Eight. Then make up your own mind.

What clauses should you watch out for in your life insurance policy?

First, make sure your policy covers you **when you travel by airplane**. It is rare to find a policy that doesn't provide this coverage, but ask anyway. You don't want to be buying flight insurance at airports. It's not only a waste of your money, but it takes the fun out of flying. Some credit cards now offer automatic life insurance coverage for air travelers when you use their card to purchase your ticket. However, don't count on this coverage to take care of your insurance needs. Without a copy of the policy, you don't know what kind of coverage you really have.

Next, look to see if there is a **war exclusion** in your policy. Today, there is rarely a life insurance policy issued without this exclusion (although some

companies offer war coverage as a way of attracting young couples who are connected to the military). A war exclusion prevents coverage of your life in the event you die in a war. If you need life insurance to cover the possibility of war, discuss this directly with your agent.

Check to see if your policy has extra insurance riders. A rider is an additional amount or type of insurance that is added to your basic policy.

Each of these riders will cost money. Sometimes they are worth the expense, and sometimes they are not. You must decide. The most popular riders are indexing, guaranteed insurability, double indemnity, waiver of premium and disability income. Let's examine these riders.

An **indexing** rider is one that automatically increases the death benefit of your life insurance policy based on increases in the Consumer Price Index. For example, if you are 24 and buy a $100,000 life insurance policy, and the Consumer Price Index goes up by 7 percent next year, your insurance company will send you a notice saying that your coverage has increased by 7 percent, too. You will also have to pay a small increase in premium, but the premium will be calculated based on the assumption that you are still 24 years old. The one limitation is that the death benefit stops increasing once it has doubled. So, for our 24 year old with a $100,000 policy, the indexing benefits cap when the death benefit reaches $200,000. You don't have to pass a physical examination or meet any other test to get the increased coverage. All you have to do is pay the higher premium. Most indexing riders allow you to stop the automatic increases at any time you wish. However, once you stop using the indexing benefit, you can't start it again.

Under a **guaranteed insurability** rider, you can purchase additional insurance at specified intervals without proving your insurability. If you choose this rider, be sure you know the cut off date or age for exercising this option. Usually, you can only exercise this option every three years between the ages of 21 and 40. After 40, you may lose this option entirely. The better companies also allow you to purchase additional insurance under this rider when you 1) get married or 2) when a child is born to your marriage. This means you don't have to wait until the next scheduled interval to increase your coverage. Such an option can be very important for two reasons. First, you can give your marriage partner or new child increased protection immediately. Second, if you have become uninsurable since you bought your policy, you can't be turned down for extra coverage because of a change in your health. However, these opportunities for increasing your coverage are "use it or lose it" options. That means *you* must request that the coverage be increased. Don't expect the insurance company to send you a special invitation to take advantage of your option.

Double indemnity riders (sometimes called "accidental death benefit riders") are popular because they pay double the amount of the insurance if the insured person dies due to an accident. However, if the accident was the fault of the insured person, the insurance company will not have to pay this extra benefit.

Waiver of premium assures that your insurance premiums get paid if you become disabled. This is very important. Just remember, however, that if you elect to purchase this rider and if you become disabled, you must be totally disabled. There is no coverage for partial disability under this rider. In addition, there is usually a six month waiting period before the insurance premiums will be paid by the insurance company. That means you have to pay the premiums yourself for the first six months. However, the small cost for this rider is usually well worth the money. The better companies tie their waiver of premium rider to their guaranteed insurability rider. This means that in the event you are disabled, you will be allowed to increase your coverage at every interval until age forty and the cost of that increased coverage (should you choose it) will be paid by the insurance company.

Disability income riders on life insurance policies are offered by many companies. They are a poor investment because they provide only a small disability benefit. Avoid them.

The final two clauses you should be especially mindful of are the **grace period clause** and the **reinstatement clause**. The grace period is that length of time a policy remains in force after you fail to pay the premium (usually 30 days). Why is this important? Because if you ever forget to pay the premium, you don't want your insurance cancelled. Usually, your insurance company will send you a notice stating that the grace period is about to expire. At that point, you had better be sure your premium is sent to the insurance company. If the grace period expires, most companies will allow you to reinstate the policy within a specified period (usually within 60 days after the lapse of coverage). However, you may have to prove you are insurable all over again.

Speaking about **proof of insurability**, you're going to find that all insurance companies want to insure the lives of people who are in good to excellent health. If you are overweight, have high blood pressure, diabetes or any number of additional health problems, you will find that the cost of your life insurance will increase dramatically. Your occupation could have a similar effect on the cost of life insurance. If you're an explosives expert (as opposed to an office secretary), your life insurance may not only cost more, you may find it impossible to buy life insurance at all. Be sure to tell your agent the absolute truth about your occupation and your health. In cases where there has been a cover-up of these facts, the life insurance company usually doesn't have to pay. Also, if you're in good health, do everything possible to stay that way.

Most insurance companies now require a physical exam before they will provide coverage.

Usually this exam will be administered by someone other than a physician. Special insurance examining services use paramedics for this purpose most of the time. In any case, you can and should expect that this exam will include blood and urine testing. Because this is true, you should do everything possible to make sure your tests produce the best possible results. Don't drink or stay out late at a party the night before an insurance exam. Watch your diet carefully and make sure you are not on medications. If you are, be sure to tell the examiner. All blood test results for all insurance companies are a matter of record and are stored with the Home Office Referral Laboratory. You *are* entitled to see your test results, but you must request this information in writing. Ask your agent to tell you how to make this request.

Of course, there are other important clauses in your life insurance policy to know about and understand. However, once you actually receive a copy of your policy, you may find *you can't understand it* because the language used to write these contracts is "legalese." Don't let that stop you. Go straight to your insurance advisor and make sure he or she takes the time to explain what the policy says. Ask the advisor about all of the clauses highlighted in this discussion and then ask him/her to explain all of your options under the beneficiary designation clause, the incontestability clause, the suicide clause, the settlement options and anything else that you want to know about. Always remember that having full knowledge about insurance is fully *your* responsibility.

Questions to Ask When Purchasing Life Insurance:

1. Should we consider using a professional life insurance counselor to help us with a review of our life insurance needs?

2. What will the life insurance coverage that we actually need cost?

3. Can we afford it, or should we settle for a little less coverage at this time?

4. Is life insurance available to us through our employer(s)? Are there limits on how much life insurance our employer(s) will provide?

5. What would it cost to purchase

individually owned policies directly from a life insurance company?

6. Can we purchase a "family plan" for life insurance and save money by doing so? If we do this, what happens to the insurance on surviving family members when one member of the family dies?

7. Are there any discounts in the cost of our life insurance if we are non-smokers?

8. Have we looked carefully at any riders offered by life insurance companies to see if we want or need them?

9. If we buy our own policies, can we save money on the cost of life insurance by paying our premiums just once each year?

10. Do we know when our insurance coverage actually begins? Will it begin when we sign an application form, when we sign our check to pay the premium or when the policy actually arrives? Did we get a receipt from our life insurance agent telling us when our coverage actually begins?

11. Did we request a copy of the application for insurance so we can check its accuracy? Did we request a waiver of a credit bureau check and other investigative procedures? If that request was denied, did we request a copy of the investigative report that will be filed with the Medical Information Bureau?

12. Do we know when and under what conditions or circumstances our life insurance coverage would end?

13. What are the conditions for annual renewal of our life insurance, and will the costs go up each year?

14. Does the death benefit (the amount paid to the survivor beneficiary) under our life insurance policy ever increase, and, if so, under what conditions?

15. Once our policy arrives, will we take the time to read and understand it? (Once your policy arrives, the law allows you 20 days to accept or reject it and regain a full refund of your premiums. This is called the "right to examine." This right must be requested in writing at the same time you make your decision to buy the policy. Otherwise, should you decide to cancel after examining the policy, you lose your premium.)

Agreement Check:

1. What is the purpose of buying life insurance at this time?

☐ Money for a surviving spouse
☐ Money to help with raising and educating children
☐ Money to pay off our home loan
☐ Money to pay off debts other than our home loan
☐ Other _____

_____

_____

2. How much money do you believe should be available for one another through life insurance?

$_____For her $_____ For him

3. How did you arrive at this decision?

4. Have you named each other as beneficiaries of your life insurance policies, and have you carefully examined the payout options and selected the one that makes most sense?

5. What will be the annual cost of your life insurance coverage during the first year of marriage?

Annual Cost of Life Insurance $_____

6. If you needed to file a death benefit claim, how would you do that?

_____

_____

_____

7. Complete the forms on the following two pages. Fill in these forms after completing a formal review of your life insurance needs.

Life Insurance: Hers

Name of Insured
_____

Policy Owner   Primary and Secondary
                      Beneficiaries
_____

Insurance Company
_____

Insurance Agent or
Employer Insurance Representative   Phone
_____

Policy Number   Annual Premium   Date Due
_____

Date Issued   Date Expires   Location
                                   of Policy
_____

Type of Policy (Term or
Permanent Insurance)
_____

Special Policy Features

_____

_____

Aviation Clause
_____

War Exclusion
_____

Indexing
_____

Guaranteed Insurability
_____

Double Indemnity
_____

Waiver of Premium
_____

Disability Income Rider
_____

Guaranteed Renewability
_____

Non-Cancellable
_____

Family Benefit Rider
_____

Dividend Provisions
_____

Classified or Rated Premiums
_____

Smoker/Non-smoker
_____

Other
_____

Life Insurance: His

Name of Insured

Policy Owner | Primary and Secondary Beneficiaries

Insurance Company

Insurance Agent or
Employer Insurance Representative | Phone

Policy Number | Annual Premium | Date Due

Date Issued | Date Expires | Location of Policy

Type of Policy (Term or Permanent Insurance)

Special Policy Features

Aviation Clause

War Exclusion

Indexing

Guaranteed Insurability

Double Indemnity

Waiver of Premium

Disability Income Rider

Guaranteed Renewability

Non-Cancellable

Family Benefit Rider

Dividend Provisions

Classified or Rated Premiums

Smoker/Non-smoker

Other

Insurance You Don't Need—and Probably Can't Afford

You will definitely receive many offers to buy insurance, especially when you are first married. Being responsible about insurance planning is important. But there is no need to go overboard with insurance coverage and make yourselves "insurance poor." Take it slow and easy and cover the basics. Simply show each other that you care enough to learn about and take action to insure against the *major* catastrophes that can occur.

There are some offers of insurance you should avoid completely. Others should be studied with great care before you buy them. Let's examine a few that you will encounter most frequently.

Insurance at Airports: These policies should be avoided completely. There is simply no need for flight insurance if you have taken the proper steps to buy life insurance and make sure you are covered when you fly.

Mortgage Insurance: When you buy a home, the home loan (mortgage) represents a large debt. You may find yourself overwhelmed by the offers to buy mortgage insurance (not to be confused with mortgage disability insurance discussed earlier). Mortgage insurance is just another form of life insurance. It pays off the balance of the mortgage if the insured person dies before the loan is completely paid off. If you already have life insurance and you own a home, then the life insurance proceeds should provide ample funds to either continue making house payments or to pay off the mortgage. You decide if you want, and can afford, the extra coverage provided by a separate mortgage insurance policy. Several years down the road, you may have ample funds to consider mortgage insurance, but even then you should study such insurance with great care before you buy. If you do buy it, make sure that the lives of both husband and wife are covered.

Liability Insurance: Your automobile insurance and homeowner's policies provide liability protection, but both have limits. If you're sued, and lose, the court-awarded damages could exceed those limits. For this reason, many couples buy an umbrella liability policy for up to $1 million. The cost is modest, but you may find that you can't afford this extra liability protection at the start of married life. Ask your automobile insurance agent how to get the maximum liability protection at the lowest cost without a separate umbrella liability policy. Then, ask your agent to help you assess your remaining risk to see if more insurance is required. You may very well need the protection, but if you need it *that* badly, you probably can't afford *not* to have it.

Credit Life Insurance: When you take out a loan, the lender may offer you credit life insurance. This type of insurance pays off the balance of your loan in the event death occurs before the loan is completely paid. Once again, if you have enough life insurance coverage, then the surviving spouse should have ample funds to pay off your debts. However, some loans may not be offered *unless* you buy credit life insurance. In that event, if the loan is critically important to you, buy the credit life insurance policy. But generally speaking, credit life insurance is an extra expense you can live without.

Cancer Insurance: Actually, any single disease insurance should be avoided. Your basic health insurance and major medical coverage are what you need now.

Auto Insurance on Rented Cars: If you're traveling on business and your expenses are being paid by your em-

ployer, your employer probably has a rule about paying for additional auto insurance on any cars you rent. Know what that rule is and follow it.

When you travel as private citizens, you can generally skip the extra expense of auto rental insurance if you have made certain your own auto insurance policy provides coverage when you rent a car. If you haven't checked this out carefully before you travel, buy the extra insurance.

What Else Do You Need to Know and How In the World Are You Going To Learn It All?

"Plenty" is the answer to the first question. You need to learn a lot more about insurance than the overview given here. That learning will come through your own continuing education program, which I hope you will pursue by reading the books suggested at the end of this chapter.

As each year goes by, you also need to have an annual insurance check-up. You can do this by scheduling a meeting with each other to review all the questions and Agreement Checks provided in this chapter.

Just update your answers, and see if your coverage is appropriate for any changes in your circumstances. Be sure you examine the changes that have introduced more (or less) risk into your lives. Look at the *cost* of your insurance again. See if there are ways to lower those costs. And finally, ask the "what if" questions that helped you decide on your original insurance coverage. What if either one of us dies? What if either one of us is disabled? What if this, what if that? Once you make your decisions (and implement them), then forget this conversation for another year.

Suggested Additional Reading:

To investigate the financial strength of an insurance company, go to the library and check the company's rating from A.M. Best, Moody's and/or Standard and Poor's. These independent rating services use different systems, and they don't rate every company. However, if the company you want to buy a policy from is rated at or near the top by all three services, you can assume that company is in good shape. You might also call your state insurance department to see if a particular company is financially sound. Also ask your insurance agent to provide clear evidence that the company is financially strong.

Abromovitz, Les. *Family Insurance Handbook: The Complete Guide for the 1990s*. Blue Ridge Summit: Liberty Hall Press, 1990.

O'Donnell, Jess, *Insurance Smart—How to Buy the Right Insurance at the Right Price*. New York: John Wiley & Sons, Inc., 1991.

Taylor, Barbara, *How to Get Your Money's Worth in Home and Auto Insurance.* New York: McGraw-Hill, Inc., 1991.

The Rules of The Financial Road:

Part V

Chapter Ten

Financial Law No. 7:
You Can't Take It With You

*"I always knew that death
was an inevitable part of living
but I sincerely thought that,
in my case, an exception would be made."*

Anonymous, deceased

Most of us have heard the expression, **"You can't take it with you,"** but married couples seldom recognize this simple statement as a financial law. Newly married couples aren't going to die anyway—they're going to live forever. As a result, they seldom give serious consideration to the reality of death and what will happen when death occurs. I sincerely hope that your life together is long and happy and prosperous. But this short course on the rules of the financial road would not be complete without discussing the responsibility you have to plan for the unlikely reality of an untimely death.

The truth is that death is always untimely. It also triggers a series of financial events and consequences that can be overwhelming and burdensome for the survivor(s).

Financially, death can prove to be disastrous for a surviving spouse. This does not have to be the case, however. Thoughtful planning can minimize the financial consequences at a time when emotional loss is all that any human can bear.

351

You live in a country where you have the right and privilege to decide how and to whom you will give your property at death. This very powerful right cannot be taken lightly. If you fail to exercise it, your state laws will make these decisions for you.

Chances are, you would not like your state's plan for distribution of your property—and your marriage partner, assuming he or she survives your untimely death, would absolutely hate it.

To complete your initial education about managing the financial side of married life, you really must examine the topics in this chapter. How you plan *now* to have your property distributed *at death* will make an important statement about your love and concern for those who remain behind after your death.

This is not a complicated subject, although some people think it is. Often, the subject only seems complicated because people don't like to talk about dying. Newlyweds, as stated above, truly believe they will live forever. As you might suspect, the absurd idea of living forever is promoted by our old friend the Neanderthal brain which will attempt to interfere with your learning the lessons of this chapter. The Nean-

derthal brain cannot tolerate death as a possibility. As a result, I've had people say to me, "If I die, I'd like my property . . ." and I say to them, "*If* you die? Think about what you're saying!! Have you known *anyone* who has cheated death *forever?*"

Let's look at this realistically. Each of us will die, and each of us has a responsibility to make sure that our marriage partner and any children born to our marriage will be cared for and protected.

From a legal point of view, death triggers a process called "passage of title." This process is designed to assure that everything you own passes legally to a new owner, one who is still living.

If you recognize this fact of financial life while *you're* still living, you can have a great deal to say about who gets your property. It's really that simple.

The best way to do this is by making a will. When you begin to plan your will and the distribution of your estate (everything you own) to heirs and beneficiaries (family members and friends), you're taking part in "Estate Planning."

Estate Planning begins when the two of you sit down and answer some fundamental questions. Not all of the questions presented in the next Agreement Check will apply to you, but some of them apply. So, as you have done many times before in this book, take all the time you need to have the discussion that follows.

Agreement Check:

1. Does either of you have a will?

Her Answer: ☐ Yes ☐ No

His Answer: ☐ Yes ☐ No

2. If either or both of you answered "YES," when was the last date your will was reviewed by you and an attorney?

His Will Was Last Reviewed_____

Her Will Was Last Reviewed_____

3. Have you had wills prepared since you became married, or (if engaged) are you planning to have your wills reviewed once you become married?

His Answer: ☐ Yes ☐ No

Her Answer: ☐ Yes ☐ No

4. What have you decided your surviving spouse would need for financial security in the event of an early death? Look back at the decisions you reached regarding life insurance to help you answer this question.

For Her Security? $_____

For His Security? $_____

5. If you have children, answer the following questions:

A. Who would you like to look after your minor children if the two of you were to both die in a tragic accident?

Our First Choice: _____

_____

Our Second Choice: _____

_____

Our Third Choice: _____

B. At what age, after you both die, do you think your children should receive substantial assets to provide for their care, support, and education? Answer this question even if you don't have any children yet.

_____

_____

_____

6. Who would you want to receive your property if something were to happen to both of you and there were no children to consider?

_____

_____

_____

_____

_____

_____

_____

_____

_____

_____

_____

_____

_____

_____

7. Are there special people in your life (other than your marriage partner) that you would want to have some special property you own, such as jewelry or a family heirloom? Make a list of those people and the property you would want them to have.

_____

_____

_____

_____

_____

_____

_____

_____

8. Do you want to benefit any charities? List them by name and what you would like them to have.

_____

_____

_____

_____

_____

_____

_____

_____

9. Who do you want to serve as executor of your estate? (I'll admit, this is not a fair question. After all, I haven't told you what an "executor" is yet. You can bypass this question and come back to it later).

_____

_____

_____

10. Do you know which properties owned by either one or both of you can legally pass to someone else under direction of your will? (There I go again, getting ahead of myself. You can answer this question later, too. Read the next section and you'll be ready to answer it.)

Property That Can Pass By Direction of a Will:

_____

_____

_____

_____

_____

_____

_____

_____

_____

_____

_____

_____

_____

How Property Can Pass To Other People at Death

If "passage of title" is the process that, at death, results in a transfer of property to someone who is living, then the natural question is, "How does this take place?" Property can pass to your heirs and beneficiaries in four ways. Before explaining the four ways, let me define what "heirs" and "beneficiaries" are.

An heir is someone who is entitled, under the laws of your state, to receive your property after your death in the event you don't leave a will. Usually, this includes your spouse and any children of your marriage. But it may also include parents and more distant relatives, depending on how your state laws are written.

A beneficiary is someone you choose to inherit property; this may include an heir. You may name anyone to be a beneficiary, as long as you leave a will. This could include a good friend or even the local gas station attendant.

O.K., back to the four ways property can pass to heirs and beneficiaries. Here they are:

By Joint Tenancy with Rights of Survivorship—Remember the discussion about this subject on pages 160 and 161? If you jointly own a home with another person and it is titled as "joint tenants with rights of survivorship," then the "passage of title" process is simple. At your death, your share automatically passes to the surviving joint tenant(s). In the Agreement Check above, Question 10 asked, "What property that you now own can pass to survivors by direction of your will?" Well, your will has no power over property that is titled as joint tenants with rights of survivorship. Now look back at your property inventory in **Appendix D** and see if you listed any

property held in this way. If you have this type of property, your surviving joint tenant(s) can secure their legal inheritance by producing a certificate of death and making the proper title transfer with the county recorder. Your will does not come into play at all.

By Contract—The best example of property passing by contract is life insurance. A life insurance policy is a contract. When you die, any life insurance benefits that are paid to your marriage partner are paid by contract. Your will can not change a life insurance contract (or any other contract for that matter). This is one very good reason to make sure your spouse is properly named as the beneficiary of your life insurance. Other examples of a contract controlling the passage of title process are retirement income contracts and trusts. If you participate in a company pension plan, or have an Individual Retirement Account, or a Keogh H.R. 10 Plan or any other retirement plans, these are retirement income contracts and they all contain provisions to pay benefits to survivors when you die. Be sure you have a complete understanding of the "survivor benefits" of any retirement income contracts you have and be sure that you both feel good about the distribution options chosen. I'll discuss trusts a little later in this chapter, and then you'll see how they fit into this definition.

By Intestacy—"Intestate" is the legal word for dying without a will. Recall for a minute what I said earlier about the state having a will when you fail to provide one. Any property you own that is not directed to survivors by joint tenancy with rights of survivorship or contractual agreements, can be distributed to your heirs by direction of the state's will. The state's will comes into play only if you fail to prepare your own will. The state's plan of distribution for your property varies from state to state. There is little justice in the state's will (not *your* definition of justice, anyway) because the needs of your survivors are not considered in the rules of inheritance. The rules of inheritance, or the state's will, are legally binding on your heirs. This means they can't go to court and fight for their needs. The only way you can assure that your family is properly protected is to provide your own will—one that is drafted by an attorney and meets all legal requirements.

By direction of your will—If you own anything at all and want to be absolutely sure who will receive it when you die, then you need a will. A will is your means of making passage of title decisions, recording them in writing and seeing that your decisions become a legal document that no one can argue about. Yes, it does cost money to have wills drafted. But by doing it now and updating your wills on a regular basis, you are implementing an important financial strategy that will allow you to harmonize with Financial Law No. 7 throughout your married life.

Before you read the next section, go back to the last agreement check and answer Question 10 by applying the knowledge you gained in this section.

...AND TO MY FAITHFUL DOG "UGLY" I LEAVE SIX DOGGIE TREATS, MY SLIPPERS, AND ONE DEAD CAT I FOUND LAST WEEK.

Financial Strategy No. 1 for Harmonizing with Financial Law No. 7: Preparing Your Wills

Preparing a will and updating it regularly is the first and most important step in the estate planning process. Estate planning was defined earlier as deciding in advance of death who you wish to receive your estate (everything you own). How you participate in this process will be largely influenced by your current financial condition and the way you want to express your love for your marriage partner, your family and your friends.

In addition to your will, there are other estate planning tools to help you accomplish your estate planning goals. This section will elaborate primarily on the importance of having a will in order to harmonize with Financial Law No. 7. Later in this chapter, I'm going to introduce one other estate planning tool—the use of trusts. After gaining an overview of these two estate planning tools (wills and trusts), you can continue your education about estate planning from the list of readings suggested at the end of this chapter.

359

The Benefits of Wills

Besides protecting your spouse against the unhappy consequences of the state's will, your will provides these additional benefits:

A. You can name your beneficiaries. Of course, you will probably name each other as beneficiary of most assets, but as already mentioned, special bequests can be made to friends and relatives and this may be very important.

B. Estate taxes (taxes paid on the privilege of directing your property to heirs and beneficiaries) can often be reduced dramatically by taking advantage of tax reduction plans that can be put in place in your will. You can also direct estate tax payments from specific assets. Keep this warning in mind, however. Unless your will is properly drafted by an expert tax attorney, these tax reduction plans will probably fail.

C. Your will can direct who is to be the guardian of your children. Guardians are those who would raise your children in the event you both died as a result of the same tragic accident.

D. Through your will, you can make sure that, in the event you die before they are fully grown adults, your minor children receive a portion of your estate only when they reach an age at which you believe they will be able to handle property in a responsible manner.

E. Your will can help protect your family by protecting your interests in a business. Once again, however, only expert legal counsel will give you the protections you might seek.

F. You can set out instructions for your funeral.

There are other advantages to having a will, and you can learn about them from your attorney or by continuing your education with the suggested readings at the end of this chapter. However, I'm going to assume you've already decided to protect each other with a well planned and professionally drafted will. In fact, in the sections that follow, I'm going to help you clear away some misconceptions about wills and prepare you to see a lawyer.

Misconceptions About Wills

When you start to think about preparing a will, it's best to begin by clearing away some misconceptions about this subject.

For example, many people believe that only a man needs a will and a wife is protected by her husband's will. This is absolutely false. Both husband *and* wife need an up-to-date will.

Why? Well, one reason is that a wife may own assets that are titled as sole and separate property (remember our discussions about title on Pages 160 and 161?). In that event, her husband's will would have no power to direct the passing of those assets. A second reason is that a tragic accident could take the life of both husband and wife. Obviously, this is an unpleasant thought. But let's imagine for a moment that a wife dies shortly after her husband, for any reason. In that case, any plans made for children or other family members in her husband's will might very well be cancelled. A husband's will ceases to control anything once he has died and his estate is settled.

Another misconception is that if you hold title to all your property in joint tenancy with rights of survivorship, a will is just not important or needed.

I hope the discussion about how property passes at death cleared away that misconception, but just in case, let me say it again. A will is the cornerstone of all estate planning. It covers property that may *not* be titled in joint tenancy with rights of survivorship. When one spouse dies and property passes to the survivor by joint tenancy with rights of survivorship, the other spouse becomes the sole owner. At that point there is no joint tenancy, and that is when a properly drafted will can take over.

Another misconception about wills is that you must itemize everything you own in the will itself so you can direct the passing of even personal property items to your heirs and beneficiaries.

You *can* use your will to direct specific personal property items, but that isn't required and may not be a good idea. Because your wishes may change from time to time, you are going to want to update your wills periodically. But since updating your wills means another trip to your attorney (no, you should not do-it-yourself when you need to change your will) it is often best to attach a special letter of instruction to your will regarding such things as family silver, heirlooms, jewelry and so forth. In this way, should you desire to change your distribution plan, simply add a new letter of instruction. Just be certain you date it and destroy the original and all copies of previous letters of instruction. Ask your attorney about this idea and take notes about what is suggested.

361

You may also have thought to list in your will all those you wish to receive cash distributions.

This is frequently done and it's perfectly acceptable. However, the preferred way to do this is by using a percentage formula rather than a cash distribution plan. The reason for this is that your financial circumstances will change from time to time. A tremendous loss in cash prior to your death could completely upset your property distribution plan unless you use a percentage formula. The result could be that some people you had designated to receive a portion of your estate might receive nothing.

The Role of An Executor

Another area of concern, and often an area of misunderstanding when preparing wills, has to do with selecting an executor of your estate.

**Your "executor" is the person you name in your will to carry out your wishes.
When you name someone in your will to serve as executor, that person is called a "personal representative."**

If you name someone who is unwilling or unable to serve, the court will appoint someone to carry out this responsibility. When the court appoints someone to serve in the role of executor, that person is called an **"administrator."**

Besides being *called* a personal representative, your executor *is* your personal representative for purposes of terminating your financial affairs and seeing that your assets are properly distributed. Your executor's judgment is substituted for your own. And that judgment will have a direct impact on your surviving spouse and other family members. Of course, as husband and wife, you can name each other to serve in this capacity and most married couples do so. However, an executor frequently will require the aid of an attorney and perhaps an accountant or even a trust officer to carry out all the responsibilities of the estate settlement process. These people (when needed) are paid for their services, whereas your surviving spouse/executor will almost certainly serve without charge.

The judgment of the executor cannot be delegated. That's why you should pick this person very carefully.

If you choose each other to serve, you should name an alternate, just in case there is some reason your surviving spouse is unable to serve. I'll come back to this point in a moment, but first let me give you some idea of the executor's responsibilities.

The common responsibilities of an executor include: paying all debts and claims against your estate, filing all necessary tax returns and supervising the ultimate distribution of your property to all heirs and beneficiaries. The law specifically says that an executor is acting in a "fiduciary capacity." A fiduciary capacity is a legal relationship which indicates that one person carries out financial obligations for the benefit of another person. The court watches over the executor's actions very carefully. Should the executor do something that is criminal or even negligent, there will be a heavy legal penalty that could involve fines and even imprisonment. If your estate is complicated and requires management of a business, then the executor may have to manage the business during the time your estate is being settled or administered. In light of this, your executor may need to have a keen sense of business. A solid understanding of the tax laws is also needed because the executor must collect and pay all taxes for the estate.

It is usually a good idea to name a co-executor to help settle your estate *and* an alternate executor. If you name each other to be executors, you might wish to consider naming a bank trust department to be co-executor.

Why? Because a bank trust department or a trust company serves in this capacity all the time. As a result, they have professional staff who know and understand the mechanics of estate settlement. That leaves your surviving spouse (or whoever else may be serving as executor) free to concentrate on judgment calls without having to struggle with learning about estate settlement mechanics. A bank trust department, or trust company, is often the best choice to serve as an alternate executor, too. An alternate executor steps in if your first choice for executor is unable or unwilling to serve for any reason. If your spouse is unable to serve, perhaps because of injuries suffered in an accident that takes your life, the settlement of your estate will proceed without interruption. If a surviving spouse is in a hospital and there are children to care for, settling your estate quickly could be critical to help provide cash to pay bills and care for the children.

364

Taking Care of Minor Children Through Your Will

If you have minor children, and here I'm talking about children under the age of 18, you'll find property distributions to them an especially challenging problem. (No, you may not have children right now, but someday you may have. So read carefully). When property is left to a minor child, he or she can't receive the property.

All states have adopted the Uniform Gifts to Minors Act, or an updated version called the "Uniform Transfers to Minors Act," that permits the transfer of property to a person 18 or under (in some states age 21 or under) only if a custodian is appointed by the court.

A custodian is a responsible adult who, under this Act, actually becomes the recipient of and controls the property left to the minor until he/she becomes a legal adult.

Often the role of custodian is combined with that of guardian. What is a guardian?

A "guardian" is an adult who is assigned the responsibility of overseeing your child's welfare in the event of your death— actually raising your child. Usually, this means that the child also lives with the guardian until reaching adulthood.

Of course, you have the right in your will to appoint who shall serve as guardian of your minor children. You're probably thinking that, naturally, your spouse will serve in this capacity should you die before the children are grown. But what will happen if you both die in a tragic accident? This possibility is frequently overlooked, but it can and does happen. The selection of a guardian, then, is a very important matter. And unless you make such a selection by designation in your will, the courts will make that decision for you. Therefore, I want the two of you to think about what type of person you'd like to raise your children should you both die before they reach adulthood. It may make you a bit squeamish, but force yourself to answer these two questions.

1. To whom do you feel perfectly comfortable assigning this task?
2. Who would actually be willing to do it?

You'll have to think of several possibilities because some of these people may turn you down. Try to think of at least three possibilities. Then take those names to your attorney.

Your attorney? Because you are newly married or planning your wedding, you may not yet have selected an attorney. However, you *will* need an attorney to prepare your wills. To ensure that your will is legally binding and valid in every respect, you must employ the services of an attorney. The idea of writing your own will is absurd, and no matter how many stories you hear about people who have left hand written ("holographic" wills) please don't attempt to do this. One error can defeat all your good intentions and leave a terrible mess for your survivors.

Drafting Your Wills

The first step in actually having your wills drafted is to select a good lawyer. When seeking a lawyer to help with your wills, I suggest you find one who specializes in estate planning and tax law. Traditionally, lawyers have handled anything that comes up. However, an ever-increasing number are now specializing in particular aspects of the law. It just doesn't make sense to expect someone who practices criminal or corporate law to be as well versed in estate planning. Bar associations are now allowing lawyers to advertise, and many cities have set up lawyer referral services you can call to obtain the name of an attorney who may help you. Always seek references from friends you respect for their good judgment when searching for an attorney. And finally, ask the attorney for references, and then check them. In the end, your own good judgment must guide your final decision.

Once you select an attorney, you'll want to prepare carefully for a will planning session. Advanced preparation will expedite the process and probably save money. Remember, your attorney charges by the hour. The more you prepare, the less time your attorney will have to spend on this process.

In addition to bringing along the names of those you wish to serve as guardians, what else should you bring to your attorney? Probably more than the items that appear on the list that follows on this page, but if you have these documents, you'll be better prepared than most to get right to work

during your first visit. Here's a starter list of what to bring with you:

1. Your birth certificates.
2. Your marriage license.
3. The birth certificates of your children.
4. Your Social Security numbers.
5. Military discharge papers.
6. Adoption papers, yours and your children's.
7. A listing of your checking accounts and savings accounts.
8. All certificates of deposit, promissory notes, deeds of trust and other proof of money owed by you or to you.
9. Insurance policies.
10. Real estate deeds.
11. Bond and stock certificates.
12. Title of ownership to boats or automobiles, for example.
13. Be sure to take along your present wills or any other estate planning documents you may have from past estate planning efforts.
14. If you have trust agreements to which you are parties or beneficiaries, take those with you.
15. Any divorce decrees and property settlements from former marriages will be important.
16. Usually, you'll have a summary of any employee benefit plans and/or contracts to which you are a party. Take those with you, too.
17. Take any partnership or shareholder agreements.
18. Take the answers you gave to the questions in the last Agreement Check.
19. Any premarital agreements.

Once you get in the door with a qualified attorney and begin the will planning process, you are demonstrating good judgment and deep caring for one another. This fundamental step in the estate planning process can have a remarkable effect on strengthening your marital partnership. However, your wills are going to be ever-changing documents. As your life changes, your wills must be updated to reflect those changes. Otherwise, your wills may become ineffective or even useless. The good judgment that prompted you to have wills drafted should also guide you in updating them. Therefore, our next discussion will highlight those occasions that ordinarily signal that a review of your wills is in order.

When To Change Your Wills

Since your wills are so important in estate planning, it is critical that you keep them up-to-date. Sometimes, this simply means attaching a letter of instruction to your wills each year (discussed earlier) that tells how you want personal property items distributed to heirs. Or, you may need a formal addition to your wills. When you make a formal change in your wills, you can do one of two things. You can add something new by attaching a codicil, or you can have your wills completely re-written.

A "codicil" is a legal document, drafted by an attorney, which may consist of a few sentences or a paragraph or two. It must be signed by you and witnesses, according to the laws of your state. It is then attached to your wills and it legally changes them.

To help you think through when to change your will, I'm going to give you a short summary of the most important events that could trigger such a change.

1. When you're first married. This is the most obvious time to change your wills, and if you've read this far, you're probably committed to make an appointment with an attorney and have new wills drafted.

2. Anytime there are changes in your family, you should re-examine your wills. The most common occurrence would be the birth of a child. However, the death of a family member might also lead to a change in your wills.

3. If you own a business, perhaps with partners or shareholders, you should consider changes in your wills if there are major changes in the business. Some wills contain plans for distributing shares of the business or for buying out the business from partners. Be especially watchful for changes that signal financial consequences for your business. If you have any doubts, ask your attorney if these changes require a change in your wills.

4. Sometimes people inherit money or property from another family member. Your wills should acknowledge such inheritances and provide for their distribution after your death.

5. In our mobile society, people often move. By changing the state in which you reside, you will be subject to the laws of that state. As a result, your wills should be changed to conform to your new state's laws.

6. Every will requires someone to witness the signing. These witnesses are frequently called upon to appear in court after your death to verify certain facts. If these witnesses have moved away or have died, you may need to make some changes in your wills.

7. As you acquire new property, you should change your wills. Your estate inventory is a list of everything you own. This list will change from time to time, and your wills should reflect these changes.

8. If you change employment and create new life insurance programs or retirement plans, your wills should at least be reviewed. Often these contracts require coordination into your overall estate plan to gain the greatest benefit.

9. Charities are often included in wills. You may wish to add a charity or remove one. This requires a change in your wills. Once again, your attorney must help you.

10. As the tax laws change (and they seem to change a lot), your wills may need to be adjusted. If you fail to keep your estate distribution plan up-to-date with modern tax laws, this could be a costly mistake.

11. Sometimes property is given away before death or title to property is changed. This happens throughout marriage. But when it does, review your wills.

As a rule of thumb, it would be wise for you as a married couple to review your wills at least once a year. Be sure to include your attorney in that review if any of the major indicators discussed in this section have occurred in your life since the last review.

What is Probate and How Can It Be Avoided?

More than likely you've heard of probate, and know it is something that people are always trying to avoid. There are lots of books in print about how to avoid probate. All of them appeal to another misconception—the idea that probate should be avoided at all costs. This is simply not true.

"Probate" is the court process of proving that the last will and testament of an individual is carried out to the letter of the law and in accordance with the wishes of the person who has died.

It is a process that is actually designed to protect your family. I believe that every estate should go through probate, at least in part, because the probate process protects any family members, friends and loved ones from claims against your estate in later years. I'll explain more about this a little later.

It is the expense of probate that has caused most people to want to avoid it.

Probate can be expensive. But with a little planning, the cost of probate can be very small. Let's examine the probate process more closely.

Recall that I said earlier that death sets off a process called "passage of title." Probate is one step in the "passage of title" process. Let me use a simple example to explain how this works.

If you own a piece of real estate, the sale of that property to another person during your lifetime is relatively simple. After the price has been agreed on, you simply sign the appropriate documents releasing title in favor of the new owner.

When you die, your executor is the only person with the power to sign over title to someone else, since you're not around anymore to sign anything. Your executor, under supervision of the probate court, makes sure that the principal purpose of probate is carried out—making sure your property is transferred to your intended heirs and beneficiaries.

Other purposes of probate are to make sure all of your outstanding debts are paid and your final income tax return and estate tax return are filed and that all income and estate taxes are paid.

To do this work from beginning to end, your executor guides your estate through five basic steps in the probate process. Here's a summary of them:

1. Your executor presents your will to the probate court. It is during this step that the probate court approves your executor (your personal representative). If you have left no will, the court appoints someone to act as an Administrator of your estate. Usually, it is more expensive to allow the courts to appoint an estate administrator. So the first way to save money for your heirs and beneficiaries is to make sure you have an up-to-date will and have named a willing and able executor. (Am I beginning to sound like a broken record?)

2. Making a complete inventory of your estate. This includes everything you owned or had interest in. This inventory tells the probate court what you owned and what your assets were worth at the time of your death. Determining an accurate assessment of the worth of your property is sometimes a complex task. But it is extremely important. Why? Because these valuations will have a direct connection to the size of your estate tax bill.

3. Payment of all your debts by the executor. Usually, this is a simple matter. But if you leave your affairs in a state of confusion, this step can be one of the longest and most expensive. There may have to be compromises reached with creditors, and sometimes assets may have to be sold under stressful conditions to satisfy major debts. If debts become a source of legal disputes, these legal battles can tie your estate up for months or even years. Keep this in mind—your family receives nothing from your probatable estate until all your debts have been paid.

4. Your executor determines the estate tax that is due and payable, as well as filing your final income tax return. Once again, depending on how you've planned your estate, this could be a relatively simple process or it could lead to disputes which last for years.

5. With all these other tasks accomplished, the court will now approve distribution of the remainder of your estate to your family and other heirs and beneficiaries in accord with the directions of your will.

Now, recall for a moment what was said about protecting your heirs and beneficiaries from future claims against your estate. Because of Step Three, your executor will send a notice to all creditors informing them that they have a limited time, set by law, to make their claims before the probate court. If they fail to respond within the time set, they lose their right to collect. Of course, it is rare that a creditor fails to respond. But once paid, and once the probate process is over, it becomes virtually impossible for creditors to come forward with additional claims. That's one real advantage of the probate process. All you have to do is have a small percentage of your estate pass through probate to protect your heirs and beneficiaries from future claims against any part of your estate. Even assets that don't pass through probate will be protected from future claims.

To limit what portion of your estate will pass through the probate process, you can use trusts, joint tenancy title with rights of survivorship and certain contractual agreements. By using these estate planning tools, your executor will be able to move through the probate process more quickly and keep probate costs very low. Ask your attorney for more information about how to keep probate costs as low as possible. But don't simply embrace the misconception that probate should be avoided at all costs.

Financial Strategy No. 2 for Harmonizing with Financial Law No. 7: The Effective Use of Trusts

There's a good chance that this subject will be entirely new to you. Yet, the idea of trusts goes back in history as far as the Crusades. During the eleventh, twelfth, and thirteenth centuries, European Christians often left their wives and families to fight in the Middle East to try to win the Holy Lands from the Muslims. To see that their families were taken care of, they would "entrust" a senior family member or friend to manage their property. The one entrusted was to provide for members of the family just as though they were his own.

Down through the ages, this idea has become formalized in our culture. The idea of "entrusting" someone with caring for the property or welfare of others is now embodied in a legal concept called a "trust." Today, every state in this country has its own set of laws that govern trusts.

In its simplest form, a trust is nothing more than a letter of instruction—your instructions! You decide what a trust will say and what the trust will do for you.

If a trust is to benefit you or anyone else, it must receive and hold title to property of some kind. That property can be in the form of cash, stocks, bonds, real estate or even personal property such as jewelry. The person who creates a trust is called a **"trustor."** Just as in the time of the Crusades, you select someone who is to manage or administer the trust. That person is called a **"trustee."** Finally, someone must benefit from the trust, even if that person is you. The person or persons or organizations (because sometimes a charity is named) that benefit from a trust are called **"trust beneficiaries."**

Most people create a trust during life to realize some personal advantage. Trusts created during life are called **"intervivos trusts" or "living trusts."** You can also establish a trust that does nothing until you die. These trusts are usually written into a person's will and are called **"testamentary trusts."** Once the trust is created, it has legal status just as a contract has legal status.

To create a trust requires the help of an attorney. Because trusts have to be in complete conformity with the laws of your state, any advantages you seek by creating one can be completely lost unless properly drafted by qualified and capable legal counsel.

What are some of the advantages of trusts? Well, for one thing, trusts can save you taxes. They can save both estate and income taxes.

But please keep in mind that I said trusts *can* save you taxes. The use of trusts for this purpose does not come into play for everyone in the same way. Usually, married couples think about how trusts can save taxes when they're much further along in life and have built their fortunes. Because this is true, I'm not going to give you a long explanation of the various ways to use trusts for tax savings. However, trusts offer other benefits which do apply to younger married couples, and we're going to look at them primarily.

Trusts are most often used by married couples under the age of forty to help plan for the care of minor children (children 18 years of age and younger) in the event both parents should die in a tragic accident.

Usually, a life insurance policy is purchased which pays life insurance proceeds directly into a trust in the event both parents die before the children are grown. If you decide to create a life insurance trust for this purpose, keep in mind that it is not only a good idea, it is very inexpensive. In many cases, a trust company or bank trust department will draft the trust document (letter of instruction) so it complies with the law. Then, if you both live until your children are fully grown, the trust won't become activated, and there won't be any trust administration costs. If a tragedy occurs and the trust is activated, the trustee (usually a bank trust department) becomes the custodian of the life insurance proceeds and works with your children's guardians to make sure that money is provided for their benefit and care. This separation of powers usually works very well.

However, while guardians don't receive a fee for raising your children, the bank trust department does charge a fee for administering the trust.

The second most common use of trusts by married couples is to help lower the cost of probate. The use of a revocable living trust, created at the same time you have your wills drafted, can be very effective in keeping the costs of probate to a minimum.

I said earlier that only property you own, titled in your name, passes through the probate process. The dilemma is to find a way to transfer title to your assets without losing control over them. The solution to this dilemma is to have most of what you own transferred to a living revocable trust. Remember, it is a living trust because you create it while you're alive. It is revocable because you can change your mind, cancel the trust at any time, and all the property can come back to you. If you don't cancel the trust, however, and you die with most of your property held by the trust, then all of the trust property avoids probate. Of course, the property held by the trust is simply distributed to your heirs and beneficiaries according to the directions you left in the trust document (letter of instruction).

When used in this way and for this purpose, a living revocable trust is a substitute for a will. However, you must fully understand this next fact. Whenever you create a living revocable trust, you must have a will anyway. Why? Sometimes trusts are not drafted properly for one reason or another. In that case, the trust fails. If this should happen in your case, your will is there to back up the trust. Another potential problem can occur when title to your property does not get properly recorded in the name of the trust. That property then falls outside the trust and your will must be there to sweep it up. Otherwise, you're back to letting the state's will take over distribution of your property. So, if you're thinking of establishing a living revocable trust, tell your attorney when you have your wills drafted. In this way, your attorney can prepare your wills in a way that supports the trust.

**Some people hesitate to use a living revocable trust because of the mistaken notion that they must give up or lose control over property placed in the trust.
This is simply not true.**

You can go right on enjoying your property as if nothing had changed. And if, for some reason, you want to sell the trust property, no problem. I've already said that you can revoke or cancel the trust. But you can also amend or change it at any time. To be honest, this is one of the most easily changed and flexible estate planning tools available.

Another widely held misconception about the living revocable trust is that it helps you save taxes as well as avoid probate. This is not true.

Avoiding probate is one thing; savings taxes is something else. The living revocable trust won't save income or estate taxes. Of the two, the tax most people think they can lower with a living revocable trust is the estate tax. Up to now, I've not discussed the subject of estate taxes. In this last section on the costs of dying, you'll learn that estate taxes are a major burden that should be planned for very carefully—and, if possible, avoided.

Common Forms Of Trusts Used In Estate Planning

Type Of Trust	Characteristics	General Benefits
Testamentary Trust	Created in your will and goes into effect after your death.	Family protection; investment supervision; income and estate tax savings.
Living Revocable Trust	Created during your lifetime with the right to revoke or amend the terms.	Management of investments; receptacle for future investments; vehicle for special purpose investments; back-up protection; avoidance of probate.
Living Irrevocable Trust	Created during your lifetime but requires you to give up forever all ownership of property placed in the trust.	Investment management of assets; distribution plan for your estate; eliminates estate administration on death; is not taxable in your estate at death.
Irrevocable Insurance Trust	Receives proceeds of life insurance when you die. You have no incidents of ownership in the life insurance contract during your life.	Provides investment management of assets for beneficiaries; not taxable in your estate when you die; helps avoid the probate process; cuts down on the cost of estate administration.
Charitable Remainder Trust	Irrevocable. Assets placed in trust during life or at death. Income paid to beneficiaries first. At death of beneficiaries, remainder goes to charity.	Provides income to trustor, family or friends; reduces estate taxes; unfreezes assets for income and reduces capital gain taxes.

The High Cost of Dying

Unfortunately, there is no such thing as dying cheaply. Settlement of an estate, regardless of the size, requires an outlay of cash. The average cost of settling an estate ranges from 2 to 5 percent. And these costs don't even include estate taxes. Let's look at some of the costs every estate has to face. The first cost faced by your estate is the cost of your funeral. You should know that in most states these costs have to be paid first as a matter of law.

If you die of a serious illness or in an accident, you may be hospitalized for weeks or months. If your health insurance doesn't cover all doctor and hospital charges, those bills will have to be paid by your estate. Once again, in most states, these bills have a high priority by law.

The next cost is for those professionals who help your spouse carry out the duties of serving as executor and the costs associated with probate. Of course, if you've taken the advice given earlier in this chapter, you will reduce these costs to a minimum. But they may still shock your survivors.

Next come your creditors. I've already told you that they have to be notified of your death. You can be sure they'll come around quickly to collect on any debt you left owing. How will you make sure your family has the cash to pay them? Will you leave your affairs in such a mess that any assets in your estate will be tied up in law suits from those creditors? I hope not.

The next big cost of dying comes in the form of "lost value." Sometimes a business, a farm or ranch can drop in value without a key man or woman who is now deceased. Therefore, just by dying you've hurt your estate because you are a valuable part of your business. Some corporations buy key man life insurance just because they know how valuable top executives are to their firm. If you own a business, what will *you* do to protect the loss of *your* value to that business in case of death? Of course, since the management of your financial affairs within your marriage is like running a small business, your family will experience "lost value" in every way possible when you die. From a purely financial point of view, the loss of your income to the family will be devastating. Having a solid life insurance plan is the only sensible way to provide ample protection.

The smaller an estate, the more it hurts to have to face these costs. Believe me, your surviving spouse will feel that these costs are a tremendous burden if you fail to do something to reduce them.

It may seem hard to believe that the government will step in and take the last big bite out of your estate. They will—if you let them.

The federal estate tax can be sizeable. It is a progressive tax, meaning that the more you own at death, the more tax you pay. It ranges up to 55% of an estate for the very wealthy. But don't forget about your state government. They probably have an inheritance tax, which, although small compared to the federal estate tax, is still a threat to your loved ones.

376

How can you protect your estate from these taxes? You can't do it by avoiding probate. The estate tax is imposed on everything you own, whether it goes through probate or not. Hiding your wealth in a trust won't help either. Neither will giving it away. So what is the answer? Actually there are a combination of tactics to use. For a married couple, there is the unlimited marital deduction.

Money or property transferred directly to your surviving spouse completely escapes the federal estate tax, as long as certain rules are met.

Be sure to ask your attorney how to make the most of the estate tax marital deduction when you go to have your wills drafted. Every will should now contain a marital deduction clause that makes sure transfers of cash and property to a surviving spouse meet the government's qualifying test.

Also ask your attorney about a marital deduction trust.

Another way to beat the high cost of dying, including the costs of estate taxes, is to make sure you have enough life insurance to pay these costs. This may prompt you both to go back to Chapter Nine and reassess your needs for life insurance. That's good. I hope that by now you've established a good friendship with an insurance counselor. Include him or her in your discussions about insurance for estate settlement costs, too.

Finally, if you have a business, and if you can arrange it, look at establishing a "buy-sell agreement." This is an agreement that makes sure your interest in the business is bought out by your partners or other shareholders when you die. Such an agreement will provide instant cash to your family at a time when they may need it most.

Your life insurance counselor and your attorney can both help you evaluate the use of a buy-sell agreement and its advantages to you.

Well, you know what they say about death and taxes...

A Final Word (or two) of Advice

The advice given to you in this chapter is general in nature and quite limited in scope. The purpose of providing it at all is to help you see that planning for the distribution of your estate is an important part of being a responsible marriage partner. The role of estate planning should be assigned to one partner with full support and participation by the other. The fundamentals of this financial management role include **(1)** making sure you have up-to-date and professionally drafted wills, **(2)** taking every step necessary to reduce the high cost of dying, and **(3)** using trusts and other estate planning tools effectively to provide every possible protection for your family.

Of course, there is much more to learn than the basics provided here. I've suggested only two books for you at the end of this chapter. Books can give you important information, but your attorney may be able to suggest a seminar or a college course that will help, too. The important point to remember is that this area of financial management requires constant learning. As you continue to educate yourselves about estate planning, here are a few topics to explore:

1. **Qualified Terminable Interest Property Trusts**

2. **Exemption Equivalent Trusts**

3. **Gifting Strategies To Reduce Estate Taxes**

4. **The Role of Bequests To Charities in Your Will**

5. **Generation Skipping Transfers**

6. **Irrevocable Life Insurance Trusts**

7. **Crummey Trusts**

8. **Minors Trusts**

9. **Charitable Remainder Trusts**

Once you create an estate plan, you'll have a new set of important documents to take care of. Please consider carefully where you will store them. I suggest that copies of your wills and trust agreements be placed in a safe deposit box at the bank (the originals should remain with your attorney). Your life insurance policies and other important contracts, stock certificates, bonds, title to real estate, birth certificates, etc., can all be kept there, too. The cost of renting a safe deposit box may be as low as $30.00 a year. The fact that these important papers are free from fire or theft will provide you important peace of mind. But most importantly, when your family really needs them, they'll know right where to get them.

By the way, if you've heard that the banks lock up safe deposit boxes when someone dies, that is generally true. But getting permission to get into your safe deposit box is not that difficult, so don't let that deter you. If it brings you peace of mind, have a copy of your will in both your safe deposit box and at home.

Agreement Check:

1. List all the reasons you can think of to avoid having wills drafted. I'll help you get started with a few suggestions:

"We don't really own very much, so it's just not important"

"We don't like to think about dying."

"We're too young, we couldn't possibly die."

"We don't really care that much."

Now list some of your own additional reasons:

_____

_____

_____

_____

_____

_____

_____

_____

_____

_____

_____

_____

_____

_____

2. List all the reasons you can think of in favor of finding a qualified estate planning attorney and having your wills drafted. Once again, I'll help you get started—then you're on your own:

"We are recently married, so we want to show how much we care."

"We need the protection of knowing exactly what will happen to our property in the event of a tragic death."

"We have a child (children) and want to provide for legal guardians in the event we both die in a tragic accident before our child (children) reaches the age of 18."

"We want to know that we have taken steps to reduce estate taxes so our survivors will realize the greatest possible benefits from our property."

_____

_____

_____

_____

_____

_____

_____

_____

_____

_____

_____

_____

_____

_____

3. Return to the Agreement Check at the end of Chapter Five. Review your decisions about the role of estate planning in your marriage. See if your answers are any different after reading this last chapter.

Suggested Additional Reading:

Corrigan, Arnold and Phyllis C. Kaufman, *Understanding Estate Planning and Wills.* Stamford: Longmeadow Press, 1987 *(This book is carried in most Waldenbooks and can also be ordered by calling toll free 1-800-322-2000.)*

Esperti, Robert A. and Renno L. Peterson, *Loving Trust—The Right Way to Provide for Yourself and Guarantee The Future of Your Loved One.* New York: Viking Penguin, a division of Penguin Books USA, Inc., 1988.

Appendix A

How To Create A Dream Book and Make It Work For Your Marriage

For those who are serious about making dreams come true in marriage, creating a Dream Book is absolutely required. If you just talk about making dreams come true, even if you talk about it over and over again, not much will happen. But when you take action by looking for and finding a picture of your dream, and then create a special page for that dream in your Dream Book, you send a signal of commitment to your brain that stiffens your internal resolve to make that dream come true.

I cannot overemphasize this point. You may consider it too simplistic or even childish to take this step. Don't let such thoughts stop you! Those who make the most significant and rapid progress toward making dreams come true in marriage are the ones who do, in fact, create Dreams Books and follow the directions below visually reinforcing their commitment. I would even go so far as to say, **No Dream Book—No Commitment—No Results!!!**

Questions To Keep In Mind as You Think About Each Dream:

1. Is this an individual or a shared dream (one that my partner and I have in common)?
2. If it is an individual dream, does my partner support me in my pursuit of this dream?
3. How will making this dream come true enrich my life and the lives of others?
4. Am I willing to go after this dream with all my might?
5. If I meet disappointment and discouragement, is this dream something I will still fight for?
6. Am I willing to give this dream enough time to put it all together?
7. What am I willing to give up in order to make this dream come true?

When You Take Time to Review Your Dream Book, Follow These Guidelines:

1. Always review your Dream Book together. Do this as often as possible. Set aside a time when you will not be interrupted. One of the best times to do it is just before falling off to sleep at night.
2. Begin by simply turning the pages of your Dream Book and by looking at the pictures.
3. Next, go back through the book, page by page, and talk over how you feel about each dream and how important it is to continue to make progress toward making each dream come true.
4. Encourage each other about realizing every dream in your book. Note any progress you have made—even in a small way.
5. If things have gotten in the way of any of your dreams, talk about them and find ways that you will work together to overcome these obstacles.

Our First Dream Book

Dream No._____

Description _____

_____

Is this dream a common (shared) dream?   ☐ Yes   ☐ No

If this is an individual dream, is my partner willing to help me make this dream come true?   ☐ Yes   ☐ No

Time necessary to make this dream come true?_____

Estimated costs to make this dream come true?_____

How will making this dream come true enrich my/our life and the lives of others?

_____

_____

    In the space below, paste in a picture from a magazine, newspaper, brochure, or other publication that is similar to your dream in as much detail as possible.

Our First Dream Book

Dream No._____

Description _____
_____

Is this dream a common (shared) dream?   ☐ Yes   ☐ No

If this is an individual dream, is my partner willing to help me make this dream come true?   ☐ Yes   ☐ No

Time necessary to make this dream come true?_____

Estimated costs to make this dream come true?_____

How will making this dream come true enrich my/our life and the lives of others?
_____
_____

   In the space below, paste in a picture from a magazine, newspaper, brochure, or other publication that is similar to your dream in as much detail as possible.

Our First Dream Book

Dream No._____

Description _____
_____

Is this dream a common (shared) dream?   ☐ Yes   ☐ No

If this is an individual dream, is my partner willing to help me make this dream come true?   ☐ Yes   ☐ No

Time necessary to make this dream come true?_____

Estimated costs to make this dream come true?_____

How will making this dream come true enrich my/our life and the lives of others?

_____
_____

In the space below, paste in a picture from a magazine, newspaper, brochure, or other publication that is similar to your dream in as much detail as possible.

Our First Dream Book

Dream No._____

Description _____
_____

Is this dream a common (shared) dream?   ☐ Yes   ☐ No

If this is an individual dream, is my partner willing to help me make this dream
come true?   ☐ Yes   ☐ No

Time necessary to make this dream come true?_____

Estimated costs to make this dream come true?_____

How will making this dream come true enrich my/our life and the lives of others?

_____

_____

    In the space below, paste in a picture from a magazine, newspaper, brochure, or other publication that is similar to your dream in as much detail as possible.

Our First Dream Book

Dream No._____

Description _____

_____

Is this dream a common (shared) dream? ☐ Yes ☐ No

If this is an individual dream, is my partner willing to help me make this dream come true? ☐ Yes ☐ No

Time necessary to make this dream come true?_____

Estimated costs to make this dream come true?_____

How will making this dream come true enrich my/our life and the lives of others?

_____

_____

   In the space below, paste in a picture from a magazine, newspaper, brochure, or other publication that is similar to your dream in as much detail as possible.

Our First Dream Book

Dream No._____

Description _____

_____

Is this dream a common (shared) dream?   ☐ Yes   ☐ No

If this is an individual dream, is my partner willing to help me make this dream come true?   ☐ Yes   ☐ No

Time necessary to make this dream come true?_____

Estimated costs to make this dream come true?_____

How will making this dream come true enrich my/our life and the lives of others?

_____

_____

In the space below, paste in a picture from a magazine, newspaper, brochure, or other publication that is similar to your dream in as much detail as possible.

Our First Dream Book

Dream No._____

Description _____

_____

Is this dream a common (shared) dream?   ☐ Yes   ☐ No

If this is an individual dream, is my partner willing to help me make this dream come true?   ☐ Yes   ☐ No

Time necessary to make this dream come true?_____

Estimated costs to make this dream come true?_____

How will making this dream come true enrich my/our life and the lives of others?

_____

_____

   In the space below, paste in a picture from a magazine, newspaper, brochure, or other publication that is similar to your dream in as much detail as possible.

Our First Dream Book

Dream No._____

Description _____

_____

Is this dream a common (shared) dream?　　☐ Yes　　☐ No

If this is an individual dream, is my partner willing to help me make this dream come true?　　☐ Yes　　☐ No

Time necessary to make this dream come true?_____

Estimated costs to make this dream come true?_____

How will making this dream come true enrich my/our life and the lives of others?

_____

_____

In the space below, paste in a picture from a magazine, newspaper, brochure, or other publication that is similar to your dream in as much detail as possible.

Our First Dream Book

Dream No._____

Description _____

_____

Is this dream a common (shared) dream?　　☐ Yes　　☐ No

If this is an individual dream, is my partner willing to help me make this dream come true?　　☐ Yes　　☐ No

Time necessary to make this dream come true?_____

Estimated costs to make this dream come true?_____

How will making this dream come true enrich my/our life and the lives of others?

_____

_____

   In the space below, paste in a picture from a magazine, newspaper, brochure, or other publication that is similar to your dream in as much detail as possible.

Appendix B

Keeping and Organizing
Your Financial Records

Setting up a system for keeping financial records is always a challenge to young married couples. There is no one "right" way to do it. You may choose a very simple system or one that requires the use of a computer. Whatever you decide, be sure your system fits your personality and is compatible with these guidelines:

1. One of you should accept the primary responsibility for organizing and keeping your financial records. However, since the system used will require the cooperation of both husband and wife, make sure you both understand the system. Also make sure that you both participate in maintaining the system. Negotiate your record keeping roles as soon as possible after your wedding.

2. Keeping good financial records is a habit. Although you don't have to work on it daily, weekly attention to your record keeping is essential. If you get lazy, you'll regret it.

3. Begin by purchasing a filing cabinet or even a file drawer. Fancy isn't important. But all filing systems require some type of container to hold your records. Although files are the heart and soul of any record keeping system, you may spend as little as $25.00 to $50.00 and end up owning all the filing capacity you need to last a lifetime. Try shopping at garage sales or at flea markets and swap meets for a used filing cabinet rather than buying a new one. Remember, this isn't a piece of furniture; it's only purpose is to store your files.

4. The first section in your filing system should contain files to hold your **income records**. At the very least have one file marked "his" and another marked "hers." If you decide to file separate income tax returns, this will make life much easier at year end. In these files keep paycheck stubs, deposit receipts, interest statements from checking and saving accounts, and a record of investment income received during the year.

5. The next section of your files should be dedicated to records of **monthly expenses**. Simply set up a file for every monthly expense item that you have. Your spending plan forms should help you identify each expense category. In these files keep both your payment reminders (including installment loan coupon books, monthly notices of payments due, etc.) and your cancelled checks. Your cancelled checks are your best proof of payment in the event of a dispute with creditors. They are also important to help document tax deductions and tax credits in preparing your income tax return.

6. Within your monthly expense section maintain a special set of files for **insurance records**. Keep the current policy, your cancelled checks for paid insurance premiums, and the business card of your agent(s) in these files. Set up a separate file for each type of insurance policy you own. Don't just stuff everything in one file. In your safe deposit box at the bank you should maintain a listing of the insurance policies you own and the policy numbers for each policy. In the event your files are stolen or destroyed by fire, your insurance company will replace your policy if you can provide them the appropriate policy number.

7.   If you own **credit cards**, have a special section for credit card records. Keep a file on each card and in those files keep the following records: a photo-copy of the front and back of each card; the purchase receipts for all purchases made with your cards; a copy of all monthly statements; and your cancelled checks for all payments on your cards. If you possess several cards, you may wish to register with one of the many credit card services that report lost or stolen cards. When registered with one of these services, just one telephone call is all it takes to contact your credit card companies and stop a thief from using your cards. If you have only one or two cards, you don't really need this service. Every credit card has an emergency number that you can call if your cards get lost or stolen. Just be sure the emergency number for reporting credit card theft (or loss) is easy to retrieve from your files. In your safe deposit box, keep a special list of your credit cards by name and number and a back-up copy of the emergency numbers in the event your cards *and* files are both stolen.

8.   Set up a special section in your filing system for **income taxes**. In this section keep all records that you will use at year-end to justify allowable income tax deductions, tax credits, and taxes paid to state and federal governments. Consult with your accountant about how to segment this section. Since the tax laws change frequently, allowable tax deductions and tax credits may vary each year. Establishing and maintaining this section will make preparation of your annual income tax return(s) a lot easier. It will also allow you to justify your deductions, credits, and tax payments in the event of a tax audit. At the end of each year, remove these files and store them separately. By law you are required to keep income tax records for a minimum of three years, but because some states require longer it is wise to keep tax records for as long as five years before trashing them. Any tax return or tax documents that will affect *future tax returns* must be kept indefinitely.

9.   While not strictly financial in nature, I suggest you set up a special section in your files for **personal property** which contains instruction booklets, warran-ties, and maintenance records for products you own or purchase. The easiest arrangement is to have a file for every valuable item in your home, including such things as furniture, appliances, furs, jewelry, T.V., stereo, computer(s), and your automobile(s). I also suggest that you take a picture of these items and place a copy in the file. Attach a copy of the original proof of purchase documents to the photograph. If you decide to etch identification numbers on your belongings, include those numbers on the back of the photographs. In this way, if there is a theft, you are well prepared to deal effectively with your insurance company. Some of you may be fortunate enough to receive a video camera as a wedding gift. In that case, a video tape can substitute for the photographs. Yet, whether you use photographs or video tape, in addition to the copy you keep in your filing cabinet, keep a back-up copy of these photo records, with I.D. numbers, in

a safe deposit box.

10. I feel compelled to urge special attention for the file(s) you keep on your **automobile(s)**. It is in your filing cabinet in the house, not your glove compartment, that you should keep all records of automobile maintenance and warranty papers. The obvious reason for this is that glove compartments seem to swallow such documents. In maintaining your automobile(s), accurate records will help you to provide the best maintenance on your car(s). Someday you will want to sell or trade your car(s), and having these papers available may boost your car's resale value if you can show that you really cared for and maintained it over the years. If you use your car as a tax deductible business expense, you are required to keep accurate mileage records to document the date, purpose, and distance traveled for business use. Any office supply store can sell you a mileage log for this purpose. Keep the current log in your car, out of sight, but readily available. Once your tax return is filed, keep last year's log in your tax return file. If you're audited, you may have to produce your mileage logs to justify your deductions.

11. Those of you who are employees (as opposed to self-employed) will receive a variety of documents explaining your employee benefits. Therefore, I suggest you set up a special section in your filing system on **employee benefits**. A separate file for each benefit is the best idea. Don't simply throw everything in one file. If you're self-employed, and maintain your office at home, you may wish to keep a special section in your files on benefits you establish for yourself through your business. However, this is not the best idea. Your business records really should be kept separate and apart from your personal financial records. I urge you to discuss this important point with your accountant or tax advisor.

12. There should be a separate and distinct section in your files for **investments**. Your savings accounts (including passbook saving accounts, certificates of deposits, and money market accounts), records of stock, bond, real estate, and mutual fund transactions all belong in this section. The proof of ownership documents (stock and bond certificates, deeds of trust, promissory notes, etc.) should *not* be kept in these files. Proof of ownership documents belong in a safe deposit box at your bank. Your objective in organizing the investment section of your records should be to assist you in tracking investment performance. Once again, consult with your accountant about the simplest way to keep these records for tracking purposes.

13. Since your **checkbook and cancelled checks** are such an important part of your financial record system, I suggest you open only a checking account that provides cancelled checks with the monthly statements. There is a new school of thought in banking that wants to do away with providing bank customers with their cancelled checks. While this may make life easier for the bankers, it won't make your financial life easier. You should keep all cancelled checks (the ones not kept in one of the files already mentioned) in a small box at the back of your filing cabinet. Keep your used check registers there, too. The easiest way to organize cancelled checks is to wrap a rubber band around your monthly checking statement which contains the remaining cancelled checks (the ones not placed in a file) and organize them in sequence by month. If you have several checking accounts, use a separate box for each account. One other piece of sound advice is this: keep your check register balanced. Don't *ever* enter a check in your register without subtracting the amount of the check from your balance. Also, when you receive your monthly bank statement(s), take whatever time necessary to reconcile the balance in your check register with what the bank says you have in your account. Do this before you start filing away those cancelled checks. No, it's not much fun, but it's also not difficult and doing it is part of keeping good records.

14. Your **spending plan forms** are a very important part of your record keeping system. Don't throw them away. Maintain a special section in your files for these records. They are your best summary of where your cash comes from and where it goes. When you want to analyze spending patterns with an eye toward changing them, these records will help enormously.

15. Some money you spend won't be recorded on your spending plan forms. I'm referring to those daily out-of-pocket expenses that can really add up. For this reason, I recommend you purchase a **calendar** that allows you to keep track of daily cash purchases. Money spent on gasoline, a meal out (especially a business lunch) and other small out-of-pocket expenses can be recorded daily in your calendar. I suggest you staple the receipt for these expenses to the date-page in your calendar so you can easily retrieve these records for income tax purposes. This system will also allow you to go back and total up all out-of-pocket expenses at the end of each week *and* at the end of the month. Enter this total on your monthly spending plan summary. If your financial ship of life has the potential to spring a leak, it could be that this is where it will occur first. Your calendered, out-of-pocket record of expenses can help you plug this leak before your ship sinks.

The form on the next two pages is called a **locator**. Its purpose is to help you remember where you keep important papers. As you set about the task of organizing your records, keep this form at hand and complete it as you make your record keeping decisions. This will help you remember where you stored important records for safekeeping. Then, when you want to do a "quick check" on specific records, you won't have to rack your brain wondering, "Where did I put that?"

Location of Valuable Papers and Assets

For _____

Social Security Number—**Hers** _____

Social Security Number—**His** _____

Our valuable papers and assets are stored in these locations:

A. Residence_____
(Address plus where to look)

_____

B. Safe deposit box _____
(Bank, address, and location of key)

_____

C. Office _____
(Address plus where to look)

_____

D. Other _____
(Detailed description of where to look)

_____

E. Other _____
(Detailed description of where to look)

_____

F. Other _____
(Detailed description of where to look)

_____

G. Other _____
(Detailed description of where to look)

_____

ITEM	LOCATION						
	A	B	C	D	E	F	G
Her will (original)	☐	☐	☐	☐	☐	☐	☐
Her will (copy)	☐	☐	☐	☐	☐	☐	☐
His will (original)	☐	☐	☐	☐	☐	☐	☐
His will (copy)	☐	☐	☐	☐	☐	☐	☐
Powers of attorney	☐	☐	☐	☐	☐	☐	☐
Document appointing children's guardian	☐	☐	☐	☐	☐	☐	☐
His burial instructions	☐	☐	☐	☐	☐	☐	☐
Her burial instructions	☐	☐	☐	☐	☐	☐	☐
List of special bequests	☐	☐	☐	☐	☐	☐	☐
Safe combination	☐	☐	☐	☐	☐	☐	☐
Trust agreements	☐	☐	☐	☐	☐	☐	☐
Life insurance policies	☐	☐	☐	☐	☐	☐	☐
Homeowner's policy	☐	☐	☐	☐	☐	☐	☐
Health insurance policies	☐	☐	☐	☐	☐	☐	☐
Disability insurance policies	☐	☐	☐	☐	☐	☐	☐
Car insurance policies	☐	☐	☐	☐	☐	☐	☐
Employment contracts	☐	☐	☐	☐	☐	☐	☐
Partnership agreements	☐	☐	☐	☐	☐	☐	☐
List of checking and savings account(s)	☐	☐	☐	☐	☐	☐	☐
Bank statements, cancelled checks	☐	☐	☐	☐	☐	☐	☐
List of credit cards	☐	☐	☐	☐	☐	☐	☐
Certificates of deposit	☐	☐	☐	☐	☐	☐	☐
Checkbooks and savings passbooks	☐	☐	☐	☐	☐	☐	☐
Stock, bond certificates	☐	☐	☐	☐	☐	☐	☐
Other securities	☐	☐	☐	☐	☐	☐	☐
Retirement plan papers	☐	☐	☐	☐	☐	☐	☐
Income and gift tax returns	☐	☐	☐	☐	☐	☐	☐
Titles and deeds to real estate	☐	☐	☐	☐	☐	☐	☐
Title insurance policies	☐	☐	☐	☐	☐	☐	☐
Rental property records	☐	☐	☐	☐	☐	☐	☐
Notes and other loan agreements including mortgages	☐	☐	☐	☐	☐	☐	☐
Birth certificates	☐	☐	☐	☐	☐	☐	☐
Citizenship papers	☐	☐	☐	☐	☐	☐	☐
Military discharge papers	☐	☐	☐	☐	☐	☐	☐
Marriage certificate	☐	☐	☐	☐	☐	☐	☐
Warranty papers for home appliances	☐	☐	☐	☐	☐	☐	☐
Personal property inventory	☐	☐	☐	☐	☐	☐	☐
Other:	☐	☐	☐	☐	☐	☐	☐
_____	☐	☐	☐	☐	☐	☐	☐
_____	☐	☐	☐	☐	☐	☐	☐
_____	☐	☐	☐	☐	☐	☐	☐

Appendix C

Tax Tips:
Preparing Your First Income Tax Return as a Married Couple

Let's get one point straight at the start of this discussion: legally paying the smallest possible income tax is your right and obligation. This undisputable "fact" has been consistently upheld by court decisions since the federal income tax was enacted in 1916. Since the tax laws, rules and regulations are constantly changing, however, it is hard to be completely certain about how to achieve this objective. The following presentation is limited in scope and general in nature, but it will give you some important points to ponder as you think about preparing your first tax return as a married couple.

1. No matter how "easy" the IRS says it is to prepare your own tax return, don't do it yourself. Engage a professional to help you—preferably a C.P.A.

2. At least once a year, sit down and read a book on current income tax laws, rules, and regulations. By doing so, you will have an overview of the tax laws so you can communicate intelligently with your accountant. Assign responsibility for this reading to the one who has the most desire to do it. Afterwards, the one who read the book should hold a book review to share any new knowledge gained with the other partner.

3. If you haven't done so before you get married, hold a meeting with your accountant right after your wedding to prepare a plan for dealing with taxes. This plan will project your taxable income for the year, and the potential deductions and credits you may have available to lower your tax bill. Most accountants can provide you with a workbook to assist in organizing your records for tax preparation. Your accountant will explain how to use this workbook to *document* your deductions and credits so you can justify them if you are ever audited.

4. For tax purposes, you are considered a married couple for the entire tax year, even if your wedding is on December 31st. This means your filing status will change the instant you are legally married. Even when you are married, you can file jointly or separately, but if you file separately you are still required to state that you are married. Taxation of married couples is determined by different tax tables than the ones used for single or unmarried individuals. This fact, and many additional tax rules and regulations that apply only to married couples, is why the IRS requires you to disclose your marital status.

5. The federal income tax is a progressive tax, which means that those who earn larger incomes fall into higher tax brackets. Your basic tax will be computed by the following formula:

a. Determine your gross income.

b. Subtract certain allowable adjustments to determine adjusted gross income.

c. Subtract certain allowable deductions to determine income before allowable exemptions.

d. Subtract allowable exemptions to determine taxable income.

e. Use tax tables or rate schedules to determine your tax for the year.

f. Subtract any applicable tax credits to determine what you owe.

6. Of course, after completing this tax computation formula, you then subtract taxes paid during the year (through payroll withholdings or as estimated tax payments) to determine what you still owe Uncle Sam. Sometimes, taxpayers have a refund due for **overpayment of taxes.** However, by planning ahead with the assistance of your accountant, you will seldom find that the government owes you a refund. Overpaying your taxes is like making an interest free loan to the federal government. It's far better to avoid overpayment and put your money to work in your own savings account where it can earn interest.

7. **Underpayment of taxes** is also something to avoid. You are required to pay at least 90 percent of your current year tax or 100 percent of your prior year tax, or you will be subject to a penalty for "underpayment of estimated tax." For those whose income is subject to payroll withholdings to meet their tax obligations, meeting the 90 percent requirement is usually easy. But those who receive alimony, self-employment-income, or dividends must *estimate* their tax and pay it quarterly. The IRS provides worksheets and vouchers, along with 1040 ES forms to help you calculate and file quarterly estimated payments.

8. Determining your **gross income** (whether projecting for the year ahead or summarizing for the year just ended) is more complicated for some couples than for others. For most couples gross income is limited to salaries, wages, bonuses, commissions and proprietorship income, interest, and dividends. But the government considers many other items under its definition of gross income. If you own a business, you have to include everything you earned from that business (although business income is reported on a special form). If you receive earnings from rent, royalties, dividends from stocks, or alimony, these all have to be reported, too. And if you gamble and win, even if you win the lottery, your *winnings* must be reported. Sometimes an employer's contributions to your fringe benefits program will also be included. It is your responsibility to report *all* income received during the year. Of course, some income is *not* reportable. Ask your accountant to help you sort out what will and won't be included.

9. When you invest, you will eventually have **capital gains** (remember what you learned in Chapter Eight?). Capital gains on investments are income, too. Capital gain taxes are imposed on the *profits* from your investments when you sell. To encourage taxpayers to make long term investments, the government offers special tax treatment to those who hold their investments one full year before selling. Profits from an investment held one year or longer are called "long-term capital gains." Profits from an investment held for less than one year are called "short-term capital gains." Ask your accountant to explain the special tax treatment provided for capital gains and losses.

10. Capital losses are what you get when you sell investments and lose money. Fortunately, you can deduct your losses from your gains and lower your tax bill. However, there are limits on the tax deductibility of capital losses. These limits are different for short-term capital losses (losses that occur from investments held less than twelve months) and long term losses. Ask your accountant to explain these limits based on current law.

11. Deductions from income are very important. Deductions are allowances against gross income which help lower your tax bill. Basically, deductions fall into three categories: (1) the cost of doing business; (2) money set aside in qualified retirement accounts; (3) standard and itemized deductions. Your accountant can be especially helpful in coaching you on deductible business expenses. If you have your own business, (or even if you only have unreimbursed business related expenses) I encourage you to meet as soon as possible with your accountant to make sure you are properly documenting *all* of your deductible costs for doing business. Your accountant can also keep you well informed on how to gain most from "socking away" money in IRAs, Keogh (H.R. 10) plans, etc. Of course, the law is quite clear about the allowable standard deductions, but itemized deductions can be more difficult to understand. Besides, the rules on itemized deductions are constantly changing. Once again, check carefully and frequently with your accountant to make sure you are properly documenting *all* of your allowable itemized deductions. This will save you a lot of agony when it comes time to prepare your income tax return.

12. After you subtract all of your allowable deductions, you have arrived at your *income before allowable exemptions*. However, to determine your taxable income, (and to make sure you pay the smallest tax) you next subtract your allowable exemptions. **Tax exemptions** are not really all that helpful because what they amount to is a special consideration for supporting someone who either *can't fully support themself* or for supporting *yourself*. For example, if you have children, you are allowed an exemption for each child you support. In 1991 the exemption was $2,150 for each child but the value of this exemption is adjusted each year for inflation. The problem is that it takes a lot more than $2,150 a year to support a child. You are also allowed an exemption if you provide more than 50 percent of the support for an aging parent. Here we have the same problem. Who can support an aging parent (or even half support one) on $2,150 a year? The final exemption joke is that you and your spouse are allowed an exemption because you support yourselves. Nevertheless, take all the exemptions to which you are entitled before computing your tax.

13. Even after your tax has been computed, you may be able to lower your tax bill through the use of **tax credits**. Tax credits are dollar-for-dollar offsets against your tax bill. Unfortunately there are very few tax credits available under current law. There are some tax credits allowed for special investments, but be careful. The tax rules and regulations on these investments are always changing and if they are going to be a part of your tax planning, make sure you work very closely with your accountant on selecting and documenting these investments. The most popular tax credit for young married couples is the childcare tax credit. The current credit available for the cost of childcare fluctuates depending on the number of children you have, the cost of care, and your income. While an important credit for young parents, it isn't exactly an incentive to have a large family.

14. Once you've subtracted all available adjustments to income, deductions, exemptions, and credits, you will have one final figure which is supposed to be what you owe Uncle Sam. However, just in case you have too many adjustments, exemptions, deductions, and credits, (and end up owing a low regular tax or no tax at all) our lawmakers have invented a special tax just for you. It's called the **Alternative Minimum Tax (AMT)**. The AMT is calculated after you determine your normal tax. Once again, it really takes an accountant to make this computation because the rules that apply to this special tax are complex. Its goal is to make sure that no one pays less tax than a certain specified rate (a rate that is constantly changing). Because the AMT is super sensitive to tax preferences offered for certain investments, you should involve your accountant in a review of the income tax implications of any tax preferences offered by investments you may be considering. Many promised investment tax benefits (especially those benefits offered by "tax shelters") can be neutralized completely by the AMT.

15. Now that I've mentioned investment tax benefits in relation to income taxes, it's important to advise you about certain other **investment tax strategies** to keep in mind.

   a. Remember that **income from municipal bonds** is not taxable on your federal return. Take a long, hard, serious look at how buying municipal bonds might work to your advantage in your overall investment plan.

   b. While **income from government bonds** (U.S.) are taxable, state and city governments do not tax this income.

   c. **Growth investments** (non-income producing investments that appreciate in value each year) are not taxed while you hold them. If you buy growth assets in the early years of your marriage, the increase in value each year will not affect your income tax situation. You only pay taxes on the growth (capital gain taxes) when you *sell* growth investments.

   d. **When you sell growth investments,** try to sell them in a way that will produce *long-term* capital gains. If it makes sense, sell losing stocks in the same year you sell your winners. In this way you can create a long-term loss in the same year you create a long-term gain. The loss will offset the gain to the extent provided by law, and thus help lower your income tax liability.

   e. If you hold real estate for commercial purposes or resale purposes, and you are considering selling it, consider a **tax-free real estate exchange.** While this is a very complicated investment tax saving strategy, your accountant can explain the fine points of how it works. The trick is to find another piece of real estate of equal type and value *and* owners who want your property as much as you want theirs. If it is done correctly, there is no income tax on the exchange.

   f. If you purchase bonds as part of your investment plan, and your bonds drop in value, consider selling them before the calendar year ends and declare a loss. This will give you a capital loss to use as an income tax deduction. Then use the money from your sale of the bonds to buy new bonds with the same face value of the bonds you sold. If you do this right, you will continue receiving the same income as before the bond sale, but you'll have to buy a new bond with a longer maturity date. This is called **bond swapping.** Ask your stock broker and your accountant for help with the fine points of this investment tax saving strategy.

g. If you consider **buying a tax shelter** to lower your income taxes, then *before you buy* ask your accountant to calculate how the tax advantages will impact your income tax situation. Often tax shelter benefits are offset by the Alternative Minimum Tax (discussed above). Tax shelters are high risk investments anyway, and should be carefully evaluated by a professional advisor (or several professional advisors) before you purchase one. But to buy a tax shelter without careful review of how it may affect your current and future income tax liability is foolish and may prove to be very expensive tax-wise.

h. Remember that **buying a house** may be one of the best investments possible for a young married couple. Since the interest on a mortgage is income tax deductible, the purchase of a home may be one of your best ways to build wealth and lower your income taxes at the same time.

i. Some young couples can't afford to buy a home in the city where they work, but they can afford to **buy a house out in the country** where the prices are much lower. Sometimes it makes sense to buy the country house and rent it out while continuing to rent an apartment near your place(s) of employment. If the country house is in an area where property values are expected to appreciate, then in a year or two the gain from this investment (assuming you sell the house) can provide the down payment for a house in the city. In the meantime the country house may become a year-round rental, or it may serve as an occasional rental and a second home for the two of you. There are different tax consequences depending on whether you rent and/or use the home for personal purposes. Obviously, your choice will be influenced most by your need for cash flow. But the tax consequences of your decision should be fully discussed with your accountant. If used properly, this investment idea can also help lower your annual income taxes.

The tax code now runs several thousand pages. In addition, there are four volumes of IRS regulations explaining them. Occasionally, everyone needs help understanding tax laws and regulations. And occasionally, everyone gets into a debate with the IRS about an interpretation of what is "right." If you find you are about to be audited, or if you face some other kind of debate with the IRS, you will be much better prepared to deal with them if you have worked closely with an accountant and followed the accountant's advice for record keeping and tax preparation. Your accountant will also help you with any correspondence or face-to-face meeting(s) with IRS officials. You *can* win with the IRS. But you must be fully prepared. Know your rights *and* your responsibilities. When you're right, and can prove it with good documentation, then you're right. But if you're wrong, or have kept sloppy records, then it may cost you dearly.

Appendix D

Detailed Assessment of Current Net Worth

The following forms have been designed for ease of use. Nevertheless, if you don't feel totally comfortable completing these forms yourself, you may find it helpful to ask for assistance from your accountant or other financial consultants. Skip any section that does not apply to your situation. Rough estimates are perfectly acceptable when determining the current value of assets or liabilities. You don't have to know the exact amount.

It may be easier to complete these forms if you have the following documents at your fingertips. They will give you a more accurate picture of your assets and liabilities.

- Tax returns (for the last three years)
- Brokerage statements or investment accounts
- Mortgage or other loan statements
- Insurance policies and statements from your insurance companies

- Employee benefit agreements as well as statements from your employer disclosing information about your benefits.
- Wills and trust agreements
- Payroll stubs
- Property records

When identifying the form of title, make your best guess for now. If you are not sure how you hold title to an asset, put a question mark beside your guess to remind you to investigate further. Use the following ownership coding for consistency:

SSP	Sole and Separate Property
TC	Tenants in Common
JTRS	Joint Tenancy with Rights of Survivorship
CP	Community Property
TP	Trust Property

Date This Inventory Was Completed _____

Marital Inventory of Assets

Item Description	Current Value	Form of Title	His	Hers	Ours
Cash					
Checking Accounts Account Numbers			☐ ☐	☐ ☐	☐ ☐
Savings Accounts Account Numbers			☐	☐	☐
Credit Union Share Accounts Account Numbers			☐	☐	☐
Money Market Accounts Account Numbers			☐	☐	☐
Certificates of Deposit Certificate Numbers			☐	☐	☐
Treasury Bills Maturity Dates			☐	☐	☐
Total Value of Cash Assets			☐	☐	☐

Marital Inventory of Assets

Item Description	Current Value	Form of Title	His	Hers	Ours
Cash Value Investments					
Money Market Mutual Funds					
Fund Name			☐	☐	☐
_____	_____	_____	☐	☐	☐
_____	_____	_____	☐	☐	☐
U.S. Savings Bonds					
HH Bonds and Maturity Dates			☐	☐	☐
_____	_____	_____	☐	☐	☐
_____	_____	_____	☐	☐	☐
_____	_____	_____	☐	☐	☐
EE Bonds and Maturity Dates			☐	☐	☐
_____	_____	_____	☐	☐	☐
_____	_____	_____	☐	☐	☐
_____	_____	_____	☐	☐	☐
Cash In Stock Brokerage Accounts					
Accounts with			☐	☐	☐
_____	_____	_____	☐	☐	☐
_____	_____	_____	☐	☐	☐
Total Value of Cash Value Investments	_____		☐	☐	☐

Marital Inventory of Assets

Item Description	Current Value	Form of Title	His	Hers	Ours

Marketable Investments

Preferred Stocks
Company Name & Quantity

Common Stocks
Company Name & Quantity

Mutual Funds
Company & Number of Shares

Bonds (Corporate & Municipal)
Company Name & Quantity

Marital Inventory of Assets

Item Description	Current Value	Form of Title	His	Hers	Ours
Marketable Investments —Continued					
Treasury Bonds Maturity Dates	_____	_____	☐	☐	☐
	_____	_____	☐	☐	☐
	_____	_____	☐	☐	☐
	_____	_____	☐	☐	☐
Treasury Notes Maturity Dates	_____	_____	☐	☐	☐
	_____	_____	☐	☐	☐
	_____	_____	☐	☐	☐
	_____	_____	☐	☐	☐
Other Description	_____	_____	☐	☐	☐
	_____	_____	☐	☐	☐
	_____	_____	☐	☐	☐
	_____	_____	☐	☐	☐
Total Value of Marketable Investments	_____				

Marital Inventory of Assets

Item Description	Current Value	Form of Title	His	Hers	Ours
Non-Marketable Investments					
Retirement Plans					
Individual Retirement Accounts Accounts with			☐	☐	☐
			☐	☐	☐
			☐	☐	☐
Vested Interest In Pension Funds Employer and Type of Fund including 401 (k)s, 403 (b)s, and SEPs.			☐	☐	☐
			☐	☐	☐
Keogh Plan Investments Invested With			☐	☐	☐
			☐	☐	☐
Real Estate					
Primary Residence			☐	☐	☐
Vacation Home			☐	☐	☐
Investment Property Location/Description			☐	☐	☐
			☐	☐	☐
			☐	☐	☐

Marital Inventory of Assets

Item Description	Current Value	Form of Title	His	Hers	Ours
Non-Marketable Investments					
Real Estate—Continued					
Other Real Estate Location/Description			☐ ☐ ☐	☐ ☐ ☐	☐ ☐ ☐
Business Interests Descriptions			☐	☐	☐
Limited Partnerships Descriptions			☐ ☐ ☐	☐ ☐ ☐	☐ ☐ ☐

Marital Inventory of Assets

Item Description	Current Value	Form of Title	His	Hers	Ours
Non-Marketable Investments			☐	☐	☐
			☐	☐	☐
			☐	☐	☐
			☐	☐	☐
			☐	☐	☐
Loans Made To Others					
Made To:					
Trust Funds			☐	☐	☐
Description:			☐	☐	☐
			☐	☐	☐
Insurance Plans					
Cash Value Life Insurance Policies			☐	☐	☐
Underwriting Company			☐	☐	☐
			☐	☐	☐

Marital Inventory of Assets

Item Description	Current Value	Form of Title	His	Hers	Ours
Non-Marketable Investments					
Insurance Plans - Continued					
Annuities					
Underwriting Company	_____	_____	☐ ☐	☐ ☐	☐ ☐
	_____	_____			
Collectibles For Investment Purposes					
Type of Collection	_____	_____	☐ ☐ ☐ ☐	☐ ☐ ☐ ☐	☐ ☐ ☐ ☐
	_____	_____			
	_____	_____			
	_____	_____			
Total Value Of Non-Marketable Investments	_____		☐	☐	☐

Marital Inventory of Assets

Item Description	Current Value	Form of Title	His	Hers	Ours
Personal Property Items					
Cars					
Make and Year			☐	☐	☐
			☐	☐	☐
			☐	☐	☐
Other Vehicles					
Make and Year			☐	☐	☐
			☐	☐	☐
			☐	☐	☐
Household Goods					
Description			☐	☐	☐
			☐	☐	☐
			☐	☐	☐
			☐	☐	☐
			☐	☐	☐
Jewelry & Furs					
Description			☐	☐	☐
			☐	☐	☐
			☐	☐	☐
			☐	☐	☐

Marital Inventory of Assets

Item Description	Current Value	Form of Title	His	Hers	Ours
Personal Property Items					
Other			☐ ☐ ☐ ☐ ☐ ☐ ☐ ☐	☐ ☐ ☐ ☐ ☐ ☐ ☐	☐ ☐ ☐ ☐ ☐ ☐ ☐ ☐
Description					

Total Value Of Personal Property Items

	Current Value	His Assets	Her Assets	Our Assets
Cash				
Cash Value Investments				
Marketable Investments				
Non-Marketable Investments				
Personal Property Items				
Grand Total				

Marital Inventory of Liabilities

Item Description	Current Balance	Interest Rate	His	Hers	Ours
Credit Cards Card Issued by and Number:			☐☐☐☐☐	☐☐☐☐☐	☐☐☐☐☐
Charge Accounts Accounts with:			☐☐☐☐☐	☐☐☐☐☐	☐☐☐☐☐
Installment Loans Loans with:			☐☐☐☐☐	☐☐☐☐☐	☐☐☐☐☐
Lines of Credit Lines of credit with:			☐☐	☐☐	☐☐

Marital Inventory of Liabilities

Item Description	Current Balance	Interest Rate	His	Hers	Ours
Personal Loans Loans with: _____ _____ _____			☐ ☐ ☐	☐ ☐ ☐	☐ ☐ ☐
Home: First Mortgage Mortgage with: _____			☐	☐	☐
Home: Second Mortgage Mortgage with: _____			☐	☐	☐
Other Mortgages Mortgages with: _____ _____			☐ ☐	☐ ☐	☐ ☐
Home Equity Loans Loans with: _____ _____			☐ ☐	☐ ☐	☐ ☐
Margin Accounts Account with: _____			☐ ☐	☐ ☐	☐ ☐

Marital Inventory of Liabilities

Item Description	Current Balance	Interest Rate	His	Hers	Ours
Auto Loans Loans with:			☐ ☐	☐ ☐	☐ ☐
Insurance Policy Loans Company and Policy Number:			☐ ☐	☐ ☐	☐ ☐
Business Loans Loans with:			☐ ☐	☐ ☐	☐ ☐
Estimated Liability for Taxes Date Due			☐ ☐	☐ ☐	☐ ☐
Other Debts Description			☐ ☐ ☐ ☐ ☐	☐ ☐ ☐ ☐ ☐	☐ ☐ ☐ ☐ ☐
Total of All Liabilities					

Grand Total

Our Current Net Worth

	Combined	His	Hers	Ours
Total Assets	____	____	____	____
Total Liabilities	____	____	____	____
(Subtract Total Liabilities from Total Assets to get Current Net Worth)				
Current Net Worth	____	____	____	____

Appendix E

Spending Plan Forms and Instructions

The forms that appear on the next six pages are designed to help you track your income and expenses on a monthly basis, increase savings, and prevent impulse spending. It is probably best if one partner is assigned to making entries in the **"Actual"** column for expenses. However, you should both prepare your spending plan estimates *and* you must both keep excellent records of your expenses in order for your entries to be accurate. You have my permission to photocopy these forms so you have an ample supply of them. Don't use the one in this book; use it as your master copy. Here are a few points to remember when making your entries.

1. Be sure to fill in the month and the year on each sheet.

2. Estimate your income first. Be sure to total the money you expect to receive during the month. If your earnings are irregular, it may be more difficult to estimate your income—but do it anyway. It is better to underestimate than overestimate your income.

3. Next, estimate your expenses. After the first month of using these forms, you can look back at each previous month's record of estimated and actual expenses to help refine your estimates. In estimating, try to use your monthly Spending Plan planning sessions to make adjustments. For example, if you spent a large amount on food last month, you may wish to see if you can set a lower estimate this month and stick to it.

4. Carry a pocket notebook around with you (or use your calendar) to keep a record of all your expenses on a daily basis. Your checkbook register(s) will also be helpful in tracking your expenses. Set aside at least one hour each week to make your expense entries. This is the purpose of page five of these forms. Keep your records up to date using your notebooks, receipts and check stubs to verify amounts.

5. At the end of each month, compare your actual income and expenses with your estimates. Always subtract the actual income and expenses from your projections and record the difference. This exercise will help you see areas where expenses are out of control.

6. At the end of each month, file your income and expense records (along with your cancelled checks, receipts, and other paper records) according to the instructions in **Appendix B.**

7. At the end of each year, complete an annual review of your income and expenses to see which areas need better management.

Spending Plan Forms—Income Record

Month_____Year_____

Income	Projected	Actual	Difference
Employment			
His (after taxes)	$_____	$_____	$_____
Hers (after taxes)	$_____	$_____	$_____
Commissions, Tips, Bonuses	$_____	$_____	$_____
Child Support and/or Alimony	$_____	$_____	$_____
Unemployment Compensation	$_____	$_____	$_____
Disability Benefits	$_____	$_____	$_____
Social Security Payments	$_____	$_____	$_____
Veterans' Benefits	$_____	$_____	$_____
Income from Trusts	$_____	$_____	$_____
Royalties/Residuals	$_____	$_____	$_____
Interest			
Source:_____	$_____	$_____	$_____
Source:_____	$_____	$_____	$_____
Source:_____	$_____	$_____	$_____
Dividends			
Source:_____	$_____	$_____	$_____
Source:_____	$_____	$_____	$_____
Mutual-fund/Capital Gain Distributions			
Source:_____	$_____	$_____	$_____
Source:_____	$_____	$_____	$_____
Rents from Real Estate	$_____	$_____	$_____
Net from Real Estate Sales			
Source:_____	$_____	$_____	$_____
Source:_____	$_____	$_____	$_____
Net from Business Profits	$_____	$_____	$_____
Second Income Stream Sources	$_____	$_____	$_____
(See Chapter Seven for a full explanation.)			
Other_____	$_____	$_____	$_____
Other_____	$_____	$_____	$_____
Other_____	$_____	$_____	$_____
Total For This Month	$_____	$_____	$_____

Spending Plan Forms—Expense Record

Month_____ Year_____

Expenses	Projected	Actual	Difference
Savings	_____	_____	$_____
Emergency Fund	_____	_____	$_____
Vacation Fund	_____	_____	$_____
Special Holiday Fund	_____	_____	$_____
Investment Fund	_____	_____	$_____
Taxes			
Federal Income Taxes	_____	_____	$_____
State Income Taxes	_____	_____	$_____
Social Security Contributions	_____	_____	$_____
Real Estate Taxes	_____	_____	$_____
Mortgage/Rent	_____	_____	$_____
Home Improvements	_____	_____	$_____
Gas/Fuel	_____	_____	$_____
Electricity	_____	_____	$_____
Water	_____	_____	$_____
Garbage	_____	_____	$_____
Telephone	_____	_____	$_____
Life Inurance	_____	_____	$_____
Health Insurance	_____	_____	$_____
Disability Insurance	_____	_____	$_____
Automobile Insurance	_____	_____	$_____
Automobile Insurance	_____	_____	$_____
Other Insurance	_____	_____	$_____
Other Insurance	_____	_____	$_____
Automobile Maintenance	_____	_____	$_____
Gas and Oil	_____	_____	$_____
Parking and Tolls	_____	_____	$_____
Bus and Taxi	_____	_____	$_____
Food	_____	_____	$_____
Clothing	_____	_____	$_____
Doctors	_____	_____	$_____
Dentist	_____	_____	$_____
Medicines and Prescriptions	_____	_____	$_____
Other Medical Expenses	_____	_____	$_____
Debts			
Loan #_____	_____	_____	$_____
Loan #_____	_____	_____	$_____
Loan #_____	_____	_____	$_____
Credit Card_____	_____	_____	$_____
Credit Card_____	_____	_____	$_____
Credit Card_____	_____	_____	$_____
Charge Account_____	_____	_____	$_____
Charge Account_____	_____	_____	$_____
Charge Account_____	_____	_____	$_____

Go On To The Next Page

Spending Plan Forms—Expense Record

Month_____ Year_____

Expenses	Projected	Actual	Difference
Child Care	_____	_____	$_____
Child Support/Alimony	_____	_____	$_____
Personal Allowance			
His	_____	_____	$_____
Hers	_____	_____	$_____
Membership Dues	_____	_____	$_____
Newspapers	_____	_____	$_____
Magazine Subscriptions	_____	_____	$_____
Books	_____	_____	$_____
Hobbies	_____	_____	$_____
Pets	_____	_____	$_____
Gifts to Family Members/Others	_____	_____	$_____
Charitable Contributions			
Church or Synagogue	_____	_____	$_____
Charity_____	_____	_____	$_____
Charity_____	_____	_____	$_____
Charity_____	_____	_____	$_____
Psychological Paychecks			
(including meals out, entertainment, etc.)			
Item or Event_____	_____	_____	$_____
Item or Event_____	_____	_____	$_____
Item or Event_____	_____	_____	$_____
Item or Event_____	_____	_____	$_____
Item or Event_____	_____	_____	$_____
Item or Event_____	_____	_____	$_____
Item or Event_____	_____	_____	$_____
Item or Event_____	_____	_____	$_____
Item or Event_____	_____	_____	$_____
Item or Event_____	_____	_____	$_____
Out of Pocket Expenses (Petty cash expenses. A record of these expenses should be kept in your daytimer/calendar.)	_____	_____	$_____
Other Expenses:	_____	_____	$_____
_____	_____	_____	$_____
_____	_____	_____	$_____
_____	_____	_____	$_____
_____	_____	_____	$_____
_____	_____	_____	$_____
_____	_____	_____	$_____
_____	_____	_____	$_____
_____	_____	_____	$_____

Total Expenses For This Month   _____   _____ $_____

Spending Plan Forms—Weekly Expense Recap

Month_____Year_____

Instructions: Only record expense items here that are untotaled expenses like food, business lunches, gasoline purchases, and out-of-pocket expenses. At the end of the month, you should total these items and record them in the appropriate place on your Spending Plan Expense Record.

Item	Paid By and Amount			Date
	Check	Cash	Credit Card	

Spending Plan Forms—Score Sheet

Month_____ Year_____

Income For This Month:

Estimated   Actual   Difference

_____   _____   _____

Expenses For This Month:

Estimated   Actual   Difference

_____   _____   _____

Total Actual Income $ _____

Less Total Expenses $ _____

**Amount available for
additional savings, investments, or debt payments** $ _____

Ideas For Reducing Expenses:

_____

_____

_____

_____

_____

_____

_____

_____

_____

_____

Ideas For Reducing Expenses:

_____

_____

_____

_____

_____

_____

_____

_____

_____

_____

_____

_____

_____

_____

_____

_____

_____

_____

_____

Appendix F

The Right MLM Company
By Doris Wood, President MLMIA

The Multi-Level (Network) Marketing Industry is experiencing a period of unprecedented growth. Many new companies are starting. People who never considered MLM Distributorships before are looking for advice on how to choose a company. Others, with experience in companies that don't seem to stay around longer than a few months, who want to remain in MLM are also searching for answers.

Many call the Multi-Level Marketing International Association, MLMIA, a non-profit trade organization for everyone in MLM, asking for advice on what to look for or the right company to represent.

Based on information obtained over the years as a Distributor, Field Manager, Corporate Staff member, Company founder, Consultant to the industry, and input from MLMIA members who are corporate executives, Product Manufacturers, Attorneys, Consultants, Data Processing companies, Distributors, etc.... and, on some studies made on companies that have been around for at least three years, we offer the following:

To Distributors

Find a product (service is a product) you can love. You must believe in the product or it is doubtful you'll ever be able to sell it, or recruit others.

Make sure the product (service):
1) Has a "real world" marketplace.
2) Is sold at an uninflated price. Price must be fair and competitive.
3) Can be purchased at wholesale or at substantial discount from prices of similar product found in retail stores.
4) Is of high quality.
5) Consumer satisfaction should be guaranteed.

If the product is consumed by Distributors, it must be one they would want to buy regardless of participation in the marketing plan.

In most (but not all) instances, give preference to consumable products or services used more than once. Repeat sales build volume and repeat customers make the best recruits for your network.

Watch out for claims of enormous overnight success. Average earnings are usually modest. It takes time and effort to truly be a "big" success.

Don't necessarily accept the first person who introduced you to the product as your sponsor. Find a sponsor who can (will) train you, inspire you, or learn with you and continue to work with you. AND don't join a (or another) company just because you like your sponsor and he/she likes you.

If you are in the industry on a part time basis, distributing for more than one company can damage your credibility. You could end up losing money because commission percentages increase with volume.

This means you will probably make more money selling one thousand (1,000) items for one company than selling 500 items for each of two different companies.

Almost everyone agrees that the majority of people who make it big in MLM market for just one company. Splitting your time splits your income.

Beware of Large Start-up Fees.

Make sure the company guarantees its product or service and that they will buy back at least 90 percent of all unsold inventory, sales kits and materials in resalable condition.

Be prepared to put in the effort, time and work it takes. In the right company, the opportunity is there. You can make it big by grasping the true principles of MLM. These are the three things that will bring larger income and make for a truly successful business.

Each Distributor should:
1) Sell his/her product, or service, weekly.
2) Sponsor monthly and
3) Train those he/she sponsors to sell, sponsor and train.

About The Company

Don't rush to become a Distributor. Read the materials. Do some checking. Is the company a memebr of the MLMIA or the DSA (Direct Selling Association)? Several days of checking to see if there have been complaints won't really make a difference in a program that will be around for a long time.

To Call: MLMIA (714) 647-7121, 2:00 to 4:30 P.M. PST M-F.

To Write: MLMIA, 119 Stanford Court, Irvine, California, 92715.

To Join: MLMIA, Distributors $35.00 yearly.

If MLMIA does not have enough information on the company for you to make a decision, they will get in touch with the company and can usually find the information you need. (Non-members—MLMIA is non-profit. To receive a packet of information about the industry and opportunities within the industry, please send a check or money order for $10.00. If you later decide to join MLMIA, your $10.00 will be applied to the cost of membership).

Do executives have MLM experience? How much? With an established, respected company? OR can they afford to hire the experienced MLM Professional Consultants (Attorney, Marketing Plan evaluator, Data Processing) that can help them? Bottom line: Are they capable of running a company?

Be sure the company has sufficient capital to adequately cover expenses. Can they meet their obligations for rent, product, phone, and data processing to ensure Distributors are paid when promised? Can they meet possible legal fees and day-to-day running of a business? Distributors' commissions and bonus are not to be used to pay company bills.

What are company ethics? Their values? Can you adhere to them?

To Determine That A Program Is A Legitimate Opportunity

The basic rule for a legitimate marketing program is that no earning representations should be made until there is a verifiable track record of average earnings of Distributors in a particular geographic area. In a start-up company, this is virtually impossible to do.

Legally, a company CANNOT make a profit on a sign-up fee. A sales kit or demonstration materials, sold at company cost, should be the only investment requirement.

Watch out for plans in which fees are paid for headhunting and/or emphasis is on recruitment rather than sale of product. Distributors (by any name) can not be paid for recruiting.

A legitimate MLM program has no minimum purchase, nor any inventory requirement, to become or remain a qualified Distributor.

Front, or inventory, loading is illegal. Mandatory purchases of peripheral or accessory products or services is illegal.

The focus of the marketing program should be to promote retail sales to non-participants.

To ensure that legitimate and ethical MLM practices are carried out, and that pyramiding schemes are stamped out, requires the cooperation of all—Companies and Distributors. The future of the industry is in the hands of all of us. YOU are the one who can help make the difference.

I encourage you to join MLMIA and keep in touch with your Multi-Level Marketing International Association. With your help, MLMIA can help all legal and ethical Companies and Distributors, and rid our industry of the troublemakers.

(This article was reprinted with permission from Doris Wood, President MLMIA with the hope that it will help my readers make intelligent decisions when exploring Multi-Level Marketing as a way to establish a second income stream.)

Members MLMIA—Sample Listing

Member	Business
Matol Botanical, Int'l Bill Melvin 8465 South Gad Way Sandy, UT 84093 (514) 639-0730	Nutrition products
Nature's Sunshine Allen Kennedy, President 1655 North Main Street Spanish Fork, Utah (801) 798-9861	Health and personal care products

Member	Business

Member

Nu-Skin International, Inc.
Steven Lund
President
145 E Center
Provo, UT 84601
(801) 377-6056

Rexall Showcase International
Lou Prescott
President
6600 N. Andrews Ave #401
Ft. Lauderdale, FL 33309
(305) 771-1446

Sunrider International
Dr. Tei Fu Chen,
Chairman of the Board
3111 Lomita Blvd
Torence, CA 90505
(213) 534-4786

Business

Health Products and Cosmetics

Nutritional Products

Chinese Herbal Products

Members DSA—Partial Listing

The Direct Selling Association is a national trade association comprising leading firms which manufacture and distribute goods and services sold directly to consumers. DSA's headquarters are located at 1776 K Street N.W., Washington, D.C. 2006. Their telephone number is (202) 293-5760. While you are free to contact any DSA member directly, you will find the trade association offices helpful to you in a variety of ways when trying to make intelligent decisions about joining a direct sales company. Contacting the association offices is the only way to secure a complete listing of DSA members.

Member

Amway Corporation
Casey Wondergem
7575 Fulton Street, East
Ada, MI 49355-0001
(616) 676-6000

Business

Autocare products, cleaning products, cookware, cosmetics, encyclopedias, fashion accessories, food/beverage products, fragrances, group buying, health and fitness, home appliances, insurance/financial planning, jewelry, nutritional supplements, security systems/ devices, skincare, travel, water filters

Member	Business
Avon Products, Inc. E.V. Goings Nine West 57 Street New York, NY 10019 (212) 546-6015	Clothing, cosmetics, decorative accessories, giftware, jewelry, skincare, toys/games
Doncaster Michael S. Tanner Oak Springs Road Box 1159 Rutherfordton, NC 28139 (704) 287-4205	Clothing, jewelry
Encyclopedia Britannica, USA Patricia A. Wier Britannica Centre 310 South Michigan Avenue Chicago, IL 60604 (312) 347-7000	Educational publications, encyclopedias
The Fuller Brush Company John Apline 3065 Center Green Drive Boulder, CO 80301 (303) 440-9448	Cleaning products, house and kitchenwares
Herbalife International Mark Hughes 9800 La Cienega Boulevard P.O. Box 80210 Los Angeles, CA 90009 (310) 410-9600	Health and fitness, nutritional supplements, skincare, water filters
Jafra Cosmetics, Inc. Robin H. Kirkland P.O. Box 5026 Westlake Village, CA 91359 (805) 494 0400	Cosmetics, fragrances, skincare
Mary Kay Cosmetics, Inc. Richard C. Bartlett 8787 Stemmons Freeway Dallas, TX 75247 (214) 630-8787	Cosmetics, skincare

Member	Business
Shaklee Corporation Rakesh K. Kaul Shaklee Terraces 444 Market Street San Francisco, CA 94111 (415) 954-3000	Cleaning products, food/ beverage products, nutritional supplements, skincare, water filters
Time-Life Books, Inc. Basil L. Ong 777 Duke Street Alexandria, VA 22314 (703) 838-7000	Educational publications
Tupperware Home Parties Augustine J. English P.O. Box 2353 Orlando, FL 32802 (407) 847-3111	Decorative accessories, house and kitchenwares, toys/games
Watkins Incorporated Richard C. Wantock 150 Liberty Street Winona, MN 55987 (507) 457-3300	Cosmetics, food/beverage products, health and fitness, house and kitchenwares
The West Bend Company Dale A. Hafeman 400 Washington Street West Bend, WI 53095 (414) 334-2311	Cookware
World Book, Inc. Frank J. Gagliardi 101 Northwest Point Blvd. Plaza Elk Grove, IL 60007 (708) 290-5300	Educational publications, encyclopedias

The listing of a company in this appendix is neither an endorsement nor a solicitation on behalf of Successful Financial Planners, Inc.

Appendix G

Prenuptial Agreements

Because trusting one another is so important to financial success in marriage, one might ask what a discussion of prenuptial agreements is doing in a book like this. "Aren't prenuptial agreements a statement about *not* trusting?" It all depends on how you look at it. The way I look at it, a prenuptial agreement is a statement of trust that says, "I respect your boundaries and I want you to respect mine." When a person owns valuable assets as sole and separate property, there is always some feeling of vulnerability that he or she might lose them through marriage or through divorce if the marriage fails. The unfortunate reality is that marriages do fail and while emotional vulnerability is required for any marriage to work, financial vulnerability is not. A prenuptial agreement can put to rest such feelings of financial vulnerability. Having said that, I have an obligation to tell you that many churches won't marry a couple who has a prenuptial agreement. Why not? The reason is that such agreements are seen by those churches as a lack of commitment to the union.

In reality, very few couples have prenuptial agreements. When couples do have them, it's usually because they are entering marriage for the second time *and* because there are *substantial* assets involved. If you believe that a prenuptial agreement is required before you enter marriage, here are a few thoughts to consider:

1. Be sure you have worked through every chapter and every discussion in this book before you try to talk about a prenuptial agreement.

2. When you do have a talk about prenuptial agreements, both of you must come to the table voluntarily. If either one of you finds the discussion uncomfortable, irritating or downright maddening, then the discussion should be suspended and your marriage plans should be postponed. Pre-marital counseling with a qualified professional marriage counselor may be called for at this point. Lawyers and other financial advisors won't be able to help solve the problem.

3. The spirit of your discussions is *most* important. Your goals will be fairness, protection and comfort if your discussions are on track and your communications are healthy. These discussions should take place long before a wedding date is set, and the agreement should be signed and in a safe deposit box before the wedding invitations are sent out.

4. Begin with full and fair disclosure of your assets and liabilities. If you read and work through this book before discussing prenuptial agreements, full and fair disclosure of your assets will occur naturally.

5. State clearly what your objectives are in requesting a prenuptial agreement. Some areas of consideration might include **(a)** a written definition of pre-marriage property ownership, **(b)** clarification of how property will be titled that is obtained during marriage, **(c)** financial responsibilities within marriage **(d)** identifying pre-existing debt and deciding how those debts will be paid, **(e)** compensation for someone who is making a financial sacrifice, **(f)** support for children from previous marriages, **(g)** support and division of property in case of divorce, **(h)** estate distribution in the event of death or divorce.

6.   Write down the objectives that you agree upon, *and* those which you can not agree upon. If you have some disagreements, that is not necessarily a problem. Disagreements can often be resolved by following the negotiating strategies outlined in Chapter Four. If you are in open conflict on some points, that could be a problem. However, your conflict might relate to issues that legally can't be a part of a prenuptial agreement. So before you launch into open warfare, go to the next step.

7.   Make an appointment with an attorney. Some attorneys specialize in matrimonial law. I suggest you find one of them to help you. Make sure the attorney is someone neither of you has used for previous legal work and decide in advance of the appointment who will pay the attorney's fee. The one who pays the fee is selecting this attorney to represent him or her. Take your written list of objectives with you and share them with the attorney (including the objectives you can't agree on). Your attorney will tell you what a prenuptial agreement can and can not cover.

8.   Have an initial draft of the agreement prepared and then sit down and review it with the attorney. The agreement, properly drafted, may resolve some of your disagreements. A good matrimonial lawyer can help you to discuss unresolved issues in a constructive way. However, if you discover that major conflict (emotional or otherwise) still remains after initial discussions with a matrimonial lawyer (including a review of a draft of the agreement), the attorney probably will be of little help to you. If this is your situation, I urge you to slow down and seek qualified, professional pre-marital counseling.

9.   If you both feel comfortable with the prenuptial agreement, then it's time to bring in lawyer number two. Each of you must have your own attorney, who counsels you separately about the agreement. Don't try to take a shortcut and save money by using only one attorney. Otherwise, the agreement may be invalidated by the courts in the event of a dispute. If you both feel good about the agreement after receiving proper legal counsel, then sign it, have it properly witnessed and notarized, and get on with your wedding plans.

10. From time to time you should update your prenuptial agreement. Things change. If you have children together, or if one of you becomes seriously ill, such changes should be reflected in your prenuptial agreement. Time is also an important factor. Your relationship ten years from now may cause you to completely void the agreement. If the tax, estate or marital laws change, your agreement must be updated to reflect those changes. When changes in a prenuptial agreement are required, or if you decide to void it completely, go together to see an attorney and make sure the document is amended or voided correctly.

Personal Notes

Personal Notes

Personal Notes

Personal Notes